BOOKS BY KATHARINE SCHERMAN

Spring on an Arctic Island
Daughter of Fire: A Portrait of Iceland

THE FLOWERING OF IRELAND

THE
FLOWERING
OF
IRELAND

SAINTS, SCHOLARS AND KINGS

By Katharine Scherman

LONDON

VICTOR GOLLANCZ LTD

1981

COPYRIGHT © 1981 BY KATHARINE SCHERMAN

ISBN 0 575 03010 0

Photographs on pages 298 and 328 appear courtesy of the Irish Tourist Board; photo on page 341 courtesy of the Board of Trinity College, Dublin; all others are from the author's collection.

The author is grateful to the following publishers for permission to quote excerpts from the material noted:

Barnes & Noble Books and Allen Figgis & Co., Ltd.: *Ancient Irish Tales,* edited and translated by Tom Peete Cross and Clark Harris Slover, 1936.

Dolmen Press: *The Tain,* edited and translated by Thomas Kinsella, 1969.

Dublin Institute for Advanced Studies: *Liber de Mensura Orbis Terrae* by Dicuil, edited and translated by J. J. Tierney, 1967; and *Sancti Columbani Opera* by St. Columbanus, edited and translated by G. S. M. Walker, 1957.

Irish Texts Society: *Lebor Gabala Erenn,* edited and translated by Robert Alexander Stewart Macalister, 1938–1941; and *Vita S. Columbae* by Adamnan, translated by W. Huyshe, 1922.

Mercier Press: *Early Irish Poetry,* edited by James Carney, 1965.

Oxford University Press (Clarendon Press): *Early Irish Lyrics: Eighth to the Twelfth Century,* edited and translated by Gerard Murphy, 1956; *Bede's Ecclesiastical History of the English Nation* by the Venerable Bede, edited by Bertram Colgrave and R. A. B. Mynors, 1969; *The Irish Comic Tradition* by Vivian Mercier, 1962; *The Irish Tradition* by Robin Flower, 1947; and *Lives of Irish Saints,* edited and translated by Charles Plummer, 1922.

Routledge & Kegan Paul, Ltd.: *Early Irish Literature* by Eleanor Knott and Gerard Murphy, 1966.

Designed by Janis Capone

PRINTED IN THE UNITED STATES OF AMERICA

FOR AXEL

CONTENTS

PART THREE · THE BREAKDOWN

PART FOUR · THE FLOWERING

PHOTOGRAPHS

PREFACE

THE GENESIS OF THIS HISTORY OCCURRED SOME YEARS AGO WHEN, READING about the origins of the settlement of Iceland, I found that the first inhabitants of that remote island were not, as I had routinely assumed, Vikings blown off course while en route to a proposed mainland foray, but Irish monks who, in the seventh, eighth and ninth centuries, directed their little curraghs thither with undeflected purpose. They not only knew exactly where they were going, they had fervently implored their abbots to allow them to make the journey to "Thule," the farthest isle. The haven of their longing was first encountered, according to legend, by the sixth-century monk St. Brendan the Navigator, who at the time thought he had touched the edge of Hell. Later voyagers sought on these cold volcanic shores something quite different, and their quest brought them there in numbers amounting, by the time of the accidental Norse discovery, to about a thousand.

The seafaring monks were not driven from their homeland by hostile forces; they were not looking for gold and slaves; they had no interest in colonizing nor in claiming new territory for their kings. Yet the island of bristling lava cliffs and wrinkled glaciers coming down to the sea, occasionally interrupted by fields even greener than those they had left, appeared to them a bourne more greatly to be desired than any earthly gift. They were looking for grace, which is a state of mind; and this made me very curious. The spiritual motive, though it may be one of the prime moving

xiii

forces of human history, does not ordinarily take men out in light boats on an uncharted ocean where the weather is nearly always foul, toward a horizon at the edge of which, according to contemporary opinion, they would probably vanish into empty space, only to settle at last — and with joyous certitude — on an uninhabited island where it is dark all winter and rains all summer. They had found what they wanted: a difficult and lonely way to worship God.

What drove them so compellingly to seek blessedness in such inhospitable surroundings? The answer took me back to prehistory, up through the origins of Irish Christianity, into the lives, partly apocryphal yet deeply moving, of the early saints, into the cloisters where some of the most beautiful manuscripts of Western art were created, to Europe of the Dark and Middle Ages, where Irish missionaries and humanists inspired amazement, delight, often fanatical devotion. It was a wonderful journey for me, akin in its spirit, though hardly in its scope, to those early voyages.

If I have even partly answered the question — Why did they do it? — I have to thank those guides who helped me on my way, the scholars of Ireland and of other countries, whose lives and talents have been totally involved with one or another aspect of this quest. It would please me greatly to be able to thank them personally. But since I know most of them only through their written words, I can make but cold reference to them in the bibliographical lists at the end of this volume, belying the debt I owe.

One I can and do thank more directly. That is Peter Harbison, archaeologist and author, who helped me from beginning to end. In the course of the work, he assisted with the bibliography, suggesting titles in specialized areas and sending me hard-to-find volumes, invaluable references. Later he kindly consented to a critical reading of the completed manuscript, a task he accomplished with a sharp eye for small factual errors, a fine perceptiveness for the larger sense and accuracy of the material and a notable forbearance with the quality of the book, which, to a scholar, must be somewhat less than profound. Though in a work of this nature, directed to an audience as ignorant as I was when I began it, profundity is neither expected nor desired, accuracy is a sine qua non, and Mr. Harbison's meticulous and sensitive reading was therefore my best outside aid.

I owe a continuing debt of gratitude to the staff at Little, Brown for their encouragement over the years, and for their expert help in giving this book its start. Among them particular thanks go to my editor, Roger Donald, as much for his kindness and patience as for his practiced editorial eye; and to my copy editor, Michael Brandon, a skilled and sympathetic professional whose perceptive editing smoothed the rough edges.

As always, I thank my husband, Axel Rosin, to whom this book is dedicated. He lived through the years of research and writing — not easy for a spouse — ever positive, encouraging, appreciative and calm; and without him I would never have got past page 1.

THE FLOWERING OF IRELAND

PROLOGUE

Mist lay over the North Atlantic near Bray Head, County Kerry, in the southwest of Ireland, a remnant of the rainstorm that had flattened the water a few minutes before. The wind had driven it off and now it lay to the south, a dark cushion of cloud hiding the horizon. Near shore the ocean was flat under the thinning fog. In the north the great massif of Brandon Mountain hulked over Dingle Peninsula, its unseen summits wrapped, as they always were even on the fairest days, in moving clouds. Over the ocean the sun broke through and the water began to shine. It looked like a lake.

The boat picked us up at the bridge over Portmagee Channel between Valencia Island and the mainland of the Iveragh Peninsula. It was a thirty-two-foot fishing boat fitted out to take a dozen or so passengers on short expeditions, with benches along the sides in the stern and a cabin forward.

For a short way beyond the bridge the channel was protected; green fields rose to mild rocky heights. But when we passed Horse Island on the left we were out of the lee. The wind off the open ocean hit us and waves came from every direction as conflicting tides and currents crossed at the meeting place of inlet and ocean. The water that had been a gray monotone from afar was a surge of flying white spray and thick green whirlpools in the wake of the breakers. Our solid little boat was picked up and tossed like an empty snail shell. For a few minutes we wallowed, making no headway at all. The motor took hold and we slowly crawled out of the

3

riptide. The open ocean was no better. Near shore the waves were short and choppy. Out in the swell they were relentless, rhythmic combers far bigger than our boat. We would climb a steep green hill and poise at the top, shuddering, the screw out of water. Our pilot cut the motor so we wouldn't dive to the bottom, and we careened down the other side, sometimes sideways or backwards, to pitch and rock uncontrollably in the trough. There was barely time to gun the motor to meet the next wave, which wasn't always directly in front but might be coming at us from the side, roughened by the gusty west wind.

We couldn't see where we were going nor where we had come from. Everywhere we looked there was only water — above us, beside us, before us, behind us, at every pitch but level. Out of the corners of our eyes we glimpsed unconcerned birds, kittiwakes playing with the wind and puffins beating low across the wave tops. Sometimes there was a seal, head high, staring curiously before submerging in its element, while we unqualified humans clung to the rails, numb to the water breaking over us, one identifiable thought in our minds (beyond the unvoiced fear that this was our last journey) — "We have to come back the same way!"

Sometimes a big bird, all white but for black wing-tips, rose out of the water near us and climbed in stately flight to circle the boat before disappearing beyond the waves: a gannet. We hardly noticed that this was becoming more frequent, until we were surrounded, the gannets hovering over the boat like gulls, wheeling in our wake, swooping close as if to see what we were and what we had with us. Unlike gulls they did not utter a sound. Their scrutiny seemed like an inspection by spirits: the gods of the bird world come down to see if we were worthy. Suddenly dead ahead appeared a tall rock of spires and castellated walls, covered with gannets, perching, nesting, landing, taking off, diving. It was the island of Little Skellig, inhabited entirely and only by gannets, twenty thousand nesting pairs of them, the second largest colony in the world, their home for possibly the past thousand years. As we came under the island's sheltering peak, the boat steadied enough so we could see, a mile or so beyond, the sharp dark triangle of Great Skellig, also called Skellig Michael, 714 feet high, which had been home to a few of Ireland's wandering monks even longer ago.

They had come across the same eight and a half miles of ocean in their curraghs, wooden-frame, hide-covered boats that bobbed lightly as thistledown over the waves. On the last part of the journey, between the two rocks, the water was no less rough, but they must have felt a somewhat startled elation, as did we, at seeing their awesome destination. The sun was so bright now that we could not look at the sea, and the shadowed island was a formidable silhouette without detail, piercing the light sky. As we neared we could see waves breaking, scattering their spray far up on bare and shining rock. We looked in wonder at the vertical slab of the wall, thinking of those ancient voyagers.

No harbor was visible until all at once we came around a corner and were in it, a small straight-walled inlet protected on three sides from open ocean. A cement dock was built into one corner and a paved walkway cut from the sheer rock led out of sight away from it. Before the walkway was built no one could have climbed from here. We learned that hand-hewn steps made by the monks ascended from another landing place on the north side, a triangular cove open to the sea, where today boats can land possibly four days in a year. But for several hundred years they had brought their little vessels into that exposed corner, where they had to haul them up on the sharp rocks above reach of the waves. They came with the few supplies they could carry in their curraghs, to an island open at every point to wind and rain, where only small hardy plants can take root in rock crevices and no animals but seabirds and rabbits can find sanctuary in weather-eroded fissures in the sheer walls.

The monks did not come here to escape. They left their quiet lives within the sheltering walls of their monasteries to set forth with hope over the savage ocean, ill equipped, unworldly, caring not what hardships they would meet at the end of the voyage. They came for love.

Today the narrow road from the harbor ascends part way up, curling around Skellig Michael's perpendicular south side, to end at a lighthouse on the southwestern tip, below West Peak, the taller of the rock's twin peaks. About halfway along the road the stairway of the monks appears, rising uncompromisingly straight up toward the rounded dome of the eastern peak: six hundred steps crudely cut in the rock face, of differing widths and not always level. Their tools must have been other rocks, and they must have worked fast. Summer off the coast of southwestern Ireland is notably cool and rainy, but winter is almost insupportable. Never does the wind cease long enough for the ocean's turbulent swell to subside. Winter gales drive the waves 30 feet up on the lee side of the island, and up to 200 on the south, where the full force of the North Atlantic hits. Nowhere on the rock is there so much as a cave for refuge, nor is there a level place anywhere near sea level that is wide enough for building. If they came in April, when the storms diminish, they had to complete their stairway to the island's only practicable terrace, 550 feet up, and build their houses all within the four spring and summer months of comparative calm.

Because when September came, with its equinoctial tempests, the monks could neither live there without shelter nor could they depart.

The flight of steps is not continuous. The slope moderates here and there, and a precarious layer of soil has had a chance to form. In these places, a few yards wide, the steps cease and we walk over pillows of sea pink and big soft clumps of sea campion, those hardy colonizers whose roots twine together in tangled mats, catching their own dead foliage and making of it their own soil. The monks took advantage of a few of these slanting terraces, erecting stone crosses where those who came later could stop and worship, or just catch their breath and look at the birds. One of these monuments is still there, a pitted stone worn almost shapeless by time and weather, rising stark out of the flowers at the threshold of the cliff, the sea fierce beyond it.

A few steps beyond the cross lichens and mosses have invaded a section of rock already eroded by wind and rain, and the spongy surface is honeycombed with puffin burrows. The stubby black-and-white birds fly straight at their holes in a businesslike manner, unconcerned with human nearness, dozens of shining little fish hanging in their triangular orange beaks for the young hiding in the moist darkness.

These oases give token that in summer, at least, the monks would not have gone hungry. Besides the puffins, which are easy to get at, the cliffs are home to hundreds of other nesting seabirds: kittiwakes, fulmars, razorbills and guillemots lay their eggs and raise their young in clefts and on ledges high above the sea. The monks could have kept a few goats, the only domestic animal unfussy enough about its diet to live on the rock's scanty pickings. Some of the plants are edible, such as scurvy grass, a low-growing succulent whose thick heart-shaped leaves contain vitamin C; and the anchorites could have grown a few herbs. In the sixth century, when it is probable that the first voyagers arrived, the climate was warmer than it is today. There could not have been much more soil, because there simply is no place for it; everything slips downward, and only in a few places can a plant take root for long enough to provide its own continuing habitat. But the summers then were not quite so short nor the winters so unkind. Fish and the few birds, such as gulls, that wintered over, would have seen them through the cruellest months.

The last few yards of the climb are in a tunnel under a retaining wall, built in modern times to protect the monastery site from the depredations of burrowing rabbits. These animals, relative newcomers, have no predators on the island and they are increasing uncontrollably. Their digging has endangered the lighthouse road, part of which is roofed against the resultant

The monastic village with beehive huts on Skellig Michael, County Kerry

rock falls, and it is undermining the foundations of the ancient buildings, a feat that the attrition of fourteen centuries of wind and rain have not sufficed to accomplish.

We climb upward through dripping darkness. Behind us is the fearsome voyage and the slow ascent up the lonely rock scourged by Atlantic storms, habitable only by birds and seals. Ahead of us, as we come out of the tunnel into the mild sunlight, is a living fragment of the sixth century. We have walked back in time, out of our own mundane earth into the world of the Irish saints and their pagan Celtic ancestors.

The pitch of Skellig Michael at this place, between 550 and 600 feet above the ocean, levels off in a series of narrow, uneven terraces before it mounts the last steep 50 feet of the eastern peak, out of sight on the rounded hillside. Six little beehive-shaped stone huts, a slightly larger stone oratory with a barrel-vault roof, and the roofless walls of a small church are clustered here at varying levels, some nestled close against the swell of the hill, some poised at the very edge, only a low dry-stone wall between them and the breathtaking cliff. Between them are winding walks lined with flat stones. A widening of the central walk into a miniature plaza is occupied by leaning tombstones, their inscriptions obliterated. In its own green square beyond them is a stele, probably originally a cross, its cross-piece two blunted knobs, the weathered carving on its face blending with lichens to form a design of geometric abstractions. It stands alone, tall as a man and somewhat resembling one, as if an anchorite had been forgotten there and still stands lost in contemplation of Little Skellig rising out of the sea, framed by the curving walls of two beehive huts.

The buildings and walls are constructed of flat stones, without mortar. From the sides of the round huts project stone corbels, which probably supported sod roofs. Each one has a hole in the top, originally closed off by a rock slab. As living quarters they offer small latitude. The highest, which is thought to have had two stories, is sixteen feet, the lowest is about nine, the walls from three to six feet thick and the square interior floor space hardly big enough for a man to lie down in. They have no windows and the doors are only about four feet high and two wide. They must have been cold in winter and damp all year round. But the people who dared the ocean waves to find their peace on this rock had no interest in comfort. On the contrary, their disregard for the everyday usages of ease was the very core of their spiritual vitality. Austerity not only pleased them, it was necessary to them.

And the rough life had compensations. Asceticism gave an intensified response to the smell of flowers, the texture of stone, the feel of rain or sun or wind, the flight of birds. When they came out of their dark cells their spirits must have lifted to heights rarefied beyond our experience. The ground they knelt on was of springy moss with flowers growing in it. Beyond the low stone walls the sea was blue, lavender, silver and green in broad uneven patches, and it appeared from this height flat as a pond. The morning clouds looked like white Skelligs, and the penitents could almost talk to the fulmars and puffins flying to feed their rockbound young. As they watched the sun rise, a curtain of rain might fly over the sea from the west, bright steel with the sun's low rays on it, to pass overhead in a few minutes leaving a rainbow and the cloverlike scent of wet sea pink. In such a setting the simple prayers to God might have been tinged with an almost pagan pantheism.

It is not known positively when the first voyagers arrived, nor who they were. Tradition attributes the founding of the monastic village to one St. Finian. Three eminent holy men of this name, teachers and founders of monasteries, lived in the sixth century. The style of the buildings goes back to this period and beyond: to the pre-Christian dwellings on which the first Christian structures were modelled. Although the earliest churches and dwellings were usually built of wood or of wickerwork daubed with mud, on Skellig Michael the builders would have had to use the only material at hand. According to the annals, the settlement survived at least four attacks by Norse raiders in the ninth century. The monks evidently turned the other cheek, because in the tenth century one of Skellig Michael's holy hermits, says tradition, converted Olaf Tryggvesson, the fierce Viking who became Norway's first, and combatively, Christian ruler. The last monks left in the twelfth century, when life had grown soft, to settle in the village of Ballinskelligs, nearby on the mainland coast.

Through all the years the name of only one monk has survived. That is Etgall, an anchorite who was apparently living there alone when Vikings arrived in 823 looking for treasure. The poor little island monastery, which could barely support six or seven ascetics, would hardly have run to the silver chalices and jewel-studded shrines that provided the freebooters such easy pickings in the mainland monasteries. In anger, or perhaps in hopes of getting a ransom, the raiders took Etgall, who died while their prisoner, say the annals, of starvation. The implication is clear: the stark rigors of Skellig Michael held no dangers for Etgall, but when he could no longer hear the cries of seabirds and the crash of waves, or taste the salty wind of his island retreat, he grieved until death rescued him.

In no other connection is Etgall mentioned. He was not a saint whose feast day is on the calendar; history records no heathens converted by him, no miracles performed, no poetry written, no manuscripts illuminated. He might have done all these things. Ireland's legion of holy men and women, the luminous quality of whose piety, learning and imagination inspirited the Western world for more than six hundred years, were most of them anonymous. Even many of the saints whose names still shine over the dimness of the centuries are probably composite personalities. Legend has blurred their outlines until they have become as large and brightly unreal as the pagan heroes they superseded.

Yet their accomplishments were very real. The intricate art of their illuminated manuscripts is still as brilliant as when it was first set to parchment. Their poetry makes the heart sing today. Greek and Roman literature and lore, as well as the authentic voice of their own Celtic ancestors transcribed by them from oral tradition, are ours to study now because these cloistered monks reached into a receding past, rescued the vanishing knowledge, and gave it back to the world. In a darkened and barbaric Europe, Irish priests and scholars kept alive the light that had burned for Greek philosophers, Roman colonizers, early Christian martyrs.

By the time dawn came to Europe again with the early Renaissance, Ireland's day was over. The Norse raiders and the Anglo–Norman conquerors between them extinguished that bright torch.

Though Ireland owed the extraordinary literary, artistic and scholarly flowering of this age to her inspired clerics, they were only secondarily artists and poets, teachers and missionaries. Their first purpose was the same that brought them to Skellig Michael: to achieve a state of grace.

It is hard for us today to understand the rationale behind this imperative yearning of the early Christian mind. What made them take their little open boats out into the Atlantic, to the Faeroes, to Iceland, possibly to America, looking for a land that had been promised in a vision? What made them starve themselves and live without sleep until the world around them was full of strangeness and the wind in the leaves became the wingbeats of angels? Why did they leave their comfortable monasteries to wander friendless and defenseless in the lands of barbarians?

Maybe we can find out by looking into the past, where their roots were, and examining the subsequent world that they themselves created. For however enigmatic are their motivations to us, it is clear that the Irish saints made something new on earth. That was what we had felt when we stepped back in time high on Skellig Michael. The little monastic village was part of a world that came out of a dream. Let us look at the people who dreamed it.

PART ONE

THE SOURCES

CHAPTER I
PREHISTORIC IRELAND

EVERYWHERE YOU WALK IN IRELAND YOU ARE CONSCIOUS OF OVERLAPPING layers of human history, visibly crumbling one into another. Nettle-guarded ruins of medieval castles disintegrate slowly; in time they will become one with the blurred mounds and tumbles of great stones that mark the cemeteries of prehistoric dead. A small square of roofless stone walls at the head of a valley could be a pre-Christian dwelling or a shepherd's croft deserted during the famine. A closer look reveals a doorway with a Romanesque arch: somewhere between the two in time a chapel was erected here for pilgrims travelling a saint's roadway. Pigs root around the entrance to an eighth-century beehive hut (like those on Skellig Michael) where the farmer keeps his mulch.

Ireland's historic and prehistoric ruins are legion. Many of them are loved and carefully tended. Many more are nameless and apparently untouched since the day they were abandoned. The presence of the spirits of the past is palpable. The very loneliness of the green and flowered fields with their mysterious man-made hillocks and decaying walls strengthens this impression. You have the sense, wherever you step, that you are walking over the bones of long-dead kings, poets, farmers, slaves and saints.

Eight thousand years ago the first people came. Before that Ireland's climate had been too arctic to support human life. Between 12,000 and 11,000 B.C. the retreating ice sheet had left the island a scoured and boggy tundra. As the climate warmed, bushes grew, to hold the earth and take up some of the excess water; and around 10,000 B.C. wild horses and giant deer crossed the land bridge from Scotland to Ireland. They spread unchecked over the rolling grassland of the interior, but the hunters from the Continent arrived too late. Long before 6800 B.C., when Ireland's first human visitors landed, the climate had moderated to allow the growth of trees. The forests had grown tall, spreading even to the tops of the hills, and the grazing animals had departed. The rising North Atlantic had covered the land bridge to Britain, but the water level was still some seventy-five feet lower than it is today, so the channel between Scotland and northern Ireland was only a few miles wide. Across this narrow strip of water the first people could paddle their dugout canoes without much danger. There was still dry land connecting Britain and Scandinavia, and it may have been from there that these Mesolithic people came. They found a thickly wooded country with a ring of ancient coastal mountains, hammered and crushed by ice and deeply eroded by time, surrounding an interior lowland that contained a formidable amount of water.

They also found a mild and agreeable climate. Lying in the path of the North Atlantic Drift Current, Ireland's changeable ocean weather is softened by the Gulf Stream, whose mild, vaporous airs, condensing over the mountains, frequently bathe the island with rain. The moisture cannot escape from the saucerlike interior, cut off from the sea by the mountain barrier that, except for a fifty-mile stretch of beach on the east coast, entirely rims Ireland; and rivers and lakes spread a watery web over the countryside, giving it the lushest pasturelands in Europe. The ocean winds that bring the rain also blow it away, usually within a few minutes, and sunlight glitters over the wet world. Sunshine and black clouds chase each other over the sky, and light and shadow fly below them, changing the colors and even the shapes of the earth. Capricious as is the weather, the rhythm of the seasons, tempered by the ocean, is gentler and more even than on the Continent. Winters are milder and summers are cooler, and this is so all over Ireland, as no part of it is more than seventy miles from the sea.

The first Irishmen were a small, dark race, very primitive. They lived close to the shores of lake and ocean, not moving far from these areas on account of the denseness of the woodland. Their food consisted of fish, birds and small animals. They cannot have seen much future in this heavily forested, overwhelmingly wet island, but they evidently did not want much, for they left no remains attesting to a settled life, neither dwelling nor altar nor burial place; only a few rubbish dumps and charcoal traces of their campsites, and some flint tools. But, however meager their impact on the new wild land and however feeble their efforts to tame it, they left a faint legacy in the bloodstreams of today's Irish, and a slight mark on history. Because, as with all the successive waves of immigration, these Stone Age people did not leave but were absorbed by the next comers, and they turned up, perhaps as a racial memory, in the fanciful inventions that passed for history with Ireland's medieval scribes.

For three thousand years the early Irishmen trod their small paths unmolested. Then came a new people, a race of Neolithic man, he who had revolutionized human history by discovering the benefits of tilling the soil and taming wild animals. These early agriculturalists, long since driven out of their original home in the Mideast by expanding population and soil exhaustion, arrived in Ireland around 3700 B.C., probably from France, the Low Countries and Cornwall. They were, like their forerunners, small and dark, and they also used stone tools, but they were not primitive in the unprogressive manner of the people they displaced. They used their polished stone axes to cut clearings in the forest, and there they plowed, sowed and reaped in an unexpectedly efficient modern manner. One of their farms has been excavated in North Mayo, where the climate changes some three thousand years ago caused the formation of peat bog, the best natural preserver.

It is hard to visualize the form of man today on the bleak, silent expanse of Erris, the big square peninsula of northern County Mayo that thrusts bluntly into the Atlantic north of Clew Bay. There is only the rolling, heather-covered bog, a single raised road winding through it, nothing to break the line of sight but the great gray dome of Nephin Mountain far away, rising alone from the sodden plain, and the crooked horizon of the Nephin Beg beyond it. But under the black peat are the clear plow marks and the ridges and furrows of an early farmer. Along the ridges he planted his barley and wheat, the excess water draining off down the furrows.

The ancient, dormant hills of Erris, bog to their very peaks, bear no witness to the energetic civilization that for a while quickened them. Yet these indefatigable farmers changed the face of Ireland. They cleared forests and pastured their sheep and cattle on the rich new fields. They made flint arrows and knives and small bone implements for household work, and adorned themselves with bone pins and stone pendants. Their fields and their flocks made them independent of the necessity to roam in search of wild game, and they began to live in settled communities. Though their earliest dwellings may have been primitive covered pits, within a few hundred years they had progressed considerably. In the North Mayo bog, near Ballyglass, postholes up to thirty inches deep have been found, disclosing the outlines of a rectangular house, probably of timber, though no remains are now evident. (A house of similar shape was unearthed at Ballynagilly, County Tyrone, with split-oak vertical planks, dating from about 3200 B.C. The Ballynagilly dig further revealed pottery shards from the surprisingly early period of 3800 to 3700 B.C.) Though mostly self-sufficient, the Stone Age farmers specialized to the extent of mass–producing axes in two known places. They must have had a stable and well-organized society with enough manpower to produce their most enduring and spectacular legacies, the monuments of enormous stones where they buried their dead and, perhaps, worshipped their gods.

The earliest of these are court cairns such as Creevykeel in County Sligo, an arrangement of great pale gray boulders lying in a level field high over Donegal Bay. A semicircle of them surrounds a grassy courtyard; at the center of the arc two tall standing stones bridged by a heavy capstone lead into a long rectangular stone-lined passage. The whole is surrounded by a mass of cobble-sized rocks that was at one time mounded over the whole communal grave. There is a sense of cheerful openness, almost modernity, about this light, airy place. The huge orderly stones could be the foundations of a new house engagingly sited on the highland above the wide bay, the bare, precipitous Sligo Mountains rising dramatically to the south. Neolithic man, like the early Christian builders, chose his holy places with the evident knowledge that his gods could be worshipped the better where the human heart could respond to the comely proportions of the landscape.

Though for over a thousand years there were no significant invasions, there is evidence that there must have been infiltration of later races of the Stone Age farming people. In their Continental history the desire for ceremonial had very gradually taken over from the simple farming mentality, and the Neolithic farmers began to build megalithic monuments. By the time the megalith builders arrived in Ireland, their techniques had developed into a high art. The results are magnificent and sophisticated structures, of which the showplace is Newgrange in County Meath, erected about 2500 B.C. (around the time of the building of the Egyptian pyramids).

Newgrange is known as a "passage grave" because the ashes of the dead were placed in burial chambers at the end of a long passage through a man-made hill constructed of about four thousand tons of stone. The megalithic tomb looms startlingly out of the gentle pastoral countryside atop a low hill in the curve of a country road. A circle of giant rough-hewn standing stones partly surrounds a mound about 35 feet high, with a diameter of

Stone Age curbstone with incised spiral designs at Newgrange passage grave, County Meath, erected about 2500 B.C.

about 250 feet. Along the base of the mound lie enormous curbstones, many carved with geometric decorations, and a rim of small white quartz pebbles surmounts these; they were found among the rubble that surrounds the building and were inserted by restorers. At one time, it is surmised, a gleaming mantle of these pebbles, quarried in the Wicklow Hills many miles to the south, entirely covered the man-made hill. Before the entrance lies a single ovoid curbstone pocked out with a brilliant asymmetrical design of spirals and diamond shapes.

Behind this beautiful stone a sixty-foot passageway leads into the hill, its side walls decorated with more geometric carving. It ends in a cross-shaped area: a circular chamber with a high vaulted roof and three small side chambers (probably the repositories of the ashes of the dead) whose floors are great slabs of stone hollowed into shallow basins. The walls and ceilings are ornamented with dazzling patterns of incised circles, double spirals, snakelike zigzags, herringbones, triangles and diamonds.

The passage and its chambers must have had significance beyond the simple burial of the dead. For it is so constructed that on the shortest day of the year the rays of the rising sun penetrate through the low, narrow corridor, to fill the inner chamber with the light of dawn. To achieve this the builders had to surmount an architectural problem: Newgrange is built on top of a hill, so its internal passage has to climb upward. The horizontal rays of the sun could only pierce to its end by the construction of a slit six feet above the entrance portal, to compensate for the six feet one has to ascend to reach the innermost chamber.

Further architectural subtleties attest to the skill of these unprimitive early builders. They clearly intended that their holy places should stay dry and sound for eternity, and they are still so after more than four millennia. The circular walls of the inner sanctum are built like an igloo: layers of flat stones, each layer narrower than the one below, rise to a single keystone twenty feet above the ground. The flat stone layers were laid slanting outward so that any rainwater seeping in from the earth above slides away from the sacred room. Channels that were cut into the roof-stones of the chamber and into the passage similarly drain off water.

The ritual marking of sunrise on the shortest day of the year — an important date in the farmer's year, for he would know that a certain number of days after this it would be time to start the springtime planting — shows that these Stone Age people had a precise calendar knowledge based on some method of calculating the positions of the sun and stars. The standing stones partly surrounding Newgrange may have been, like the later Bronze Age stone circles, an early astronomical observatory. For the great mound is sited off-center within their circle, suggesting that one or the other was built first, and the second oriented according to clues from the first.

The careful positioning of Newgrange, the architectural dexterity of its internal building, and, above all, the luxuriance of its carven designs, suggest that the mound meant far more to its creators than is consonant with a tomb for the dead. The symbolism of their art is obscure to us; we have no idea of what language they spoke or how they worshipped their gods. But the whole splendid structure expresses the soul of a people with at least the sophistication of the pyramid-builders of Egypt, their near-contemporaries, or the much later Mayan civilization of southern Mexico and Guatemala.

Lovingly restored and carefully tended as it is, Newgrange represents more a copy than an echo of an early civilization. To feel the presence of Stone Age man one must see those passage graves less diligently restored. About three hundred have been discovered in Ireland, most of them clustered in groups on the tops of isolated hills, well off the beaten track. One of the most evocative is Carrowkeel, in the Bricklieve Mountains of County Sligo, a group of very old hills whose eroded, rocky summits rise from valleys and slopes of bog where no one goes but the peat-cutters with their carts and donkeys. Though Carrowkeel is not as magnificent nor as highly decorated as Newgrange, its untouched loneliness renders it affectingly suggestive. Its hilltop is a bleak mesa surrounded by vertically split rocks, like walls. A grass-grown cart track leads to the foot of these rocks, where it ends, and the visitor climbs through heather among the stones and boggy potholes to the mounds grouped on the flat summit. They are low, much smaller than Newgrange, with square entrance holes leading downward into blackness, their passage walls fallen in.

On a neighboring hilltop, circled by the same cracked perpendicular rock walls, are the remains, invisible from Carrowkeel, of a village of the living, the stone foundations of forty-seven circular huts. It is thought that they were the dwellings of the same people who built the mounds; if so, it is their only known village in Ireland. Among these crumbling hills time is forgotten and the Stone Age farmers seem very close. The only living being is a skylark that floats above the cemetery, its clear high song loud in the empty silence. It flutters down and lands, still singing, on the edge of one of the broken entrances. Probably it has a nest among the sedge cotton whose downy white heads wave in the hollows beside the grave mound. It is easy to think of its predecessor singing the same long sweet song to warn away the mourners of 2500 B.C. when they brought the ashes of their dead to bury them on this lonesome hill.

Low clouds have hidden the sun and a rain shower is speeding over the mottled blue and green of lake and pasture below the mountains. The storm wind blows the clouds over the hilltops and fog suddenly eddies between the mounds, followed by a curtain of rain that obliterates the haunting image of the past.

The people who built Newgrange and Carrowkeel did not long have Ireland to themselves. With the discovery of the uses of metal and the consequent inception of the Bronze Age, trade became a dominant influence over most of the inhabited world. Instead of the populating of new lands by the drift of hunters or the overflow of agriculturalists driven out of their homelands by soil exhaustion, the purposeful search for raw metals —

copper, tin and gold — by merchants and adventurers signalled new ways of life for the countries in their paths.

Throughout history and prehistory Ireland has been at the edge of things, but she has never been isolated. Her coastlands on the Irish Sea were part of the "Atlantic Ends of Europe," a Bronze Age province of the western islands and peninsulas that were the natural stops for seafarers from Spain and Portugal to Brittany, Cornwall and Ireland, thence northeast around Great Britain to the coast of Norway. Spain, the southernmost link of the chain, had close contacts with the North African coast, Greece and the Near East. So whatever happened in the cradle of civilization found its way without too much time lag along the edges of the Atlantic, and gave the remote ends such as Ireland a share in all the latest in technical skills and artistic development.

When gold was discovered in the Wicklow Hills, around 2000 B.C., something in the nature of a gold rush brought new art and new industry to Ireland, and she soon became one of the focal points of trade, not only with the Atlantic ports but with northern Europe. At the time the Minoans were painting their consummate frescoes on the walls of Knossos, Irish lunulae — crescent-shaped, delicately chased gold neck ornaments — as well as beautifully decorated pottery vessels, were in the markets of Europe. In this same period amber from the Baltic, bronze daggers and axes from Portugal and faience beads, possibly from Egypt, were turning up in the ports of Ireland.

Some scholars now surmise that the extraordinary flowering of Ireland in this period, the Earlier Bronze Age, was the result of a large-scale invasion, the last one in the prehistoric period.[1] The arrival and establishment of the new people, it is thought, covered the centuries from about 2100 B.C. to 1300 B.C. The deductions are based on archaelogical evidence. During this time a new type of burial was introduced: single-inhumation graves in place of the great stone communal tombs of the Neolithic people. The proliferation of these graves suggests an extensive influx; further, the skeletons recovered show a round-headed people of a racial type completely new to Ireland. The graceful decorated pottery of the period has a style that has little continuity with anything of an earlier age in Ireland, though it is similar to contemporary finds in Britain and continental Europe.

These people, the Beaker Folk (so called for their pottery style) were, it is now thought, possibly Indo-Europeans, the great family from which the Celtic nationality later developed. Their arrival in Ireland in force toward the end of the third millennium B.C. marks the true genesis of Celtic Ireland. Throughout the following centuries — as one branch of the Indo-

European peoples coalesced into an extraordinarily tough and spirited new race, the Celts — small waves brought to Ireland new colonists and masters, new ideas and discoveries. They left their mark upon a population that was of the same proto-Celtic race. The continued infusion of fresh blood and the assimilation by the older inhabitants of the powerful but relatively few newcomers resulted in an accretion of culture that has been called "cumulative Celticity."[2]

The Celts are a branch of the Indo-European family from which most of the present-day European, Middle Eastern and Indian races are descended. Their forebears probably lived on the plains of western Russia, the region of the Volga steppes. The ur-people were originally hunters; later they became seminomadic shepherds, pasturing sheep and cattle on their broad plains; finally, around 3000 B.C., they domesticated the horse. Endowed by nature with an energetic and adventurous spirit and now by their own initiative with unrestrainable mobility, they began drifting away from the plains, driven by drought and other adverse conditions. West of the Carpathians the forage was richer and the climate more equable than on their native prairies. Hordes of horsemen descended inexorably on the lush valleys of Europe, where they easily vanquished and ultimately mingled with the indigenes, imposing their own language and customs but marrying the women of the subject races and adopting many of the old ways. Out of this mixture came, among others, the Copper Age people known as Beaker Folk. Immeasurably strengthened by their development of slashing swords and riveted spears, their probable descendants extended their conquests, reaching the British Isles, as noted, in the third millennium.

Around the same time, other branches of the Indo-Europeans went south and east. Uniquely mobile, fearsome on their powerful steeds (it is thought that their descent on Thessaly gave rise to folk legends of centaurs), far more active than the people whose lands they coveted, and remarkably well organized, they pursued their conquering way with little resistance. They occupied Greece, Persia and parts of India (where their superiority in strength combined with their relatively small numbers gave rise to the caste system) and about 1750 B.C. they established the Hittite Empire in Anatolia.

In the Alpine region of Austria and Switzerland, meanwhile, the invaders had found an unadventurous and largely contented farming people. The mounted warriors easily overran the undefended countryside and, finding the peasantry easygoing, patient and hardworking, settled among them to establish a tripartite caste system of aristocratic warrior-lord, farmer and serf. In this area and among these people, changed over the years by the admixture of other invaders both belligerent and peaceable, arose between 1300 and 600 B.C. the coherent society that we know traditionally as the Celts. At no point in their history were the Celts a separate, blood-pure race. They were a blend of many peoples, an amalgam of adventurers, traders, farmers and fighters bonded by intermarriage, similarity of religion, custom and language, who developed a binding and potent sense of identity: they were a nationality.

Their development was spectacular; and it was given a strong impetus by the onset of the Iron Age. The use of iron, learned in the Caucasus, was brought into western Europe starting around 1100 B.C., and reached the Celtic cradle around 900 B.C. The new technology in the hands of a driving and talented people, added to the growing sense of an emergent nationality, gave the Celts an urge for expansion beyond their borders. Beginning about 500 B.C., the rest of Europe became increasingly familiar with roving bands of shaggy-haired, mustachioed, half-naked warriors, irresistibly armed and mounted, and unleashing a wild, unnerving fury in battle. The fragmentary raiding resolved into a wholesale drive to conquer, and by the beginning of the third century B.C. the Celts had become Europe's dominant power, their sway extending south to Italy and parts of Spain and Portugal, east to Rumania, Yugoslavia, Bulgaria, Thrace and Macedonia and north through France and southern and central Germany to the British Isles. This period of the ascendancy of the Celts is known as the La Tène era (from the site in western Switzerland where the first artifacts were identified).

The Romans considered the Celts to be oafish and unkempt barbarians unable or unwilling to speak a civilized language or to write any language at all.* But the Celtic society that developed in the five centuries before Christ — the La Tène culture — had a degree of accomplishment far beyond anything yet seen in that part of the world.

In their hierarchical society, aristocratic warriors shared the highest place with druids, who were priests, philosophers, teachers, judges and poets. Artists and artisans ranked only a little lower. We know little about their religion, as the Continental Celts did not develop a written language. The druids, highly educated as they were, preferred to transmit their lore orally to chosen disciples; to record it, as they could easily have learned to do had they so chosen, would have lessened its magic. They did not want too familiar a congregation: the less available the mysteries the more potent

*It was actually the Greeks who originally coined the word *barbarian,* from the "ba-ba-ba" sounds uttered by those they considered too uncouth to be able to learn Greek — including the Romans.

their effect. The rituals were practiced not in temples but outdoors, usually in groves of their sacred tree, the oak. It was a complex faith, which had gone beyond the primitive peopling of hills, rocks, rivers and trees with spirits, to the worship of the great forces of nature: moon, sea, sun and wind. Beyond these was a pantheon of gods governing every facet of human life: agriculture, commerce, healing, fertility, war. The functions of these gods corresponded closely with those of the Greek, Roman and Norse pantheons, all of them derived from their common Indo-European ancestors. The Celts believed in the immortality of the spirit, and in reincarnation. Their priests placed strong reliance on magic, augury and human sacrifice.

Music and poetry, in the regard of these fierce pagans, reached a level almost divine. Eloquence was valued as highly as bravery in battle and could stay the arm of the most berserkly inspired fighter. Diodorus Siculus, a Greek historian of the first century B.C., observed that when "two armies are in the presence of one another, and swords drawn and spears couched, [the Celtic poets] throw themselves into the midst of the combatants and appease them as though they were charming wild beasts. Thus even amongst the most savage barbarians anger submits to the rule of wisdom, and the god of war pays homage to the Muses."

Of all the evidences of Celtic sophistication, the richly sensuous ornamental art of the La Tène era gives the clearest indication of the cultivated imagination of these talented people. Artists in metal covered the smallest surfaces of pots, weapons and personal ornaments with mazes of arabesques, arches and curving tendrils entwining fantastical stylized plants, animal figures and faces. The rhythmic multiplication of abstract figures is carved with infinite perfection of detail, as if the artists had worked with magnifiers. They mastered the art of enamelling, learned from Eastern sources the secret of producing highly colored glass, excelled in weaving and dyeing, devoted meticulous care to the manufacture of beautiful weaponry: chain mail, tall ornamented bronze helmets, enormous shields, fine-wrought swords.

They were endlessly inventive, not only in art but in the conveniences of daily life. Their smiths, who learned to cast soft iron and developed a new kind of brass, made a variety of excellent utensils and tools. Their carpenters and wheelwrights, as well as fashioning the swiftest and most elegant chariots, originated barrels and buckets, which replaced the pottery jug over most of northern Europe. They lightened the labor of the farmer and his wife with the invention of the scythe and the rotary hand mill for grinding grain. They introduced to Europe the use of trousers for men, a necessity to a people devoted to the cult of the horse. In dress and adornment, men and women of the upper classes were dramatic and colorful.

They had a high regard for education. In the schools of the druids, students trained for as long as twenty years to attain knowledge of astronomy, geography, philosophy, law and religion. There were also lessons in the druidic order; some were instructed in civil affairs, others learned the duties of lawyers and judges, others studied to become poets — besides those who were to function solely as priests. Teaching and learning were entirely oral, everything being cast in verse form for easier memorizing. Not only fledgling druids attended school but also the male children of the highborn — those who were destined, on reaching manhood, for the Celts' most enthusiastic occupation, the practice of war.

Though their level of education was high, their sense of justice strong and lively, and their devotion to art, music and poetry fervent, the Celts were mainly notorious in their own day for their fearsome aptitude as fighters. Their long fair hair, clear white skin and great height were attributes as startling to the small dark southern peoples into whose world they intruded as were their manners in battle: the furious rush of horsemen and horse-drawn chariots, the chanting shout of harsh voices, the discordant music of horns, the rhythmic beating of swords against shields. Before going into combat they whipped up a war spirit with ritualistic imitations of battle, shouting insults, challenging one another to mock duels, dancing and leaping. By the time they were ready to go they were so overheated with frenzy that many threw off their chain mail and helmets and went into the fray naked and entirely without fear. Their four-wheeled chariots were manned by two warriors, one driving the horses, the other flinging javelins at the enemy. When the latter had thrown all his spears, he leaped into the conflict on foot, while the charioteer turned the vehicle around. The horsemen were similarly mounted: two to a horse — one to manage, the other to fight. They further appalled the enemy by cutting off the heads of their victims and attaching them to the necks of their horses, to be embalmed later in cedar oil and displayed as trophies on the walls of their houses.

After the fight Celtic warriors were wont to feast hugely, swallowing an abundance of wine and mead and listening to bards sing lays of the deeds of redoubtable ancestors as well as lyrical encomiums of themselves. Even at the banquet they were liable to quarrel. The smallest pretext would provoke a duel, often fatal. Death meant little. It was but the "mid-point of a long life," according to Lucan, a Roman poet; their spirits would survive in another body, or perhaps in a re-creation of the present one.

Fighting was the heart's blood of the Celts. Yet with all their savagery as warriors, their spiritual outlook was imbued with grace and honesty. They honored their women and were generous and hospitable to strangers. They were an outdoor people, loving and understanding the ways of nature. Having no towns, they had not learned the decadent luxuries nor the accompanying miseries entailed in urban living. Their moral code was uncluttered by sophistry and their life-style was spontaneous.

Their virtues bred flaws, and deep in the Celtic character lay the seeds of their downfall. Free, individualistic and proud, they could not envision the concept of subservient cooperation that was essential to a strongly organized central government. They never managed — in fact they never even tried — to make a working empire out of the vast territories they dominated. They tended to operate in small groups ordered around the family or an economic unit, and political integration eluded them. They were too sure of themselves. Their natural superiority was great, and they appear to have had a distaste for the hard work of expanding it in the direction of self-government. The detailed, self-denying exercise of exploiting their resources and consolidating their conquests was alien to them. The closest they came to acknowledging a central power was their loose obeisance to the national assembly of the druids in Gaul.

In an unexacting way the multitrained druids and their easygoing compatriots managed very well until the Romans arrived with their superb military machine and their superefficient network of civil bureaucracy. For all the Celts' numerical superiority and brilliance as individual fighters, they had nothing but their death-defying courage with which to confront the measured advance of the legions. Once the Romans had won on the field of battle it was only a matter of time before the whole discrete Celtic structure fell apart and the fiery barbarian was transmuted into a new European anthropos: the Roman citizen.

Caesar completed his conquest of Gaul in 51 B.C. That was the last step in the submergence of Celt in Roman. With the exception of a few pockets, Celtic culture on the Continent ceased to exist. Its usages are known only through accounts, biased at best, by those who displaced it.

As Celtic power in Europe flooded, then ebbed, Ireland, on the periphery, got the last edges of the ripples. Everything came more slowly there; in turn, the old ways lasted longer. After the major invasion of the Earlier Bronze Age, smaller ones of the Later Bronze Age brought a constant flow of fresh ideas and discoveries, as well as a changing but ever-strengthening aristocracy. There was increasing turbulence, but there was apparently little real danger. The people of Ireland, wealthy and conservative, changed their mores very slowly. The aliens were always absorbed into the stream and the new thoughts blended with the old ways. Life continued its stormy yet homogeneous course. A few fortifications were built, and many people buried their treasures for safekeeping, but most did not consider it necessary to build defensive walls around their dwellings.

With the advent of the Iron Age, the arrival of La Tène Celts from Europe brought a new set of masters to Ireland. Though the incursions were small and widespread in time, ranging probably from the third century B.C. to the first A.D., their effect was potent. These fierce heroes, seething with war fury and invincibly armed with iron swords, easily made themselves masters of a confident, disjointed country still in a Bronze Age culture. By the time Caesar had completed his conquest of Gaul, Ireland, the last niche of the Celtic nationality, had acquired the character she was to keep, hardly changed, for the next thousand years. Mostly eradicated in Europe, Celtic society was to live on in Ireland, as fresh and proud as in the centuries before the first Roman legions marched north to metamorphose Europe. In the Irish sagas and legends is the very voice of the Celtic pagans themselves, speaking directly to us from a time before history.

They were not quite the same pagans who had dominated Europe. Like all their forerunners in Ireland, the La Tène Celts had gradually adopted the ways of their new country as they changed those of the older community. The spirit of these Iron Age warriors — their martial vigor, their ardent and irascible temper, their poetic imagination and physical skill — fused with the ancient alloy of races and customs they found in Ireland. The result was an exciting blend of tenacity and temperament, self-discipline and anarchy, poetry and casuistry, which the Christian religion would transform into a clear flame of genius.

CHAPTER II
PAGAN IRELAND·
THE PEOPLE

THE LOWEST COMMON DENOMINATORS OF PAGAN IRELAND WERE THE SOIL and the cow. The pastoral society built upon these foundations grew from the simple primitive family unit into an edifice of intimidating complexity. Its culmination, in the time shortly before the advent of Christianity, was the flamboyant and sophisticated period known as the Heroic Age.

This epoch is preserved in colorful and extravagant detail in the series of tales known as the Ulster Cycle, handed down orally by many generations of poets and storytellers, and later inscribed by Christian monks who prized their native heritage. The tales describe the feats, journeys, loves and battles of the warriors of the court of King Conchobar of Ulster, a circle called the Red Branch Knights, from the name of the hall where they traditionally feasted. They operated, it is thought, in the first century B.C., and their center was Emain Macha (said to be at Navan Fort, a prehistoric hill-fort in County Armagh). Ulster was a haughty province perpetually at odds with the rest of Ireland. Its hereditary foe was the equally contu- melious province of Connacht, ruled at that time by King Ailill and his combative queen, Maeve, from Rath Cruachan (on the site of the present Rathcroghan in County Roscommon). The Connacht court had its own circle of knights, and contention between the two sets of hero-warriors was a usage indulged in with ardor: "I swear what my people swear," says an Ulsterman, "since I first took spear and weapons, I have never been a

27

day without having slain a Connachtman . . . nor have I ever slept without the head of a Connachtman under my knee." [1]

The classic contest between the two proud realms is enshrined in the magnificent epic *Tain Bo Cuailnge (The Cattle Raid of Cooley)*. Its main hero, Cuchulain, embodies the contemporary ideals of the Irish-Celtic warrior-aristocrat: courage, honor, physical beauty, a deep respect for women, unmatched arrogance and a nonchalant disregard for death. He is *sui generis*: he leaves no descendants (he kills his one son in a tragic duel) and he is indestructible on the field of battle. Being the spirit of unconquerable youth, he can only be defeated, in the end, by the stratagem of magic. His character, his deeds and his trappings have counterparts in Homer's Greece and the India of the Mahabharata, a throwback to the stories and beliefs of their common Indo-European forebears.

Though the *Tain Bo* is the longest and most spectacular of the Ulster stories, they are all classics of high drama and literary felicity — the latter quality being a contribution as much of their Christian transcribers as of Iron Age storytellers. In addition, they are, along with the several other story cycles, a treasure house of information on the life-style of the pagan Irish-Celts, the civilization that was to give Irish Christianity its unique lineaments.

Even at the time of the *Tain Bo*'s bravura aristocracy, the base of society's extreme structural intricacy remained that primal unit, the family. The family, all members of it equally, owned its land; the family avenged wrongs done to any member of it; the family was made to suffer in toto if one of its members transgressed. The legal family, the *fine*, consisted of all relations in the male line of descent for five generations. Included were a man's sons, his father's brothers, his grandfather's brothers: an unwieldy throng of relatives all sharing alike in the family's goods and privileges, victories and misfortunes.

A cluster of families constituted a *tuath*. The word designates a body of freemen, ruled by a king, which could support from 700 to 3,000 soldiers in emergency; by extension, the term applies to the land occupied by this group. There were over a hundred of these semi-independent petty kingdoms, grouped into five over-kingdoms. Each of these was presided over, in prehistory as well as in recorded history, by a high-king, or *ard-ri*.

The *tuaths* were the ruling force in pagan Ireland. Their king was elected — by the freemen, who alone had the franchise — from among the many eligible members of the ruling family. He was their judge and their war leader, but he did not make the laws, which were decided by the association of freemen in assembly. He was more a sacred figurehead than a ruler: his presence — if he was the rightful king, descended from the ancestor-god — insured the fertility and contentment of his country. An unjust or usurping king brought the land famine, plague and inexpedient war.

The local king might be an over-king as well, but only in his own *tuath* did he have any political authority. Like the other princelings in his dynasty, he was trained in the arts of battle from the age of seven, when he received his first weapons. War was his chief duty and his chosen diversion. The allegiance of his freemen, his tribute, the songs of his bards — he owed these all to his accomplishments on the field. If he died in battle, he was assured of probable reincarnation in a later, presumably still appreciative age. And it could indeed be preferable to die on the battlefield: if he was disfigured by a wound he could no longer be king. This prescription was so stringently observed that sometimes the elected king, in order to insure his continued rule and suppress possible rebellion from eligible cousins, uncles and nephews, would keep a few potential contenders as hostages and see to it that they received a slight disfigurement, such as a needle through the eye, to certify that they could never become king.

The territories conquered by a king were obliged to pay him tribute but in no other ways were they disturbed. He appointed no viceroy to rule the subject people, who continued to elect kings from their native dynasty. Similarly, he chose no general to conduct his battles. His followers were in the enterprise not for victory but for him; if he died on the field, the battle was generally over.

A prince usually tried to prove his fitness to be elected king from among his many eligible relatives by deliberately provoking battle. The country-wide measure of wealth was cattle, and the surest way to get a fight going was to organize a cattle raid. Stealing was not the object. It was not that the raiders really wanted the cows; they were merely offering a gratuitous insult. The king of the territory so affronted was bound to raise his forces in reprisal. The battle that ensued was rarely a prolonged affair, though a great deal of rodomontade went into it. The preliminary noises alone were enough to daunt a timid man: "a rush and a crash and a hurtling sound, and a din and a thunder, a clatter and a clash . . . the shield-cry of feat-shields, and the jangle of javelins, and the deed-striking of swords, and the thud of the helmet, and the ring of spears, and the clang of the cuirass . . . the whirr of wheels, and the creaking of the chariot, the tramping of horses' hoofs."[2]

The noisy approach of the armies was followed by a series of insulting predictions hurled back and forth between the camps: "As numerous as hailstones . . . will be your cloven heads and skulls and the clots of your brains, your bones and the heaps of your bowels. . . . the fragments of you will be fit to go through the sieve of a corn-kiln." [3]

With all its bombastic prelude, however, and despite the subsequent accounts of dead as numerous as "grass on a green," a single day usually saw the battle through. The contrived quarrel might also be resolved by a duel of heroes, each with his chariot and charioteer, his two javelins, his broad slashing sword, his round shield of wood and cowhide and his self-induced, near superhuman battle fury. The hero Cuchulain, when he worked himself into his "warp-spasm" in preparation for battle, became a figure with the monstrous deformity of one of the Celtic gods (after all, he was a demigod):

> His body made a furious twist inside his skin, so that his feet and shins and knees switched to the rear and his heels and calves switched to the front. . . . On his head the temple-sinews stretched to the nape of his neck, each mighty, immense, measureless knob as big as the head of a month-old child. . . . He sucked one eye so deep into his head that a wild crane couldn't probe it onto his cheek out of the depths of his skull; the other eye fell out along his cheek. . . . his cheek peeled back from his jaws until the gullet appeared, his lungs and liver flapped in his mouth and throat. . . . The hair of his head twisted like the tangle of a red thornbush. . . . if a royal apple tree with all its kingly fruit were shaken above him, scarce an apple would reach the ground but each would be spiked on a bristle of his hair as it stood up on his scalp with rage. . . . Then, tall and thick, steady and strong, high as the mast of a noble ship, rose up from the dead center of his skull a straight spout of black blood darkly smoking. [4]

The contest that followed was never a letdown. One of these splendidly savage duels, described at length in the *Tain Bo,* occurred when Cuchulain was forced to fight his best friend and foster brother, Ferdia, a champion from the other side. "They took up their two solid broadshields and their big burdensome stabbing-spears and began piercing and drilling each other and felling and overwhelming from the gray of early morning until the evening sunset. If ever birds in flight could pass through men's bodies they could have passed through those bodies that day and brought bits of blood and meat with them out into the thickening air through the wounds and gashes." The quarrel did not last beyond sunset, when the heroes "came up to each other and each put his arm around the other's neck and gave him three kisses. Their horses passed that night in the same paddock and their charioteers by the same fire." But they were at it again at dawn the next morning, and the days following, until the contest ended with Ferdia's death. His closest friend and mortal enemy clasped him in his arms and mourned:

> *What have I to do with spirit?*
> *Stupor and sorrow weigh me down*
> *After the deed that I have done,*
> *This corpse that I have hacked so harshly.*
>
> . . . .
>
> *Ill-met, Ferdia, like this*
> *— You crimson and pale in my sight*
> *And stretched in a bed of blood,*
> *I with my weapon unwiped.*
>
> . . . .
>
> *Misery has befallen us,*
> *Scathach's two foster-sons*
> *— You dead and I alive*
> *Bravery is battle-madness!*[5]

Hotheaded the Celtic heroes might be, but they were never coldhearted. Love, honor and chivalry were as important as valor in the field and carelessness toward fate.

The battle infatuation of kings and heroes, with the active concurrence of their followers, would seem to preclude normal attention to the homely business of daily life. Such a pitch of continuous belligerence, one would think, should have reduced the country to a permanent condition of anarchy. However, though the pagan Irish were not notably peaceable, their day-to-day existence was elaborately structured. They were hemmed in by a complex body of common law, called the Brehon Laws, which had grown gradually out of custom, hereditary habit and public opinion. Their smallest actions were governed by prescriptions and strictures, from the rules covering the imposition of different fines for bee stings in various parts of the body, and the stealing of a needle from an embroideress, to the exact articles of clothing that must be provided a child, depending upon his family's place in society, when he entered fosterage.

Bodily injury and homicide were atoned for with a fine called an *eric*, calculated, like all financial transactions, in cows. The *eric* entailed payment for the injury — the amount depended on its severity — plus the honor-price of the victim. The higher the rank, the greater the honor-price (a poet's being equal to a king's). Injuries were enumerated with minute precision. If a wound was inflicted on the face, for instance, the *eric* was greater than if the blemish was hidden by the clothing. The system was regulated so that the rich did not have all the advantages. It did not quite work out that way, but it was preferable to the notion of more primitive societies that the law was the tool of private vengeance, and that justice should be dispensed by direct retaliation.

If a man (or his family, because all five generations of it were liable for the indiscretion of one) did not pay his fine, the plaintiff often had recourse to the procedure of fasting, a device of peculiar potency. He went to the house of the wrongdoer and sat before the door, eschewing food and drink, until the defendant paid or pledged the fine. He always did pay or pledge because, according to law, "he that does not give a pledge to fasting is an evader of all: he who disregards . . . shall not be paid by God or man."[6] Fasting was regarded with superstitious awe, a resource as powerful as the poet's satire; furthermore, he who was fasted against and did not regard it lost his character and was universally boycotted.

The death penalty was frequently invoked. A man who got in a fight at a fair, where peace was sacrosanct, and killed his opponent, was put to death — generally thrown into the water tied up in a sack. A woman caught in adultery was burned to death.

Society was straitly classified, its degrees based, at the top, on nobility, wealth and learning, and going on down the scale to the hapless refugee or escaped criminal. The highest were the kings and nobles, who owned the land. Below them were various grades of freemen, starting with the highest-ranking *bo-aire* (cow-lord), who must have property (but not land; this he rented from the resident noble family) worth thrice seven *cumals*. A *cumal* was a female slave and she was worth four milch cows. The lowest grade was the great class of free farmers, who owned no property but who were the bedrock foundation of the country, the ultimate source of all law and authority. The peasants, though they owned no land, had rights in the tribal land, which included forest, heath, river, lake and seashore. A man could kill one salmon for his family's need if the stream ran near his dwelling, and could cast his net once thereon. The wild garlic of the woods was his, as was the nut-gathering. He could take from the forest one night's supply of kindling, timber enough for a coffin, a spear shaft, a churnstaff and the hoops for a barrel. He could pluck the dulse that grows just below tide line and take the jetsam that the waves wash ashore. He could pasture his sheep and cattle on "the common mountain" — that is, on the highlands above the arable fields.

Below the freemen was the class of the nonfree, again divided into grades. "Nonfree" did not mean slaves only, though there were slaves (well into the Christian era, the English sold their children as slaves to the Irish through the great slave market at Bristol). The nonfree classification signified people who did not have the legal rights of freemen nor claim to any part of the common land. Included were laborers, herdsmen, squatters on wastelands — down to the lowest, the *fudir* (fugitive), the best of whom were "kin-wrecked" refugees from other territories and the least regarded of whom were escaped criminals, battle captives or convicts respited from death. *Fudirs* were not popular in the *tuath;* they lowered its tone. But the chief felt otherwise. He was pleased to have on call a large body of expendable fighting men.

No one below the rank of noble could travel, except with special permission, outside the borders of his *tuath.* Soldiers of the king stood on guard to challenge travellers at the river fords and mountain passes that marked the boundaries. Beyond his native soil a man's rights ceased and he became an outcast. The only people allowed the freedom of the roads were members of the highly privileged class — the *aes dana* — whose members came from all the other classes. The phrase *aes dana*, which means "people of poetry," was applied not only to poets but to historians, jurists, physicians and skilled craftsmen. A principle of pagan Ireland was that "a man is better than his birth." No matter how poor or lowborn he was, learning elevated a man to the status of freeman; a higher level of attainment, that of *ollam* (master), equated him with a king. The poet or harper, the doctor or the lawyer could travel anywhere in Ireland. "Each of Ulster's heroic warriors," it is written in the *Tain Bo,* "had his day on Sliab Fuait, to take care of every man who came that way with poetry, and to fight any others."[7]

Not only was the roving scholar free to use the highways, he was welcome everywhere. Men of learning were considered as essential to the well-being of the king as his fighting heroes. In a country intensely family-proud, eaten by petty strife and divided into fiercely guarded tiny states, the freedom of the *aes dana* and the high regard shown to them was a benison. The blessings of education spread equally over all of Ireland, giving her a singular cultural unity and grace of outlook. By the time of Conchobar and the Red Branch Knights in the first century B.C., one-third of Irish men, it is written, were either teachers or poets. There were not schools as we know them: the poet took his pupils with him on his travels and taught them when it was convenient, usually out of doors. He was entitled to hospitality wherever he went, along with his entire company — a privilege, as we shall see, that was sorely abused in later years. Allied to the reverence for education was the system of fosterage: children, both boys and girls, were sent at an early age to live with foster parents, who were responsible for their care and instruction. The bonds of sympathy and affection that grew from this relationship were often stronger than the ties of the blood family and lasted a lifetime; the foster child, in return for his early care, was responsible for his adoptive parents in old age, poverty or illness.

One of the more important gods was Ogma, the "honey-mouthed," who was the god of literature and son of the chief god, the Dagda. Ogma was described by Lucian of Samosata, a Greek satirist of the second century A.D., as drawing "a willing crowd of people, fastened to him by slender golden chains, the ends of which pass through his tongue." His devotees, among the highest regarded of the *aes dana,* were the *filid* (poets). This class went back to Ireland's legendary beginnings, to Amergin, the druid, a son of Mil, who chanted a poetic incantation to the beings of earth and sky as he stepped on Ireland's shore in the fifth and final mythical invasion. But poetry as we conceive it — a distilled and euphonious expression of emotion — did not exist in the Heroic Age. The poems in the sagas, many of felicitous charm, were composed later by those anonymous poets, the monastic scribes. The *filid* class developed to a fine pitch in the years just before the Christian era, many of its members reaching equality with kings. This order comprised historians, who kept alive the deeds of heroes and recorded the genealogies (most important in a society based on hereditary aristocracy); *brehons* (lawyers) to expound and clarify the law according to tradition and precedent; and straight poets, men of "poison in satire and splendor in praise,"[8] who composed not abstract verse but eulogy or satire for the glorification or debasement of its object.

Forms of verse were many, complex and sophisticated, and the straight poets had to go through as elaborate a training as all the other men of learning to achieve the status of *ollam.* When they reached that stage they could wield a weapon of fearful authority: satire. This ranged from the simple "insulting speech without harmony" to the *glam dicend* (satire from the hilltops), which was an elaborate ritual of magic.

The satirizing of Caier, the king of Connacht, is an illustration not only of the mystic and awful power of the poet but of the pervasive force of the taboos and rules governing the life of the pagan Irishman. Caier's wife fell in love with his nephew and adopted-son Nede, a poet. She asked her lover to produce blemishes on the king with satire: a disfigured king must be deposed, and Nede would reign in his place. Nede could not oblige: to strike with satire he had to ask for something and be refused, and Caier would not refuse anything to his loved adopted son. The disloyal wife pointed out that her husband could not give up his knife because it was taboo that he should part with it. Nede asked for the knife, was regretfully refused, and thereupon extemporized a satire. The next morning, when the hapless king went to the fountain to wash, he found three blisters on his face — "disgrace, blemish and defect" — which the satire had raised in red, green and white. He fled in shame, and when later Nede, who had become king in his place, repented and went to find him, Caier hid in a cleft of rock. There he was discovered by his own dog. Nede approached with words of atonement but on seeing him the unhappy man fell dead of humiliation. The rock of his hiding place boiled up and burst, and a splinter entered one of Nede's eyes and broke in his head.

Not all learning was oral. The Irish had an alphabet, though it was cumbersome, before Christianity made writing easy with the Roman alphabet. The earlier system was named *Ogam,* after Ogma, the Celtic god of literature, who invented it. It consisted of horizontal strokes along a stem line, a certain number and position of strokes for each letter. The twenty letters were based on the Roman alphabet but arranged differently. The pages of a normal-length book, printed in this alphabet, would cover about a mile. It was used mainly for inscriptions for the dead, carved on wood or stone.

Awe of the sorcery of words was equalled by belief in the spell of music, which was bequeathed to the Irish by their hero-god Lug. He in turn derived it from an older source, the Dagda, chief god of a more archaic Celtic pantheon. When the Dagda's wife, the goddess Boann (the river Boyne), was in labor, he played upon his harp, crying and mourning with her in her pains. When her sons were born he brought laughter and joy to her, then he made the sounds of sleep, to bring her rest. When she awoke she named her sons, in gratitude to her husband and his harp, Goltraighe (crying music), Geantraighe (laughing music) and Suantraighe (sleeping music).

Two of the compelling strains were used when Labraid Loingsiuch courted Moriath, daughter of Scoriath, in *The Destruction of Dindrigh.* The lovers were never allowed to be alone together, as her parents did not approve of him, and they called at last on her father's harper to help them.

He played at a feast, making the company joyous with the *Geantraighe*, then invoked on his harp the *Suantraighe,* the sleeping music, and put the whole assemblage into the sleep that was like death. The young couple, absent during the lethal lullaby, became lovers in the interval. When the queen awoke she took one look at her happy daughter and said to her husband, "Arise, Scoriath, thy daughter respires the breath of a plighted wife; hear her sigh, after the secret of her love has passed away from her."[9]

The Dagda's harp, the first Irish harp, was probably a quadrangular instrument with six strings tuned to the pentatonic scale (the black notes on the piano keyboard), very like the lyre of the Thracian Orpheus in Greek classical sculpture. It is thought to be the harp still in use in early Christian times, for it turns up in an appealing bas-relief Bible scene on a ninth-century granite high cross at Castledermot, County Kildare: a small four-cornered instrument held in the lap of a seated David. The Irish harp was plucked with the fingernail, and the law was minutely circumstantial about the reparation due to a player whose plucking finger was injured:

> If the top of his finger, from the root of the nail . . . has been cut off . . . he is entitled to compensation [for his injured body] and a fine [for his outraged honor], in proportion to the severity of the wound. If the blood has been drawn while cutting his nail off, he is entitled to the fine for blood-shedding for it. If it be from the black circle out that his nail has been taken off him, he is entitled to the same fine as for a white [bloodless] blow. Then there is a quill for him besides, by way of restitution.[10]

The harper was a freeman, not quite as high in rank as a poet; he was placed just below the poet at the king's banqueting table. But the chief harper, the *ollam* of his profession, was up there among the best grades of the gentry, entitled to four cows as his honor price.

Besides the harp, there were wind and brass instruments: horns, which were not used for music proper but to call men together for war or for hunting; and bagpipes, the musical instrument of the peasantry. Performers on the latter were classed, with jugglers, among the inferior professions. They sat at the bottom of the king's table, in the corner near the door, next to the mercenaries, and they were not in the class of freemen.

The decorative art of the Heroic Age was a rare achievement of beauty in abstract imagery. The latest masters of Ireland had brought with them from the Continent the La Tène techniques and styles of metal- and stone-work; and they found in Ireland an already flourishing artistic tradition.

What developed was an art style peculiar to the island, which would set its mark on the inimitable creativity of the Christian era.

The workers in gold, bronze, iron, wood and stone, while they were highly respected, were not in as elite a class as poets and historians. They belonged to an upper circle of artisans, called the "base professions" because they had to use their hands. What came out of their shops and forges, however, is no less true art: forms of dramatic simplicity covered with cryptic geometric decoration. Circles and spirals, zigzags and trumpet shapes intertwist in graceful, complex patterns that seem to have a secret meaning. Weapons and personal ornaments were the chief vehicles, though their horses' bits were also decorated, as well as the knobs and feet of their furniture, their cooking caldrons, their musical instruments — in fact, almost any object that offered a surface.

What remains is almost all of metal and stone, but the artisans used wood extensively. The trees were designated by law (which regulated their cutting and use) according to their quality. "Chieftain" trees were oak, yew, ash, pine, holly, apple and hazel: all noble because of their superior usefulness. An oak was beneficial for its fine building timber, for its acorns (to feed pigs) and its bark (to tan leather) and, not least, for its lordly beauty. The hazel carried their favorite nuts, and its flexible branches formed the wickerwork of their houses and boats. Yew wood was used for building, for the finest furniture and for household vessels. From the ash came wood for furniture and for the shafts of spears. Barrels and casks were made of pine. Apples were valued for their fruit and their tanning bark. Holly provided chariot shafts. In a lower category were "common" trees: alder, willow and hawthorn. Then came "shrub" trees: blackthorn, elder, arbutus. At the bottom of the list — but also useful in their ways — were "bramble" trees: furze, bog myrtle, broom and gooseberry.

The metalworkers were specially skilled in creating and developing alloys and utilizing in one object several metals — as two different-colored bronzes, or bronze with gold — to create striking artistic effects by surface contrast alone.

The stonework has the same curvilinear, interlacing patterns as those on the metal ornaments and household tools. Probably the most splendid example is the Turoe Stone in County Galway (illustrated on page 61), of which we will speak later. Though the Celts, both on the Continent and in Ireland, were rarely representational in their art, there remain a few human figures, deliberately grotesque as were the gods in the old stories, such as two- and three-faced idols.

Aside from the few examples of human depiction and some highly stylized and unrecognizable animals, the pagan art of Ireland is nonrepresentational, geometric and sophisticated. It is overlaid with mysticism, a deliberate obscurity like that of the druids who did not want the common people to understand too much. This abstract, enigmatic imagery, specifically Celtic and totally alien to idealistic Greco-Roman artistic concepts, was to turn up later in the pages of the *Book of Kells* and other fantastic and beautiful illustrated Gospels produced by monks who were direct descendants spiritually as well as physically of pagan priests and artisans.

Love of battle and reverence for the arts were two facets of the Irish-Celtic character. A third, equally vital, was their delight in outdoor activities, along with which went a sensuous pleasure in nature and a fondness for animals. Among their domestic animals the spectacular wolf-dogs, "big as an ass," were in demand all over Europe; they were presented as gifts to kings. When seven of them were brought to Rome in the fourth century A.D., a Roman observer thought, from their size and savagery, that they must have been conveyed thither in iron cages. The wolf-dogs needed to be fierce because wolves, in those days when there were still extensive forests, were a numerous and formidable menace. The great dogs were also used for sport hunting, chiefly of boars and deer. There were beagles for hunting hares, greyhounds for racing and lapdogs for the ladies of the aristocracy.

The horse was, as it had been on the Continent, the Celtic passion. The Irish-Celts rode them from their earliest years (a prince received his first horse when he was seven), drove them and raced them. Horses were their friends in life and guardians at death. When Cuchulain went into his last battle, his horse, the Gray of Macha, foreseeing his master's death, "let his big round tears of blood fall on Cuchulain's feet." When the hero stood, fatally wounded, the horse came "to protect him as long as his soul was in him. . . . And the horse wrought three red routs all around him. And fifty fell by his teeth and thirty by each of his hoofs."[11]

In the tales of Finn Mac Cumail and his followers, the *Fianna,* love for the out-of-doors was at its pre-Christian height. These stories form the Ossianic (or Fenian) Cycle, named for the poet Ossian, Finn's son; their period is later than that of the gallants of the Heroic Age — probably the third century A.D. In contrast to the court of King Conchobar, where the emphasis was on the arts and sports of the aristocracy, the main bent of the Ossianic Cycle is toward the man's world of the untamed woodlands and the attractions of nature. One can see here clearly the hand of the monastic scribe, in the tenderness and passion with which scenes of nature are limned. Who would be better attuned to this world than the ascetic recluse? — free from everyday vexations, sensitized by extreme austerity and exquisitely receptive to the few events of his life: the song of a bird or the color of the sky in the morning. The life-style of the *Fianna,* who subsisted on the fringes of society, would further have appealed to the inveterate wanderlust of early Irish clerics. Penitential exile was the ideal of many young monks: eschewing home and family life, they sought a "desert in the ocean," or an alien barbarian land, or they simply spent their lives in never-ending itineracy in their own country.

The *Fianna* was an army of the forests, led by the folk hero and demigod Finn, starkly Spartan in his perspective yet in touch with the world of magic. The *fian,* band of warriors, was originally a group of seminomadic hunters living off the land. In later stories, which savor more of peasant folklore than of the high knightly ideals of Cuchulain and his allies, they came to be King Cormac Mac Art's standing army, the defenders of their country against invaders.

To enter Finn's band one must foreswear all ties with family and home, and undergo a stringent training. One must, first of all, be a poet versed in the twelve traditional forms of poetry. The physical ordeals of initiation were harsh. The candidate stood in a waist-high hole armed only with his shield and a short hazel branch; with these he must ward off the spears thrown by the warriors, and if one touched him he was disqualified. He must braid his hair and run through the forest pursued by the others: he must not be wounded or captured, his weapon must not tremble in his hand nor a twig crack under his foot nor a branch disturb one braid of his hair. He must be able to draw a thorn out of his foot while running, leap over a stick as high as his forehead, and streak under one level with his knee.

When he was accepted he was, with his companions, in the anomalous position of being outside society but not outside the law. The *Fianna* could not claim compensation for injury but, though they lived by hunting, plundering and warfare, they were not considered brigands. In the winter months, from Samain (November 1) to Beltine (May 1), they lived off the people, keeping their foraging to a necessary minimum. At the same time they acted as the king's defenders, upholding justice and guarding the coasts and harbors from foreign invaders. In the summertime, while continuing their work of national defense, they roamed the forests and led the life of footloose hunter-warriors. Though ascetic in their ideals they did not foreswear women: they had first right to the girls of the tribe, who could not be given in marriage before they had been offered to the *Fianna.*

Finn Mac Cumail's country, the lakes and forests of southern Ireland

This on occasion made the *Fianna* considerably unpopular, and it was the cause of their final downfall, when they demanded too important a princess.

Though they were outside the conventional rules of society and their exploits and forays were not always condoned, the *Fianna* were in the main a force for good. They "expelled from Ireland marauders and reavers and monsters and many beasts and full many a fleet of exiles and every other pest. And there came a plague to Ireland from one corner to another; and for a whole year Finn fed the men of Ireland and put seven cows and a bull in every single farmstead." [12]

It is in their relations with animals and their love of nature that the spirit of the *Fianna* shines most brightly. One of Finn's wives was a doe. Her child could be human if she did not lick it; if she did it would turn into a fawn. She could not quite resist — so Finn's son Ossian, the poet, had a tuft of fur on his forehead. Finn's two most faithful companions were two dogs who were also his nephews, by a sister who had been changed to a bitch by a jealous rival. By turning his magic hood, Finn could change himself to a deer, for his wife, or a dog, for his nephews. One animal beloved in the heroic tales is conspicuously absent in the Fenian: the horse.

The *Fianna* operated entirely on foot, and this endeared them to the peasant class, whose idols they were to become in later years.

The *Fianna's* joy in hunting was attributable as much to the attraction of nature as to delight in the chase: "It was sweet music to Finn's ear the cry of the long-snouted dogs as they routed the deer from their covers and the badgers from their dens" and "the melodious chase by beagles after the swift and gentle hares," and "more melodious than all music . . . was to give ear to the voices of the birds as they rose from the billows." Of an island that was one of their hunting grounds, the Fenian poet Cailte, cousin of Ossian, says:

> Skittish deer are on her pinnacles, soft blackberries on her waving heather; cool water there is in her rivers, and mast upon her russet oaks. Greyhounds there were . . . and beagles; berries and sloes of the dark blackthorn . . . and the deer fed scattered by her oaken thickets. A crimson crop grew on her rocks, in all her glades a faultless grass; . . . her wild swine, they were fat; cheerful her fields, her nuts hung on her forest-hazels' boughs; . . . under her rivers' brinks trout lie; the sea-gulls wheeling round her grand cliff answer one the other.[13]

In a conversation with the nobles, Cailte tells of the division of Ireland between Tuathal and Fiacha, sons of King Feradach Fechtnach. One, he said, took "the treasure, the herds and the fortresses," the other "the cliffs and estuaries, the fruits of the forest and sea, the salmon and the game."[14]

The storyteller is interrupted by the nobles, who maintain that the division was unequal. "Which of the two parts would you have chosen?" asks the poet.

"The banquets, the dwellings and all the other precious things," they answer.

"The part you despise," says Cailte, "seems more precious to us."

Finn's band may have been an actual social institution, an army dedicated to helping the people and defending the realm. Or its origin may lie deep in Ireland's mythology — Finn has attributes, as does Cuchulain, of the Celtic god Lug. Regardless of where the tales come from, they have been refined and transmuted by the pens of cloistered monks and secular poets of later centuries, until the *Fianna,* dwellers in the wilds and champions of the poor, have become the Irish myth par excellence of the romantic outlaw. What comes down to us, the essence of the *Fianna,* filtered through centuries of oral and written retellings, is best expressed by Cailte in his conversations with St. Patrick in *The Colloquy of the Old Men.* "Were but the brown leaf which the wood sheds from it gold — were but the white billows silver — Finn would have given it all away," [15] said the poet.

"Who or what was it that maintained you so in your life?" asked St. Patrick.

"Truth that was in our hearts, and strength in our arms, and fulfilment in our tongues."

The pagan Irish, while adoring their turbulent, fearless heroes and revering the mystic power of their poets, obviously savored the fleshly side of life. They dressed opulently and they ate and drank well. Men and women alike delighted in clothing of bright primary colors, and in heavy gold, silver and bronze ornaments. The gaze of the cloistered monk, setting down on parchment the gaudy descriptions of his forebears' dress, must sometimes have wandered ruefully over his own simple habit of undyed wool. When King Eochaid first saw the maiden Etain, one of them wrote,

> she held in her hand a comb of silver decorated with gold. Beside her, as for washing, was a basin of silver whereon were chased four golden birds, and there were little bright gems of carbuncle set in the rim of the basin. A cloak, pure purple, hanging in folds about her, and beneath it a mantle with silver borders, and a brooch of gold in the garment over her bosom. A tunic with a long hood about her . . . made of green silk beneath red embroidery of gold, and marvelous bow-pins of silver and gold upon her breasts in the tunic, so that the redness of the gold against the sun in the green silk was clearly visible. . . . Two tresses of golden hair upon her head, and a plaiting of four strands in each tress, and a ball of gold upon the end of each plait. [16]

The men were no less addicted to brilliance and complexity in their dress. When Cuchulain was not fighting he outshone even the king. "This is what he wore," wrote the scribe, his mouth perhaps watering: "a fitted purple mantle, fringed and fine, folded five times and held at his . . . breast by a brooch of light-gold and silver decorated with gold inlays. . . . A fretted silk tunic covered him down to the top of his warrior's apron of dark-red royal silk." When dressed for battle he wore

> twenty-seven tunics of waxed skin, plated and pressed together and fastened with strings and cords and straps against his clear skin, that his senses or his brain wouldn't burst their bonds at the onset of his fury. Over them he put on his heroic deep battle-belt

of stiff, tough tanned leather from the choicest parts of the hides of seven yearlings, covering him from his narrow waist to the thickness of his armpit. . . . Then he drew his silk-smooth apron, with its light-gold speckled border, up to the softness of his belly. Over this silky, skin-like apron he put on a dark apron of well-softened black leather.[17]

Types and colors of garments were decreed by law with tortuous exactitude, according to the class of the wearer — from the king, who might wear seven colors, down to his lowest servant, who was allowed only one. A poet could wear six colors, which was one more than was allotted to a chief. Most clothing was of wool and linen locally raised and dyed with colors from the field flowers. Irish dyers were expert, and it was a common fancy for the young aristocrat to wear a cloak of many colors. Fur was valuable, and constituted a large export item. For home consumption skins of seal, otter, badger and fox were fashioned into capes and garment edgings for chieftains and kings.

Jewelry — finely chased with the Celtic geometric patterns yet with shapes of the most elegant simplicity — was so heavy that it must have been a chafing discomfort on the aristocratic body. Queen Maeve, when she was persuading Ferdia to fight against the Ulster champion Cuchulain, offered him — along with her daughter's hand in marriage and "my own friendly thighs on top of that if needs be" — her "leaf-shaped brooch . . . that was made out of ten score ounces and ten score half-ounces and ten score cross-measures and ten score quarters of gold."[18] This adds up to about four pounds.

There was almost no part of the person of a princess or a chief that was not weighed down with precious metals and stones. Besides brooches — which were worn by everybody to fasten the conventional loose-hanging cloak at the throat and which were made of gold, silver and bronze for the aristocracy, of iron for the poor — they wore finger and thumb rings (a ring for every king killed in battle), ankle circlets, neck torques of twisted gold ribbon or etched design, bands of gold, silver or white bronze around the forehead, earrings looped over the ears and golden balls for the ends of the braided hair. Much of this jewelry was studded with gems: amethyst, topaz, emerald, sapphire or garnet.

Food was never a problem in fertile Ireland. Nearly everyone, no matter how high his rank, was basically a farmer. Though there were no towns, each farm was a self-sufficient settlement endowed with prodigal sources of food, domesticated and wild, in the fields, the rivers, the forests and the barnyards. Cattle, as well as being the measure of wealth, also supplied the main part of the food and clothing. In the fall the animals were slaughtered on account of the impending shortage of fodder, and beef cured with salt became the winter staple. The cutting of a beef at the king's banquet was a class ritual. The meat was given according to rank: "A thigh for a king and a poet; a chine [backbone] for a literary sage; a leg for a young lord; heads for charioteers; a haunch for queens." [19] The king's hero always got the choicest bit, and mortal fights sometimes ensued between rival heroes who were not so much jealous as arrogant. The story *Bricriu's Feast* centers around such a quarrel of outraged vanity, as Bricriu goads each of three heroes into competing for the champion's portion. The monkish scribe who wrote it down in his quiet cell caught the spirit of Celtic ebullience as the three hotheaded heroes went to it, first flinging fulsome insults at one another, then sallying forth after giants and lake monsters — all for the honor of a better cut of beef.

Other domestic food animals were pigs (blood sausage and bacon were popular in Ireland then as now), goats and sheep. Though the Irish of that time were primarily pastoral, they grew some grains: oats, barley, wheat and rye, from which they made unleavened bread and porridge, called stirabout, the staple of the masses. In the kitchen gardens they grew cabbages, leeks, onions, garlic, parsnips and carrots. They ate some wild vegetables: watercress for salad, and dulse and laver from the ocean, which they dried and ate with wildfowl. Among their fruits were the blackthorn, or sloe (a kind of wild plum), strawberries, whortleberries and rowanberries. Apple trees were carefully cultivated, and hazelnuts were a choice food. Most fruit and nuts were eaten raw, though some apples were made into cider, and there was a kind of wine made from whortleberries.

Milk products were the summer staple: butter, thick sour milk, curds and cheese. A preferred kind of cheese was made of curds compressed until they were stone-hard. Queen Maeve's nephew, annoyed at her for some slight — it was not hard to be angered by that high-handed lady — put a clod of this cheese into his sling and shot her on the forehead, killing her instantly.

Hunters brought in venison of the red deer, considered a princely dish, wild boar, badger, hare and wild birds. There were no domestic chickens, but people ate the eggs of wildfowl, especially those of the goose. Ireland being a country lavishly supplied with lakes and rivers, there was always fish for the table, among which salmon was revered as food for kings.

Beekeeping was a very big item, and regulation of the industry takes up much space in the Brehon Laws. Honey was the only sweetener, eaten with everything and even used to baste the roast. Its chief use was its fermentation into mead, "the dainty drink of nobles." Everyone else drank beer, made from fermented barley malt boiled with aromatic herbs of oak bark and brewed in oaken vats (an invention of the Continental Celts).

Meat and fish were roasted or broiled over open fires, baked underground between hot stones, or boiled in great bronze caldrons on wood- or peat-burning hearths (cow dung was used in the poorest homes). The size of the household cooking pots is indicated in the Brehon Laws relating to the mandatory possessions of a middle-class farmer: "A bronze caldron into which a hog fits."

Flavoring included butter, salt, bacon, lard and vegetables. Salt was greatly prized, as it was not as easily come by as it is now. Bread was baked in loaves or cakes of "man-size" or "woman-size," and a larger cake was kept whole for guests, before whom should never be placed a cut loaf.

The plenitude of good native food insured that the Irish-Celts were basically healthy; besides, they had a care for their general physical well-being. Doctors, members of the *aes dana*, went through a long training period — the students, like the novice poets, living with the master and travelling with him. On attaining *ollam* status they had reached the elite of the *aes dana* and sat high at the king's table. The law dealt minutely with insurance for the care of the patient and the demands made of the doctor. If a man wounded another, not only was he liable for a specified fine but he must stand the costs of doctor and hospital as well; further, if the doctor failed through negligence or lack of skill to heal the wound, he had to pay the patient the same fine that the assailant had.

The original doctor, a Celtic god named Diancecht, had killed his son Midach through envy of his greater medical skill; from the son's grave grew 365 herbs, one for the healing of each part of a man's body. Midach's sister, Airmeda, also medically wise, picked the herbs and classified them, but her jealous father emptied them out of her mantle, mixing them all up so that later generations could never quite sort them out again. But Diancecht's descendants, however limited by their forerunner's ill nature, were known even on the Continent for their knowledge of medical botany and their successful use of herbs to heal a variety of ailments. Besides the use of herbs both orally and in medicated baths, Irish doctors were skilled in surgery, from the simple stitching of a wound to cesarean sections and the complex brain operation of trepanning. They also knew well the importance in the healing process of fresh air, clear running water and general cleanliness. Every physician was obliged to build his house over a running stream; a mere spring would not do. Further, his house must have doors on all four sides, at least one of which must be open for ventilation of the sickroom.

Medical superstition, of course, was extensive: a druid could produce hideous malaises — from boils, ulcers and falling hair to driveling insanity — by pronouncing evil words over a wisp of hay, which he then threw in the face of his intended victim. But in general the practices of the medical profession were not only respectable but remarkably sound.

Though cleanliness was a prerequisite for the treatment of disease, in the normal way of life sanitation was not a major consideration. The floors of the houses were strewn with alternating layers of refuse and rushes, with now and then a new flooring of clay to cover it all up and begin again. The smoke from the central hearth added to what must have been a pungent effluvium. (It should be noted that sloppy housekeeping was not a peculiarity of the pagan Irish; archaeologists have found a similar situation — a bonanza to them — in the dwellings of the early Anglo-Saxons.)

The wealthier farmers lived in settlements called *raths* (ring-forts), a group of buildings enclosed by earthworks with hedges or palisades on top to keep out unwanted guests and wild animals. The buildings were mostly wattle and daub: a round or rectangular wall of poles was interwoven with supple rods of hazel and plastered over with mud or clay. In parts of Ireland where wood was scarce, notably the southwest, building was of stone. Some of the smaller of these ancient dwellings still stand, testifying to the skill of their builders. The stonemasons did not know how to construct an arch and had not learned the use of lime in mortar (though they used lime to whiten their walls). So they built with overlapping stones, the corbelling method that was ancient in Ireland even then, having been used, as mentioned earlier, by the Stone Age architects of Newgrange. The beehive-shaped huts were uniquely durable, though as homes they must have been dark and damp. Most of them are one-story and windowless, with a low door and the rooftop opening serving as the only sources of light and air.

This prehistoric building style was taken over by the monks of the early Christian period — the monastic village on Skellig Michael is an example — and even up to the last century the little huts were being constructed for farm purposes. In Slea Head barnyards on the Dingle Peninsula, County Kerry, are some very old ones, possibly dating from pagan times, their tops fallen in but their round walls still intact. They are so small that they could never have been used as dwellings; more likely they were shepherds' shelters. Lately they have been used for storing hay and for other farm purposes. Since their antiquity has been discovered, however, the farmers realize that the tourist value is greater than their own immediate convenience, and a few pence are charged to view them. But the little gray stone buildings are still an integral part of the farmyard. Puppies play among the fallen roof slabs, chickens peck at the old hay on the dirt floors, and cows nibble the grass growing out of the curving walls.

A more protectible kind of homestead was the *crannog* (lake dwelling), an artificial island in a swamp or the shallow part of a lake, made of layers of peat and brushwood on a foundation of logs, all held together by a circle of timber pilings. On top of this round islet were several small thatched and plastered wickerwork houses, round, oval or rectangular, enclosed by a palisade of vertical logs interwoven with saplings. Though the floors were paved with flagstones, there could have been little protection against the pervasive dampness. The inhabitants must have felt almost as uncomfortable as secure in their humid sanctuaries.

Chieftains had larger residences, called *duns* (fortresses), similar to the *raths* of the wealthy farmers but having two or more walls of earth or stone, with a water-filled ditch between them. They were always built in defensible places, on a mountainside, a hilltop or the edge of a seaside cliff. Those still standing are difficult to date, as they have been used through the centuries, some up until the seventeenth. But the hill-fort style of dwelling undeniably originated before the Christian era, and some of these massive piles may have been strongholds of the Celtic Iron Age chieftains in the first and second centuries A.D., the personae of the Heroic Age.

Staigue Fort, in County Kerry, is the archetype. Its position at the head of a narrow valley is dramatically commanding: a small dirt road winds up through the boggy flower-strewn valley, and at the end of it there is the great somber circle of the fort rising from the green to challenge the bare stony hills on either side. The dry-stone walls are thirteen feet thick and up to eighteen high, and they enclose an area ninety feet in diameter. All around is loneliness; there is not a farm in sight, and it may have been so in the Iron Age too. Forts had dwellings inside them then, but the farms of their demesnes were widely separated. The people would have resorted to the safety of the great walls only in times of serious danger. The position of Staigue Fort is almost invulnerable: before it nothing impedes the view down the valley to the ocean two and a half miles below, while behind and on both sides is the high bristly terrain of the interior of the Iveragh Peninsula.

Dun Aenghus, on the island of Inishmore in the Aran Islands, County

Galway, is a cliffside fort of equally sovereign position. Legend has it that the Fir Bolg, Ireland's third invaders, after being defeated and banished from Ireland by the Tuatha De Danann at the conclusion of the first battle of Mag Tured, returned several hundred years later, in the first century B.C., as Clann Umoir, whose chief was Aenghus. They were pardoned by King Ailill and Queen Maeve of Connacht, and granted the seaboard of Galway and Clare, and the Aran Islands. On Inishmore they built fortresses, of which the greatest is Dun Aenghus. The visitor climbs steeply from the island's central road to the cliff edge, through a field of flat light-gray rocks. Scarlet pimpernel and bloody cranesbill alternate with pillows of purple wild thyme on the grass between them. The broad avenue of straight-edged rocks with the motley-hued edging has the look of a man-made promenade, its goal the enormous roofless mass of Dun Aenghus, dark against the bright sky. The approach is accompanied by the dull heavy boom of the invisible ocean, like a roll of drums, imparting to the scene a tangible sense of formality and portent.

The reality of Dun Aenghus is even more impressive. Though much of it was restored, not too accurately, in the nineteenth century, it retains a primitive look of forbidding majesty. The cliff forms the seaward wall, a straight sheer scarp dropping two hundred feet to the sea. Back of it three massive semicircular walls enclose eleven acres of the hilltop. As if the high

Dun Aenghus — prehistoric fort on Inishmore, Aran Islands, County Galway

dry-stone walls (parts of them over twelve feet thick) were not enough defense, there is outside the outermost circle a thirty-foot band of jagged upright stones, known as chevaux-de-frise, to discourage intruders before they reached the first wall. But they could hardly have got even as far as the bottom of the hill. The defenders not only had a comfortable view over the stony pastures of Inishmore, they could spot their enemies before they left the mainland. From the eighteen-foot height of the inner wall, the coast of Connemara is sharply visible to the north.

According to early Christian poets and historians (our only sources of information on pagan Ireland), this is the way it was when St. Patrick came in the fifth century A.D.; and this was the way it remained, with not much modification, for the first five hundred years of Christianity. With all their originality, their imagination and their zest for living, the Irish were a deeply conservative people. Though not precisely out of Europe, they were on the edge; and their isolation excluded them from the progress, for good or ill, of the rest of Europe.

They had no towns and no centralized authority. Farms were isolated, homesteads were walled, provincial boundaries were fiercely guarded. Family members were dangerously jealous; heroes bristled with prideful, easily bruised honor; princes had an immoderate addiction to battle. Irish pagan society, it seems, should have been discrete and unkempt, if not downright anarchical. Yet it cohered. It not only cohered, it had an exuberant grace. Partly this was because it was pagan. The religion, though we know little of it, must have been an expression of the Celtic high style. It must have given significance to their ardor and justified their extravagantly spirited way of life. Above all, it must have informed and inspired their art, music and poetry.

CHAPTER III
PAGAN IRELAND·
THE RELIGION

THE RELIGION DEPOSED BY CHRISTIANITY WAS CLOSELY AKIN TO THAT OF the Continental Celts, diluted by distance and mutated in fusion with the religious practices of the earlier inhabitants. The Celts were a tolerant people in religious matters, easily adapting to the cults of those they conquered, and fitting the resident deities into their own pantheon.

The chief gods of pagan Ireland were those the Iron Age Celts brought with them, representing their ideals of masculinity. They were the deities of society: the prototypes of the warrior, the magician, the craftsman and the father-leader; in one case all these qualities were embodied in a single god. The goddesses were more universal and more primitive. They were legacies from a pre–Iron Age matriarchal system, and they personify the forces of nature: fertility and destruction.

The tales of the gods' and goddesses' activities are flamboyantly dramatic, often to a grotesque degree. The theology appears to have no symmetry. This is the fault neither of the system nor of its later recorders. Much of it was veiled from the beginning, due to the reluctance, exhibited by the Continental druids as well, to allow secular familiarity with their rites, lest the enchantment fade. Further, the Celtic pantheon has not had the literary artistry of a Homer nor the synthesizing genius of the compilers of the *Edda*s to resolve its contradictions and give it esthetic coherence.

Most of our knowledge we owe, paradoxically, to the Christian monks who wrote down the old stories. These scribes may have contributed to the cloudiness of our understanding of the ancient ritual by their disposition to block out heathen practices. In general, however, they respected the spirit of the old tales. In Ireland, because Christianity came easily, without martyrdom, there never existed the fear of and hostility to pagan gods that made the religious orders on the Continent so fanatically evangelical. There was little conflict between the old ways and the new, and Irish Christian scholars delighted alike in the love poetry of classical Rome and the lusty, war-oriented legends of the gods and heroes of their own heathen ancestors. They treasured their mother tongue as much as they esteemed the language of the Church, and wrote most of the sagas in the vernacular. Ireland was the first country, by many centuries, to appreciate the literary value of its native language.

However, the concept of false idols was intolerable even to their easy-going intellects. So when the scribes in the monasteries came to record the oral tales they changed the emphasis: they made the gods mortal. *Lebor Gabala* (or *Book of Invasions*) is the synchronized history devised by medieval Irish scholars to dovetail their country into the mainstream of world history based on the Old Testament. It describes the five successive conquests of Ireland, starting before the Flood. Most of the account is pseudohistory, with racial memories of early population groups providing a substratum of fact. But with the fourth invasion, that of the Tuatha De Danann (People of the Goddess Dana), history turns to straight mythology. The Tuatha De Danann are the gods of the Celtic pantheon, which the chroniclers lifted whole out of the context of religion and put into the framework of the synchronized history. Though the flexible priestly historians reconciled their consciences with this token genuflection, they still could not forbear to describe with relish the magic arts and attributes that the invaders brought with them from Greece.

The Tuatha De Danann had two chieftains, Lug and the Dagda, of which the second was the representative of an older, more generalized pantheon. The Dagda is not a name, but a title meaning "the Good." It was given to him when, before a great battle, he announced that he could wield by himself all the powers that the other gods would individually use to confound the enemy. Therefore they called him "the Good," meaning not that he was good in a moral sense, but was good at things. In addition to being the patriarchal head of his people, his knowledge made him their chief magician. With his invincible club, so heavy that eight men had to carry it and its track made the boundary-ditch of a province, he defended them against enemies; his magic caldron fed them endlessly; and his sexual unions with the goddesses of the earth ensured his people protection against the ancient, sometimes hostile deities. His activities, gross as they appear to the more delicate sensibilities of this age, are ritualistic manifestations of his all-embracing godliness. His eating prowess in particular, a stylized ritual of plenty, is obscenely magnificent.

> They filled for him [with porridge] the king's caldron, five fists deep, into which went four-score gallons of new milk and the like quantity of meal and fat. Goats and sheep and swine were put into it, and they were all boiled together with the porridge. . . . Then the Dagda took his ladle, and it was big enough for a man and woman to lie on the middle of it. . . . "Good food this," said the Dagda. . . . Sleep came upon him after eating his porridge. Bigger than a house-caldron was his belly. . . . Not easy was it for the hero to move along owing to the bigness of his belly. Unseemly was his apparel. A cape to the hollow of his two elbows. A dun tunic around him, as far as the swelling of his rump.[1]

Lug, the younger chieftain, probably belongs to a later period of Celtic development. Where the Dagda was good at everything in a nonspecific way, Lug's skills, also encompassing everything, were yet particularized. He could build chariots, work metal, cure the sick, compose poetry, work sorcerer's spells, defeat an army single-handed. Besides his deadly prowess with the casting spear and the sling (he was called Lug of the Long Arm for his use of the latter), he was able to charm the company at a feast into sleep with his harp, so that they slept from night until the same hour the following night, then to wake them into tears and lamenting with his wail-strain, finally to bring joy and merriment with the laugh-strain (music is the one specific skill he inherited from his otherwise archaic predecessor). As the acme of the Irish-Celtic hero, he was the favorite god of the Heroic Age, and the father of the most beloved of all the mortal heroes, the ever-young Cuchulain.

The god of the sea was Manannan, son of Lir (a sea-god of greater antiquity), who travelled over the oceans in his chariot. The god once spoke of his dominion: "That is a happy plain with profusion of rosy-colored flowers. . . . Sea-horses glisten in summer. . . . Speckled salmon leap from the womb of the white sea, on which thou lookest: they are calves, they are colored lambs."[2] Legend on the Isle of Man, named for Manannan, and in parts of Leinster, sees him as rolling on three legs like a wheel through the mist. In *Cormac's Glossary,* a tenth-century work attributed to Bishop Cormac Mac Cuilennain, king of Munster, Manannan was a merchant of the Isle of Man, an accomplished seaman who knew "through seeing the face of the heavens" when the weather would be fine and when stormy.[3] From his skill as a mariner, the lexicographer goes on, the Irish called him the god of the sea. This is another example of the god made mortal by a prelate with a tender conscience, who felt at the same time a responsibility to the tradition of his fathers and a reluctance to acknowledge a pagan divinity.

Some of the goddesses were mother and fertility figures; others were agents of death. There is an amorphous quality to them: they are figures of multiple personality veiled in shadows behind the clear, bright singleness of the male deities. In some cases three goddesses shared the same dominion. Brigit, Anu and Dana were generally deities of fertility and prosperity. Anu and Dana, confused with each other, were the mothers of the gods, while the similar Brigit watched over childbirth and brought plenty to the houses she visited, leaving her footprint in the ashes of the hearth. She was also the goddess of poetry. Other threefold goddesses presided in battle. The Morrigan (great queen), Badb (carrion crow) and Macha (also a crow, whose food was the heads of slain warriors) caused confusion in the ranks of the enemies of their favorites, or materialized in animal form to persecute a single fighter. While Cuchulain singly defended a ford against the challengers that Queen Maeve sent against him, the Morrigan came as an eel, to wind itself around his legs, then changed to a wolf, frightening herds of cattle to stampede against him.

Some goddesses embodied the functions of fertility and war in the same figure. One of these was Maeve, namesake of the Connacht queen who initiated the war against Ulster in which Cuchulain was the hero-defender. Queen Maeve herself, a near-legendary mortal, was a figure with the qualities of fable: a woman who commanded her own armies (as well as her meek husband), and on occasion engaged in battle personally, being a good hand at spear-throwing. The archaic Maeve, she who was worshipped in Ireland long before the Heroic Age in which the queen of Connacht flourished, was believed to be the goddess of sovereignty, whom every Tara king married symbolically. In another guise she was the queen-wolf. She could outrun a horse, and when a warrior looked on her he lost two-thirds of his strength. Her lover was Fergus, who ate seven times as much as an ordinary man and had the strength of seven hundred; his nose, mouth and penis were each seven fingers long and his scrotum was as large as a sack of flour. When his wife was away he needed seven women. The strongly sexual and at the same time bellicose character of the various Maeves illustrates the combined fertility and destructive functions of the female deities. It is clear that myth has overlapped myth here, that many layers of folklore have coalesced, and the qualities of earlier legendary figures have been grafted onto the personalities of later ones, producing an effect of double vision.

A monument that strongly evokes this sense of the mystery of goddesses is Maeve's Lump, a prehistoric mound atop a mountain some thousand feet above the city of Sligo. The walk up to it is a straight path along bedrock, climbing through pasture scattered with flowers — the bright orange and yellow pealike blossoms of bird's-foot trefoil, small fragrant white wild roses, sun-yellow tormentil, wild strawberry. Near the top, pasture and rock give way to bog, where the heath spotted orchis, a delicate, many-flowered field orchid, grows in profusion, shining palely through the heather. Below, Sligo Harbor, Lough Gill and the high mountains to the north near Drumcliffe are sharp in the sunlight, but ahead a cloud flies over the pile of the grave mound. From sea level it had looked like a pimple on the mountaintop; close to, it hulks enormous through the mist, a pile of loose stones fifty feet high and two hundred in diameter. Around it are smaller rock piles and stone circles — satellite tombs. Though the great mound is known as the grave of Queen Maeve, it is impossible that the Iron Age Connacht queen is buried here. The mound is of the same period as Newgrange, about 2500 B.C., and it is considered to be a similar passage grave, built by the Neolithic forerunners of the Celts.

Many of Ireland's prehistoric mounds were thought by pagan worshippers to be the abodes of gods, and in fact, as is surmised at Newgrange, may have served other religious purposes than that of graves. This belief was transmuted by time, aided by the medieval Christian scribes, into superstition and fairy lore. The mounds marked the dwellings of the *sid* (fairies) — the Tuatha De Danann and earlier gods gone to establish their kingdoms under the earth. It is an unwarranted but tempting surmise that Maeve's Lump was a place of worship long before the rule of the Celtic gods, and that the primeval Maeve, the mother-destroyer herself, was the deity that inhabited it. The awesome pile stands alone in the cloud, untouched and profoundly mysterious, while the wind flies silently around it over the long level mountaintop, flattening the heather and bending the fragile-appearing, tough little orchids. Whoever or whatever lies beneath those forty thousand tons of stone is lost in a mist far deeper than earthly fog.

The antique goddesses have not much play in the medieval account of the invasion of the Tuatha De Danann, because this is the story of the new young gods who took over Ireland. It is the best place, however, to see the Celtic deities in action, in their medieval disguise as the fourth race to occupy Ireland.

The Tuatha De Danann, so the historians tell us in the medieval annal *Lebor Gabala,* arrived in Ireland with four gifts: the *Lia Fail* (Coronation Stone), which notified the accession of the rightful king of Ireland by screaming when he put his foot on it; the spear of Lug, which fought by itself; the sword of Nuada, which slew its victim at the first touch; and the caldron of the Dagda, which perpetually refilled itself. When they landed on Ireland's shores they burned their ships so that neither could the enemy use them nor would they themselves be tempted to retreat; then they wrapped themselves in a black fog and marched inland. When the residents, the Fir Bolg, awoke to discover their peril, the Tuatha De Danann were entrenched on a mountain in Sligo, from which they challenged the opposition to battle or surrender. Battle was chosen, and Mag Tured (Moytirra) — "Plain of Pillars" — was the scene of a notable conflict in which after four days most of the Fir Bolg were slain and the rest were routed to "the outermost isles and islets of the sea."

Moytirra is a green and fertile area of pastureland and small rounded hills high above the crooked shores of Lough Arrow. In its sloping fields are the remains of prehistoric graves, perhaps the inspiration for the legends of the two great battles, which may represent true memories of struggles between the ancient resident farming population and the better-armed newcomers. It was probably more thickly settled in the third millennium than it is today. The only sound is the call of a cuckoo; the sun shines hot on the stones of a prehistoric court cairn and a little wind brings the scent of hawthorn blossoms and the faint whiff of a distant barnyard.

The Tuatha De Danann did not hold the land unopposed. They were assailed by the Fomorians, a race of infelicitous savages (possibly a brutish survival of an earlier pantheon) who had come out of the sea time and again to attack previous inhabitants. The second battle of Mag Tured took place between these forces, and the whole of the Irish-Celtic pantheon appears in this classic conflict. Fought between the primeval spirits and the young usurpers, it is strongly reminiscent of other wars in Indo-European myth, another indication of the common ancestry of most of the peoples of the Western world. The defeat of Cronus and the Titans by the family of Zeus has a similar cast of characters, as does the continuing struggle between Odin and the children of Ymir, the Frost Giants.

The Tuatha De Danann summoned every man, from the chief sorcerer and the cupbearer to the smith and the charioteer, to contribute his special talent to the confounding of the enemy. The sorcerer promised to cast upon the enemy the twelve mountains of Ireland "and roll their summits against the ground." The druid would cause "three showers of fire to pour on the faces of the Fomorian host, and . . . take out of them two thirds of their strength . . . and bind their urine in their own bodies and in the bodies of their horses." The leech Diancecht would make whole the bodies of the slain, provided their heads had not been cut off nor their spinal marrow severed. The Fomorians had powerful help too, especially that of Balor of the Piercing Eye. His one eye was never opened but on the battlefield, when four men thrust a polished handle through the lid to lift it. Then men died by the thousand from the venomous fumes that emanated from it. On this occasion Balor — challenged by Lug, the bright and fearless one — opened his baleful eye that he might "see the babbler who was conversing with me" and received a sling stone that carried the eye right out through the back of his head. After the slaying of as many men "as the stars of heaven . . . flakes of snow . . . or grass under the feet of herds,"[4] the Fomorians were at last beaten back into the sea, from which they never again emerged.

Despite all their magic, the Tuatha De Danann could not withstand the final conquerors of Ireland, the sons of Mil. Arriving with thirty ships at Kenmare Bay on the southwest coast, the Milesians demanded the customary surrender or battle. The dispute was, in the Celtic manner, referred not to the king of the invading warriors but to their chief poet-druid, Amergin, one of the nine sons of Mil, who justly declared against his own people: they would withdraw "nine waves from shore" to give the inhabitants time to make ready. The Tuatha De Danann used the postponement by raising a "druidic wind," which could blow no higher than a ship's mast but sufficed to scatter and wreck the fleet, killing five of the nine brothers. The remaining four, including Amergin, succeeded in landing. When they stepped on shore Amergin chanted a strange song of creation, the haunting strains of which echo back, perhaps, to the earliest invocations spoken by priests of the Indo-European forebears of the Celts — for it has a close parallel in the song of Sri Krishna in the *Bhagavad-Gita:*

> *I am wind on Sea,* [sang Amergin]
> *I am Ocean-wave,*
> *I am Roar of Sea,*
> *I am Bull of Seven Fights,*
> *I am Vulture on Cliff,*
> *I am Dewdrop,*
> *I am Fairest of Flowers,*
> *I am Boar for Boldness,*
> *I am Salmon in Pool*

I am Lake on Plain
. . . .
I am Word of Skill,
I am the Point of a Weapon
. . . .
I am God who fashioneth Fire for a Head.

Who smootheth the ruggedness of a mountain?
Who is He who announceth the ages of the Moon?
And who, the place where falleth the sunset?
Who calleth the cattle from the House of Tethra?
On whom do the cattle of Tethra smile?
Who is the troop, who the god who fashioneth edges?
. . . .
Enchantments about a spear?
Enchantments of Wind? [5]

Two battles were fought, one in the harsh high mountains of the Slieve
Mish in Kerry, the other at Taillten in Meath. The Tuatha De Danann
were defeated and the poet Amergin divided Ireland. He awarded the upper
earth to his brothers, and to the Tuatha De Danann he gave the territory
under the earth and under the sea, and the islands of the sea beyond man's
horizon. In these places, out of the ken of mortals, the Tuatha De Danann,
now the *sid*, fairies, lived splendidly in palaces glittering with gold and
jewels. They emerged at times from their caves and mounds, to mix, not
always benignly, into the lives of the upper residents of the earth. A few
mortals chose to visit the country of the *sid*. But if a man went there he
lost contact with the mortal world: several centuries seemed to him as a
few days, or weeks of adventure appeared to pass although he had been
away from home but an hour. Usually he could not return except for short
visits, and then only by horse or by boat. If he touched the earth he turned
to ashes.

Though the old tales give us eventful, fantastical and richly detailed
accounts of the nature and attributes of the Celtic gods, the ritual of their
worship remains largely in darkness. No temples remain, and it is thought
that woodlands were their sanctuaries. In Ireland the rowan was the sacred
tree and the yew was the wood of which the druids' wands were made.
There may have been significance attached also to the oak, the sacred tree
of the Continental Celts, because later Christian churches and monasteries
were sometimes built in oak groves or beside a lone oak in deference to an

older sanctity. Springs, rivers, lakes, mounds, caves — each had its presiding spirit, or was itself divine, like the river Boyne, who was a goddess. The gods were all around; on occasion they directly invaded the lives of mortals or themselves became mortal. The dividing line between god and human was very fine. Taboos controlled men's lives, and even such human concepts as numbers, riddles and verses had mystic powers.

Like the Continental Celts, the Irish had no thought of an afterlife in which the good were rewarded in heaven and the wicked tortured in hell. Virtue was unimportant, as was death, which was but a stepstone from one life to the next. A person would reappear, sometimes several times over many centuries, in the form of an animal, another human, sometimes as the re-creation of his own self. Transformation occurred also without death, by a supernatural agency whose nature might be either wicked or benign.

A pretty example of this occurs in the romantic love tale *The Wooing of Etain*. Etain, the wife of Midir, a fairy king, was changed to a dragonfly by her husband's jealous second wife, and carried by a great wind for seven years above the world, until she was borne to the palace of Aenghus Og, son of the Dagda. He knew who she was and cherished her, even in her insect form, in a crystal bower filled with flowers and fruits, with windows so that she could fly in and out. But the jealous wife found her and again she was whirled around over Ireland, until she fell through the roof of Etar the Warrior and into a golden cup from which Etar's wife was drinking milk. The woman swallowed the dragonfly with the milk, was impregnated, and in due course gave birth to a child. This was again Etain, born a thousand years after her first birth. In her latest life Etain was wooed by King Eochaid Airem in a delightful courtship, and they were wed. Midir, her husband in her first life, came to claim her but she refused to leave her beloved. So he challenged Eochaid to a chess match, won Etain as his prize, and spirited her away to his fairy mound. After a fierce battle, in which the fairy mound was destroyed (an event of dire and distant consequence in another story), Eochaid rescued his love, and Midir's power over her was ended.

There was a paradise, but it was not a place you went to after you died if you'd been good on earth. It was the place of the heart's desire, a land of singing birds and beautiful women, usually across the western sea, that frontier of mystery whence no invaders had ever come and from which few venturers returned. It had several names, the most familiar of which is *Tir na n'Og* (Land of Youth). It is alluringly described in *The Voyage of Bran*, an eighth-century retelling of an old tale:

There is a distant isle,
Around which sea-horses glisten:
A fair course against the white-swelling surge, —
Four pillars uphold it. . . .

. . . .

Unknown is wailing or treachery
In the familiar cultivated land,
There is nothing rough or harsh,
But sweet music striking on the ear.

Without grief, without sorrow, without death
Without any sickness, without debility,
. . . .

A beautiful game, most delightful,
They play sipping at the luxurious wine,
Men and gentle women under a bush,
Without sin, without crime.

Along the top of a wood has swum
Thy coracle across ridges,
There is a wood of beautiful fruit
Under the prow of thy little boat.

A wood with blossom and fruit,
On which is the vine's veritable fragrance,
A wood without decay, without defect,
On which are leaves of golden hue.[6]

Such was the fascination of the western sea to the pagan Celts and later to their Christian descendants — the lure of misty distances, the flickering horizon hiding a land no one had really seen but everyone knew must be there, the overwhelming desire for a fresh new country, younger and purer than the tired old world — such was the passionate longing, expressed again and again, for this cloudland, that it is all too easy to conclude nowadays that some of them actually did get there. The real *Tir na n'Og*, some say, was the shore of America, and voyagers from Ireland, having braved the North Atlantic in their little wooden-frame, hide-covered curraghs, did come back to tell the tale — by the time of their return exaggerated beyond recognition. But those journeys belong to Christian times.

The Christians inherited *Tir na n'Og,* a dream too seductive and too firmly entrenched in the Irish soul to fade away easily. During the Heroic Age, the Land of Promise was still magical, still the territory, glimpsed by a few favored mortals, of the *sid,* where gods and fairies sported and life was forever young.

Besides their beliefs, clothed, to us, in cloudy vagueness, and the rituals of worship, now largely unknown, there were definite festivals to honor and propitiate the gods. November 1, Samain, was the day on which mortals made peace with the spirits. On this day the feast of Tara was held; it was probably the day on which the high-king of Tara celebrated his ritual marriage with the goddess of the earth, to insure the prosperity of his reign. The eve of Samain was a night of confusion, when the spirits came out of the earth to tease, confound, and often destroy. Sometimes men returned the attack, driving the spirits back into their darkness. On May 1, Beltine, two ceremonial fires were lit and the cattle were driven between them, to protect them against disease. These two chief festival days are thought to be survivals of an ancient pastoral way of life, marking the times when the herds must be moved to and from their summer pasture. Little is known of other festivals. Imbolc was the day the lactation of the ewes began. On Lugnasad, August 1, the god Lug was honored with games and races. Some of the festivals were adopted by the Christians, notably Samain, which became All Souls Day, preceded by the similar night of truculent spirits — only under the new rule there was to be no reciprocity. People might suffer, but they were not to fight back.

Though there were no temples built, there were ritual stones, and it is thought that there were also idols. A peculiarly savage one turns up in the legends associated with St. Patrick. Crom Cruaich was said to be a great stone figure standing in the Mag Slecht (Plain of Prostrations), in County Cavan. It was covered all over with gold and silver and surrounded by twelve lesser idols decorated with brass and bronze. To this fierce symbol must be offered "the firstlings of every issue and the chief scions of every clan." The king and his people would prostrate themselves before it "so that the tops of their foreheads and the gristle of their noses and the caps of their knees and the ends of their elbows broke." When St. Patrick came on this abomination "he lifted against it the staff of Jesus; when suddenly by the power of God the idol fell on its left side, and all the silver and the gold passed from it broken and powdered into dust; but on the hard stone of the image was seen impressed the mark of the staff, though it had touched it not: and the earth swallowed up the twelve inferior gods even to their necks; and their heads continue above the ground unto this day."[7]

The Turoe Stone — Celtic ritual stone (probably of the third century B.C.*) incised with La Tène designs*

Among the sacred stones was the *Lia Fail,* the Coronation Stone brought to Ireland by the Tuatha De Danann, which roared when the proper king stepped on it. It lies at Tara, the deeply venerated hill that was at one time a place of great religious significance associated with the goddess Maeve, and which became the seat of the local priest-kings and later housed the high-kings of northern Ireland in an immense palace. Layers and layers of history and prehistory permeate this gentle green hill rising out of the soft Meath countryside. Under the mild mounds that mark the sites of the buildings of the Heroic Age are passage graves dating back to about 1800 B.C. Buttercups and daisies fill the long, sunken corridor that once was the banqueting hall where sounded the sweet harp, as well as the place where the king symbolically mated with the earth goddess; and sheep graze on the Mound of Hostages where the Coronation Stone lay. The ancient pillar-stone said to be the *Lia Fail* was moved from its original place and now stands to commemorate the spot where insurgents died in a skirmish with the English in 1798.

A curious little group of holy stones lies on an old stone altar in an early medieval monastic village on the island of Inishmurray in County Sligo. These are known as cursing stones, and they were used as lately as the Second World War, to bring perdition upon Hitler. One progresses around them the wrong way (against the sun's course), turning the stones as one utters one's curses. Today these stones embody Christian superstition — backwards Christian, as one of the islanders put it, because the observers perform the rites backwards. Nothing at all is known of their nature before the monastery was founded in the sixth century, except that they were there when the Christians came, and they had properties that were not of this world.

The Turoe Stone is a pagan monument of extraordinary potence, probably dating from the third century B.C. It stands in the middle of a lush green field in County Galway: a fat, rounded stone about three feet high and two in diameter, looking like a monumental penis, which is probably what its creators intended. It is incised all over its upper part with harmoniously flowing linear patterns — the profoundly mysterious interweaving designs of the La Tène Celts — abstractions that appear to have an arcane significance. The stone has a purity and simplicity about it, an absolute dedication to its own purpose, which brings to us as no words can the vitality of the heathen religion that once governed this island. Its aura of supernatural power is almost incarnate. One feels that if one knew the right words or signs something awesome would at once happen.

CHAPTER IV
CHRISTIANITY ON THE CONTINENT

WHILE HEATHEN IRELAND PURSUED HER COURSE OF ORDERED TURBULENCE, a new transcendental philosophy had come out of the eastern Mediterranean. A religion combining mystery and logic in a system of austere simplicity, early Christianity seems at first sight the antithesis of the joyous and lusty animality of the Irish-Celts.

The monotheistic religion of the Jews was the first source, revealed by Christ in a simple, appealing, profoundly mystical faith. In its early years, despite the refusal of the first Christians to be contained within the strict confines of the Jewish ritual, the new sect came near to being assimilated into Judaism. About fifty years after the death of Christ, St. Paul rescued it from obscurity by investing its basically Eastern mysteries with an explicit form and logic that was purely Greek: and here was Christianity's second source. For centuries Greece had been the fountainhead of enlightened abstract thinking. The subtle and supple language, developed by a people in whom these qualities were supreme, was ideal for the expression of sophisticated philosophies. In giving Christianity a Greek context Paul made it accessible, universal and flexible; in its new guise it inevitably became a force in the Greco-Roman world.

In its first two centuries, however, Christianity was an underground force, a counterstream to the pragmatic and orderly Roman world, answering a deep need among the disadvantaged and powerless who could not or would not conform to the materialistic structure. It provided their cheerless lives with a fresh infusion of beauty, hope and love. It offered them one God in place of the pantheon of aristocratic Roman prototypes, a God who materialized on this earth with forgiveness on his lips and healing in his hands. Above all, they had the promise of another world, where the crueller the suffering here, the more beatific would be the euphoria there.

With its powerful appeal to the meek and miserable and its acknowledgment of no authority but that of an indefinable, invisible God, Christianity was considered by the Roman Empire's tidy bureaucracy to be dangerously revolutionary. The early efforts of the Roman establishment to stamp it out served only to make it stronger. The glories of martyrdom added to the young faith the dimension of passion and laid the basis for a new mythology, the hierarchy of saints.

Christianity was more than simplistically mystical. It could not be dismissed as a mere panacea for the poor, a fad of which time would comfortably dispose. Besides the potency of faith, it had the authority of abstract reasoning — the heritage of Greece — on which to build a new dialectic. Such was the intellectual atmosphere of the early Roman Empire that the most modest Roman citizen, along with the educated elite, could follow the logic of philosophic debate and grasp the subtler concepts of a new ideology.

After two centuries of persecution, during which the Christian faith inconspicuously spread its roots and opened its flowers like the periwinkle thriving on the dim forest floor, it became evident that the new religion could not be eradicated by punishment or ostracism. Converts were coming from the highest social ranks, and officialdom itself was riddled by the sedition of the faithful. Christianity was in fact becoming a kind of spiritual Roman Empire, its administration parallel and similar to that of the materialistic world, having as its main difference a fresh and ardent commitment. The old gods, on the other hand, had grown sterile and uninspiring, their worship a perfunctory formality upheld officially but not enkindling any fervor.

Emperor Diocletian, in a last, desperate gesture, decreed in 303 that Christians be deprived of Roman citizenship and the right to hold property. He ordered the razing of churches and tried to force the clergy, through torture, to sacrifice to the Roman gods. But he could not stem the tide. His successor, Constantine, perceived that it would be extremely useful to Rome to have this youthful and well-organized enthusiasm on its side. He saw to it that a dramatic occurrence clothed his practical reasoning in the proper other-worldly guise: on the eve of his bold march on Rome to consolidate his legal title as emperor, he saw or dreamed a vision of the flaming cross in the noonday sky, with the legend "By this conquer." He announced his acceptance of Christianity and in 313 issued the Edict of Milan, guaranteeing religious tolerance for Christians and restoring their rights and property. Constantine's nephew, Julian the Apostate, took advantage of official neutrality by announcing himself a pagan. But the trend was irreversible. In the late fourth century Emperor Theodosius rejected religious sufferance, closing the temples and outlawing pagan rites.

When Emperor Constantine made Christianity the ruling religion of the Roman Empire, in one stroke he assured its permanence and determined the shape of its development. No longer was it a secret cult glorying in its martyrs and relying for its appeal on the mystic faith that had come out of the East and the abstract logic of its Greek philosophic forebears. It gradually took on the intellectual discipline and the orderly legal framework of Rome. As the empire was ruled centrally through a bureaucratic network operating out of civic centers, so the clergy became organized along similar systematical and hierarchical lines, extending the authority of the faith through the countryside from town-based sees. The urban bishops were in turn accountable to a high bishop, the pope, who symbolized the final divine authority as the emperor represented the temporal.

Another action of Constantine had equally far-reaching consequences. Between 324 and 330 he built the city of Constantinople on the site of the Greek Byzantium and moved there the seat of government, shifting the focus of imperial power from the West to the East. It was a necessary move for the Roman Empire of the fourth century; it had been foreshadowed forty years before, in the reign of Diocletian. Since the state was no longer ruled by the senate and the people of Rome, but authority was vested in a single man, the Eternal City had lost her claim to political supremacy. That single man, the emperor, could elect to found a new Rome wherever wisdom dictated, and Constantine made an astute choice.

The empire was no longer expanding. It was on the defensive, and its unwieldy bulk was menaced on all frontiers — not only by attack from the outside but by the overweening ambition of successful generals. It was as difficult to control the danger points from a single center as it was to administer government. The division of power between Rome and Constantinople, with the eastern city the main capital, was an essential for survival. It was a boon as well to the empire's spiritual health. The East had become the liveliest area of the empire, increasingly important politically and commercially, and a fertile ground for Christianity. It was also the most liable to attack at that time. Situated on the Bosporus, the narrow channel that divides Europe from Asia, Constantinople was a vital trading center for the two continents. Its position between two inland seas made it a natural, almost impregnable fortress. The frontiers of both East and West were more easily controlled from this strong median point than from Rome.

Constantine's decision was brilliant; it was a secondary consideration that he wished to remove himself from a still-pagan Rome, to build Christianity in a more receptive environment, and at the same time to found a city in his own image, a supreme memorial. It is hindsight to recognize that Rome's loss of supremacy would inevitably entail the decline of the West. And no one could foresee the deterioration that would overtake the young religion in those beleaguered provinces, cut off from the source of its inspiration, weakened by heresies, and beset by the heathen importunities of barbarian invaders.

In the East the emperor envisaged a lustrous and enduring capital — and so it was, for eleven hundred years. All through Europe's Dark Ages, Constantinople was the wellspring of Christian theology and the repository of the classical learning of Greece. When the city finally fell to the Turks in 1453, the priceless lore of earlier centuries that had lain protected and fostered in its citadel was dispersed to a Europe no longer dark but ready to wake up to the morning of the Renaissance.

There was one other place in Europe where the classical tradition would be kept green and learning cherished through the chaotic years that followed the fall of Rome: that was Ireland.

In the fourth and fifth centuries corrosion ate at the foundations of the western section of the Roman Empire. Its being rested on the mass of peasant serfs who grew the crops — a class ruthlessly squeezed between ever higher government taxes on profits and increased rents imposed by absentee landlords. Trying to wrench a modest living from their land, the farmers spoiled its yield with overproduction. Then they moved away, and large tracts of countryside became desolate areas of eroded earth and abandoned dwellings. Meanwhile the barbarians pressed at the edges. More soldiers were needed to patrol the precarious frontiers and the deserted farm areas, and many of the new recruits were members of tribes that had but recently known the civilizing touch of Rome, at best haphazard in their allegiance.

With the machinery of government running rustily under a corrupt civil service, with most of the wealth concentrated in decadent and sybaritic cities, with a farmer class thoughtlessly exploited and an army of 300,000 men, most of them fledgling Roman citizens shaky in their loyalties, the empire was a sick and easy prey. Invasions came from all sides as Visigoths, Ostrogoths, Vandals and other tribes nominally under Roman rule spilled over the borders. In the beginning they were not specifically invading; rather they were fleeing before the onslaughts of the Huns, the Turco-Mongolian hordes described by an appalled Roman historian as squat men with "horrible faces," cemented to their horses, on whose backs they ate, drank and slept, and who could neither plow nor cook. The invading refugees set up their own tribal kingdoms within the boundaries of the empire, which continued in a mock existence, its figurehead emperors controlled by barbarian generals. The last of these, a feeble puppet whose name, sadly, was Romulus Augustus, was deposed in 476. Thereafter Rome was but the capital of Italy, another little kingdom among the fragments of the empire, its first ruler being Theodoric the Ostrogoth, a Christian educated in Constantinople.

Though the political machinery of the empire existed no longer, its contours remained. Christianity, modelled along the lines of the empire, had reached the barbarian tribes along with the temporal power of Rome, and had taken hold. So strong was this foundation, so awesome the reputation of the empire even after its dissolution, that Christianity, in the old framework, became the centralizing influence of Europe. Though in the early centuries after the fall the new kingdoms were only technically Christian, the outlines were there. Western Europe was cut off from Byzantine civilization and the balance of power shifted from the Mediterranean to the kingdoms of the north — France, Germany and the Low Countries, whose governments were separatist and autonomous.

Christianity, shadowy as was its dominion at first, would survive through its centralized bureaucratic structure and gather strength from new movements of spiritual ardor, to dominate the spirit of the Middle Ages as the only institution with a universal character. This rise was foreshadowed in St. Augustine's beautiful *City of God,* begun three years after the sack of Rome by Alaric the Visigoth in 410. With rare prescience — considering the tenuousness of Christianity's hold on barbarian Europe — he envisioned the new sacred empire rising out of the ashes of the old profane one.

In St. Augustine's own time, however prophetic he was, Christianity in the West had degenerated into a mere outward form, the lip service of people who had only yesterday worshipped heathen gods. In the eastern Mediterranean a more insidious erosion had set in long before the fall of Rome. Christian worship had become fashionable in the luxurious cities of the Middle East. Martyrdom was extinct, asceticism was out of style, the true believer no longer wore the mantle of adversity. Priests were wealthy and materialistic and their congregations were apathetic. The teachings of Christ were nearly forgotten.

There were a few who remembered, and in the late third century, out of Syria and Egypt, came the beginning of a new movement that looked to an earlier spiritualism for its inspiration. The first to emerge from the shades of legend is the real though dim figure of St. Anthony of Egypt, born about 250 A.D. He chose to exile himself to the desert, following the exhortation of his leader: "If any one comes to me and does not hate his own father and mother and wife and children and brothers and sisters, yes, and even his own life, he cannot be my disciple."[1] St. Anthony's place of lonely trial was a mountain near the Nile called Pispir, where for twenty years he cleansed his soul with prayer and fasting. His example was soon followed, in a return to the immaculate austerity of the first followers of Christ — a reaction against the hedonism of present-day Christians. Like most reactions it took extreme forms. Not only did the anchorites of the fourth and fifth centuries seek to reinstate the chaste virtues of earlier times, they longed for a substitute for martyrdom, for the mortification so eagerly sought and so fiercely worshipped by the Christians of imperial pagan Rome. In St. Anthony's day, a time of freedom of worship, it had to be self-flagellation. "I kill my body, for it kills me" was the credo of the more rabid practitioners of the hermit life. St. Anthony was not one of these. He wrestled with subtle demons who came in the shape of dreams of family joys, or appeared in the guise of pride, or tempted him with bread and with women. He succeeded at last in defeating his devils and emptying his heart and mind to receive God. But he never let the life of renunciation erode his rationality. His body remained healthy and his perceptions lucid, it is said, into his 105th year. In the early years of his solitude a group of like-minded souls followed his lead, and after twenty years he emerged from isolation to rule the little colony that had grown up in his desert. Like the Carthusians later, it was a community of silence and contemplation, the anchorites gathering only for meals and worship.

Not all religious hermits were as sane as St. Anthony. Some carried the act of humiliating the body to purge the soul to hysterical lengths, indulging in self-torture, inviting filth and disease, eschewing all social contact to serve God to a repulsive and useless dead end. One of the more notoriously holy of these was Simeon Stylites (from the Greek word for pillar) of Antioch, born about 389, who, after being expelled from a monastery for overdoing his penances, chose to live for some years chained to a stone inside a cistern infested with worms. Then he built himself a six-foot pillar in the Syrian desert and sat on it. During the next ten years he built pillars higher and higher, until he reached sixty feet, and there he squatted on a platform, praying and performing hundreds of prostrations every day, until his death thirty years later, in 459. He must have become rancid, but his fervent disciples evidently did not mind, for they gathered around the base of his roost to hear him preach in the intervals between his strenuous devotions, carried food to him by means of a ladder and, many of them, went off to build their own pillars.

Unappetizing fanatics such as St. Simeon Stylites were the immoderate cases. There was a true and deep-felt longing among many for escape from the stagnant voluptuousness of the cities to the arduous purity of desert life. But few of these sincere escapists had the strength of a St. Anthony to contend with their demons alone. The life of a religious hermit on the eastern desert was too severe, its isolation too frightening. The stringent self-command was extremely difficult — beyond the capacity of any but the strongest, both physically and mentally. The anchorite was under no discipline except his own; he needed neither to work nor to consider any man but himself. He must school himself to empty his mind of all conscious thought until he reached the stage of complete passivity. Then he would be in a state of grace, ready to be possessed by God. The long hours without sleep or food that were necessary to achieve this state were likely to have other effects. Among the most distressing was the mental prostration called acedia, a frustration neurosis in which the recluse suffered an onslaught of anxious torpor, unable to concentrate, unwilling even to move. Other secondary effects of extreme self-penance were hallucinatory phenomena, often ecstatic and miraculous, which were welcomed as signs of holy transport. But desert theology held that these visions were not the primary purpose of contemplation — that the sole aim was the achievement of a silent, all-embracing oneness with God. It was in a way a destructive movement: it led nowhere and helped no one. But the best of the desert fathers did not lose themselves entirely in ascetic discipline, nor were they all perfervid fanatics. There was gentleness among them, a perceptive love of nature and a willingness to share their experiences with others by example and instruction.

As the hermit life demanded more than ordinary mortal strength, there appeared an alternative for the truly religious: communal living. Contemplation was still possible and desirable, but it was supplemented by work, by responsibility to others and by obedience to an authority outside oneself. About the same time that St. Anthony meditated by the Nile, another

Egyptian, Pachomius, a soldier in the service of Constantine, became converted to Christianity. He retreated to Dendera, on the Nile, where he lived the life of an anchorite under the direction of a venerable hermit, until called, so says legend, by an angel to found a commune of like souls. He was not the first to gather men together for a life dedicated to the worship of God. His creative contribution was to organize his followers into a structured community, economically self-sufficient and subject to specific rules laid down by him as the chief moral authority. His original monastery grew, under his organization and direction, into a great order. By the time of his death in 346 it included nine monasteries with a total of about three thousand monks, and a nunnery. Though his order, which was under his absolute control, was punitively austere, his monks and nuns had the sympathy of companionship and the pleasure that came from altruism: facing outward to the world instead of inward on their own visions, tortures and ecstasies.

Basil the Cappadocian, who lived a generation later than St. Pachomius, 330 to 379, gave monasticism a new perspective. As bishop of Caesarea in the Roman province of Cappadocia (present-day central Turkey), he showed brilliant if autocratic ability in stamping out the Arian heresy and gathering diffuse practices of the Eastern Church into orthodox coherence. But the longest-lasting influence of his organizational genius was in his monastic rule. Though he had gone in his twenties to learn the practices of ascetic piety from the desert fathers of Syria and Egypt, he came to see the eremitic life as futile, deploring especially the extravagant self-mortification of some of its devotees.

St. Basil's ideals were the reverse of those of St. Anthony's followers, who escaped from the cities to find sanctity alone in the silent desert. Basil taught that true piety lay in mingling with, not avoiding, humanity. In his monastery near Neocaesarea in Pontus on the Black Sea (present-day northern Turkey), his monks were not to be isolated from the world. Not only were they to lead a constructive community life, they were to do so near a town in order to follow the precepts of Christ by doing good to others. An almshouse, a hospital and a school attached to the monastery were the mediums for carrying out this precept. Contemplation, prayer and austerity were still practiced, but they were no longer ends in themselves. And work was not merely an occupation to prevent acedia but an active and holy participation in life. St. Basil was a kindly and generous man in spite of his hothcaded imperiousness. He was beloved in his time, and such was his influence on the cenobitic life that his monastery became the model for those of the Middle Ages and his rule is still the basis for the monasticism of the Greek and Slavonic Churches.

The early monasticism of the East, having started as an escape from the fleshpots of the towns and the apathy of formal Christianity, was not much influenced either by the demands of society or by the ecclesiastical organization. Each monastery was run according to the beliefs and the personality of its founder. Some were dedicated solely to ascetic contemplation; in some the monks were involved with social welfare; some became centers of learning. One thing most of them had in common: detachment from the Church establishment. While this was a great attraction to the free soul who looked to the teachings of Christ as his only authority, it could have led the monastic movement into schism, or into a cul-de-sac — the rarefied, unreal world of the perennial social rebel.

It happened otherwise. Athanasius, bishop of Alexandria, an eminent fourth-century Greek theologian who lived at the same time as St. Anthony and St. Pachomius, reconciled the individualism of Egyptian monasticism with the formalized structure of the Church. His friendship with the two great Egyptian recluses and his own reputation for asceticism endeared him to the Eastern monks. He was the first high churchman to promote monasticism, and he made a place for the ascetic contemplative within the discipline of the Church. His influence went far beyond his see. The new Christian theology that had arisen in the Egyptian desert had begun to seep into the West through the teachings of pilgrims and missionaries. But it took the inspired authority of the revered bishop to bring the ideals of Anthony and Pachomius to Rome, providing the young movement with its first great impetus beyond the Mediterranean.

In the West, Christianity was in an increasingly unsound state in the years just before and after the fall of Rome. Political power, moving away from Italy, came to be centered in the north, where the Frankish tribes had taken over Gaul. In between Catholic Italy and the northernmost tribes, which were still pagan, was a large area nominally Christian. It was under the hegemony of centralized church administration, the heritage of the empire. The organization was efficient but, cut off from the refreshing flow of ideas from Greece, Egypt and the Middle East, the Church had lost much of its spiritual force.

A heresy had taken over: Arianism, which taught that Christ had been created by God from nothing before He created the rest of the world, and that this Son of God had the divineness of God in him. Arius, the Alexandrian priest of the early fourth century who thus interpreted the origin of Christ, was a monotheist who firmly believed in the unity and simplicity of the eternal God. It did not occur to him that he was reasoning like a pagan philosopher: beside the all-encompassing oneness of God he had set up a separate deity. Because the Son of God was a created man, he could not have the perfection of God: neither perfect God nor absolute man, the Arian Christ was in essence a demigod. This view of Christianity was attractive to the once-heathen tribes of Europe. It was much easier for them to understand the worship of a visual symbol, a God who looked and acted like a man and who was different only in his point of view from the semimortal gods they had but recently foresworn.

The Catholic Christians in Europe, distressed by the pervasive heathenism and heresy around them, were ready for the teachings of Athanasius — a persuasive and determined opponent of Arianism — and for the ideals of ascetic monasticism he brought from Egypt. Others followed him, some coming from the East, some native Europeans. Jerome was a late-fourth-century Dalmatian who lived, studied, and taught mostly in Rome. In reaction against the worldliness of the Byzantine Church and the heterodoxy of the West, he advocated a harsh austerity that in effect divorced Christian sanctity from normal life. He preached the virtues of the eremitic life, though he himself had tried it for five years and found he could not tolerate it. His own internal conflicts made him embittered and contentious. But his influence was profound. He was a great Christian scholar — his masterwork was the translation of the Bible from Hebrew into Latin, the basis of the Vulgate — who was made a saint despite his abrasive personality, because of his scholarly erudition, his exalted intellectual spiritualism and his great services to the Church.

Joannes Eremita Cassianus — St. Cassian (360 to 435) — was a monk from Bethlehem who spent several years with the desert fathers near the Nile. He was ordained priest at Rome and went to Marseilles, where he founded the abbey of St. Victor and a convent for nuns. Though he was Eastern born and educated, he saw that the monasticism that had grown up in reaction to the decadent wealth of the Eastern cities could not exist in the West. The Byzantine fathers taught that austerity and reclusive contemplation were ends in themselves. Their institutions were dependent upon charity; and the concept of being self-supporting, or, in most cases, of having any secular contacts at all, did not arise. Even St. Basil's monks, though they went among the people to teach and heal, were supported entirely by alms. The West, impoverished and politically chaotic, could not afford to subsidize parasitic monasteries, however sanctified their inhabitants. They must be economically independent, a functional part of the working community. St. Cassian was the first to envision the need for constructive work as a necessary adjunct to a life of reclusive holiness. Though his bent was toward the life of the ascetic recluse, he saw to it that his monks had a use: they were to educate and proselytize, and their cultural purpose would bring them not only the respectability but the patrimonies of their upper-class converts.

Honoratus — St. Honoré, Cassian's contemporary, born probably in northern Gaul of a noble family — became bishop of Arles and founded a monastic community on one of the islands of Lérins off the coast of southern France near Cannes. St. Honoré went further than St. Cassian in bringing the monastic movement toward a healthy integration with the lives of the people. Where Cassian was inflexibly, almost cruelly austere, St. Honoré had a happy and sociable disposition. He believed not only in helping one's neighbor but in seeing to it that he was never depressed. "Let the hearts of those who seek the Lord be glad" was the axiom ascribed to him by his kinsman, disciple and successor, St. Hilary of Poitiers. St. Honoré and his disciples enriched Lérins with their patrimonies and took care of fugitives from lands ravaged by barbarians. Their monastery became an illustrious seat of learning; so many came to study and left to enlighten others that it was called "the nursery of bishops."

St. Martin of Tours was born in 316 of heathen parents in Pannonia (now Hungary), received rudimentary Christian instruction at ten, and became a reluctant soldier at fifteen. While stationed at Amiens he exercised his embryonic Christianity by dividing his cloak with a beggar. This occasioned a vision the following night in which Christ told the angels of his neophyte's act of charity. Martin was baptized and joined St. Hilary of Poitiers, who wanted to make him a deacon. Martin, humble then and always, said that he was not ready to be anything higher than an exorcist (a respectable but lowly religious office in those days). For a while he lived as a hermit on a desert island near Genoa, then returned to St. Hilary and eventually founded a monastery near Tours. He came to be so highly respected by the people of Tours that they chose him for their bishop. Monasticism, still very new in fourth-century Gaul, was looked at askance by the clergy, as outside the regular organization of the Church. Martin himself appeared an unseemly choice as bishop to the Gaulish high churchmen, very much on their dignity as representatives of the august discipline of Rome. To them he was an insignificant and lowborn ex-soldier, excitable in temperament and uncouth in manners, who dressed very badly and had "disgraceful hair." But the people prevailed, exalting their beloved, bedraggled, unassuming priest. His renown endured: 206 miracles were attributed to him after his death in the year 400, and he was to become the patron saint of France.

The vicissitudes of the Church in Italy and Gaul, and the rise of monasticism there, are fairly well documented. The civilizing influence of the Roman Empire, the strong tradition of Roman authority, the spread of the Latin language and the consequent emphasis on learning long outlasted the demise of Roman temporal power. In the British Isles the story was different. Christianity had reached Britain from Gaul by the third century, possibly earlier. But, though a few luminous figures stand out of the darkness of those early years, the faith does not seem to have penetrated very deeply into this fringe colony.

Between 410 and 442 the Roman legions were withdrawn and Britain was left to mind her own borders. This was a hopeless prospect: her neighbors were far too strong. Scots (the contemporary name for the Irish) crossed the Irish Sea to loot the western ports, and Picts swarmed south across Hadrian's undefended wall. These were strike-and-run attacks much like the Viking raids of later centuries, their main purpose being pillage and the taking of captives. Far more serious were the invasions of Germanic tribes from northern Europe: Angles, Saxons and Jutes. The southeastern shores of the island colony had been defended against these piratical depredations while the Romans still guarded their outlying territories. After the withdrawal of the legions, the freebooters crossed the North Sea to plunder with impunity. Their actual settlements started around 450 — according to the sixth-century Welsh historian Gildas, the first chronicler of British history — when the Britons called on the tough Germanic warriors to help them protect their borders from the incursions of the Picts and the Scots. The aliens then turned their arms against their hosts, claiming they had not been paid enough. Another version has Hengist and Horsa, two exiled Jutish leaders, seeking the protection of Vortigern, the king of Britain. They expelled the Pictish invaders for him and he gave them land as a reward. They then treacherously induced him to let them send for large numbers of their countrymen, who settled irremovably in Kent. Whatever the truth, the occupation was inevitable: with population pressures behind them and a fair, fertile and vulnerable country before them, nothing could have stopped the conquerors. By the beginning of the seventh century, all of present-day England to the borders of Wales on the west, Cornwall in the south and Scotland to the north was Anglo-Saxon.

Toleration of indigenous folkways was no part of the Anglo-Saxon culture pattern. As their Teutonic warrior-run kingdoms took over the imprecise Celtic political arrangements, so did the celestial phalanx led by Thor and Odin displace whatever remained of Roman Christianity. The troubled course of British history is obscure for the two centuries between the removal of the Roman military establishment and the final conquest by the Teutonic tribes, but it is clear that Christianity had little part in it. The faith was pushed out to the edges, along with the civilized traditions of Roman Britain. Wales became a stronghold of Christianity; there were pockets in Cornwall, Britain's southwestern corner, and in Cumberland to the north. Some of the hard-pressed Britons crossed the Channel to settle in Brittany, continental Europe's last refuge of unconquered Celts.

The light of the new ideology that had arisen in the Egyptian desert shone even into these remote corners. Ninian, a northern Briton educated in Rome, came back to his native land to build a church and monastery on the Isle of Whithorn, off Galloway, southwestern Scotland, where he worked to convert the southern Picts. Very little is known of St. Ninian. He probably lived in the late fourth century, at the time of St. Martin of Tours, for he dedicated his church to the French saint. He built of stone, reputedly with the aid of masons supplied him by St. Martin. In fourth-century Britain — particularly in the primitive backwater of Pictish Scotland — the use of stone was rare. St. Ninian's church must have shone out among the little mud-daubed wattle houses of the natives, for it was known as Candida Casa, the White House. The monastery became a center of learning for the British Isles, and was to have a great influence on Irish scholars.

At about the same time as St. Ninian, another native of the British Isles, Pelagius (360 to 420), originated a heresy more subtle — because its basis was sound — than that of Arius. Pelagius was a monk with an excellent education, including a knowledge of Greek. His origins are not known; he was probably Celtic, from Ireland or southern Scotland. At the beginning of the fifth century he went to Rome, which he found decadent in the extreme. Coming from the purity and austerity of the north, where the life of the pious was modelled on the spiritual regeneration of the Egyptian desert fathers, the moral degeneracy of the capital of Western Christianity shocked him to the soul.

In rebuttal to his remonstrances, the excuse was given that man was born to original sin and human weakness was his natural state, to be redeemed by God's grace. Pelagius responded by reasoning that man is born with free will, and that there can be no such thing as original sin, sin being a function of will and not of nature. If we accept as a fact our inborn evil, the will is crippled and we have no longer any incentive to effort. We are, in essence, blaming God for our shortcomings and living in the passive hope of salvation (available only to a few of the chosen) through his eventual forgiveness.

Pelagius was not only speaking out against the corruption of Rome, he was inveighing against that passionately eloquent scholar St. Augustine, whose doctrine of total depravity, of man's inheritance forever of the sin of Adam, seemed to the high-principled northern monk a peremptory denial of man's dignity and an excuse for lax morals. Pelagius's arguments for greater moral responsibility through higher freedom of the will seem in retrospect more sensible than alarming. He certainly had no intention of initiating a heretical doctrine, nor did his contemporaries, in the beginning, consider him a threat. In fact he became very popular in Rome. His precepts, succinctly expressed ("If I ought, I can" was his favorite maxim), touched a chord and his reforming idealism attracted many among the more earnest and literate of the aristocracy. His disciple, Celestius, much bolder and more assertive, gave to Pelagius's refreshing words of wisdom a backing of philosophical absoluteness that the teacher had possibly not intended. Celestius was probably an Irishman: St. Jerome, who was not above peevish invective, wrote of him that he was "a great fool and had his wits as heavy as his paunch from eating Irish stirabout." Both master and pupil fell afoul not only of Augustine and Jerome but other influential functionaries of the Church.

The great controversy that ensued showed how widely accepted were the doctrines of the Celtic monk. It was in fact a dividing line in the history of the Catholic Church. St. Augustine, expressing the fearfulness of the European ruling classes consequent on the fall of Rome and the influx of the barbarian tribes, was endeavoring to make the Church narrowly and unquestioningly conformist. Pelagius expressed the eminently reasonable point of view that the Church should be tolerant and all-inclusive, that barbarians could make as good Christians as anyone else and that no soul was irretrievably lost.

Augustine won and the Church, in retrospect, was not the better for his victory. The reasoning of the orthodox as to Pelagius's heresy was that if human will, capable alike of good or evil, is the natural endowment of man, independent of God's grace, then a man need not be a Christian to be blessed. The heathen can live according to his own precepts and be as perfectly righteous as the Christian. Once this premise is accepted, Christianity becomes redundant. If human will takes the initiative, then the Holy Spirit is no longer necessary to the erring human soul, and divine will becomes by implication nonexistent.

However philosophic the reasoning, in denouncing Pelagius's doctrines the Church took the road to totalitarianism, and the way was open to the abominations of the Inquisition. Pelagius's viewpoint seems far more sensible and appealing today than Augustine's constrictive view of Church doctrine and his dogmatic and dispiriting assertion of man's inborn wickedness. Still, there was something to be said, in the fifth century, for the Augustinian position. Christianity was still floundering among its own conflicting creeds, and the implicit denial of the Holy Spirit was potentially an extremely dangerous heresy.

Pelagius's teachings were officially condemned in 418. But he had sown a seed in the British Isles that was difficult to eradicate, and his doctrines remained popular there long after they had been banned on the Continent. Whether it was his altogether laudable moral honesty that appealed to Irish scholars or the fact that he was one of their own — his independence of official dogma appealing to a like sentiment among his proud-spirited countrymen — they were still quoting his writings several centuries after his death.

More conventionally correct — and probably more pervasive — was the influence that came to Ireland from Wales. By the time of St. David, who lived in the sixth century, Wales was firmly Christian. Little is known of David's life. It is thought that his father was a prince; if so, he would have been accustomed from his childhood to the uses of authority and, as a powerful aristocrat, would have been in a strong position to organize the Welsh Church. He became primate of South Wales and founded churches throughout the area (fifty-three bear his name today). But evidently the reclusive ideals of monasticism appealed to him, for he removed the seat of ecclesiastical government from Caerleon, the conveniently located town on the Bristol Channel, to the isolated headland of Mynyw (Menevia), later called St. David's Head. On that remote tongue of land, Wales's westernmost point, he built a monastery that became, like St. Ninian's Candida Casa, a mecca for scholars.

The promontories on which St. David's monastery and Candida Casa were situated were easily accessible from Ireland, Mynyw being separated from County Wexford by the narrow width of Saint George's Channel, and Whithorn, off Galloway, being even closer across the North Channel from County Down. They had been prime landfalls for piratical forays, and after Ireland's conversion they became goals of a different sort. A large part of the spiritual fervor that came out of Egypt filtered through these two great centers to the site of its most exciting realization, across the Irish Sea, at the opposite end of Europe.

Ireland had somehow remained inviolate, untouched except peripherally either by Rome or the barbarian invasions. In 82 A.D. Gnaeus Julius Agricola, governor of Britain, judged the time ripe for the taking of the western island. It could, wrote his son-in-law Tacitus, "be invaded and conquered with one legion and a moderate number of auxiliaries. The result would be of advantage even with reference to the coercion of Britain, if Roman arms were to be seen everywhere and independence swept from the map." It is not clear why this project never materialized. Though the interior of Ireland was unfamiliar to the Romans, the approaches and the harbors were well known. Ireland had for many years had commercial contacts with Rome, pottery and glass from the south being exchanged for Irish hides, cattle and the popular wolf-dogs. Possibly it appeared so easy a takeover that Agricola judged he could accomplish it whenever he had the time and a free legion or two. Then in 84 A.D. he was recalled by Emperor Domitian because the German frontiers were in need of strengthening. His successors evidently did not consider Ireland a serious threat to the Romanization of Britain and she remained happily outside the pale. The years of anguish and disruption that followed the withdrawal of the Roman soldiers from Britain also left her closest neighbor unscathed. The unconquered southern and western parts of Britain lay between the Teutonic invaders and the crossings to Ireland, and Britain's new masters were in any case too busy subduing a fractious population to look beyond their troublesome borders.

In the same century that St. Anthony prayed alone in the Egyptian desert to bring to a tired and decadent world the radiance of a new mystical experience, the heathen Finn Mac Cumail and those who would follow him pursued their own Spartan paths in the wild forests of Ireland. Christ's words, exhorting men to sever all other ties and to adhere to him, would have struck a familiar note to those hardy soldiers of the woods. Boisterous and combative as were the Irish-Celts, the quality of their life came closer in spirit to the Christian ideals of the early monasteries than that in many an Eastern city. Pre-Christian Ireland had no towns; the farms were self-sufficient and their people — buoyant, enduring and arrogantly free-spirited — were ready to cope with whatever life brought them. They were proud, but they were accepting. Neither alarmed by change nor dismayed by adversity, they had a resilient native tolerance. It cannot be said that these tough farmers were anywhere near ready to be converted when the first

Christian missionaries walked among them. But the pagans could respect the undaunted, self-reliant apostles of a strange creed, whose attitude toward life was not so dissimilar to their own. And, with a certain expectant, receptive forbearance, they were ready to listen.

For the first time in its history Christianity was to come to a people who had never been conquered. Early Christianity had taken fire from the sufferings of the martyrs; later the logic and order of Rome had shaped it; then had come the passionately rebellious escape from the corruption, apathy and heresy of the post-empire, giving Europe a novel idea in piety: monasticism. Though none of these fluctuations hit Ireland, they all added up to the faith that was to be once again changed. Christianity, modified by the vicissitudes of four centuries, would come to a country with an ancient continuity of tradition and a proudly independent, if barbaric, culture. It would take over a people vigorous, imaginative and artistic. A different kind of Christianity would arise, a rare, one-time flowering, and the Irish would bring back to a darkened Europe the faith they had received, freshly illumined by their own peculiar genius.

PART TWO

THE SAINTS

CHAPTER V
ST. PATRICK

SAINT PATRICK, IRELAND'S SPIRITUAL FATHER, DID NOT THROW HIS CHAL-
lenge to a country altogether hostile, to take on and vanquish one by one
its barbaric chieftains and druids like Cuchulain at the ford downing in
single combat the heroes of Connacht. The legends of Patrick's life, mixed
inextricably with the truth, are indeed reminiscent of the zestful heroism
of an earlier time; as with many of the other Irish saints, the stories of
whose deeds replaced in popular mythology the bardic lays of heathen
stalwarts, his life shines with the unearthly light of the more-than-human.

But he had predecessors. Through the nimbus of myth that surrounds
early Irish church history there emerge four holy figures who were there
when Patrick came. When he received his visionary call to return to Ireland
and proselytize, he found not only a people ready to listen to his passionate
words but, it is recorded, already existing churches, where these saintly
men had gathered around them a modest following of the new faith. The
groups flourished largely in the south, the part of Ireland most readily
accessible to intercourse with Britain and the Continent. Not much remains
to us but the names — St. Ciaran of Saighir and Ossory, St. Ailbe of Emly,
St. Ibar of Beg Erin and St. Declan of Ardmore — and some lively legends
of their miraculous activities.

St. Ciaran was born possibly in 375 A.D. on Clear Island in County Cork
— a craggy islet, the most southerly point of Ireland, that was home to
about four hundred people whose herds of cattle had to eke out such a

83

frugal living that the animals were very small. Before Ciaran was born, his mother had a vision wherein a star seemed to fall into her mouth. While still a boy, unbaptized but already "in a state of holiness," he saw a kite pluck a small bird from its nest. Ciaran prayed in his grief, and the kite returned and dropped the little bird at his feet, wounded almost to the point of death. The boy soothed it and put it back in its nest, miraculously healed. This early proclivity endured, outshining even the eloquence, saintliness and wisdom for which he came to be revered. After his baptism at age thirty and some years of study in Rome and Lérins (in the course of which he was said to have met the much younger Patrick), he returned to Ireland to found a church on the present site of Kilkenny, County Kilkenny. The place, when Ciaran chose it, was tenanted only by wild animals, and his first disciples were a fox, a wolf, a deer and a badger. A wild boar fled at his approach but returned to be tamed. With its tusks it cut the materials for his first dwelling, a house of woven twigs daubed with mud and roofed with grass. Ciaran lived alone and austerely in his retreat until knowledge of his sanctity, his gentleness and the sweetness of his words spread and attracted a nucleus of converts to what was to become probably Ireland's first monastery.

The figure of St. Ailbe is almost as nebulous as that of St. Ciaran. His life is said to have spanned 167 years, from 360 to 527. He is probably a composite: the saints of early years, the recording of whose deeds was dependent on the spoken word of recent converts steeped in the magic and mysticism of their pre-Christian youth, tended to blend together. Their deeds, later recorded in writing by monks themselves enveloped in the climate of unquestioning faith, took on a cloudy aura, and several saints merged into a single hyperbolic monument to saintliness.

Ailbe was born to a maidservant in the house of Cronan, lord of Eliach in County Tipperary. Cronan, for reasons unrevealed, disapproved of his birth and directed that he be exposed to "dogs and wild beasts, that he might be devoured."[1] The baby was found by a wolf, who tended him until an unidentified passerby, possibly a Christian from Britain, noticed his beauty and his potential Christian grace, and took him away to be reared in the faith. After study and consecration in Rome, Ailbe was directed by the pope, along with "fifty holy men from Ireland," presumably recently converted followers, to proselytize the heathens in an unrecorded corner of Europe. Then, like "a sagacious bee loaded with honey," he embarked for Ireland with his companions in an unseaworthy boat. By blessing the sea, he brought them all serenely to port in northern Ireland, where he converted the king, Fintan, and brought back to life Fintan's three sons, slain in battle.

St. Ailbe traversed Ireland, as did St. Patrick after him, converting as he went, and at last settled in Emly, County Tipperary, near the place of his birth. There he founded a church and a school, and promulgated the "Law of Ailbe," supposedly the first codification of ecclesiastical rule in Ireland. In the huge span of his life he was a friend to many holy men, including, of course, St. Patrick, who reputedly named him archbishop of Munster. When he was very old he wished to retire to Tyle (Thule), the island that is now Iceland, to flee worldly honors and to meditate among the holy hermits already established on that bleak shore. But King Aengus of Munster (converted by St. Patrick) refused permission and placed guards at the seaports so he could not escape his responsibilities to the multitudes of his adoring followers. Ailbe is called "the second St. Patrick," and he may be one of those whose deeds and persons fuse into the great shadowy form of Ireland's patron saint.

The features of St. Ibar are the dimmest of the four holy men who preceded Patrick. He was probably born in Ulster, of high lineage, but his chief sphere of activity was County Wexford, in the southeast, where he built a monastery on Beg Erin, an island in Wexford Harbor (now attached to the mainland). One hundred and fifty monks lived under his rule, and the school attached to his monastery attracted students, it is said, from all over Ireland and even from the Continent. The latter fact is interesting, as it indicates that Gaulish scholars fleeing the invasions of the Huns were already at this early date seeking sanctuary in Ireland. The barbaric island on the outer edge of Europe, it appears, acquired a reputation for sanctity — or at least for the toleration of Christianity — well before its official conversion. Apart from the renown of his school, Ibar is chiefly known for his early resistance to Patrick. He objected, it is written, "for it was displeasing to him that a foreigner should be patron of Ireland." [2] His obduracy melted, however, and he later joined the Synod at Cashel where the four holy men of the south met with Patrick to discuss church matters and arrange their respective ecclesiastical jurisdictions.

St. Declan was, like St. Ailbe, epically venerable, his life spanning those of St. Patrick and St. David of Wales, who died over a century apart. He must have been greatly beloved, for the little stone oratory at Ardmore, County Waterford, built probably in the eighth century and said to contain his ashes, is still a place of annual pilgrimage. His life, according to his eighth-century chronicler, consisted of the familiar series of miracles, many of them repetitive, that turn up in the lives of one saint after another. The early scribes regarded their subjects with uncritical eyes: the more miracles they could attribute, the higher and holier was the object of their adoration. The medieval monastic view of life was unsophisticated and romantic, as naturally receptive to the marvelous as that of a child. Then too, the saints were their heroes. They composed their *Lives* not with the intent to teach, but to entertain the recently converted, the naive new believers still in touch with the old magic. As with the bards of earlier years, whose warriors outdid one another in the audacity of their exploits, each devoted biographer liked to brag of the superior proficiency in holiness of his own saint. Personalities and facts, while they can sometimes be deduced, were unimportant to the chronicler. The portraits have the bright primary colors and the bizarre, childlike shapes of medieval stained glass.

Declan was of the clan of the Deisi, a northern family that had left its home territory to settle in Munster, and he was descended from kings of Tara. Some of his antecedents are outrageously pagan: three of his ancestors slept with their own sister, and the one son she bore was marked by three wavy red lines, the marks of his three fathers. A ball of fire was seen blazing above the house where Declan was born — a nearly universal mark of holiness attending the births of Irish saints, and almost heretically reminiscent of the Star of Bethlehem. When his mother lifted him she struck his head against a stone. The baby was not hurt but the stone retained the hollow image of his head, and the rain that fell into it cured sickness. He was obviously destined for sanctity, and indeed, as early as age seven, when he was sent to study, "he avoided every fault and every unlawful desire."[3] When he was grown he went to Rome to continue his studies, and was ordained bishop by the pope, who sent him back to Ireland to preach and convert. Many Romans, it is written, accompanied him "to perform their pilgrimage and spend their lives there under the yoke and rule of Bishop Declan . . . amongst them Runan, son of the king of Rome; he was dear to Declan." After all, though his garb was of homespun and his patrimony belonged to God, Declan would hardly forget that he was a scion of kings.

In Rome he had met Ailbe, already prominent, and they had formed a deep friendship that was to last their lives. When leaving Italy Declan encountered Patrick on the road; the young Briton was on his way to the Holy City for his ordination. When Declan and his followers reached the Channel, they had no money and could not find a boat to transport them. The saint had received a little black bell from heaven; he struck it, asking

God to help them, and there appeared an empty ship with no sails. It wafted them over to Ireland, then glided away, to vanish over the waves. But the little black bell was forgotten, left by one of the Romans on a rock at the edge of the shore of Gaul. Declan, distressed, asked God to bring it back, and the rock itself floated over the ocean with the bell upon it, to come to rest on an island on the south coast of Ireland, in County Waterford. It lies there still, a great ice-age boulder with a hole through it, and only he who is without sin is able to crawl through the hole. In the last century a parish priest tried to have this object of superstition broken or removed, but he could find no workmen to perform such an act of desecration to the memory of a still-loved saint.

Declan chose to settle where his floating rock had come to rest. The center of the island rose to a mild height, and Declan named it Ardmore (Great Hill), which is its name still, although it is no longer an island. On this hill he built his church and monastery, the land being granted to him by the king of the Deisi, his own family. But the people of the nearby mainland did not want the holy men on the island: they were afraid the coming and going of the monks across the water would cause them to be expelled from their homes. Declan struck the ocean with his crosier, and it dried up "so swiftly . . . that the monsters of the sea were swimming and running and . . . it was with difficulty they escaped with the sea."

Declan was dedicated to his mission: he founded churches, converted pagans without number, and gained the reputation of a man "wise like a serpent and gentle like a dove and industrious like a bee." But like many of the Irish saints he was as ready to raise his left hand in a curse as his right in a blessing. It added to the stature of a saint, in the view of his biographer, if he could successfully smite the aggressor. Turning the other cheek was rarely an attribute of the early Irish Christian: it was a luxury unaffordable to one who had to vie for supremacy with druids and chieftains still in the mentality of the Heroic Age. In Declan's travels he once came to a settlement where the villagers refused him hospitality. He spent the night in a bare stable with no food and no fire to warm him. In the morning he cursed the people and "there came fire from heaven on them to consume them all [and their] homestead and village, so that the place has been ever since a wilderness accursed." On another occasion, when a fleet of pirates approached the shore, Declan "held his left hand against it and, on the spot, the sea swallowed them like sacks full of lead, and the drowned sailors were changed into large rocks which stand high out of the sea from that time until now."

St. Declan lived long enough (probably a second Declan overlapped the first) to visit St. David in Wales. David, who died about 600, was bishop of the Deisi colony in Wales, kinsmen of the southern Ireland family who comprised Declan's see. About a hundred years earlier, Declan had seen St. Patrick convert Aengus of Munster at Cashel, an act the older saint had been unable to achieve because of the king's traditional enmity to the Deisi. Declan then took part in the Synod of Cashel with Patrick and the three fellow bishops of the south. The dearest of these to Declan was Ailbe, and when the former felt death near he summoned his equally elderly friend. The final fourteen days were passed in pleasant colloquy on Declan's lovely hilltop.

The high promontory of Ardmore might have been an island once, and appears to be becoming one again. On both sides of it the sea pokes gently into the land, seeping between level fields where the grass grows green, flecked with the yellow of wild iris, right to the water's edge. The North Atlantic is uncommonly placid here. No rocks interrupt its peaceful flow, and many shallow little harbors with pinkish beaches hold the water calm. The first sight on Declan's rounded hill is a tall, tapering round tower, one of those beautiful and unique Irish monuments probably originally intended as bell towers and later used for defense against the Viking raids of the ninth and tenth centuries. On one side of it is an attractive small church of Irish Romanesque, the "Cathedral"; on the other sits the primitive oratory called St. Declan's House, where perhaps lie the saint's remains. About fifteen feet by nine, the oratory is a simple rectangle of stone, possibly built in the eighth century, with a slate roof added in the eighteenth. A stone-lined pit in the corner is, it is said, the receptacle of the holy ashes. The sea wind blows the wildflowers and long grass of the cemetery surrounding these buildings, and far below, the ocean ripples quietly, light gray under a misted sun and a white sky. Declan chose his spot well. The words of the new faith would not have sounded strange here, to farmers attuned to the worship of the deities of hill and ocean.

Foggy as the facts are surrounding the four holy men of the south, a basic truth is evident: before the beginning of the fifth century, Ireland had become known, in Britain and on the Continent, as a good place for a Christian. True, it was still looked upon as a barbaric country with no towns and a population of ignorant and irascible cattle lords. But its heathens seemed to have more interest in bludgeoning one another than in molesting Christians, and it was still untouched by the storms that were tearing at most of Europe. Christians who found their way there, whether out of devotion to one or another of the good bishops, or for safety in this unruffled backwater, or simply from curiosity, found an unexpected climate of serenity and simple piety.

In the early fifth century the administration at Rome decided that the signs of grace in the remote island were discernible enough to warrant the sending of an official representative to strengthen and spread the faith. The choice fell on one Palladius, who was sent in 431 by Pope Celestine to be bishop to "those of the Irish who believe in Christ."[4] Palladius's origins and background are obscure. He may have been a Greek; he probably studied at Auxerre; his reputation was strong as a scholar and an opponent of the Pelagian heresy so dangerously popular in the British Isles. The only thing sure about his antecedents is that he was not Irish. He knew neither the language nor the life-style of the people he was sent to proselytize, and he failed entirely.

Though most of the Christians were in the south, Palladius chose to land on the coast of Wicklow and to start his preaching in the central and northeast sections. The local king, Nathy, opposed him at once, and the "wild and rough people . . . did not readily receive his teaching, nor did he himself desire to spend a long time in a land which was not his own. . . . His resolve was formed, to return with the first tide which served."[5] After founding three little churches on the coast of Wicklow (no trace of which remains — not even knowledge of their locations), he departed for Rome. Chance landed him first on the shore of Galloway in western Scotland, and there he carried on a more successful mission among the Picts until his death a year later, in 432.

Out of the murky past of facts magnified into legends and legends superimposed on one another arises the extraordinarily clear vision of Ireland emerging into the full sunlight of Christianity in the middle of the fifth century. Folklore would have it that this happened suddenly, as St. Patrick swept across the island mowing down druids and confounding heathen chiefs. The four saints of the south recede into misty vagueness before this bright onslaught. In truth the figure of St. Patrick is just as phantasmal as theirs. Tradition chose him from among Ireland's early missionaries because tradition needed a single hero, like the figure of Cuchulain or Finn, on whom to place the halo of the fresh young faith.

It was not an entirely capricious choice. There must have been a man like St. Patrick — or several men embodying the one great figure — of remarkable attributes. One cannot now disentangle history from fantasy; one can only repeat the story as it is told, and try to discern something of the character behind the myth.

He was born, probably, in the district of the Severn in western Britain, about 390 A.D., the son of a British official of the Roman administration, who may have been a Christian. When Patrick was sixteen he was taken prisoner in a raid by Niall of the Nine Hostages, king of northern Ireland, and sold to a farmer named Milcho, who lived in Dalaradia, County Antrim. He was set to herding cattle on Slemish Mountain. This is one of Antrim's dramatic heights, Ireland's only remnants, eroded and ragged, of the flood of liquid basalt that arose from volcanic fissures in the ocean floor in the Eocene Epoch fifty million years ago, to form the great land-mass called the Thulean Province, comprising southern Greenland, Iceland, northern Ireland, the Faeroes and the Hebrides.

The ancient mountain is high and lonely, and the boy, though he performed his duties conscientiously, was inspired by the magnificently bleak scenery to contemplation of the God who had been but a faint figurehead of his childhood. He lived on roots and herbs, it is written, and through winter frost and summer rain he prostrated himself day and night in prayer. Along with his self-taught faith the impressionable young slave absorbed the language and the fables of pagan Ireland, and he came to love the country of his enforced exile.

After six years of slavery, years of patient hard work and devotion that strengthened his spirit and toughened his body, he escaped and took ship for the Continent. The history of his European years is vague and contradictory, confusedly entangled with the life stories of various others of Ireland's holy men. Somewhere (possibly Auxerre) he learned a passable Latin; somehow (maybe by Amator, the bishop of Auxerre) he was ordained priest; someone (possibly St. Germanus, the succeeding bishop of Auxerre and missionary to Britain) appointed him bishop of the Irish and sent him back to propagate the faith. In Patrick's eyes the call was extra-terrestrial: "I saw, in the bosom of the night, a man coming as it were from Ireland . . . with letters . . . and he gave one of them to me. And I read the beginning of the letter containing 'the voice of the Irish' . . . and they cried out then as if with one voice, 'We entreat thee, holy youth, that thou come, and henceafter walk among us.'"[6]

In 432 he returned with twenty-four companions, landing first on the Wicklow coast where Palladius had been discomfited the year before. Patrick was received with the same lack of warmth and he retaliated, in the accepted manner, with a curse, converting King Nathy's domain into a salt marsh. The party then sailed slowly up the coast, making a final landing at Strangford Lough, County Down. It may have been that there the travellers had no choice, perforce riding the tide that rips through the half-mile-wide channel at ten knots, carrying four hundred million tons of water into that great, nearly landlocked inlet of the sea.

The local chieftain, Dichu, inhospitably set dogs on Patrick. Taking refuge in a barn, the saint cried out a curse in Latin and the dogs stiffened into stone. Dichu then lifted his sword, found his right arm suddenly paralyzed, and decided on the spot to embrace the faith. Patrick restored him to health, and the chief presented him with the barn where the miracle had happened. It was called Sabhal Padraic (now Saul); and though, un-conventionally, it was aligned north and south, the young priest made it his first church.

Patrick knew that in order to convert the people he had first to convince their lords. His initial step was to make a bold stand at Tara to face down the fierce opposition of Laoghaire — son of Niall of the Nine Hostages, Patrick's captor — who was now high-king of northern Ireland. King Laoghaire feared the new religion, and specifically he feared it in the person of Patrick, who already in his short sojourn was exhibiting an alarming flare for attracting converts. Laoghaire had heard dire predictions of the young missionary from his druid, Matha Mac Umotr:

> One shall arrive here, having his head shaven in a circle, bearing a crooked staff, and his table shall be in the eastern part of his house, and his people shall stand behind him, and he shall sing forth from his table wickedness, and all his household shall answer — So be it! — and this man, when he cometh, shall destroy our gods, and overturn their altars. . . . He will seduce the people and bring them after him. . . . He will free the slaves. . . . He will magnify kindreds of low degree . . . and he shall subdue unto himself the kings that resist him . . . and his doctrines shall reign for ever and ever.[7]

The ominous forecast of equality was by itself enough to induce the high-king to gather his druids and his warriors around him and instruct them to lay low the sinister apostle and his friends without delay. But Patrick eluded them, rendering himself and his companions invisible, so that the assassins saw only a herd of deer as the Christian travellers passed. It is likely that the years on the lonely northern mountain had taught the young shepherd well how to melt into a natural background.

To reach Tara they sailed down the coast to the mouth of the river Boyne and walked along its shores through the modest hills and wide green valleys of Meath. The countryside was soaked with heathen associations. Patrick knew that the mild, sinuous river whose shores he followed was the personification of the goddess Boann, wife of the ancient chief god, the Dagda. He passed the vast pyramid at Newgrange, where were buried, it was said, the three sons of the Dagda and where worship of the deities Patrick had come to combat still took place. He knew their strength but he never doubted his own.

He arrived before the great palace on top of the Hill of Tara on the eve of Beltine, the pagan celebration of May 1. It also happened to be Holy Saturday, the day before Easter (by the old reckoning). On Beltine Eve, so the legend goes, a fire was traditionally lit at Tara, accompanied by ceremonial rituals (a made-up legend, it must be said, invented later by an adoring biographer with a nose for drama, to point up Patrick's conflict with and victory over the druids; no evidence exists that there was ever a cult fire at Tara). On that night no other fire was to burn before the Tara fire. But Patrick, honoring his own Christian festival, set a challenging fire on a nearby hill before the pagan flame was kindled. He was summoned into the king's presence, where he amazed the assembled chiefs and druids with a series of magical miracles more reminiscent of druidical conjuration than of missionary godliness. The druids were confounded, many of the company were converted, and the king was, if not inwardly convinced, outwardly subdued, to the extent that he promised tolerance to Patrick's mission.

The success at Tara opened the way for conversions throughout Meath. Besides concentrating on the cattle lords, whose relatives and vassals would follow the lead of their chief, Patrick made a point of appearing at sites of pagan worship, where many people would be gathered together in a mood for religious exercise. Whatever the original character of this, Patrick made sure that it would eventually turn in the direction of Christian worship. His most famous legendary exploit of this nature was the miracle at the notorious stone idol Crom Cruaich (aforementioned), the worship of which occasioned such peculiarly abysmal prostrations. His destruction of the idol was followed by the wholesale baptism of its worshippers, an act accomplished by means of a fountain produced by Patrick's holy staff out of the dry earth. The real miracle here, as elsewhere, must have been the simple and vibrant fervency of the young man's words, his spirited courage and his lambent sincerity.

After some years of purposeful wandering, Patrick paused near Ireland's western edge at the place now called Murrisk Abbey, County Mayo, on Clew Bay under the shadow of a great brooding mountain. It was the beginning of Lent, and Patrick decided to spend the forty days of fasting on the mountain, now called Croagh Patrick. It is a loaf-shaped massif, its main peak a shapely pyramid of quartzite, 2,510 feet high, alive with birds and rabbits up to the base of the rocky summit cone. On the lower flank he walked (according to the tracing of today's broad pilgrim track) beside a fast, stony little stream, straight up to the saddle below the peak's sheer north face. Below him the blunt, tree-covered Murrisk peninsula jutted into the great square of Clew Bay, whose landward surface was dotted with hundreds of drumlins, resembling a host of surfacing porpoises. He turned through the saddle to climb the summit cone from the back. The final ascent was a steep scree of loose, jagged stones that slid downward as he stepped on them, a purgatory for the feet whether bare or sandaled (today's pilgrims accomplish it barefoot). It is likely that the bitter north-west wind off the ocean whipped rain-filled clouds unceasingly around him, as it is a rare day when the top of the mountain is unveiled. Up here on the unsheltered summit, where it was too cold and wet for rabbits and no bird could survive the unremitting wind, Patrick meditated "in heavenly rapture" for the forty days of Lent. At the end of that time "he gathered together from all parts of Ireland all the poisonous creatures. . . . By the power of his word he drove the whole pestilent swarm from the precipice of the mountain, headlong into the ocean."

This legend was invented some seven hundred years after Patrick lived, to explain the then-unaccountable fact of Ireland's freedom from snakes. The island actually lost its reptiles and amphibians fifteen to twenty thousand years earlier. Most of the plants and animals of the British Isles had been killed or driven south as the ice cap grew. When the glacial sheet waned they began to come back. But before they could reach Ireland the melting ice raised the water level, and the land bridge that had connected Wales and Ireland during the Ice Age was broken by the re-creation of the Irish Sea. A junction between Scotland and northern Ireland existed somewhat longer, but to get there the animals had to travel all the way through England. Most of them did not get that far before that bridge too was submerged. The only animals that got back to Ireland were those that could swim or fly. Two amphibians and one reptile made it: the natterjack toad, the smooth newt and the brown lizard, all innocuous little creatures. Ireland's snakelessness was commented on as early as the third century A.D. by the grammarian Gaius Julius Solinus: "In that land there are no snakes, birds are few, and the people are inhospitable and warlike." In the eighth century the Venerable Bede wondered at the fact: "No reptile is found there, nor could a serpent survive; for although serpents have been brought from Britain, as soon as the ship approaches land they are affected by the scent of the air and quickly perish."[8] And though Giraldus Cambrensis, the Welsh historian who came with the conquering Anglo-Norman forces in the twelfth century, complained peevishly of the lechery, irascibility and superstition of the conquered Irish, he found their country admirably wholesome, particularly in its lack of snakes. "Sometimes," he wrote, "for the sake of experiment, serpents have been shipped over . . . but were found lifeless and dead as soon as the middle of the Irish Sea was crossed. Poison also . . . was found to lose its venom, disinfected by a purer air." Even the harmless toad, he added, could not survive the atmosphere of sanctity — for a merchant, finding toads in the bottom of his ship's hold, threw them on Ireland's shore, whereupon "they immediately turned on their backs and, bursting their bellies, died."[9]

None of these early commentators mentioned St. Patrick. It was his twelfth-century biographer, Jocelyn, credulously reverent, who chose to explain his country's odd deficiency by tacking yet another legend to the top-heavy halo surrounding the saint.

Apocryphal as are most of the stories around the hazy figure of Ireland's patron, it is a historical fact that the framework of a Christian organization modelled loosely on that of Rome began to take shape under the aegis of a single or composite strong, vibrant personality. It started, probably, when Patrick went to challenge the heathen stronghold of Cashel. (This was the seat of King Aengus, the over-king of Munster, which was one of Ireland's five provinces and at that time, with Tara, the most powerful.) Cashel was the traditional rival of Tara in the ages-old division of Ireland into a northern and a southern half, and Patrick knew that the conversion of its king was just as important for his mission as the convincing of King Laoghaire at Tara. The eloquent young man succeeded where his elders, Ireland's first four holy men, had failed. Aengus became one of his strongest supporters, and Cashel was the site of Ireland's first meeting of ecclesiastics, as Patrick summoned to him Declan, Ibor, Ailbe and Ciaran for the disposition of local ecclesiastical affairs.

As one crosses the intensively farmed plain of Tipperary, named the Golden Vale for its fertility, the eyes are soothed by its long, mild undulations. St. Patrick's Rock in Cashel (shown on page 225), a tall limestone knob rising suddenly out of the flat fields, is all the more startling for its unassuming surroundings. The natural citadel is crowned by an ancient stone wall surrounding a group of buildings and towers, sharp shadows in the wide blue sky, a vision improbably romantic like an illustration for a troubadour's ballad. Within the walls it is no less hauntingly beautiful (in a later chapter we will look at some of its structures). Though nothing remains from the time of Patrick and though all the ruins are of different periods, such is Cashel's composite harmony that the strength and grace of the religion he inaugurated is a living presence.

Patrick continued his circuit of Ireland, going, as did the kings on their tribute-collecting progressions, with the sun. Like the kings, he collected around himself a retinue of the sons of chieftains and various household functionaries, including a cook, a brewer, a bell ringer, a scribe, smiths, shepherds and embroideresses (nuns). He made handsome gifts to his followers, as well as to those whose lands he visited. His generous life-style was looked on askance by the Continental clergy, but they did not understand the peculiar requirements of a mission to a country still living in a barbaric age. Patrick's stature as an apostle of the Church required that he travel like a prince; he attracted a great deal more favorable attention than if he had gone his way in humble poverty. He left behind him a trail of churches under the governance of the flower of the land.

One of the two most important collections of ancient law tracts is attributed to St. Patrick. When he came again to Tara, such was his prestige that King Laoghaire was persuaded to detail Dubhtach, his chief poet and a devout Christian convert, to expound to Patrick the whole of the extant law, an awesome recital. Then the king, at Patrick's request, appointed a committee to revise the code. Three kings, three churchmen and three historians were gathered for the purpose, and after three years they produced the civil code known as the *Senchus Mor,* the Great Tradition. It contained no new laws but was a codification of the old, with the addition of some church canons and the deletion of measures that were cruel or arbitrary. Patrick, broad-minded and eminently sensible, saw to it that most of the common law was left untouched and the customs and quirks of the ages respected. His only opposition was to open pagan worship and idolatrous rites, and in that he was fierce and fearless. The introduction to the *Senchus Mor* states that "what did not clash with the word of God . . . and with the consciences of the believers was confirmed." Like all the old law, which was recited orally, the *Senchus Mor* is in verse. Dubhtach "put a thread of poetry around it for Patrick.'

At some point the itinerant bishop thought it advisable to establish a main church. He chose a hilltop at Armagh, County Armagh, a site that seemed expedient, probably because of its nearness to Emain Macha, the ancient capital of northern Ireland, a place still in his time regarded with religious and political reverence. He intended to make Armagh his primal see, but until his old age he spent little time there. In his lifetime it never grew much beyond a simple church, the nearest settlement two miles away. He had not the inclination to be a proper bishop like his Continental brothers, with a seat in an ecclesiastical city. All his life he preferred to move about, calling himself simply "resident of Ireland." Despite his elaborate retinue, his personal life was austere. He slept on stone and said his prayers, night and day, immersed up to the neck in cold water. He wore the simplest clothing: a rough hair-shirt next to his body and over it a hooded robe of unbleached wool. He fasted often, but it is said that, except during Lent, he had no prescriptive rules for eating, following Christ's sensible and courteous precept of eating whatever was laid before him. Most of the many gifts he received he passed on immediately to the poor. He further endeared himself to those around him by joining in whatever manual labor was necessary, fishing, tilling the ground, building churches. He travelled on foot until age overtook him; only then did he resort to chariot.

When he got too feeble even for this, he retired to Saul, the place of his first church, to spend the remainder of his life in prayer and contemplation. He still ventured as far as Armagh, however, to hold council with his younger priests about matters that needed reform. When he was near death, Brigid came to him and offered him a winding sheet that she had spun and woven. He had loved Brigid since, as a girl, she had come to hear him preach. She had fallen asleep in the midst of his words, and Patrick forbore to wake her. When she awoke by herself, saying, "I sleep but my heart waketh," she related her dream to Patrick, who explained to her its holy and prophetic meaning. Now, at the end of his life, he accepted with touching gratitude her artless intimation of his coming demise. There seems to have been little unnecessary tact among the early Irish ecclesiastics. In any case, death held no shadows; it was but the prelude to a bright awakening. His last benediction was given to Brigid's nuns. He died in 461 and was buried at Downpatrick, County Down, where, in due course, his remains were joined by those of St. Brigid and St. Columba.

The fledgling Church that Patrick left behind him was based on the conventionally Roman ecclesiastical organizations of Britain and Gaul. Deeply committed Irishman though he became, Patrick had received his first lessons in Christianity in Roman Britain and had studied in even more thoroughly Romanized Gaul. There were intended to be bishops, ruling their flocks from sees, with a central administration at Armagh. Patrick optimistically appointed a successor to the office of this focal see, one Benignus, whose name has not made an indelible mark on history. If it did not work out as Patrick planned, it was from no weakness on his part. Rome was far away and Ireland was conservative. The Irish had always absorbed their masters, and the hand of the new spiritual master rested lightly on them. Patrick himself had started the trend, deviating from the Roman model of the inflexible and exacting proselytizer. He followed the ancient customs, he appreciated the pagan tales of Celtic heroism, and he tolerated the eccentricities of a people he loved. Further, he never settled long enough in one place to get around to administering it in the meticulous Roman manner.

The ease with which Christianity took over a totally barbarian country is an indication of how little it displaced. The new religion moved flexibly into the niches of the old. Since Ireland had no towns, the bishops set up their sees in the framework of the *tuath,* the convenient geographical and political unit based on the family and only large enough so that a man could ride to the assembly place and back in the same day. Often the bishop had himself been the chief, so that a whole *tuath* would go Christian at once, druids, poets and all. As his see was rural, every bishop was a farmer and many of them, aristocrats or not, worked in the fields along with their people as Patrick had. The bishop knew his flock well, far better than if he had ruled from an episcopal palace in a city: they were his family, physically and spiritually. All the attributes of a monastic system were here, ready for the rise of the distinctive Irish brand of Christianity that was to bring Europe to a new awakening.

There had been monasteries in Ireland before Patrick came, and he encouraged the founding of new ones. They rested easily on the foundations of the Celtic family structure, so easily that it was not long before the title of bishop became subsidiary to that of abbot and the most important churches were ruled by a monastic house — almost a dynasty, since the abbot was generally chosen from the founder's family. Even the pope came to be called "Abbot of Rome."

The ascetic way of life had always been attractive to the Irish: the virtues preached by Christian missionaries were not far from those practiced by the *Fianna.* For a cattle lord to become a monk did not entail a profound sacrifice, and there was little change in the way of life of his followers. The main change was for the better: the shift away from combativeness, toward tolerant tranquillity. No longer need they follow their lord in the mandatory raids dictated by pride and status. Squabbling, for the time being, was in abeyance.

Aside from the practicality and naturalness of the new way of life, monastic Christianity appealed to minds already imbued with poetry and mysticism. In the place of *Tir na n'Og* over the western sea, it offered a heaven of not dissimilar beatitude, attainable to one who lived a life of austerity and strict obedience. The cloistered monk paring his life to the minimum in his quiet cell, or the ascetic recluse communing with God and nature on a rock in the ocean, could achieve a state of grace even on this earth. This benignity was open to everyone. The new religion recognized no social barriers to grace. What was even better, the anchorite understood what he was doing and why he was doing it. The religion of the druids had reserved its mysteries, fearing the profaning touch of common knowledge. Their practices were wrapped in obscurity, where Christianity hid no secrets: it offered a clear and beautiful mysticism and it promised an accessible happiness to anyone who had the desire and the strength for it. It is also likely that the people had grown tired of the old religion with its hosts of capricious deities and multitudes of peremptory, often contradictory taboos. The new creed was refreshingly simple.

Above all, Christianity came to a country that had no reason to fear it. Ireland, small and unimportant as she was in the European scheme, had remained unassailed in her ocean fortress for a thousand years. Her masters might fight among themselves, but they had not to repel an outside invader who could come in the armor of a warrior or the habit of a monk. No suspicion attached to the gentle-seeming clerics with their message of salvation, that they might be the forerunners of an alien power. They asked only to be listened to. Since the message was appealing, they were. These spokesmen for a new order were themselves its best advertisement. Starting with Patrick, Ireland produced a series of extraordinary personalities in which sensitivity, sympathy, humility and passionate earnestness were backed up by an invincible courage worthy of the heroes of the sagas. They could perform feats of physical endurance with the toughness of the old-time warriors. Like them, they had no fear of death. In their intolerance of evil they exercised a weapon worthy of the feared master poets: they could curse with formidable effectiveness. After all, they were the children of these very warriors and poets, and the lusty vigor of their race was not weakened by the consecrated serenity of their lives.

Among the gifts brought by Christianity, that most happily appreciated by the pagan Irish was the love of learning. Patrick is said to have introduced the Latin language; once it was accepted, the art of writing followed with almost unbelievable quickness. The replacement of the clumsy and laborious *Ogam* with the convenient Latin script was like the touch of a magic wand on spirits ready to be awakened. As we have seen, the Irish already had an extensive oral literature and a sophisticated skill in the use of words and the ways of poetry. Christianity brought them not only the means of transcribing their spoken tales to parchment but a fresh assemblage of stories and characters, those of the Old and New Testaments. A new literary class, the masters of Christian scholarship, came into being under the influence of Patrick and his successors. They were rendered the same awed respect that had been accorded to the *aes dana,* the learned men of the Heroic Age.

Patrick himself was not a polished Latin scholar; he described himself as "a rustic, a fugitive, unlearned." [10] But his *Confession* and his *Letter to Coroticus,* both in Latin, are Ireland's earliest known pieces of written prose. He may have felt easier in the native language. A sacred poem in Irish, *Faedh Fiada (Cry of the Deer),* is said to have been composed by Patrick as he approached Tara. King Laoghaire's men, sent to ambush and murder him, saw only a herd of deer in the hills, with a fawn following them, and mistook the chanting of the hymn for the call of the fawn after its mother. The hymn, which we will consider in chapter 14, has curious pagan overtones: Patrick owed much to his youthful years among the heathens.

Patrick is said to have gone even further in his response to native lore. Though he is believed to be the first to introduce Latin, the Christian creed and the laws of the Church, Patrick is also represented as the first to encourage his lately baptized flock to write down their own tales in their own language. In this guise he appears in *The Colloquy of the Old Men,* a charming, semihumorous entertainment written about 1200 A.D. Ossian, the poet son of Finn, and Cailte, Ossian's cousin, are the only surviving members of Finn's army. A century and a half after the final destruction of the *Fianna,* Patrick and his companions meet these two very old men, giants with huge wolf-dogs, before whom the little Christian band quails. But Patrick boldly sprinkles holy water on them, banishing the "thousand legions of demons" that have been floating over them, and bids the two large warriors rest awhile with him and tell him of their lives. The Christians wonder at the size of the ancients, "for the largest man of them reached but to the waist . . . of the others, and they sitting." Soon all their qualms are forgotten in their delight at the stories told by the two heathens, of the noble adventures of Finn's army of the forest. But Patrick is uneasy at his own pleasure: "Were it not for us an impairing of the devout life, an occasion of neglecting prayer, and of deserting converse with God, we . . . would feel the time pass quickly, O Warrior." [11]

Patrick calls on his two guardian angels, Aibellan and Solusbretach, who reassure him: "Holy cleric, no more than a third part of their stories do those ancient warriors tell, by reason of forgetfulness; . . . but by thee be it written on tables of poets, and in learned men's words, for to the companies and nobles of the later time, to give ear to these stories will be a pastime."

Patrick thereupon blesses the heathen storytellers, saying, "Victory and blessing wait on thee! For the future thy stories and thyselves are dear to us."

However imaginary the part assigned to St. Patrick in the preservation of pre-Christian lore, the phenomenon occurred very early in Ireland's Christian history. The very first missionaries, as well as those who came later, displayed an easy tolerance, often an open enthusiasm, for the customs, usages, even the mythology of the heathen Irish. Ireland's heritage of pagan literature, the most extensive in existence, would have sunk long since into the abyss of the forgotten if not for the inspired support of these sympathetic priests. That is the greatest legacy of the early Christians.

CHAPTER VI
THE INNOVATORS·
ST. ENDA, ST. FINIAN
AND ST. BRIGID

AN EIGHTH-CENTURY HISTORIAN DIVIDED IRELAND'S SAINTS INTO THREE orders, not according to the degree of their sanctity but to delineate their periods and their orientation.* "The first order . . . ," wrote the scribe, "was in the time of Patrick; and then they were all bishops, distinguished and holy, and full of the Holy Ghost . . . founders of churches. They had one head, Christ, and one chief, Patrick. They had one mass, one liturgy, one tonsure from ear to ear. . . . They did not reject the service and society of women, because, founded on the rock, Christ, they feared not the blast of temptation." [1] The second order of saints, the writer continued, had few bishops but many priests who, although they also acknowledged one head, Christ, had different methods of celebrating the mass, and different rules for daily life. These, overlapping with and succeeding Patrick's bishops, were the founders of Irish monasticism, the movement for which Ireland was so peculiarly suited. (The third order, to be discussed in chapter XI, consisted of anchorites and hermit communities.)

Patrick's clergy labored hard during his later years and after his death, but none of them had his magnetism, and the glow of his teaching began

---

*The word *saint,* the usual designation of early Ireland's holy men, is used here in its old sense of a Christian distinguished either for martyrdom or for his exceptional piety, purity, kindness and general all-around goodness. None of Ireland's premedieval saints were canonized, not even St. Patrick: too little could later be proven of their deeds and miracles, even of their actual existence.

to die away. Much of Ireland was still pagan at Patrick's death, and now, with the first combative apostle gone, the druids began to revive their old power. The honest, beleaguered missionaries found their popularity waning and the spread of their teaching discouraged.

During these arid years some of the young clergy left Ireland to seek a more congenially sanctified atmosphere in the monasteries of Wales and Scotland. There they found the dedicated zeal they had missed in their own country, and after a while, full of enthusiasm for the monastic movement, they came back to light some fresh fires.

The originator of Irish monasticism, and the bridge between the first and second order of saints, was St. Enda, born in the middle of the fifth century. Less than twenty years after the death of Patrick, he founded Ireland's first historic monastery. Its fame, both as a retreat of the most rigorous and inspired sanctity and as a school, spread far beyond the borders of his country. His disciples included many of those who, with their own monastery-schools, were to bring Ireland to the threshold of her golden age and carry the bright flame abroad.

Enda was the only son of Conall, king of Oriel, a small state in what is now County Dublin, and when his father died the young prince, audaciously warlike in the pagan tradition, celebrated his inheritance in the time-honored way by making a raid on his neighbor. Returning from the successful engagement, in which one of the enemy was killed by one of Enda's soldiers, the party sang a triumphant song in praise of victory. They were overheard by Enda's sister, Fanchea. This beautiful girl, who was to become a saint in her own right, had been sought in marriage by Aengus, king of Munster, but she longed for the life of a nun. She persuaded the king to take her sister Darenia instead, and herself went, later, to found a nunnery on Lough Erne, County Fermanagh. When she heard the song of her battle-gorged brother she cried, "Do not approach . . . for thou art contaminated with the blood of a man."[2] Enda protested that the blood had not been shed by him, and that anyway he was justified in defending the inheritance of his father. Their father, Fanchea rejoined sternly, was in hell at that very moment. Enda, unreformed, then asked his sister for one of the girls she was educating. The novice was given the choice of bridegrooms; she chose Christ, and soon thereafter she died. Fanchea brought her brother to the girl's bedside. "Look now upon the face of her whom thou hast desired," she said.

"It is sadly pale and ghastly," answered Enda.

"And so shall your features hereafter be," said the unsparing nun. Enda was at last convinced, but not so his followers, who tried to dissuade him.

The relentless lady then prayed, saying that men so assiduous in earthly pursuits should find themselves even more firmly attached to earth itself — and the clansmen found their feet stuck to the ground.

Enda went to study at Candida Casa, St. Ninian's school in Whithorn, in western Scotland. Returning to Ireland he asked his brother-in-law, King Aengus, to grant him the Aran Islands, County Galway, for his church. Aengus, who liked the company of educated ecclesiastics (he was the one who had kept St. Ailbe, the pre-Patrician bishop, at home when he wanted to exile himself to Iceland) and who had never seen this far area of his jurisdiction, said he would prefer to enjoy Enda's company at Cashel. Aged Ailbe himself then spoke up on Enda's behalf, and Enda helped things along by making the earth "swell upward" so the king could view his distant islands. When Aengus saw how fair they were, he gave in willingly.

Enda's islands lie across the entrance to Galway Bay, protecting the great square harbor from the full force of the North Atlantic. Their gray limestone ridges lift cleanly out of the bay in straight-edged terraces that rise to three-hundred-foot cliffs on the southwest side, toward the open ocean. On the northeast shore the flat fields of rock surface imperceptibly out of the calm water of the bay. Enda found them fair indeed, but very, very bare. This suited him. When he had given up his patrimony he had chosen the road of "white martyrdom." This was a category of piety that distinguished the Irish saints from their more comfortable contemporaries on the Continent. The faith had taken hold in Ireland with relative painlessness, its coming nowhere accompanied by the persecution out of which "red martyrs" were created. Ireland's holy men, revering the early Christians who had died for their faith, and longing for the rapt purification of pain, devised their own forms of self-sacrifice. "Now this is white martyrdom," ran a seventh-century homily, ". . . when for God's sake [a man] parts from everything that he loves, though he suffers fasting and labor thereby. And green martyrdom is when he endures labor in penitence and repentance. And red martyrdom is the submission to the cross and tribulation for Christ's sake."[3] Enda was the first thus to renounce the world, and this was the life he directed for all who sought his island retreat.

They had little choice. The Aran Islands had been scraped clean of their topsoil by the ice sheets of the Pleistocene; what little could form later was scavenged by ocean winds or sluiced down into the porous limestone. The islanders made soil by carrying sand and seaweed from the lowlands, filling in the cracks in the limestone with rubble so the earth would not wash into them; they then built dry-stone walls to protect their crops, using the

St. Enda's Church on Inishmore, Aran Islands, County Galway

stones they had laboriously dug out of the fields. The islands were cob-
webbed with the lacy gray walls — today there are about seven thousand
miles of them on Inishmore alone — that represented this arduous toil.
Once the soil has been gathered, however, the land responds with astounding fertility. Washed by the Gulf Stream, the islands enjoy a climate even
milder than that of the mainland. Flowers range from Mediterranean to
Alpine and Arctic species, and among the few trees that can survive the
wind in protected inland depressions there grows an occasional palm,
scrawny and bent, but enduring.

Enda came to Inishmore, the largest of the islands, about the year 480.
He landed on its southeastern shore, not far from the southernmost point,
where the island meets the ocean gently. He walked up a mild incline
where wild roses grew between the loose paving-stones of the bedrock,

and stopped below a steep hill that was the beginning of the great square-cut cliffs. After winning over the hostile pagan chieftain of the islands, Corban, the exile decided to build his first church at this place. Over the years, Enda's monastery attracted increasing numbers of young would-be ascetics and students from all classes. They built their little churches all over Inishmore and surrounded each with a cluster of low round-domed huts, their sleeping cells. Half the island came to be known as the special property of Enda's home establishment, the other half was given over to ten daughter monasteries, each with its own superior. At the head of this conglomeration of monastic villages, Abbot Enda was, until his death around 530, the supreme authority. The masterful and willful young prince-warrior had not relinquished his character along with his birthright. Under his autocratic and talented leadership, a monastic school grew that was renowned even on the Continent.

Little is left of St. Enda's great establishment but a sprinkling of tiny chapels over the island, much weathered by the centuries, with attendant graveyards, fragments of cells, crosses and towers. The church called St. Enda's, on the shore where he landed, is an ancient structure (possibly eighth century or earlier) of simple and attractive proportions. It appears to have sunk: its floor lies well below the level of the surrounding cemetery, where high grass and pink daisies grow unchecked around the graves. The cemetery is sanctified; it contains, tradition holds, the bodies of 120 saints. Some of the graves are very old, possibly even going back to the time of the founding saint, who is said to be buried here; others are of this century. Ireland's holy places stay holy forever. But of St. Enda all that remains is the little sunken church, lonely under the wide sky.

One has to imagine the monastery peopled. The teacher may have gathered his pupils around him on the hill behind his church, where they could spread out on a large level space of flat rocks rippled with watermarks and pocked with sea-smoothed holes where the ocean tides of an earlier epoch had washed over them. Along their borders and in their cracks grew sweet-smelling thyme, vivid yellow pansies and orange-yellow bird's-foot trefoil. Around the gathering of students and monks lay the crooked pattern of dry-stone walls fencing in the little fields of unexpectedly rich green grass. The monastery's sheep roamed the higher hills toward the ocean, grazing on what appeared to be a pale gray desert but was actually, on closer look, a rock garden of extraordinary variety. Many kinds of ground-hugging flowers and grasses grew luxuriantly in the crevices, encouraged by the absence of inhibiting trees and shrubs, and nourished by the mild damp climate and the lime-rich soil. Below the group of disciples, just beyond Enda's church, the calm water of the bay crept over a broad flat beach, where lay their hide-covered fishing curraghs. In the near distance were the sharp rocks of Aran's two smaller islands, and far across the water rose the heavy black line of the Cliffs of Moher. Possibly Enda built a church on this hill. There is one here now, a small rectangular oratory with side walls of enormous stones and steep-pitched gables, which probably supported a stone roof. It is called Temple Benen, or St. Benignus's Chapel, named for Patrick's disciple, whom he designated his successor to the see of Armagh. Benignus was older than Enda; he died in 468, twelve years before Enda came to Aran, so he could not have built the chapel himself. It is very old, however, built in the style of Ireland's earliest churches, and it is oriented, like St. Patrick's first church at Saul, north and south. Around it are the foundations of the beehive-shaped cells of the monks, each just big enough for the bed of stone on which they spent the brief hours of rest; and enclosing the little settlement are the crumbling remains of the cashel, or wall.

Aside from the gatherings on the hill, the disciples hardly had a moment of leisure. Under Abbot Enda's rule, for which he set the example, life was rigorous in the extreme. The monks' day was divided into fixed periods for prayer, labor and sacred study. They cleared and planted their fields entirely by hand, by order of the abbot, who refused to use any tools. They ate silently and frugally in a common refectory, their food consisting mostly of oats and barley from their hard-won fields, and the fish they caught around the islands. They drank no wine and they ate no flesh. They never had a fire, no matter how wild the weather (the absence of trees precluded this luxury anyway). They made their own clothing from the undyed wool of the few sheep they could pasture on the rocky uplands. They slept in their day-clothes on the bare ground, or at best on a bundle of straw.

In spite of the severe austerity of his discipline — or partly because of it — the fame of Enda's monastery school spread over the Christian world. Most of the students who came to him from the Continent went back to teach and to sing the praises of Irish sanctity and scholarship; a few left their bones on the island. At the church dedicated to St. Brecan — a tiny, beautiful eighth-century oratory with late medieval additions, lying deep in a grassy hollow — one grave is inscribed "*VII Romani.*" (This may refer either to students from Rome or to seven famous martyrs of an earlier century.) Among Enda's Irish disciples were several who would carry on and surpass the work that he started, notably Finian of Clonard, Ciaran of Clonmacnoise and Kevin of Glendalough. Brendan the Navigator came to him for three days and three nights, to receive his blessing at the start of his voyage over the western ocean to find the Land of Promise.

What made Enda's school, and those that followed its model, so widely revered? A school needs more than piety and uncompromising discipline to attract so many devoted scholars. The austere abbot must have had a personal magnetism enhanced by a deep-seated kindness. Padraic Pearse, describing the humane ideal of education that existed in pagan Ireland and was carried over into Christian times, wrote:

> A Kieran [Ciaran] or an Enda or a Colmcille gathered his little group of foster-children around him; they were collectively his family, his household, his *clann*; many sweet and endearing words were used to mark the intimacy of that relationship. It seems to me that there has been nothing nobler in the history of education than this development of the old Irish plan of fosterage under a Christian rule, when to the pagan ideals of strength and truth there were added the Christian ideals of love and humility. And this, remember, was not the education system of an aristocracy, but the education system of a people. It was more democratic than any educational system in the world today. At Clonard Kieran, the son of a carpenter, sat in the same class as Colmcille, son of a king. To Clonard or to Aran or to Clonmacnoise went every man, rich or poor, prince or peasant, who wanted to sit at Finian's or at Enda's or at Kieran's feet and to learn of his wisdom.[4]

In 515 one of Enda's disciples, Finian, established a monastery at Clonard on the river Boyne, County Meath. Enda had shown the way; Finian, learning from him — as well as from the great Welsh churchmen of the sixth century, David, Gildas and Cadoc — was to become the patriarch of Irish monasticism. Where Enda had attracted disciples by his piety, austerity and kindness, Finian excelled as a teacher and organizer.

When he returned to Ireland from long study abroad, Finian found that his fame had come before him. At his landing place he was met by Muiredach, king of Leinster, who, wrote the scribe, "carried him on his back three journeys over the three fields that were nearest the harbor,"[5] and offered him any place he wished for a church. (Ireland had come far in the two generations since St. Patrick had been set on by the king's dogs on the shore of Strangford Lough.) Finian chose a field of apple trees. The farmer who kept his pigs there objected and was backed up by King Muiredach's son Bresal. Finian at once anathematized the prince: "Before this hour tomorrow the hand that was stretched forth to refuse me shall be in a hawk's talons and laid before me." Bresal was killed that day in a raid and a hawk seized his hand, as ordained. The field of apple trees was the site of one of several churches founded by Finian before he finally settled at Clonard.

Little or nothing remains today of the sixth-century establishment at Clonard. The valley of the Boyne was directly in the path of rampaging Vikings coming inland from Dublin Bay, and whatever was salvaged then did not survive the destructive plundering of the Anglo-Normans at the instigation of their Irish leader, the infamous Diarmait Mac Murrough. The monastic village must have been very large, even allowing for adoring exaggeration, which poses three thousand monks under Finian's rule. Out of the throngs of novices and bishops, priests and lay students who came to sit at the feet of the "tutor of saints" stand the shining figures of Finian's "Twelve Apostles of Ireland," the saints of the second order, founders of the great monasteries. They are Columba of Derry and Iona, Ciaran of Saighir, Ciaran of Clonmacnoise, Brendan (the Navigator) of Clonfert, Brendan of Birr, Colman of Terryglass, Molaisse of Devenish, Canice of Aghaboe, Ruadhan of Lothra, Mobhi of Glasnevin, Senell of Cluain Inis and Nannidh of Inis Maighe Samh.

Finian, like Enda, set the example for austerity — going, in modern eyes, to an unappealing extreme. "Senach," wrote the scribe, ". . . beheld Finian's meagreness . . . so great that his ribs could be counted through his inner raiment. Moreover Senach saw the worm coming out of Finian's side, and this was the cause — from the cold girdle of iron which he wore around him as a penance for his body, and which cut to his bone." Physical penances such as this, displeasing as they are in a softer age, were customary in the sternly sanctified atmosphere of early monasticism. A man learned to suffer pain in order to strengthen his soul. Pain gave him a heightened sensibility, and in time the mind, sharpened by torment, rose above the agony, forgot the body and reached the tranquillity of awareness of God. Self-denial — eating sparely and sleeping little — had a similar effect, a state akin to hallucinatory ecstasy. Yet it was not, as the phrase implies, a diseased condition, because these people were honestly and deeply aware of God as a living presence. Their profound faith does not strain credibility: the monks of the fifth and sixth centuries were still close to an era of magic, when the rocks and trees had voices and a man could travel to another world or another body and back again without displacing a hair on his head.

The monks under Finian's rule willingly met his severe standards of asceticism — standards that would not have been strange to the Egyptian desert fathers of an earlier time but were by the sixth century quite unacceptable in Continental monasteries. Their lives were reduced to an extreme of simplicity. Daily labor insured the self-sufficiency of the monastery: they grew and ground their own corn, kept their own cows and sheep, wove and spun wool for the coarse robes, girdled by rope, that they wore day and night. Food was limited to the barely essential: bread, milk, eggs, fish, fruit and nuts, with meat allowed only when guests arrived, and on Sundays and festival days. Even the Spartan fare was reduced, in accordance with the self-denial that was the usage of their lives, on Wednesdays and Fridays, when they fasted all day until late afternoon; and during Lent, when every day but Sunday was a fast-day with but one light evening meal. Finian himself customarily ate only barley bread and water, except on Sundays and holy days, when he indulged to the extent of wheaten bread, broiled salmon and a cup of mead.

They prayed alone and often, both day and night. The brief hours of sleep were on beds of stone or wood in the little cells that surrounded the church, each hardly big enough to stand up in. The other buildings in the monastic village were also strictly functional, except for the church, which, though small and unpretentious, was usually a structure of simple architectural grace.

In the course of their mostly private, arduous days, the monks gathered in small groups for meals and for the saying of offices. The only times that approached social occasions were Finian's teaching sessions. So many came to hear him expound the truths of the Church that the monastic enclosure could not hold them and they assembled, churchmen and laity, on the grass outside, where the mentor sat on a knoll to teach and converse. The art of writing was still so new that manuscripts were rare and highly valued. Most teaching, therefore, was oral and outdoors, so that as many as possible could participate.

There were some books, however, and an important part of the monk's day was labor in the scriptorium, work that consisted mostly in copying. There the precious vellum manuscripts, encased in leather satchels, hung on wooden pegs around the walls. The writing materials — parchment of goat-, sheep- or cowhide, carbon ink, quill pens, metal styles for writing on wax tablets — were all made by the scribes themselves. Not only scholarship was valued; a fair hand was greatly prized, and the artistry of the skilled scribes was to flower later in the production of some of the world's most exquisite illuminated manuscripts.

The school was open to everyone who wished to learn. If a student could, he paid a little; if he was poor, he learned free. The Bible as interpreted by the Church Fathers was the basis for study. The texts were in Latin, either original or in translation; in later years the more advanced students would learn Greek but in Finian's time Latin was the only language of study. As well as ecclesiastical works, the students learned the classics — Virgil, Horace and the Roman poets — study that was forbidden in Continental church schools, where delight in the beauty of words outside of strictly religious connotation was suppressed as a dangerous pagan luxury. Latin became so easy to the Irish scholars that they could compose their own fluent prose and poetry. A happy grace with words was then, as it still is, a talent as natural as singing.

The study that most clearly set Ireland apart from the Continent was that of pre-Christian works of history and law, the pagan lore of Ireland. On account of the ease with which Christianity had taken hold, Ireland's new teachers had no reason to fear her old ones. The knowledge of heathen deities and customs presented no threat, unlike old Rome, where the gods, tools in the hands of vengeful and imperious masters, had loomed, an ever-present menace, over the faithful. This tolerance gave Irish learning a continuity unique in Europe, and Irish scholars an extraordinarily well-rounded view of the world. Physically, Finian's disciples and their successors might be the most inflexible ascetics; but their unfettered minds soared in realms of learning and poetry unknown to the rigid dogmatists across the sea.

Finian was not only a teacher, he was father-confessor and counselor to all who needed direction. To guide the penitents who came to him for advice and absolution, he devised a penitential rule that became the model for later monasteries. The local sinners, if their errors were petty, worked out their penances at home. The more grievous transgressors, many of whom came from far away, stayed in the monastery for months or years to purify their souls under the guidance of the abbot. Finian's rule specified much heavier penances to clergy than to laity, for "the blame to be attached to a layman in this world is lighter, even as his reward in the next will be less."

Penance was exacted for crimes of thought as well as deed. If a cleric so much as angled his mind toward the striking of another, he was due for six months of bread and water and another entire year without meat or wine. If he wounded, he must live on bread and water for a year, during which time he was distrained from exercising his priestly functions. If his victim died, he must suffer ten years of exile; he must, as well, give financial satisfaction to the bereaved family. The layman, on the other hand, who inclined his thought toward violence had only to fast for seven days, while his penance for bloodshed was a mere forty days of fasting, along with the law-imposed payment to the victim.

A significant difference between the penitential discipline laid down by Finian, which was followed in succeeding Irish monasteries, and that observed on the Continent involved the privacy of the confessional. In Gaul it was considered important that atonement be out in full view. In Ireland a man's confession and penance were between him and his priest. He need not be conspicuously wicked or about to die, but could confess to the minutest of improper intentions, whenever he thought it necessary for the good of his soul. The consequent frequency of confession, while it could become obsessive, undoubtedly led to a remarkable cleanliness of mind. This is a small example of the disparate practices that set Irish monasticism apart from the Continental variety, and that exhibited the determination of the Irish to go their own way. Later differences, while hardly more weighty, would lead to serious friction. The devotion of the Irish monk to his Church was as earnest as that of any holy man across the sea — possibly fresher and more ardent because of the nature of the people — but from the beginning the Irish set their own rules.

In the time of the first order of saints, the presence of women in holy precincts was not shunned. The celibacy of priests was still a matter of choice in Rome. The Irish chieftains who became priests saw no reason to discard their wives along with their lands, although some wives, upon conversion, chose to become nuns. Women who had taken the vow were accepted within monastery grounds as workers; St. Patrick set the example by including embroideresses in his entourage. Some nuns, however, preferred to gather together to found their own houses. In the late fifth and early sixth centuries there were already convents, the most outstanding of which, and probably the mother-convent of Ireland, was St. Brigid's remarkable coeducational establishment at Kildare.

Ireland's female patron saint was born about 450, the daughter of a pagan chieftain, Dubhtach (the Dark One) of Fang, County Louth, and a Christian bondswoman. Dubhtach's jealous wife made him sell the pretty servant before the child was born, and Brigid's birth took place in the house of a druid who lived nearby, in Faughart. This is said to be the site of the ford that Cuchulain defended single-handed against Queen Maeve's Connacht forces; not far from here is the pillar-stone to which the mythical hero tied himself in his last combat so that he would die on his feet. Brigid's childhood, in a pagan household, must have been filled with stories of ancient glory. The druid was a kindly man with a Christian uncle, and he early recognized and respected Brigid's strong-willed piety. When she was about ten she returned, by her own choice, to her father, and proceeded to discommode his household by giving away to the poor most of the food from the kitchen and dairy. She further irritated her father by insisting on returning to her foster home to help her mother, who was still a slave, and ailing. The girl took on her mother's dairy work, singing as she churned the butter:

"O my prince
Who canst do all these things, Bless, O God . . .
My kitchen with thy right hand!

My kitchen, the kitchen of the white God.
A kitchen which my King hath blessed,
A kitchen that hath butter.

Mary's Son, my Friend, cometh
To bless my kitchen.
The Prince of the world to the border,
May we have abundance with him." [6]

The butter multiplied until it filled an immense creel and the druid, in gratitude, not only freed Brigid's mother but allowed himself to be baptized and became Brigid's servant for life. He also gave her the butter and the cows, which she at once gave away. On her return home, where she followed the same generous habits as before, her exasperated family decided to marry her off. A good offer was received from a poet — for Brigid, despite her unauthorized prodigality with the household supplies, was a miraculously practical housewife and, besides, a girl of great beauty. Brigid refused the poet, offering him another pretty maid in her place. When her father insisted she defiantly disfigured her face, marring her beauty so no man would want her. Her unswerving purpose at last prevailed; Dubhtach allowed her to take the veil and gave her money for her new life.

Though Brigid had been treated, in general, with unwonted kindness, her outlook was fundamentally different from that of the heathen households of her upbringing. All over Ireland, women, converted by Patrick, were living with their pagan relatives, sustaining their faith with lonely fortitude. This strong, imperious young woman decided to found a house where such women could work and pray in community. After taking her vows (whereupon, it is said, her ruined face became beautiful again),

Brigid, with seven companions, asked for a piece of land, the Curragh, in County Kildare. It was refused by the local king, and the nun said she would be content with whatever her mantle could cover. Whether it was the ardent intensity of her purpose, her persuasiveness or her beautiful face that won him over, the king saw the holy mantle grow until it covered the whole of the Curragh (today the largest piece of unfenced arable land in Ireland, and the headquarters of horse racing), and Brigid had her land.

At the edge of her fair grassland, on the site of present-day Kildare, she built a church and convent. She may have chosen a place of heathen worship, a move wisely favored by the early founders, for the convent kept a curious pagan holdover: a sacred fire in a hedged enclosure outside the church, kept burning always and guarded by twenty nuns, including Brigid, day and night. After Brigid's death, it is said, the nun who watched on the nineteenth night would always cry, "Brigid, guard your own fire, the next night belongs to you." The fire burned until it was ordered extinguished in 1220 by Henry de Londres, the Anglo-Norman archbishop of Dublin. Later rekindled, it was finally quenched forever upon the Dissolution.

The warmth of Brigid's personality and the animation of her leadership attracted so many to her convent that it became one of the showplaces of Ireland, containing, it is grandly asserted, ten thousand nuns. Its abbess could no longer handle such a complex establishment alone. Though Brigid had had no interest in marrying, she never eschewed the company of men. As her convent grew and her interests and undertakings became ever more wide-ranging, she invited a bishop to take up residence at Kildare to help her. Under the aegis of this man, Conleth, a metal craftsman (later called "Brigid's brazier"), a monastery grew whose monks excelled in the making of chalices, missal covers, shrines and other beautiful metal objects for religious use. He and Brigid, bishop and abbess, ran the double monastery as coequals.

Though nothing remains of her church, her first biogapher, Cogitosus, who wrote in the seventh century, describes it as being a building of timber, spacious and high-roofed, with many windows and walls adorned with frescoes. Its sanctuary was cut off by a screen painted with figures and covered with linen hangings made, no doubt, by Brigid's nuns or their successors, skilled in weaving, dyeing and embroidery as in every other domestic accomplishment. Beautiful shrines were decorated with ornaments of gold and silver fashioned by the famous metalworking brothers. Down the center of the nave ran a screen dividing the nuns from the monks. In its day-to-day work Brigid's convent practiced a cheerfully efficient, unselfconscious sexual equality. But in praying, as in private life, men and women must separate.

Brigid was a shining exponent of good housewifery. She taught her nuns the dignity of a woman's manual labor among animals, in the dairy and in the house, setting the example by tending her own sheep, milking her cows (which she could persuade to give milk three times a day, it is said, when she needed to feed visitors), churning, spinning, weaving. As well as for her practicality, she was known for her generosity, that joyfully hospitable trait of giving everything away, which had so irritated her family and which, in a woman less transparently good, would have appeared as reckless improvidence. Rich vestments brought by Bishop Conleth from Rome went immediately to the poor, as did all gifts of money or food brought by her wealthy and highborn visitors, of which there was a continuous stream. But a leper was as welcome at her board as a prince; no one was ever turned away. She supplied the countryside round about with the bounty of her farm and her kitchen, even brewing ale one Easter time for all the neighboring churches. A sunny little poem is attributed to her, celebrating her generous spirit:

> I would like a great lake of ale for the King of the kings;
> I would like the people of heaven to be drinking it through time eternal.

Though this first verse is perhaps more reminiscent of the pagan hero's happy islands than of an ethereal Christian heaven (after all, Brigid was nourished on barbaric tales of valor in Cuchulain's own country), the poet goes on to less heathen reflections:

> I would like the viands of faith and pure piety;
> I would like the flails of penance in my house.
>
> I would like the people of Heaven in my house;
> I would like the baskets of peace to be theirs.
>
> I would like the vessels of charity to distribute,
> I would like the caves of mercy for their company.
>
> I would like good cheer in their drinking,
> I would like Jesus, too, to be among them.
>
> I would like the Three Marys of illustrious fame,
> I would like the people of Heaven there from all parts.

I would wish that I were a rent-payer to the Lord,
That I should suffer distress, and that he would bestow on me a good
   blessing.[7]

Brigid's friends among the clergy were numerous and warmly admiring. Finian came to Kildare before he built at Clonard, to learn from her bright example the art of organizing a monastery. When Brendan, returning from his spectacular voyage, arrived on a visit, Brigid, it is written, came in from her sheep pasture to welcome him, hanging her wet cloak on a sunbeam to dry. Brendan, impressed, succeeded only after the third try in doing the same thing. The miraculous voyager asked her how she had gained so much more power than he — especially since his piety was such that, he said, "I never crossed seven furrows without turning my mind to God."

"Since I first fixed my mind on God," she answered, "I have never taken it off." She added tactfully, "Thou . . . art so constantly incurring great danger by sea and land, that thou must needs give thy attention to it, and it is not because thou forgettest God that thy mind is fixed on Him only at every seventh furrow."[8]

Like most of the missionaries of her period, Brigid travelled a great deal, to found churches and convents and to show Ireland's women that Christianity promised a new kind of freedom for them. Her conveyance was a two-horsed chariot. Though she habitually gave her horses away, fresh ones were always forthcoming. Two that were given to her by a grateful prince were unbroken but became docile as soon as Brigid harnessed them. Along with her other skills she was evidently a good horsewoman. In a contemporary hymn she is described as "the nun who used to range the Curragh."[9] Though it is unlikely that the sixth-century servants of God used the great field for the purpose it now serves, the picture of the nun flying over the greensward behind her two young horses is irresistible.

Even allowing for the customary hyperbole, Ireland's foremost female saint must have been a blithe and warmhearted lady, her joy in life glowing through the stringent discipline of her calling. Easy with both sexes yet never less than womanly, she was an attractive example to women of the virtues and benefits of Christianity. She did not illustrate so much the equality of the sexes — though her double monastery was a surprisingly liberal and imaginative innovation — as the strength of women and the power for good they could exercise within the framework of the Church.

CHAPTER VII
THE FOUNDERS
OF THE MONASTERIES

THEY WERE THE INNOVATORS, BRIGID AND FINIAN AND ENDA, WHO LED the way. The Irish Church changed direction, gaining strength and a new dimension, under the persuasive guidance of these spirited teachers. The monastic ideals and practices that were to bring Ireland into the light as the "Island of Saints and Scholars"[1] had their foundations in the sixth-century houses that were founded by their pupils. By the end of that century, Patrick's episcopal system was giving way to the monasticism that was to dominate the Irish Church for six hundred years. We will look at a few of these early monasteries, greater and lesser, and at the holy men whose influence was to be so far-reaching.

One of those who came to Brigid was a gentle youth named Kevin. Brigid was old when he was very young, and she spoke to him in the guise of a mother, counselling him to a life of austerity — advice that confirmed his natural bent. Kevin was born in 498 (perhaps — he died, it is written, 120 years later, in 618) at the edge of the sea in County Wicklow. Though of a royal race, descended from the first kings of Leinster, he never had the wish to rule nor to fight nor in any material way to honor his inheritance. His spirit inclined toward piety, a disposition that was so early recognized that at age seven he was sent to receive literary and religious training with one Petrocus, a clerical scholar from Britain. While living in fosterage with this man he worked in the fields, sustaining himself, at his own wish, by the labor of his hands.

At the age of twelve Kevin began to display an asceticism so extreme as to seem warped. A pretty girl saw him working in the field and fell in love at once with the beautiful youth. As she approached in an overfriendly manner, the frightened boy made the sign of the cross and fled, hiding in a patch of nettles. She followed him with seductive intent, whereupon he made a bundle of the nettles and defended himself, stinging her badly. She then perceived, wrote a biographer,[2] that he was a lad of holy persuasion, fell on her knees, and asked his pardon, promising thereafter to devote her virginity to God. This unpleasing little tale was recorded by a chronicler whose intention was not to record his subject's neurotic celibacy but, like the pre-Christian bard who sang of the inordinate fearlessness of his hero, to demonstrate the superlative purity of his saint, thus attesting to his higher godliness.

Kevin's excessive reaction indicates a new orientation, toward an inflexible moral chastity that had not been embraced by the earlier teachers. It was characteristic of the second order of saints who, according to the historian quoted above, "denied women . . . , separating them from the monasteries." But it is unlikely that Brigid had counselled her young student to quite such an immoderate attitude. Virtuous nun as she was, she had never turned her face away from the opposite sex, nor had her earliest mentor, St. Patrick. Gone were the days when saintly men and women "feared not the blast of temptation."

Resolving to follow the way of "white martyrdom" — to retire from the world and lead a life of solitary contemplation — Kevin went to the Valley of Luggala in the Wicklow Hills, where he built a wattled hut on bare stone. Luggala is a long heath-covered vale closed in by ancient, rounded peat-bog mountains, brown and purple with bright yellow patches of gorse, crisscrossed by the wandering paths of sheepherders. There, amid the lonesome, muted scenery, the pale sky enormous above him, the young penitent stood in cross-vigil (an exhausting pose, the arms outstretched in the attitude of Christ on the cross) for the forty days of Lent. A blackbird perched on his hand, and so still did he stand that she built her nest there. An angel appeared to him, to tell him that he had done sufficient penance and should go back among men, to lead them. He answered that he would remain thus through the bird's brooding, for "the pain of his hand being under the blackbird till she hatched her clutch was little compared with the pain which his Lord suffered for his sake."

Kevin was not allowed his solitude for long. Would-be anchorites sought him out, wishing to learn from his pious example, and eventually he left his retreat to found a monastery in Hollywood Glen, a long glacial hanging

The Wicklow Gap, County Wicklow — St. Kevin's route to Glendalough

valley near today's enormous man-made Poulaphouca Reservoir, site of the Liffey hydroelectric works. But this place became too populous for him and he left his followers to find a spot shut off from the world. He went southeast, following one of the winding tracks that were old then, over the brown windy hills where prehistoric miners had found the gold that had brought Ireland into the trade orbit of Europe 2,500 years before; past a great boulder covered with the spiral designs of the Bronze Age and through the Wicklow Gap, a desolate stony pass (Ireland's second highest, at 1,567 feet) in nearly perpetual cloud, where nothing grew but ling and the only moving beings were sheep grazing the thin pasture and skylarks floating in sweet song above them. There he left the wide spread of moor and mountain to make his way down a precipitous, rocky defile into the isolated, nearly inaccessible ravine of Glendalough (Valley of the Two Lakes), a deep glacial trough surrounded by forested mountains. His path from Hollywood to Glendalough was later named St. Kevin's Road and paved over for the pilgrims who wanted to visit both the saint's shrines.

Kevin stopped at the upper lake, a narrow, shadowed pool closed in by Conavalla Mountain at its head and steep overhanging banks along its western side, with wild little rivers coursing through the dark spruce woods to fling themselves over its cliffy edges. He lived there, it is written, in the hollow of a tree and "he had no food but the nuts of the wood, and the herbs of the earth, and fair water for drink, and for bed, only a pillow of stone under his head . . . and his clothes were the skins of wild animals." He would walk into the cold mountain water of the lake to pray for long hours. Or he would crouch in a hole in the cliff later called St. Kevin's Bed, about twenty feet above the lake, seven feet deep and just wide enough for a man's body. The cave was partly man-made and may have been a prehistoric burial place. So gentle was he, it is told, that the animals of the woods and mountains forgot their natural savagery and drank water from his hands. When he prayed, birds perched on his head and shoulders, and flittered around him "warbling sweet hymns in honor of God's servant. . . . Even the branches and leaves of trees . . . chanted sweet hymns to St. Kevin." The only bird that did not respect him, wrote the scribe, was a crow, who drank the milk brought by a wild deer for a child under Kevin's foster care, overturning the vessel. Kevin did not quite curse — his nature was too mild — but he scolded: "Thou, and birds of thy species, for a long time shall repent this fault. . . . Much food shall be prepared, yet you shall have no part of it. . . . You shall be in sorrow on the tops of the mountains, cawing and contending in discontent." Every year, on Kevin's birthday, it is said, the crows fast, screaming in annoyance in the hills above Glendalough.

Many stories are written of Kevin's friendship with the beasts of the forest and lake: of an otter that brought him food, of a boar that sought his protection against hunting dogs, of a lake monster that swam tamely around him as he prayed up to his waist in the water. Such occurrences grow familiar in the perusals of the saints' lives. But the prevalence of friendly animals is not simply gratuitous repetition on the part of gullible biographers. No matter what their rank at birth, the early holy men were all country people with a natural affinity for animals. The gentleness of their natures was such that wild creatures responded to them without fear. The tales of their rapport, whether believable or miraculous, present a beguiling foretaste of the spirit of St. Francis.

The anchorite did not spend all his hours cleansing his soul in arduous penitence. He divided his time, as ordained in the monasteries where he had studied, between prayerful meditation, labor of the hands and labor of the mind. It is said that he wrote several learned works there, including a life of St. Patrick. That he was scholarly there is little doubt; the monastery-school that grew up around the two lakes during his lifetime became a mecca for students from all of the Western world. For he was found again, of course, and brought, against his wish, out of his wild and beautiful hermitage, to teach and minister to hosts of the faithful who had heard of the extraordinary compassion and piety of this saintly man.

The lower of the two lakes, though elongated like the upper by the gouging of the glacial finger, had a more gracious aspect, and the milder incline of its shores lent itself more readily to habitation. A parklike forest of larches, pines and ancient mossy oaks bordered one side; on the other, and below the lake, watered by its outlet stream, was a long stretch of lush meadowland where the monks could grow their barley and pasture their cows.

Though the buildings of St. Kevin's monastery were ravaged by fire nine times before the eleventh century, inundated by flood, repeatedly pillaged by the Vikings, and laid waste by the English in 1398, the remains, carefully and lovingly restored, are a felicitous illustration of the growth of an ecclesiastical village over six centuries. Though little but foundations remains of St. Kevin's original monastic settlement, the one-and-a-half-mile stretch of lakefront contains stone buildings dating from shortly after his death up to the twelfth century. The oldest, Temple-na-Skellig (Church on the Rock), probably the site of Kevin's first church on the upper lake, is a little rectangular building of the unassuming plainness of Ireland's earliest churches, with the remains of a stone enclosure outside it that probably held the monks' cells. Nestled in the trees along the shores of the lower lake are many buildings: they include the gateway to the monastery, a solid square stone structure with low, round-arched entrances; a lovely round tower lifting over the treetops; the cathedral, the largest building (but still small — its nave is only forty feet long), which was built and added to from the tenth to the twelfth centuries; St. Kevin's Kitchen, an enchanting small peak-roofed church; and St. Saviour's Priory, probably the latest building, said to have been founded in 1162 by St. Lawrence O'Toole (one of Ireland's few canonized saints), a little Irish Romanesque church hidden in a grove of tall Scotch pines, with charming and grotesque carvings of stylized animals and flowers in an extravagantly intertwined design.

St. Kevin's Kitchen — twelfth-century stone-roofed church in the monastery at Glendalough, County Wicklow

Though Kevin chose Glendalough for its wild and rough isolation, a spot where the world's importunities would not assail him, he must have seen at once, as he came through the rocky defile out of the bare peat-bog mountains, that he had reached a place where the worship of God would be easy. The two little lakes shine like bright eyes in their deep mountain-shaded trough, and through the high trees the hazy Irish sunlight softly touches the stone of the old buildings like a blessing of the saint. The sacred village that grew up in the place where Kevin soothed a lake monster with psalms is an eloquent tribute to a man who must have had an incandescent goodness even in an age of exceeding sanctity.

Clonmacnoise — St. Ciaran's monastery on the Shannon, County Offaly

Among Finian's "Twelve Apostles" was a very young man named Ciaran, born possibly in 516, the son of a chariotmaker of County Roscommon in Connacht. Since his parents were poor they could not pay for his tutelage at Clonard, and he asked them to give him a cow to bring as an offering to the master. They refused, but a dun cow and her calf followed him when he left home. He blessed her and she gave milk, it is said, for all the household at Clonard, with their guests. When Ciaran left Finian's establishment he gave the dun cow to another disciple, saying to him that "though a multitude would be helped by her milk, there would be more to whom her hide would give help."[3] The hide of Ciaran's milch cow became, legend has it, the parchment used for the *Lebor na h'Uidre (Book of the Dun Cow),* one of the two oldest and most important Irish literary collections, compiled by a Clonmacnoise scribe in 1106, containing tales, poems, history and genealogy, annals and other miscellaneous literature of ancient Ireland in the vernacular.

Ciaran was an apt pupil at Clonard, quick to learn, gentle in manner and chaste in habits. When a king's daughter was sent there for her education Finian saw fit to entrust her to the care of the youth, who was so pious that throughout the period of the lessons he never once looked at her face, and saw nothing of her body but her feet.

After studying a few years at Clonard, Ciaran went to Enda of Aran, who advised him to found a church in the middle of Ireland, at Clonmacnoise (which means "the field of the hogs of Nos"), County Offaly, beside the Shannon. When he came to the spot he saw there a young man near his own age, Diarmait (son of Fergus Cerrbel), a prince of the Ui Neill family, kings of northern Ireland, who had been exiled by the reigning king, Tuathal. The young scion set to work with the priest to build a wooden church. Grateful Ciaran prayed for Diarmait, saying to him, "Thou shalt be a king tomorrow." The next day Tuathal fell in battle and the exile returned to Tara, to become the first Irish high-king to be crowned as a Christian.

Since the stakes of his first church were planted by a royal prince, who later "offered a hundred churches to God and to Ciaran," and since the abbot, young and gentle as he was, exhibited a remarkable aptitude for organization, the monastery flourished. Ciaran lived only seven months after he had founded Clonmacnoise, dying in 549 at age thirty-three of the yellow plague, a pestilence that appeared out of the East, raging across Europe and killing half the people of Ireland. But the school founded by him was to become, by the time of Charlemagne, one of the most illustrious seats of learning in the Christian world, the center of Irish art and literature.

Today the silent stones of Clonmacnoise are a dream of the past, the afterglow of an ancient glory. It was a monastic city with at least 105 buildings (that many were destroyed by the Anglo-Normans in 1179 in a typically savage foray) and a wealth of art and artifacts beyond that of any Irish ecclesiastical establishment except Armagh. The city has had more than its share of the ill haps that have blighted Ireland: it was burned thirteen times, pillaged by Vikings eight, attacked by the Irish themselves twenty-seven, by the Anglo-Normans six times, and finally despoiled in 1553 (by agents of the Dissolution) of every book, shrine, bell, altar, even window-glass, that could be carried away. The remains — miraculously extensive considering their savage history — lie open to the sky in the mildly rolling midlands, on a flat meadow above a bend in the quiet Shannon: a group of little, plain, mostly roofless churches, round towers and carved high crosses and graves of extraordinary richness of design. The haphazard growth of the early Irish monastery is evident in the number of small churches — eight are left of an original twelve or thirteen — in contrast to the European model coherently organized around one great many-faceted church. Though the tiny rectangular chapels and oratories are unpretentious, the artistry of the crosses and some of the gravestones gives evidence of the radiant imagination that those devout artisans dedicated to the service of God. We will look later in some detail at the most splendid of these, the Cross of the Scriptures (shown on page 322); for now we will only note, on its lowest panel, a possible representation of the young prince Diarmait, kilted, with a sword at his belt, planting with the long-robed saint the corner-post of Ciaran's first church.

Many of the renowned sixth-century monasteries, like Glendalough and Clonmacnoise, reached their highest eminence after the deaths of their founders. Bangor, founded by St. Comgall, another of St. Finian's accomplished alumni, was a major school during his lifetime, and the center from which started the first great missions abroad.

Comgall was born in Dalaradia, County Antrim, about 515, to modest, elderly parents who adored him. Despite his loving home, he exhibited early in his life a sternness that registers, even through the reverent biography, as rather bleakly unforgiving. His first teacher, in whose house he lived, spent nights out "in the commission of sin." Comgall appeared one morning in a dirty garment. Reproved by his tutor, he said, "Is it more dangerous, master, to have our garment soiled, than our soul? That defilement of soul and body, in which you spent last night, is worse than the condition of this habit."[4] When the master, silenced but unrepentant, continued to visit his mistress, the pupil defected, to seek his education in surroundings more morally congenial. Besides his notable severity, which was to stand him in good stead in organizing the discipline of a large and diverse monastery school, Comgall was known for a bizarre talent: he could spit hard enough to break a rock. Sometimes, added the biographer defensively, this flinty saliva turned to pellets of gold.

As well as demanding moral flawlessness in others, Comgall was humble as to his own fitness. For many years he refused to take holy orders, believing he did not deserve them. After his education at Clonard, he retreated to an island on Lough Erne, County Fermanagh, to commune with God and achieve purity of soul through extreme self-denial. Of the handful of monks who joined him there to follow his stern example, seven died from cold and hunger. He would later relax his discipline for others, but never for himself.

Comgall emerged from retreat about 555 and went east, past his home territory of Antrim, to found a monastery at Bangor, County Down, on the gracious southern shore of Belfast Lough, the fjordlike harbor of Belfast. The monastery, at its height, was said to have housed four thousand monks, but this may have included daughter houses. The school attached to it became a great center of classical learning, with special emphasis on historical studies. The first Irish annals were compiled there; in its scriptorium was also transcribed from oral storytelling one of ancient Ireland's most beautiful poems, *The Voyage of Bran*. And from Bangor priests and scholars first began to look outward, toward the benighted lands across the sea. From here the first missions started, to bring back again to Europe her treasures of learning, and to infuse her faltering Christianity with the fresh zeal of the lately converted. Out of Bangor, still in Comgall's lifetime, went, among others, Columbanus, the founder of the great houses of Luxeuil in Gaul and Bobbio in Italy.

Excessively rigorous though Comgall continued to be with himself until his painful death at age eighty-five, his monastic discipline aroused lavish admiration in his monks, one of whom described in it a Latin hymn as "the good rule of Bangor, right and divine, strict, holy and careful — the best of rules, just and wonderful." [5] Comgall's rule was one of the eight chief monastic rules of Ireland, along with those of Patrick, Brigid, Brendan, Ciaran, Columba, Molaisse and Adamnan.

Though the rule was extremely strict, the abbot, who could be compassionate, relaxed it supernaturally when need arose. St. Finian of Moville, aged and ailing, visited him. The old man needed milk to sustain him, but according to custom there was nothing in the cupboard but bread and herbs. Comgall sent a messenger to the cellar, and he found there a vessel miraculously filled with enough milk to feed everyone. While travelling in winter, the saint, who for himself never paid any attention to the weather, was asked by his weaker companions to make a fire. With his breath he kindled a pile of dry sticks to warm the chilly brethren.

Comgall had the Irish saint's customary tenderness with animals. On another journey the travellers stopped at the edge of a lake with swans floating upon it. The monks were hungry, but no food was forthcoming. They asked Comgall if, for consolation, he would call the swans to them, that they might stroke them. "'If such is God's will,' said the saint, 'be it so done.' And as he spoke, the swans, constrained by God's command, took wing towards the servants of Christ, and one of them stayed in his flight in the bosom of the holy Comgall. And thereafter, when he gave them leave, they resorted again to the lake." [6]

Besides the large, important establishments of organizing geniuses like Comgall, the fame of which resound through the centuries, the sixth century saw the founding of numerous smaller houses. Their proliferation signified the gradual conversion of Irish Christianity from the centrally organized Roman episcopal model to the peculiarly Irish system of autonomous monasteries, each obedient only to the rule of its founder, with nothing to tie them together but the admiration and sometimes very close friendships between the ruling abbots. This discrete structure appealed to a rural, pastoral society whose framework, the family and the *tuath,* was an almost direct parallel to the monastic system, and whose patriarchal chiefs were easily replaced — often in the same person — by equally paternalistic abbots. Disjointed as it was, it worked where a more formally coherent scheme would have foundered.

Another strong appeal of monasticism was to the native character: the Irish-Celt's penchant for asceticism and the simple life, and his love of nature. In most cases the holy men who founded the monasteries went away first, as had the Egyptian desert fathers, to purify themselves by exile in a wilderness. But there was a difference: Ireland's saints had an eye for scenic surroundings. They were not solely obsessed with the practice of intense inward communion; they reached outward to the lonesome world of their isolation, which was lonesome only in that it was unpeopled. Invariably their wilderness retreats were places already blessed by the graces of nature. When they accepted disciples, men and women of like mind, they saw no reason to desert the fair scenes of their lonely penance. The remains of Ireland's monasteries are not by chance situated among her most pleasing natural surroundings; they are there because early cenobites found it appropriate to contemplate heaven amid surroundings of earthly beauty.

The monasteries that grew over several centuries into monastic cities remind us of the greatness of spirit, combined with simple piety, that led to the glory of medieval Ireland. The smaller places, settled into their surroundings as harmoniously as the trees and rocks and flowers around them, give evidence with a touching reality of the early Irish monk's affinity to the natural world. Among these are the islands of Devenish, on Lough Erne in County Fermanagh, and Inishmurray, off the coast of County Sligo.

Devenish was the province of St. Molaisse, another of St. Finian's twelve illustrious disciples. He was born in Carberry, County Sligo, the latest of a resplendent lineage, being eighty-fifth in descent from "Adam son of the Living God."[7] (These exalted family trees were a favorite device of historians of the period — not only in Ireland — who sought to correlate the history of their country and their great men with events and personages in the Bible). More recently his antecedents were of the royal houses of both Tara and Cashel. After studying at Clonard he went to Devenish (Ox Island), a lake island not far from his birthplace, which he had known and loved since his early youth. There, about 563, he founded a monastery and school that, though not large, attained a choice reputation for sanctity and learning. His was one of the eight rules, aforementioned, that became models for Irish monasticism. To his monastery came the other eleven of Finian's apostles, with Finian himself, to stay with Molaisse for a year. There he advised his schoolmate Columba, with some sternness, to go into exile across the sea in penance for having caused a battle. Devenish was known, in addition to its fame as a school, as "a resort of poor and of naked, of orphans and of such as were in distressful straits; every one too that from none other in Ireland could find help . . . that he should help them against cold and famine, against thirst and hunger." This kindly and learned man lived to be very old. He died around 570 and was buried on his own island; a remarkably small stone coffin (six feet two inches long on the outside), said to be his, was found there.

A lovely and difficult way to reach St. Molaisse's Devenish is to row from Enniskillen, three miles distant, over the reedy, shallow waters of Lough Erne. This is a lake of many low-lying islands in a county, Fermanagh, that is barcly above water at best. One-third of Fermanagh is permanently under water, much more of it in unusually wet seasons. The lake floods easily, sometimes reaching twice its normal size of twenty-nine square miles.

The journey by rowboat is an uphill one against the prevailing northwest wind. The traveller cannot see the island until nearly upon it; after a couple of hours of pulling, one begins to think that Devenish is not really there at all. The island appears suddenly, as if its patron saint had brought it out of the water for the occasion — a low green rounded hill, its grass and trees growing right down to the water, the pointed top of a round tower just showing on its far side. The visitor moors the boat among the floating cow lilies at a little stone dock, and walks up the hill through a grove of old gnarled hawthorn trees, their wrinkled roots exposed and coiling around each other like the mythical interlaced animals in Celtic stone carvings. A curlew flies up, disturbed by unwonted intruders, and gives its long bubbling call, a kind of musical gargle. The trees give way to the wet long grass of a pasture grazed by a herd of fat steers. Beyond this is the enclosure — its grass short and thick as a golf green — of the monastery, which is a group of small roofless stone buildings. A perfect twelfth-century round tower rises from below them, at the edge of the lake, and beside the squat round-arched church is a very ancient cemetery with a singularly beautiful stone — a decorated cross atop a tall slim column, its curves a dark and graceful silhouette against the white sky.

As one walks on Devenish the feeling grows stronger that the island has just risen out of the water. The land seems an outgrowth of the lake; along its shores grow alders whose roots are underwater and whose lower branches float, entangled with reeds and lily pads. The still, steamy air is kind to life of all kinds, and the luxuriant vegetation, surrounded by dampness, in turn creates its own extra dampness. Swallows circle and dip, attracted by the multitudes of insects that proliferate in the deep grass; wading birds probe for the small marine life sheltering in the branches of the half-drowned trees. The little group of stone buildings on the island's hilltop, safe from flooding, seems a natural outcropping, blending into its surroundings as if it too was there when the island surfaced. The lives of St. Molaisse's monks must have been encompassed by the teeming world of their island, of which their comings and goings were but a small part.

Inishmurray, equally involved with water, has a totally different ambience. It is a plateau island, one mile by one-half mile, of rocks and wind-flattened herbage, with a shoreline of low cliffs, scoured by the unshaded sun and the uninterrupted salt-laden storms of the North Atlantic. Ocean birds nest by the thousand in seaside clefts and grassy hummocks. The island also supports great numbers of rabbits; no predatory animal, not even a rat, exists to control them. The ruins are a cluster of small, primitive stone buildings possibly going back to the sixth century, in the style of stone corbelling seen on the south coast and at Newgrange, surrounded by a wall fifteen feet thick and originally twenty feet high, built probably in the ninth century as a hopeless gesture of protection against Norse raiders. The ancient monastic settlement lies directly behind the more recent remains of a one-street town, which was deserted in 1947.

The monastery's founder was another St. Molaisse, who lived, confusingly, at the same time as the abbot of Devenish. He is believed to have studied at Candida Casa, in Whithorn, and later to have been an associate of St. Columba. The latter, it is said, helped him build on Inishmurray but departed soon, possibly on account of temperamental disaccord. The history of the monastery is dark, because no records remained after a thoroughgoing Viking raid in 807.

Neatly enclosed by its wall, the silent little holy village is a capsule of
the past: churches, oratories, ancient altars (one of them, containing the
cursing stones described on page 62, may go back to a time of pagan
worship) and beehive huts, all of mortarless stone, as solid and evocative
as if the monks had left no later than the villagers next door. Now the
island and its entrancing ruins belong entirely to the seabirds. They rarely
see intruders, because their home is a fastness unreachable by boat except
on unforeseeable days of windless calm. The only landing place is a high-
walled natural rock slip barely wide enough for the little fishing boats that
ply the Sligo coast. The merest hint of a sea, and a boat caught in there
would break up against the pitted stone. On top of the rock begin the thick
healthy carpets of seaside vegetation that cover the island: colonizers all,
with furled or fleshy leaves and creeping stems to withstand the constant
beating of ocean weather, and small bright blossoms, yellow, purple or
blue, close to the earth and wide open to the sun. In a few places where
the land dips grow fields of wild rhubarb with gross elephant-ear leaves,
and thickets of blackberry bramble. Along the edges of the seaside cliffs,
where nesting gulls wheel and dive and scream with indignant alarm, are
pillows of thrift and sea heath. A little road runs around the outer edge of
the island; spaced along it are praying stations, stone slabs or pillars incised
with crosses, some as old as the monastery buildings, which barefoot
penitents traverse clockwise after the fashion of their pagan forebears. At
the northern end is Tobar na Cabhrach — the Well of Assistance, said to
have been blessed by St. Molaisse — an ancient wellhouse with a bath
attached. If the weather was dangerously stormy, it is said, the islanders
emptied three handfuls of water from the well into the ocean and recited
prayers for calm weather, which then materialized. The pilgrims' road is
overgrown with nettles and wild hyacinth today, and oyster catchers,
sharply black-and-white with long heavy red bills, run along it, calling
shrilly.

The monks could have grown a few crops in the hollows and pastured
a few sheep along the higher edges. But if they wanted to be self-sufficient
— and it was inescapable on an island so difficult of access — they must
have relied for their food mainly on fish, caught on fair days from their
curraghs. Life must have been frugal and strenuous in the extreme. That
was what they wanted; that was why they went to Inishmurray instead of
establishing on the fertile Sligo mainland. The struggle to stay alive was
compensated for by the wild beauty around them. Their small island world
was always in motion, alive with sound and scent: the salty sea wind

Natural landing slip on the island of Inishmurray, County Sligo

The monastic village on Inishmurray (altar in foreground holds cursing stones)

mingled with the smell of the fragrant-flowered hummocks; the graceful, ever circling, sharp-crying seabirds; the sounding pulse of waves against the cliffs; white clouds racing across the sun and sea.

Though Inishmurray's St. Molaisse is little more than a name, there remains a thirteenth-century oaken statue of him. It stood within his own monastery walls, in the oldest of the buildings, the little stone-roofed chapel that bears his name. Now it is in Dublin's National Museum: a figure of primitive, detached purity, the very essence of medieval saintliness. It is easy to picture him on his island, directing his monks in prayer and study, working beside them in field and fishing boat, presiding in silence over the long, lightly laden refectory table, teaching, advising, chastising, with austere kindliness.

Through him one can see his monks, and those of the many other monasteries that arose throughout Ireland in the wake of the innovators, seeking God in a way perhaps alien to us but spiritually credible. The life of the sixth-century monk was stern, abstinent, toilsome, yet of an extraordinary subjective freedom: the freedom that comes to one shed of the world's cares and temptations, his body careless of discomfort, his senses awake to the beauties of nature, his mind, sharpened by active use, delicately attuned to the exactions of reason and poetry.

CHAPTER VIII
THE TRAVELLERS ·
ST. BRENDAN
THE NAVIGATOR

THE SAME DESIRE TO SHED THE IMPEDIMENTA OF MUNDANE LIFE THAT LED
Ireland's holy men to gather their disciples around them on islands in the
rough ocean, hidden valleys and lonely mountaintops for the nearer and
purer worship of God sent some anchorites, in another form of self-exile,
out of the tranquillity of the cloister to a life of wandering. Starting with
St. Patrick, Irish clerics were inveterate travellers. A spirit of restless energy
possessed them. It was given many names, but its cause must surely be
sought in the peculiarly Irish development of Christianity in the early
centuries: a seeking curiosity, the desire to expand mental boundaries along
with physical, to find new ideas in new settings. The questing urge is a
youthful proclivity, and in Ireland this was a youthful time.

To begin with, they called it exile and regarded it as white martyrdom.
Following the Lord's command to Abraham — "Go from your country
and your kindred and your father's house to the land that I will show
you"[1] — they left their homes and families in a spirit of penance, to seek
a state of grace through the pure and difficult life of the recluse or the
lonely life of the stranger. The disposition was not stilled with the coming
of disciples and the building of monasteries. Many saints, still footloose,
travelled with the intention of proselytizing, founding new churches, learning from their elders, furthering friendships with their peers. A familiar
sight on the road was the travelling monk, carrying his leather water bottle,
his crosier and his bell, and little else. Neither weather nor privation

dismayed him: if at nightfall he was far from shelter, a tree and a stream were his hostel, with wild fruit for food and animals for companions. He spoke to everyone as he passed, helping the ill and old, lending a hand to the farmer and his wife in the fields or the dairy, preaching to anyone who would listen, begging his keep but giving it away to anyone more destitute. Though he was unstinting in his kindness to one who needed him, inhospitality brought a startlingly efficient curse.

A typical holy itinerant was the seventh-century St. Moling, who roamed Ireland for sixteen years before founding his monastery. Among his adventures is a brisk contest of words with an Evil Specter, strongly reminiscent of the flinging of insults practiced by warriors of the Heroic Age to work up their battle fury.

> EVIL SPECTER: By me thy wallets will be destroyed. . . .
> ST. MOLING: By my father's hand, thou doest it not until I consent.
> EVIL SPECTER: I will drive this spear through thy side.
> ST. MOLING: By my fosterer's hand, I will rap thy head with the staff.
> EVIL SPECTER: 'Tis easier for me to fight thee than boiled flesh.
> ST. MOLING: By a host of thrusts thy hair will go on its hole [sic].[2]

On his way the saint befriends a leper who takes outrageous advantage of him. "For God's sake," begs the leper, "take me with thee to the church."

"I am willing," says St. Moling.

"I cannot travel till I get myself carried comfortably," the leper responds.

"Come on my back then."

"I will not go lest there be some of thy raiment between me and thee, for the raiment [probably a hairshirt] will leave none of my skin upon me." So the saint removes his clothing and takes the invalid upon his naked back.

But the insolent leper is not through. "Blow my nose," he demands. The saint reaches a hand to comply, but the leper says, "Nay, for thy fingers will strip my skin off: put thy mouth around it."

So St. Moling "puts his mouth around the nose and sucks it to him, and spits the mucus into his left hand." This unappealing — and refreshingly outspoken — episode has echoes in many of the lives of the saints: the admiring biographer wishes to illustrate not only his subject's determination to succor the lowest and the most wretched, but also his deliberate courting of illness, which his body will bear cheerfully, that suffering may bring his soul closer to heaven.

St. Moling took an intense personal interest in the creatures that came into his lonely life. Among his animal friends were a fly and a wren. The fly cheered him after his prayers with its little buzzing song, until one day the wren hopped on it and killed it; then St. Moling, grieving for his friend, cursed the wren, saying: "He that marred for me the poor pet that used to make music for me, let his dwelling be forever in empty houses, with a wet drip therein. . . . And small people shall be destroying him." According to the biographer, boys hunt and kill the wren on one day of the year ever since that day.

Though many of the wandering monks, like St. Moling, made their travels in Ireland, others chose the even harder road of leaving the homeland entirely, to return only in old age, or never again. Whatever the internal reasoning for their travels, the external results were to be momentously beyond the original motivation.

One of the first of the seekers abroad was Brendan. He was born in 484 in Fenit, County Kerry, a village on the narrow neck of a flat peninsula, the northern arm of Tralee Bay. Fenit is a jumping-off place for the Atlantic Ocean. The calm, protected waters of bay and inlet touch the village on two sides, lapping almost to the dooryards of the houses, and sailors can pull their boats right out of the sea onto the grass of their home fields. Whichever way the child Brendan walked he could see the quiet water with the black fishing boats on it, and beyond them the cloudy reaches of the western ocean, uncharted and endlessly alluring. He must have known all about boats and water before he even knew that he knew.

Legend, in an Irish echo of the birth of Christ, has a bright light shining over Fenit the night Brendan was born, and the thirty cows of a local farmer giving birth all at once. "Three purple wethers," the story goes on, "leaped out of the well [of baptism] as the fee for baptizing Brendan."[3] He was only two when he was sent out to fosterage, after the pagan manner, to St. Ita of Kileedy, County Limerick, known as Foster-Mother of the Saints. She was a lady who, while probably kindly (a tender poem about the Christ-Child was later composed in her name), had formidable self-control: she allowed a *daol* (stag beetle) to feed upon her body, so that she was in perpetual martyrdom. Although in real life this large horned beetle preys on flora, not fauna, St. Ita is said to have finally died of its foragings.

At age seven Brendan was taken over by a local man, Bishop Erc, to

Curragh on the beach at Fenit, County Kerry — St. Brendan's birthplace. Curraghs are still made much as they were in Brendan's time.

continue the training in toughness and godliness begun by his foster-mother. Perhaps the boy was exposed too young to too stringent a moral discipline, for by the age of ten he already exhibited the same sexual apprehension as his contemporary Kevin. Bishop Erc once took Brendan with him on a journey, leaving him in the carriage reading the Psalms while he went to preach. A "young maiden, gentle, modest, flaxen-haired . . . came close to the carriage and saw his face beautiful and bright; all at once she makes a sportive bound into the carriage, in order to play her game with him." Brendan, crying in horror, "Go away at once, and curse whoever brought you here," laid about her with the carriage reins. He was scolded by his teacher, but the scar was deep; all his life Brendan would shun the company of women except for his sister Brig, a very holy nun in whose arms he would die.

After completing his religious training in Galway and being ordained priest by Bishop Erc, he was ready to devise his own rule. He received a grant of land from the local king at Ardfert, five miles northeast of Fenit, and with a small group of followers founded a monastery there. Though nothing remains of that first establishment, the place remained holy, and buildings still stand from later years — three remarkably beautiful small churches built between the twelfth and fifteenth centuries.

Brendan was not satisfied for long. Though he was a good and beloved leader, simple and sensible in his rule and generally kind in his administration, he felt the need to become closer to God. Like others of his period, he saw the best road to redemption as the hard life of the exile. His thoughts went always to the sea, the promise beyond the long waste of waves that had haunted his childhood. There were tales, of course, from far before Brendan's birth, of those who had found *Tir na n'Og,* the Land of Youth, over the ocean. The stories persisted into Christian times, the country of flowers and singing birds and beautiful women now transformed into "The Land of the Saints." One Barinthus, a holy man, grandson of King Niall, told Brendan he had sailed there with another monk, and his description of the island of "resplendent beauty, full of fragrant apples" aroused Brendan's never-dormant desire to see for himself.

As he slept one night, "he heard the voice of an angel from heaven who said to him: 'Arise, O Brendan, for God hath given thee what thou soughtest, even the Land of Promise.' " To prepare himself spiritually, he went away alone, south to the tall, inhospitable mountains of the Dingle Peninsula, and walked to the top of Brandon Mountain. There he built a stone oratory and lived on what small fruits and mushrooms and leafy plants the bleak mountaintop afforded. In the spirit of tranquil ecstasy that came to him then, he had a vision: "He saw the mighty intolerable ocean on every side, and then he beheld the beautiful noble island, with three trains of angels rising from it. . . . Then the angel of the Lord came to commune with him there, and spoke to him thus: 'I will . . . teach you how to find the beautiful island of which you have had a vision, and which you desire to attain.' "

Brandon is a mountain that generates visions. Ireland's second highest, towering 3,127 feet from the ocean shore, its rocky north and west faces catch the full force of the mositure-laden sea winds, and its upper half is nearly always fog-shrouded. A pilgrim track, the Saint's Road (disused since the eighteenth century), ascends, following the course of a small stream. The stream soon loses itself in the boggy slope, degenerating into puddles and marsh, and so does the track. The mountain cloud creeps down and envelops the broad view of the green Dingle farmland with the inlet of Brandon Creek, whence Brendan set sail, at its edge. We cannot see each other ten feet off and keep in touch by voice alone. We climb by guess, putting one foot before the other in a direct upward slant, to make sure we are not going off to the side into the fearsome gash on the mountain's southeast flank. Sheep blunder across our way unnoticing, and wheatears flutter up before us in short-lived alarm, to land immediately, only their white rumps visible in the mist. Tall gravestones loom up; we go close to each one, to find they are only boulders, and climb on, without hope. Then, dead in front, is a purposeful pile of stones, an extraordinary, man-made object. Quite unbelievably we hit another, also straight on. We have inexplicably made contact with the Saint's Road again. But the cairns give out while we are still climbing steeply. The steepness ends too, and we are on a discouraging mild incline, sure that we have missed the top and waiting for our feet to tell us we are going down the other side.

All at once the sea wind hits us full, and through the torn and flying clouds we see the penitents' final goal, the summit cairn with a tall iron cross leaning against it; and beyond it, at the edge of the precipice that drops off some thousand feet on the mountain's northeast face, the stone heap that legend says is the remains of St. Brendan's oratory. In the strange state of transport — compounded of relief and exhilaration — that comes at the top of a mountain, there is no reason to doubt that it is indeed St. Brendan's chapel, any more than there is to question that we were guided to this place.

Following his vision Brendan went down and gathered the monks who wished to voyage with him. They built "very light little vessel[s], ribbed and sided with wood," which they "strengthened with iron and ox hides. . . . And they smeared their joinings within and without with myrrh and bitumen and pitch and rosin. . . . And in this wise were Brendan's boats, with three rows of oars to each boat, and sails of the skins of animals both wild and domesticated, and twenty men in each boat."* They put in the boats food enough for forty days, along with butter and tallow to dress the hides, water in goatskins and wine for mass. Their beds were of heather and grass.

They went first to Inishmore, to receive the blessing of St. Enda. Three days later they left the Aran Islands and sailed westward, into the unknown, "over the wave-voice of the strong-maned sea, and over the storm of the green-sided waves, and over the mouths of the marvelous, awful, bitter ocean, where they saw the multitude of the furious red-mouthed monsters, with abundance of the great sea-whales."

*Some accounts postulate more than one boat; others specify one boat only, with the number of monks varying from twelve to twenty.

The story of Brendan's voyage, *Navigatio Sancti Brendani,* was written in the tenth century and was a huge literary success, translated into many languages. Its sources are not totally original. Some of its occurrences have parallels in Greek literature, others illustrate the strong hold the pagan tales of *Tir na n'Og* had kept through the centuries. St. Brendan was not the only monk attracted by the western sea, nor was he the first Irish Christian to seek a land over its horizons. Tales of other seafaring monks looking for a dream island where they could worship God in undistracted seclusion are undoubtedly blended into a single account. But the *Navigatio* is not a patchwork conglomeration. It has a charming and straightforward unity: the integrated narrative of the voyage of one holy man, high-minded and unafraid, used to the sea but surprisingly innocent, sustained through every peril by spiritual fortitude and unswerving faith. And fanciful as the voyage is in the legendary account, it contains tantalizing glimpses of fact. It is hard to escape the conclusion that someone, or several people — an amalgam that has blended into one St. Brendan — actually made much of this journey. Sights and events accord with actualities in the mid-Atlantic; and the later accounts, crisply factual, of Atlantic voyages undertaken by Norse seafarers in the ninth and tenth centuries place the Irish across the sea before the Norse got there, in Iceland and possibly on the North American shore.

The play of the medieval imagination in the *Navigatio* is like the sparkle of a prism in sunlight. It takes the sailor monks in a dreamlike sequence from one fantastic island to another, each one exhibiting its special enchantment — some fearsome, some delightful.

Among the alarming landfalls was the Isle of Mice, wherein "hideous furry mice as large as cats" ate a jester who had begged at the last minute to be included in the voyage, leaving "nothing but the bare bones upon the shore." It is to be hoped that his soul was sensible of compensation upon his being declared by his companions a "glorious martyr."

The grisly Isle of Mice was followed by the intoxicating Paradise of Birds, where "there were many excellent fruits . . . and little bees gathering and collecting their harvest . . . and a beautiful stream flowing . . . full of wondrous jewels of every hue." One tree was covered entirely, so that not one leaf was visible, with white birds singing. One of them flew down to perch near the saint, and its "wings in flight had a tinkling sound like little bells." It explained to the company that the birds were the souls of those who were "partakers in the great ruin of the ancient enemy, having fallen, not by sin of our will or consent, but soon after the creation our ruin resulted from the fall of Lucifer." God had not thrust them into eternal torment, but had doomed them "to this place, where we suffer no pain, and where we can partially see the divine presence, but must remain apart from the spirits who stood faithful. We wander about the world, in the air, and earth, and sky, like other spirits . . . but on festival days we take the shapes you see, abide here, and sing the praises of our Creator."

The travellers came on Judas, sitting on a stone in the middle of the sea, "tossed about like a small boat in a storm." When Brendan asked him why he was so wracked, the unhappy man replied: "Through the forebearance and mercy of Christ . . . I have this cooling relief, as it is now the Lord's Day; while I sit here I seem to be in a paradise of delights, considering the agony of the torments that are in store for me afterwards; for when I am in my torments, I burn like a mass of molten lead, day and night, in the heart of the mountain. . . . But that you may know the boundless mercy of God, I will tell you of the freshing coolness I have here every Sunday." The devils, coming for him at sundown, were balked by Brendan's prayers, so the unfortunate soul could enjoy for a few extra hours the lesser agony before the serious week's tortures began again.

When Easter neared, and the featureless ocean offered no sanctuary, Brendan promised that "God is able to find a land for us in any place he pleases." And so it came to pass: on the day before Easter, an island raised its smooth expanse above the waves. After Brendan had said mass at dawn "the brethren took out some uncooked meat and fish . . . and put a caldron on a fire to cook them. After . . . the caldron began to boil, the island moved about like a wave; whereupon they all rushed toward the boat, and implored the protection of their father. 'Fear not, my children,' said the saint, 'for God last night revealed to me the mystery of all this; it was not an island . . . but a fish, the largest of all that swim in the ocean, which is ever trying to make its head and tail meet, but cannot succeed because of its great length.' " Every year for the seven years of the voyage, the "fish" (whale) surfaced beside their boat in time for the celebration of Easter.

At one time the voyagers came to the edge of Hell. They saw a mountain rise out of the sea

full of clouds and smoke about its summit. . . . They saw the peak of the mountain unclouded and shooting up flames into the sky, which it drew back again to itself so that the mountain was a burning pyre. . . . They heard the noise of bellows blowing like thunder. . . . Soon after one of the inhabitants came forth. . . . he was all hairy and hideous, begrimed with fire and smoke. When he saw the servants of Christ . . . he withdrew into his forge, crying aloud: "Woe! Woe! Woe!" St. Brendan . . . armed himself with the sign of the Cross and said to his brethren: "Put on more sail and ply your oars more briskly that we may get away from this island." Hearing this the savage man . . . rushed down to the shore, bearing in his hand a pair of tongs with a burning mass of slag . . . which he flung after the servants of Christ. . . . Where it fell into the sea it fumed up like a heap of burning coals and a great smoke arose as from a fiery furnace. . . . Then all the dwellers of the island crowded down to the shore, bearing, each one of them, a large mass of burning slag which they flung . . . after the servants of God; and then they returned to their forges, which they blew up into mighty flames, so that the whole island seemed one globe of fire and the sea on every side boiled up and foamed like a caldron set on a fire well supplied with fuel. All the day the brethren, even when they were no longer in view of the island, heard a loud wailing from the inhabitants thereof, and a noisome stench was perceptible at a great distance. Then St. Brendan sought to animate the courage of the brethren, saying: "Soldiers of Christ, be strong in faith unfeigned and in the armor of the Spirit, for we are now on the confines of Hell."

Leaving out the fiendish smiths, this passage would be an apt and spirited description of the volcanic birth of the island Surtsey in 1963 off the southern coast of Iceland. That little country, the most actively volcanic place on earth, has at times within recorded history seen islands similarly rise out of the sea, only to sink again, the fiery force beneath the ocean floor exhausted, under the action of waves and weather. It is quite credible that the monks witnessed such a spectacular occurrence. Even their interpretation accords: by the sixteenth century Iceland's dangerous volcano Hekla, visible from the ocean off the southern coast, had become notorious all over Europe as the gateway to hell, and its smoldering, bubbling, stinking interior known as the abode of the damned.

The mysteries of the North Atlantic unfolded apace before the monks, and quite a different ambience enveloped a succeeding encounter, the vision of a transparent column. "It seemed . . . to be all of the color of crystal from top to bottom. . . . Everything could be seen through it . . . and it was harder than glass." They entered through one of the many doors, "and there was . . . a mile of sea from the enclosure on every side. . . . They were a whole day skirting a quarter of it. . . . Brendan . . . bade the monks praise the Creator . . . for the great delight which they found in the column." This encounter puts Brendan and his monks well west of Iceland. Surrounded by the Gulf Stream, that island gives birth to no icebergs, nor could any Greenland ice survive its warm waters. Icebergs calving from Greenland's east coast are caught in the East Greenland Current, which, clinging close to the coast, swings west around Cape Farewell, Greenland's southern tip, to meet the Davis Strait between Greenland and Baffin Island. The iceberg route, therefore, even of those that survive to drift south of Newfoundland, is entirely in the western part of the Atlantic.

It is also possible that the voyagers got as far south as the Tropic of Cancer, because for three days they were becalmed on a sea "like a thick curdled mass," which may have been the Sargasso Sea, a huge, ever-changing but permanent mat of floating seaweed that hovers in the mid-Atlantic east of the Bahamas and was a continuing hazard to early mariners.

After many adventures, their buoyant little vessels floating where the caprice of ocean and weather dictated, the long search was rewarded:

> Towards evening a dense cloud overshadowed them, so dark that they could scarce see one another. Then [their guide] said to St. Brendan: ". . . This darkness surrounds the island you have sought for seven years. . . ." And after an hour had elapsed a great light shone around them. . . . They saw a land . . . thickly set with trees, laden with fruits. . . . All the time they were traversing that land, during their stay in it, no night was there; but a light always shone, like the light of the sun in the meridian, and for the forty days they viewed the land in various directions, they could not find the limits thereof.

After their explorations they met a young man who said: "This is the land you have sought after for so long a time; but you could not hitherto find it, because Christ the Lord wished first to display to you His divers mysteries in this immense ocean. Return now to the land of your birth, bearing with you as much of those fruits and of those precious stones as your boats can carry. . . . After many years this land will be made manifest to those who come after you." After leaving the island, Brendan "set sail in a direct course, under God's guidance, and arrived at his own monastery."

The whereabouts of St. Brendan's Promised Land is a source of endless, fascinating — and idle — speculation. It has been held that the geographical description can be interpreted to fit Florida or Nova Scotia. St. Brendan himself has been placed in Mexico, where his appearance, tall and fair-skinned, was supposed to have identified him to the Indians as the golden-haired Toltec god Quetzalcoatl returning over the ocean from the east in fulfillment of an ancient promise. But all hypothesis, unless positive archaeological proof be unearthed some day, remains as cloudy a dream as the wondrous lands and creatures of the saint's voyage.

The tenth-century writer of the popular *Navigatio* culled his combination of myth and experience from several centuries of seagoing adventure, not all of it Irish. The Brendan legend, however, is only one source of possible evidence that westbound Irish voyagers reached land officially discovered much later. The Irish seafaring monks were not only pure souls secure in God's custody, without fear of earthly suffering and spiritually ready for death; they were also very good seamen. Their light boats were superlatively seaworthy, big watertight baskets riding high on the waves, dry in the heaviest seas. The monks guided them with the expertise that came from years of navigating the rough seas around home in search of their main protein food. The sea held no terrors for the voyagers, nor did the earth's geography. The lands beyond the horizon might be unknown, but these cloistered monks had no fear of falling off the edge of the world. In an age of the blackest geographical ignorance, Irish mariners knew the earth was round. Lacking the superstitious fear of studying heathen classics — the fear that kept most of Europe ignorant for centuries — Irish scholars had unearthed this ancient Greek knowledge, transmitted by two fifth-century Latin savants, Macrobius and Marianus Capella. Further, they knew of the voyages of the Greek explorer Pytheas of Marseilles, who, sailing north in 300 B.C., found "the farthest island of the ocean, lying between north and west six days voyage beyond Britain, getting its name [Thule] from the sun, because at the summer solstice there is no night, when the sun passes out of the Crab."[4]

To early Irish sailors, Thule (Iceland) was the volcanic island first glimpsed by St. Brendan, later sought and found by others looking for a remote wilderness where they could lead undistractedly hard and holy lives — their only company seals and seabirds, their only food the fish in the stormy ocean and birds' eggs on the sheer and slippery cliffs. We have seen that St. Ailbe knew about the Irish anchoritic settlements on Thule (his mythically long life makes him a contemporary of St. Brendan as well as a precursor of St. Patrick). The Irish monks' presence in Iceland is attested to by the Irish geographer Dicuil, who wrote in 825:

> It is now thirty years since clerics, who had lived on the island from the first of February to the first of August, told me that not only at the summer solstice, but in the days round about it, the sun setting in the evening hides itself as though behind a small hill

in such a way that there was no darkness in that very small space of time, and a man could do whatever he wished, as though the sun were there, even remove lice from his shirt, and if they had been on a mountain-top perhaps the sun would never have been hidden from them.[5]

By 874, when the first Norwegian voyagers, blown far off course, hit Iceland by mistake, the island's southern shore had been occupied for some eighty years by as many as a thousand monks. The Norse account states that "the Christian men, whom the Norsemen call Papar were here; but afterwards they went away, because they did not wish to live here together with heathen men, and they left behind Irish books, bells and crooks. From this it could be seen that they were Irish."[6]

By the ninth century, the Irish already had firsthand knowledge of the savage interest of buccaneering Vikings in undefended monasteries. At the first sight of the bulky ships with high-curved prows and striped woolen sails nosing around the rocky headlands of their bleak and peaceful sanctuary, the anchorites would have abandoned their few belongings, fled to their beached curraghs, raised their masts, and skimmed away over the waves, either to make for home or to seek a spot even more desolate and unreachable. But if they were hunted out of their retreat, they left their curses behind them in true Irish saintly style. One of their communities had been at Kirkjubær (Farm of the Church), a green oasis between the ice cap of the interior and the black lava sands of the southern coast. The Norwegian settlers coveted these fertile fields, but ill luck and death attended all efforts of the worshippers of Thor to farm it. "Ketil [a Christian] made his home at Kirkjubær, where the Papar had been living before and where no heathen was allowed to stay. . . . Hildir [a Viking] wanted to move house to Kirkjubær after Ketil died, not seeing why a heathen should not farm there, but as he was coming up to the fence of the home meadow, he dropped down dead."[7]

It may be that the holy men dispossessed from Iceland actually did sail west and discover a retreat forever secure. For a provocative reference turns up in *Eirik's Saga,* an account of the short-lived Norse adventure in Vinland. The last of the Norse settlers in North America was a small group led by an Icelander, Thorfinn Karlsefni. Soon after the birth of his son, the first white child born on this continent, the little band left those lovely shores forever, terrorized by natives they had whipped into hostility. They sailed northward along the coast before turning east across the narrow Davis Strait to Greenland. Reaching Markland (probably Labrador), they caught two *Skraeling* (Eskimo) children, whom they took on board and taught to speak their language. The children, describing their lives, added the information that near their home was a country "where the people went about in white clothing and uttered loud cries and carried poles with patches of cloth attached. This is thought to have been Hvitramannaland, White Man's Land." *Landnamabok,* the thirteenth-century chronicle of the settlement of Iceland, has a further reference to this place: "Ari Marson was driven by a tempest to Hvitramannaland which some call Greater Ireland; it lies to the west in the ocean near to Vinland the Good."

It is only the word of two frightened children, possibly misunderstood by their captors, repeated in a tale written down about a hundred years later. The merest hint — but what a picture it evokes and what a possibility it opens up! A little company of white-robed anchorites celebrates a feast day with banners and shouted prayers, keeping up their spirits on a cold and alien shore two thousand miles from Ireland. They have come across the ocean in their featherweight boats, impelled only by the search for grace. Blown and battered, cold, wet and hungry they must often have been on the journey, but asceticism pleases them. Nothing holds them on this wintry shore but piety, nothing sustains them but trust in God. The deep desire for penitential exile may have been animated in part by a certain native wanderlust. And they surely have found unexpected beauties in their lonely northern sanctuary that gladden them even so far away from their mild and misty homeland. Still their insouciant courage is incredible, as is their shining faith.

This is a digression from our sixth-century monk. Yet it is not so far afield. The impulse, the courage and the ideal that sent St. Brendan over the western sea were the same that motivated succeeding ocean-oriented pilgrims. If he was not the first, he was one of the earliest, and the success of the *Navigatio* would later make him a prototype. Not only was he emulated by those seeking holy exile, explorers with far other intent sought through the *Navigatio* for guidance and information. Even Columbus, it is said, went to Ireland looking for amplification of the "facts" of St. Brendan's voyage, and the explorer made sure that several Irishmen were included in his own expeditions.

But in the sixth century the voyage, while full of marvels, would not have seemed so momentous. Exile was desired and miracles were expected. For Brendan it was but the first step toward sanctity, the preparation for his chosen life. He came home after seven years ready to take up the work for which God intended him, as a leader of souls. For the rest of his life he was a working abbot, founder of several houses in Connacht and Munster, and framer of one of the famed eight monastic rules, the tough but sane discipline for which Irish monasticism was noted. He was styled Brendan of Clonfert, for the best known of his monasteries, in the mild rolling countryside of southeast Galway, far from the mountainous shores of his native Kerry. Where Brendan's monastery once stood is a small twelfth-century cathedral, its main door a masterpiece of stone relief in the Irish Romanesque style.

He lived out most of his remaining years in Ireland at one or another of the houses he had founded. His energy remained unimpaired to the end and his miracles were many, both kindly and irritable. Though he was beloved, he was also regarded with a certain amount of prudent awe, as he sometimes gave way to unreasonable flare-ups. He was known for odd quirks of personality, such as a testy intolerance to music. When he heard the strains of the harp, he petulantly refused to listen. A young cleric visiting the monastery at Clonfert played to the monks at a meal, and they blessed him for his music. He asked then to play for the saint, but the brothers discouraged him, saying: "He will not admit thee . . . for Brendan . . . has never listened to any music in the world; but two balls of wax tied together with a thread are always on the book in front of him. And whenever he hears any music, he puts the balls into his ears." Evidently this discourteous ritual caused him some guilt, for he explained that the archangel Michael had once played for him. Coming in the shape of a bird to the altar at Clonfert, "he drew his beak across the wattle of his wing. And I listened till the same hour on the following day, and then he bade me farewell." After hearing this heavenly music, the saint never again could tolerate the mundane harmonies of humans.

On the other hand, Brendan performed innumerable small acts of kindness, such as disposing of a local pestilence: "There was a great affliction in this place, viz. an immense quantity of fleas, numerous as the sand of the sea. . . . And Brendan said, 'O Lord, let this people by thy mercy be freed from this plague in thy name.'" The fleas disappeared at once.

Brendan was also a capable curser. Denied fish by the local fishermen on one of his journeys, he "refused to allow the river to have any fish in it thenceforth forever." A farmer killed one of the monastery oxen, which had mistakenly wandered into his field to graze. Brendan turned the man into an otter and he "remained thus [wandering] up and down the lake till he died."

A distressing episode concerned one of Brendan's monks who was set to guard the boat when a tempest came up. Another monk went to Brendan to say the brother would drown. In an indefensible burst of anger, Brendan said: "If thou art minded to have more pity on him than I, go in his place, and perform the duty." The second brother drowned and Brendan, overcome with remorse, went to his foster-mother, Ita, who bade him, for penance, once more to cross the sea. At this time in his very old age, he did not attempt to go west but "after labor of great rowing, and after traversing rough strange barbarous lands" he came to Wales, where he stayed with Gildas, the monk-historian. Here, in the only country besides Ireland where Christianity was still imbued with the dedicated simplicity of an earlier century, Brendan, with his old-fashioned piety and his innocent purity of soul — to say nothing of a charming miracle whereby he tamed a whole valley-full of lions, who followed him "like young calfs following their mothers" — won the affection of all. Gildas asked him to stay, offering him lands and authority beyond anything he had in Ireland. But the saint refused, saying, "I bear witness before the King of the stars that the things of this world are no more to me than sand of the sea or leaves of the wood." He had never been a coveter of the appurtenances of success. And now, over eighty, he wanted to die at home.

He went back to western Ireland, to the convent at Annaghdown, County Galway, which he had built for his sister Brig, the only woman whose company he could endure; and there he waited — but not idly — for death. As in pagan times when a king would call on a poet or a druid to intervene in strife, the king of Connacht called on the aging saint to dissuade the men of Munster from a projected raid on his lands. Though it was probably no more serious than a spot of cattle thievery, Brendan was unsuccessful. He did manage, however, to enlist God's aid in causing the trespassers to stumble around in circles (probably in a timely fog); foiled in their purpose, they finally gave up and went home.

Brendan died in 577, aged ninety-three. In the near century span of his life, his country had changed vitally. When he was born, much of Ireland was still heathen, and Brendan lived and worked in the mystical aura of a land barely emerged from the clouds of paganism. To a people attuned to the cult of the hero-warrior, courage and charisma were more telling than organizational ability, and conversion was a matter of the personality and style of the individual saint. Brendan was the last of this era: he remained to the end a saintly Christian hero in the old mold, heedless of peril, ever restlessly on the move, of changeable temper, as quick to curse as to bless and wonderfully effective in both offices. If he was also sometimes eccentric and fractious, much could be forgiven a saint so transcendently gallant. Though his earthly accomplishments were respectable, his appeal is rather that of the romantic adventurer than the revered and inspired leader.

By the time of Brendan's death, his country had almost entirely accepted the Christian doctrine, which it fashioned in its own image, that of the agrarian, familiar society ideally adaptable to the monastic system. A different talent was needed in the late sixth century to handle the new modus operandi: that of the creative organizer.

CHAPTER IX
THE TRAVELLERS·
ST. COLUMBA OF IONA

WHILE BRENDAN WAS THE LARGER-THAN-LIFE EXPONENT OF A VANISHING period, Columba was the epitome of the sixth-century modern man. Born in 521, thirty-seven years after Brendan, he was another of Ireland's great adventurous abbots, one in whom the impulse to seek a new horizon led out of Ireland and gave the Christian impulse a fresh direction. Though only a generation separated the two abbots, their outlooks were an age apart. So firmly had the new religion taken root that Ireland was ready by now to export what she had so recently imported: her ardent young faith and her extraordinary learning, the knowledge dormant or lost entirely in continental Europe during the barbarian invasions. Columba was the first to carry the message out of Ireland. If he lacked the irresponsible charm of the semilegendary voyager, he had attributes better suited to his age: a practical genius for organization, a passionate desire to convince and convert, and a proud and martial spirit that brooked no officiousness in kings — or in other abbots. He was also an *ollam* (master poet), which meant that he commanded the respect of Ireland's most prestigious class, the *aes dana,* men of learning. His resolve for exile took him not into the unknown ocean to seek a dream, but only over the North Channel, where his intention for penance canalized itself into a practical direction, the conversion of the heathen Picts of Alba.

Columba was a prince by birth, a great-grandson of Niall of the Nine Hostages and one of the heirs to the throne of Tara, the high-kingship of northern Ireland. He was born in Garton, County Donegal, above long, narrow Garton Lough, whose waters reflected the darkness of deeply forested, overhanging mountains, the haunt of wolves. His baptismal name was Crimthann — which, aptly, means "wolf" — and was a name often bestowed on the scions of warrior-kings. Later he was given by his friends the name of Columba, or Columcille, Dove of the Church, in recognition of his extraordinary piety. This was presumptuous: the dove is the representation of the Holy Spirit, and a strict purist might see in the designation an implied analogy to Christ. The Irish Church, individualist from the first, indulged in many such near-heresies, arousing deep though not actionable suspicions in Roman clerical circles. Nothing could ever be pinned down as false doctrine, but the Irish spirit of lofty independence, however pious the motives, was deplored by the proper Roman establishment. And in the case of Columba, he was from early youth one to whom presumption came naturally.

When still a boy, Columba chose to renounce his birthright, bringing his personal wealth and his family influence into the Church. This was an arrangement that would become familiar practice, and it was mutually advantageous. The ruling family, having jettisoned its druids, could still maintain its power, and the Church received the benison of lands and money. The system had the perhaps dubious result of making the Church — never the most democratic of institutions — firmly aristocratic, even dynastic.

Though he had destined himself for a holy life, Columba was brought up like a young lord, to be well versed in letters as well as hardy and knowledgeable in the outdoor skills of the farmer. He was sent out to fosterage to a priest, Cruithneachan, at Kilmacrenan, County Donegal, near the place of his birth. His teacher taught him his letters, it is said, by giving him a cake to eat, whereon were inscribed the letters of the alphabet. Presumably he absorbed the knowledge well, along with the cake, for his next step was a renowned school, that of Finian of Moville, a learned abbot trained in St. Ninian's Candida Casa in Galloway. Thence he went to the Aran Islands to learn at the feet of the beloved Enda. Finally he studied at the great school of Finian of Clonard, where he became in time one of the "Twelve Apostles."

Finian received him, as had the other two abbots, with the specially gracious deference due to a prince who brings to the Church both money and family consequence. The young student asked where he should build his little cell of mud and wattles. The master, favoring his star boarder, told him to build it by the door of the church. "Columba built his bothy then, and not at the door that the church had then did he build it. And he declared that he would build his bothy in the place where the door of the church should be afterward. And what Columba said was fulfilled."[1] Not only did the abbot respect his new student's rather imperious wishes, but the other students also deferred to him in small ways. Everyone, according to Finian's rule of daily labor, took turns to grind the monastery grain with the big stone quern. But legend has it that angels took over Columba's stint — probably in the guise of poor students ready to do menial work for a prince.

So far the young aristocrat appears to have had a haughty arrogance ill suited to the monastic spirit of self-renunciation. In his favor, he was conscious of his flaw; all his life he would fight his own pride and seek to stifle the contentious nature bequeathed to him through generations of belligerent warlords. If he never quite succeeded, he managed to sublimate his tempers and to redirect his hotheaded energy. He became a superb organizer and a brilliant leader, second only to St. Patrick in his accomplishments in a heathen country.

By the time he was ready to be ordained, however, he had not yet calmed his temperament. The bishop who was to consecrate him was out plowing his fields when Columba arrived. The young man's reputation had gone before him, and the bishop, with the intention of inducing a touch of humility, refused to unyoke his oxen until his regular hour. Before this, Columba had been the favored pet; this was the first recorded setback. It is not written whether the wait cooled his impatience. Presumably it did, because the sacrament was duly performed.

At the end of his schooling, Columba went north to Donegal, where he was born, and where his relatives held sway from the great stone fortress of Aileach, at the foot of the peninsula of Inishowen. His cousin Ainmire was king at that time, and when he was not holding court at Aileach he lived near the river Foyle on a steep hillside called Doire-Calgaich (the Oak-Wood of Calgach), today the industrial city of Derry, County Derry. The king gave this oak-covered hill to Columba, and there, in 546, he built his first monastery, placing the little wooden huts near the river's edge, the church high on the hill amid the oaks. If Columba was not oversensitive toward his fellowmen, he was all his life responsively tender to other creatures of nature. From the beginning, he had a deep fondness for his oak grove. He could not build his church with its chancel facing to the east, according to custom, without cutting some of the trees. Rather than desecrate the beloved forest, his chancel faced north. "Though I fear death," he is reputed to have said, "I fear still more the sound of the axe in Derry wood."

Columba's studies at Clonard had included not only the obligatory Latin language and the Scriptures but also the history of Ireland and the art of poetry. He developed a lively interest in the literature of the vernacular. Following the lead of St. Patrick, who, as we have seen, was said to have conversed with the heathen ancients and found their message felicitous, Irish monastic education had become the most liberal in Europe. Study of the pagan classics of Europe was encouraged, and special homage was paid to the heritage of the bards, Ireland's own classics in Ireland's own language. In Europe most of the oral literature was lost and the old languages forgotten or unrecognizably mutated, as the schools stressed learning in Latin only, with the Scriptures and the Christian fathers the prescribed reading matter. Columba, in whose ancestral home must often have been heard the voice of the bard chanting of the glorious doings of old, knew well the beauty of his native literature. He had chosen to study Irish poetry under a Christian scholar trained in the druidic tradition, one Master Gemman, who taught him orally in the old style, a method that fostered the development of a well-muscled mind. In time he himself became a master poet, composing many lays, in joy at nature's blessings and in sorrow at exile.

Columba's love of literature and books eventually led him into a shockingly un-Christian performance, the action of a spoiled and peremptory lordling. Paradoxically, this outburst of temper, a kind of last youthful fling, had the end result of taking him out of Ireland and into the life for which his commanding spirit was most aptly fitted.

On a visit to his former teacher Finian of Moville, he was shown a copy of the Book of Psalms that had recently arrived from Italy and that may have been the first copy of St. Jerome's Vulgate to be seen in Ireland. On account of the barbarian wars, books were increasingly hard to come by in Ireland. Their rarity invested them with a mystical value far beyond their contents. Finian treasured his beautiful manuscript, and though he allowed Columba to read it, forbade him, as the younger priest wished, to copy it. In his customary high-handed way, Columba ignored the prohibition, and in a few secret nights he had copied it all. He was discovered at the work, and Finian demanded that the copy be rendered to him, along with the book. The two could not solve the problem, so together they went to Tara, where the annual fair was in progress. There the high-king,

Diarmait (he who had befriended St. Ciaran, and had now grown autocratic with age), was holding court, and they asked him to judge between them. Finian deposed that as the book was his, so was the copy. Columba held that the book was not harmed by being copied; further, that the holy things in the book should be read by many, not withheld for the pleasuring of one. The king judged in favor of Finian, saying, "To every cow her young cow, that is her calf, and to every book its transcript. And therefore to Finian belongeth the book thou hast written, O Columcille." Columba, with conspicuous ill grace, returned his copy.

Shortly thereafter, King Diarmait gave him a more serious cause for annoyance. At a game of hurling, the son of the king of Connacht killed one of Diarmait's servants. The penalty for breaking the peace at the fair of Tara was death, and the young prince fled to Columba, who was his kinsman, for sanctuary. King Diarmait's officers broke the sanctuary and seized the boy. Priest or not, Columba was the heir of warrior blood, and at the direct insult his native conbativeness rose uncontrolled. He stormed out of Tara full of threats and went north to raise an army among his people, the northern branch of the Ui Neill, descendants of Niall of the Nine Hostages. Though Columba's action was deplorably unpriestlike, he had good reason for his anger. The breaking of sanctuary was a clear and inexcusable act of defiance to the Church. It is thought that Diarmait was anticlerical; consequently Columba's fierce stand can be regarded as a stroke, belligerent but effective, against lingering paganism. It turned out actually to be the final blow — for not only Diarmait but Tara itself fell as an indirect result.

Columba's side of the Ui Neill was opposed to that of Diarmait, who was the offspring of another branch, the southern Ui Neill, and both parties were happy to have an excuse for war. They met at Culdreimhne, County Sligo, and in the ensuing battle three thousand men (it is said) fell, while the archangel Michael hovered in the clouds above, smiting with his bright sword the hosts of the enemy of Christ. Tradition further has it that the two priests, Finian and Columba, while they did not go so far as to lift a weapon, prayed enthusiastically for the victory of their respective sides. The forces of Diarmait were defeated, and the leaders of the victorious army came to Columba to propose that he himself should replace the high-king on the throne of northern Ireland. He would have made a fine king. But he was already suffering intense remorse and turned them down, asking them to make peace with Diarmait, for the sake of Ireland, and to allow him to continue on his throne.

Columba's conduct is not so extraordinary when one reflects that monks were not exempted from military service until the ninth century, and that intermonastic strife was an everyday affair, whether resorted to for defense or indulged in for the redress of an insult. What damaged his prestige was the size of the conflagration and the huge glare of publicity that attended it. He was excommunicated at once, and though the punishment was revoked following the able pleas of some of his admirers, the errant priest had no mercy for himself. His self-reproach was as extreme as his anger had been, and in agony of soul he saw that the only restitution he could make was to convert as many souls as had perished by his fault.*

The saint's immediate object was penance by exile. He went, as afore-mentioned, to the island of Devenish in Lough Erne, to take counsel with his Clonard schoolmate Molaisse, whom he judged to be, at the moment, a man of wiser vision than himself. Molaisse confirmed his decision, adding the extra penance that Columba must never again set foot on Irish soil.

The land of exile Columba chose was Scotland, which was then called Alba or Pictland. It was not entirely strange territory to an Irishman. Finian of Moville, who had been Columba's teacher before they became enemies, had studied at Candida Casa in the small Christian area of western Scotland. There had been an Irish settlement there from the early third century, when the family of Carbery Riada, escaping famine in Munster, migrated to the north of Ireland, to settle in County Antrim, and thence across the sea to Argyle in southwestern Scotland. In both these places they established themselves permanently as the Dalriada (Riada's Portion). The tiny Scottish colony languished until 503, when three brothers, Fergus, Angus and Lorne, direct descendants of Carbery Riada, led a group across the sea from Irish Dalriada and, meeting little opposition, took over a much larger piece of land. Fergus was their first king; his descendants ultimately became

---

*A sidelight to this tale is the fate of the book that came between Finian and Columba. Known as the *Cathach,* or *Battler,* because it led indirectly to an armed conflict, it is thought to have come back into Columba's possession, and to have become an heirloom in his family, the O'Donnells. For all the saint's subsequent penitence, he could not even in death escape his martial reputation. For, so the tale goes, his book was a talisman: if carried (in the hands of a priest free from mortal sin) three times around the army before the chieftain went into battle, it would insure victory. In the seventeenth century, one of the O'Donnells, a supporter of James II at the time of his forced abdication of the English throne, fled in exile to the Continent, taking the *Cathach* with him. When it turned up in 1802, the vellum pages were stuck together in a lump. Carefully moistened and separated, they revealed the Psalms written in Latin in a "neat but hurried hand." Tradition has it that that hand was indeed Columba's, though the writing shows one characteristic that probably could not have appeared until early in the seventh century, after Columba's death. The book is now in the Royal Irish Academy in Dublin.

kings of all Scotland, and from them derive, through the Stuarts, the present royal family of Great Britain.*

At the time of Columba, most of Scotland was ruled by the Picts, who had been, according to the Venerable Bede, converted by St. Ninian of Galloway but had since slid back into paganism. These people were a mixture of Celts and an older race, the Neolithic farmers who had dominated both Ireland and Great Britain until successive invasions reduced them to a remnant everywhere except in parts of northern Ireland, the Scottish highlands and the promontory of Galloway in southwestern Scotland. The Celtic Picts were the ruling class in Pictish Scotland, and their language was similar to that spoken in England before the Anglo-Saxon invasions. Here and there the older civilization showed through in unintelligible words (names such as Bliesblituth and Uipoignamet), in the remarkable artistry of their decorated stone tombs and in a sober, dignified demeanor quite different from that of the volatile Celts.

In 563, when Columba left Ireland, he was forty-two years old, at the beginning of middle age, a time when he was probably ready to make a decision for fundamental change. He had accomplished a great deal in Ireland, founding monasteries — each one outstandingly successful — that were endowed with the stamp of his dynamic organizational talent and his devotion to scholarship, poetry and art. As with many Irish clerics, travel seemed as necessary to him as breathing, and he had never stayed long in one place. It is possible that at this stage in his life he decided that he had done all he could in his native land and, still vibrantly energetic, looked for a new kind of challenge. Life among the pagan Picts, a people not altogether alien, would have been an attractive prospect to a man with Columba's driving vitality. Possibly his decision to expiate his sin in this particular direction was moved as much by his natural bent as by the need for atonement.

But when the time came, he left Ireland in sorrow. He sailed down the Foyle in a curragh with a leather sail, accompanied by twelve clerics; and as the little boat left Derry, he looked back a last time, speaking (is is said) a sad verse.

*The origin of the name Scotland goes back to the Dalriada: the Irish, during these centuries, were known as Scots, and their settlement in Argyle was therefore said to be "Scottish." When the north-Ireland family of Fergus extended its rule, the name "land of the Scots" (meaning Irish) came to be applied to the whole country.

> *There is a gray eye*
> *That will look back upon Erin;*
> *Never again will it see*
> *The men of Erin or women.*

Even the birds grieved at his going. "And in token of this, the seagulls and the birds of Lough Foyle were . . . screaming and screeching for grief that Columba was leaving Erin. And he understood that they were uttering speech of sorrow. . . . No greater was his sorrow in parting from the human folk than his sorrow in parting from the seagulls and the birds of Lough Foyle."

The North Channel, between Ireland and Scotland, is a rough stretch of ocean full of rips and eddies where the tides of the North Atlantic and the Irish Sea meet. It is notoriously unkind to mariners, and even the buoyant little Irish curraghs were hard put to negotiate its capricious currents. But it presented no threat to Irish monks secure in the hand of God and knowledgeable from childhood in the ways of water. Columba and his companions sailed across it with no accident, making their first landing at the peninsula of Kintyre, the Scottish mainland nearest to Ireland, where the Irish Dalriada had a colony. They rested there a few days before continuing to Oronsay. Ireland was still visible from the highest point of this tiny island, so Columba directed that they should put to sea again.

The next landfall was Iona, about one mile off the large island of Mull and about seventy-five miles from Ireland.* They put in at a small cove at its south end, an inlet guarded by rock islets and on its shoreward side by a ring of knobby hills. The beach was stony but just beyond it was a sheltered meadow. They pulled the boat over the pebble beach, and the leader crossed the flower-filled field to climb the highest of the surrounding hills. He looked southwest and his eyes met only the empty ocean. "Here we will stop," he said in effect. "I can no longer see Ireland." His landing place is named Port of the Coracle (curragh) and an ancient cairn on top of the hill where he stood is called the Cairn of the Back Turned to Ireland.

The clerics walked inland from their landing place, among the rocky little heather-covered hills, the valleys between them fragrant with thyme and clover. There was underground water; they crossed boggy patches

---

*Iona's name was originally *I* or *Hy*, Gaelic for "island"; hence came *Ioua*, which means "pertaining to I." Later it was called *Icolmkill*, "the Island of Columcille." A medieval scribe, misreading the name *Ioua*, wrote it as *Iona* and the name, easier for the English tongue, persisted.

where grew yellow flag and cotton grass, and here and there a pond shone in the bottom of a hollow. The rough terrain of the southern end gave way to beaches of white shell sand and rolling grassland, thin-soiled, exposed to the west wind off the open ocean. But lime from the shell sand made the sparse earth unexpectedly fertile (it is called in Gaelic the *Machair,* Sandy Plain, and is the soil that covers most of the Hebrides). It would make good pasture for the monks' sheep and cattle. The northeastern part of the island, facing away from the storms of the west and sheltered by higher hills, had broad level meadows where they could grow their crops. The ocean was full of flounders, and seals basked on the offshore skerries or played in the coastal waters: a plentiful supply of meat, skins and oil for lamps.

It was all very small, only three and a half miles long and one and a half at its widest: too small to be self-sufficient if, as Columba is supposed to have said, "it yet shall be mighty." But for the few monks of that first landing and the monastery of the first years, Iona was proportioned just right; it evinced a kind of peaceful certainty. It still does today. Whether its serene beauty gives rise to the emanation of spirituality that almost every visitor finds there, or whether its history has invested its soft green fields and wild little hills and bleached sands with a kind of saintly halo, it is an intensely affecting place. Samuel Johnson felt it: "We are now treading that illustrious Island, which was once the luminary of the Caledonian regions, whence savage clans and roving barbarians derived the benefits of knowledge and the blessings of religion. . . . That man is little to be envied, whose patriotism would not gain force upon the plain of Marathon, or whose piety would not grow warmer, among the ruins of Iona."[2] Felix Mendelssohn's companion on his Scottish journeys, Karl Klingemann, found it deeply moving in another way: "Sometimes, when I sit in lively company with music and dancing around me, and the wish arises to retire to the loneliest solitude, I think of Iona, where there are ruins . . . which were shining once."[3]

Columba's monastery was on a mild rise above the eastern coast, looking over the gentian-blue sea toward the green hills of Mull. It consisted of the usual beehive-shaped wattle-and-daub huts surrounding a rectangular wooden church with a heather-thatched roof. Other buildings included a guesthouse, refectory, barns, mill and bakery, and the whole was enclosed within an earthen bank. Of all this neat, busy establishment, nothing is left but a heap of stones on top of a rocky outcropping behind the Norman cathedral, said to be the foundation of Columba's hut, where the saint slept on bare rock. Near it is tiny St. Oran's Chapel, built in the ninth or tenth century and probably the image of the original wooden church; and a fine ninth-century high cross, St. Martin's, carved on one side with scenes from the Old Testament, on the other with curving, abstract design. This is the only cross left of the eighty-six that the island is said to have had, most of them destroyed by Puritan iconoclasts.

Columba's rule, like that of all Irish monasteries, was severe. The brothers were enjoined to the strict Christian principles of celibacy; caution and reason in speech; humility; hospitality; and kindness to animals (this stricture was one particularly after Columba's heart). The daily discipline was divided between work and prayer. Food and sleep were scanty, sometimes dispensed with altogether. Besides the daily manual labor pertaining to the functioning of the monastery, there was a greater than usual emphasis at Iona, as in Columba's monasteries in Ireland, on the work of the scribes. Columba himself was an expert copyist and was said to have made in his own hand three hundred copies of the Psalter. Out of the Columban scriptoria were to come some of the most beautiful manuscripts in the world: the *Book of Kells* (shown on page 341) and the *Book of Durrow,* though their provenance is not entirely certain, may be directly attributable to Columba's ardent interest in books and writing.

Iona was on the edge of the territory settled by the Irish Dalriada. Beyond it was the land of the pagan Picts. The Dalriadan king at the time was Conall, great-grandson of Fergus, the first Irish king in Scotland. But Scottish Dalriada was in trouble. Brude Mac Maelchon, king of the Picts, had marched against the colony three years before Columba's arrival, driven out its then king, and reduced it to the status of a tributary state. To make good his claim to Iona, Columba had to gain the favor of the pagan king. He went to Inverness, the king's seat, but Brude, on the advice of his foster-father, a druid named Broichan, had barred the gates. Columba performed the customary miracle: he made the sign of the cross as he knocked, and the great doors swung open before him. It is likely that the apparent miracle was an outgrowth of King Brude's favorable predisposition toward Columba, for the saint's chief biographer, Adamnan, writes that the king then "issued forth to meet the blessed man with all reverence; and addressed him gently with words of peace. And from that day forth, this ruler honored the holy and venerable man all the remaining days of his life, as was proper."

The druid Broichan was still unregenerate; after all, his position rested on the continuance of the old religion and the discouragement of the new. His obstructive strategy was to create a discordant noise to drown out the sound of the mass Columba was celebrating in the palace courtyard. But he reckoned without Columba's peculiar physical trait, a voice of stupendous carrying power, which, wrote Adamnan, was "sometimes heard for eight furlongs, that is a mile." The saint, according to his biographer, "began to chant the 44th Psalm, and in a marvelous manner his voice was at that moment so lifted up into the air, like terrible thunder, that both king and people were affrighted with fear intolerable." It must have been an electrifying scene: the strange holy man standing tall, light eyes flashing, fair hair flowing long down his back, shaved off in front from ear to ear in the Irish tonsure, arms raised in a blessing, great voice strong above the pagan din, pealing over the hills to carry the word of God to those in the farthest valleys: "Thou didst drive out the heathen with thy hand. . . ." In spite of his long habit of rough wool and his monk's tonsure, he must have appeared to the awed Picts the very image of the royal Celtic warrior. Broichan was silenced, though not for good: the saint yet had to chastise him with an effective curse before he admitted the superiority of Christian miracles.

For all the aggressive power of his presence, however, Columba brought to the country of the Picts not war but peace and a new awakening. Following his conversion of the court of King Brude, the Highland Picts easily adapted themselves to the way of life preached by the eloquent and commanding apostle from Ireland. To begin with, Columba must have impressed them deeply: here was a magnetic personage, of great consequence, who had given up his birthright to a throne to live the spare, chaste life of an ascetic. The word he preached was appealing to a people who already had a dim belief in a higher power and in the immortal soul of man (as one can see by their splendid tombs). Evidently intelligent and perceptive, they soon came to appreciate not only the spiritual benefits of Christianity but the material advantages of a more advanced civilization. The Irish missionaries brought them the techniques of a more efficient agriculture and the benefits of medical skill; they also introduced an exacting yet humane system of education. And whatever body of mythology the Picts possessed, whatever deeds of bygone heroes they related to one another (they had no written language, and their lore is lost), they evidently gave it up without a sigh when the wonderful realm of Bible stories opened to them.

Columba's missionaries went all over the Highlands and beyond, and daughter foundations grew up under the aegis of Iona, with Columba competently holding all the strings. It would have seemed natural, considering the prestige of his position and the weight of his family background, that he should have been a bishop. But he chose not to aspire to this reverential position, which would have put him above the mundane bustle of the abbot's concernment. He preferred to operate from the simple position of priest. This gave him all the leeway he needed — and enjoyed — for the day-to-day politics involved in managing his multifaceted organization.

When the first monastery grew too big for Iona, Columba received grants of several of the neighboring islands. Many of his monks were skilled seamen, and as well as negotiating the currents and eddies of the waters around the Hebrides, they began to explore farther. The most audacious of the voyagers was Cormac, a monk from Durrow and a feverent admirer of Columba. Like his abbot, Cormac longed for exile, but he looked for a sterner and wilder solitude. He "sought with great labor . . . a desert in the ocean." When he came to Iona, he desired Columba to send him as a missionary to the farthest islands. The abbot, ever sympathetic to the would-be exile, complied and sent Cormac forth with a letter to King Brude, saying, "Some of our people have lately gone forth, hoping to find a solitude in the pathless sea, and if perchance after long wandering they should come to the Orcades Islands [Orkney], do thou earnestly commend them to the under-king, whose hostages are in thy hand, that no misfortunes befall them within his territories."

Cormac sailed around the northern tip of Scotland to land in Orkney, where he was received in a friendly manner. Thence he crossed the channel between the Atlantic and the North Sea, one of Europe's roughest passages, to bring the word of Christ to the Picts who scraped out a thin living on the steep and rocky pastures of Shetland. His yearning for isolation not yet satisfied, he made journeys still farther afield, reaching the Faeroes, Iceland and probably Greenland, where he encountered "loathsome creatures . . . which smote the keel and sides and stern and prow. . . . They were about the size of frogs, with very terrible stings, and more like swimming than flying creatures." (They were probably stinging jellyfish, though one commentator seriously suggests mosquitoes.)

While Cormac was on this journey, Columba, who had second sight — not so much miraculous as a function of informed intuition and a keen perception of the ways of the natural world — knew that his disciple's boat was beset by storms. He prayed that God would change the wind and bring his brother home, and so it came to pass. When Cormac sailed in on the favorable wind, he begged Columba to let him stay in Iona. But the abbot told him that his fate was in Durrow and ordered him home, adding a mournful postscript.

O Cormac, woe to one that quitteth Erin when he might still be there; for sweet are the voices of her birds and the rippling of her rills. Smooth are her plains and sheltered woods. . . .

> Better death in Erin without stain,
> Than life forever in Alba.

Despite his busy, fulfilled life, the exile Columba still looked toward Ireland, invisible over the sea, and specially to his beloved Derry, as is poignantly expressed in a poem attributed to him

> If mine were all of Alba
> From the center to its border,
> I would liefer have space for a hut
> In the middle of fair Derry.
> . . . .
>
> This is the reason why I love Derry:
> For its level fields, for its brightness,
> For the hosts of white angels
> From one end to the other.
>
> There is not a leaf on the ground
> In Derry, lovely and faultless,
> That hath not two virgin angels
> Overthwart every leaf there.
> . . . .
>
> My Derry, my little oak-grove,
> My dwelling, my little cell,
> O eternal God in heaven above,
> Woe be to him who violates it.

This cry of love and longing comes strangely from the pen of the hardheaded organizing virtuoso of Iona. That there is sensitive perception behind the practical strategist can be seen in his loving solicitude for animals (and for some men) and his alert observance of natural phenomena. Columba was a poet, and though little remains that can be surely ascribed to him (even the songs of exile quoted above were probably written two centuries later), he was renowned in his day. He wrote both in Latin and in Gaelic, he knew and loved the pagan literature of the vernacular, and he respected the poetic tradition as the very spirit of Ireland, something that would not die without crippling his county.

When Aed Mac Ainmire, high-king of northern Ireland, decreed the suppression and exile of the bards, Columba saw this as an acute danger, a threat so serious that it brought him to break his vow. He returned to Ireland in 575 (wearing clods of Scottish earth on his feet, it is said, so he would not touch the soil of his homeland) for the Convention of Drumceatt, County Derry, where the future of the bards was to be settled. Another question before the convention, also of close concern to Columba, was that of the authority of the Irish Dalriada over its Scottish colony.

The bards were a powerful class. They were the sole keepers of the genealogies, the arbiters in matters of lineage and property; their voluminous legal and historical knowledge was committed to memory and recited in elaborate — and very expensive — verse. To stay on their right side was vital to the leading families, and the poets, knowing their favor was essential, had become insufferably arrogant. Each master poet had a company of thirty and each poet of the second rank had fifteen. Being of the learned class, the enormous parties crossed borders with impunity. At each house they stopped at they had the right to demand refection. Further, they carried with them a great silver pot called the Pot of Avarice, into which went the arbitrary and exorbitant fees they demanded for their services. If proper entertainment was lacking or the pot's contents were lean, they would circulate damaging lampoons or even wreck the offender's life with the dreaded weapon of satire.

The reaction of their victims, long overdue, was therefore oversevere. Columba, a master poet himself, was naturally sympathetic to his class. Though he perceived the provocation, he was aghast at the extremity of the sentence. He saw behind it an even more serious threat. Christianity had brought to Ireland the art of writing, along with the Latin language and culture. Ecclesiastical scribes, writing in Latin, could keep the records that had until now resposed only in the memories of the poets. Many churchmen saw this new education as a weapon against the last echoes of paganism. If they could go a step further and eliminate the bards, they reasoned, then the lingering tradition of heathen glories and the adulation of heroes and demigods would vanish at once, leaving the Christian ethic supreme. It was an ugly confrontation of cultures — a clash, as Columba understood, that could eradicate the Irish language and destroy the historic individuality of Celtic Ireland.

The saint was a shrewd political negotiator as well as a statesman of vision, and he brought the convention to a brilliant compromise. The sentence of banishment was revoked on the condition that the numbers of the bardic companies be reduced, their exaction of hospitality curtailed, and their prices fairly fixed. At the same time, a system of secular education was devised, each master poet to be given free common land for the purpose of establishing schools. There was to be a chief college for each of the five provinces; under its administration were to be minor colleges, one for each *tuath*. All were to provide free education.

Secular schools were not new in Ireland, but the sons of the nobles had been taught orally, in the old tradition, and there had been no intercourse between the ecclesiastical schools and these essentially pagan institutions. Now there would be a give and take between the heretofore separate worlds of the imported Latin culture and the hereditary native. The result would be the growth of Ireland's remarkably coherent continuity, a kind of nationalistic Christianity far in advance of the Continental variety. On the mainland, the suppression of pagan lore (which included the stored knowledge of ancient Greece) in favor of a strictly Christian Latin culture would severely impede the free development of learning and scholarship.

The man chiefly responsible, with Columba, for framing the new educational system was the saint's good friend Dallan Forgaill (whose first name means "blind"), Ireland's most revered poet. Like Columba he was both poet and Christian, symbol of the promise of harmony in Ireland between her pagan past and her Christian future. When the convention ended, a banquet was given for Columba, for which Dallan Forgaill wrote a poem in his honor, the *Amra Columcille (Hymn to Columcille)*. It was in Irish, the first known Christian composition in the vernacular (the provenance of St. Patrick's *Cry of the Deer* is uncertain). The poet began to sing his eulogy with the choral accompaniment of the time, a deep-throated murmured crooning at the end of each verse; and Columba was caught again in the trapfall of his own pride: "When he heard all the poets praising him . . . there came upon him such exaltation of mind and heart, that the air above him was filled with evil spirits. . . . Then Columba covered his head and wept sore. . . . And when he lifted his head . . . a great smoke rose up . . . and that smoke did scatter the demons. . . . Columba said to [Dallan] that he should not praise a man so long as he is living." Dallan Forgaill's paean, he added, should be reserved for its subject's funeral.

The other problem before the Convention of Drumceatt was also settled favorably for Columba, with his active participation. The Scottish Dalriada was declared free of all tribute to Ireland, and its king, Aidan, was declared independent. The only remaining condition was that Ireland and her erst-while colony should join forces against enemies to either one or the other. The alliance, cultural as well as political, was to endure for centuries as Ireland and Christian Scotland exchanged their saints and scholars and made common cause against the heathen invaders, Saxon, Dane and Viking.

Aidan, the first independent king of Scottish Dalriada, was also the first Christian king in Great Britain (excluding Ireland), succeeding to the throne upon the death of King Conall in 574. As well as being a direct descendant of Fergus, Aidan had the inestimable advantage of Columba's backing. The inauguration was a composite of heathen and Christian rites, as the new king sat upon the Stone of Scone, brought from Ireland by Fergus seventy years before, and the priest laid his hands upon his head, blessing him as if he were being ordained. At the same time that Scottish Dalriada became independent of Ireland, the little kingdom, by now a power in Alba, also declared its freedom from the control of the Pictish king, Brude. This was the beginning of Gaelic Scotland. In 842 the whole country was united under the aegis of the Dalriadan kings and Aidan's descendants ruled until 1285, when the last one died and the ancient Irish bloodline passed maternally to the family of the Stuarts.

Columba was responsible for the conversion of the Highlands to Christianity. He also brought that land freedom from outside domination and saw the start of its eventual unification under a strong and lasting dynasty. Equally vital was his introduction of education, reading and writing to a people who had not before had these boons of civilization.

After his death, the spirit of Columba's Iona moved out beyond the border of Pictland into northern England. At the same time, southern England was coming under the sway of Rome. In 597, thirty-four years after Columba had come to Iona, Pope Gregory I had sent a papal mission under Augustine to bring the Gospel to the backsliding Britons. The natives did not like their new ecclesiarch, who had come with the hated recent enemies, the Saxons. The Rome-oriented bishop, moreover, was tactlessly haughty toward the Britons and impatient with their shaky Christianity. His mission foundered. Some years later it was to revive under Paulinus. In the meantime the Irish missionaries coming down from the north fresh with the inspiration of Iona were signally successful. Their tolerance of human frailty (lay, not clerical; their personal discipline was unsparing), combined with an attitude toward Rome respectful but not meticulously docile, was empathetic with the native outlook. And their monks and priests — simple-living, hardworking, friendly, withal shiningly pious — were greatly loved wherever they went.

As the Augustinian missions spread north from Canterbury, eventually reaching York, the Irish influence was extending southward through Northumbria. At this time, the early seventh century, the rightful heir to the kingdom of Northumbria was the Anglo-Saxon Oswald. He had been exiled by a usurper, Edwin, had fled to Scotland, and found sanctuary at Iona, where he was baptized and received an education. In 633 Edwin was killed and Oswald, in a battle to reclaim his throne, saw Columba (whose martial proclivities persisted even into the hereafter) up in the sky over the field "gleaming with angelic beauty, and his lofty figure seemed to touch the clouds with the crown of his head."[4] The battle was won, and the big slice of England over which Oswald proceeded to reign became an Irish Christian stronghold. Politically, Oswald was a strong king, ruling successfully over four nationalities, two of them mainly heathen, each with its own language. Spiritually, he had the vital support of St. Aidan, an Irish priest educated in Iona, who came at Oswald's invitation to strengthen the faith of the Britons and Scots and introduce to the heathen Picts and Angles the blessings of Christianity. In 635 Oswald gave his spiritual aide the island of Lindisfarne, off the coast of present-day Northumberland.

Lindisfarne is a low sandy island accessible on foot from the mainland at ebb tide. Except for undulating, grass-covered sand dunes and an excrescence of rock at the southeastern point, jutting into the North Sea, where rises a grim Norman castle much restored, the island is flat and amorphous, shrinking and growing out of the shallow seas with the fifteen-foot tides. The monks must have subsisted, as do the islanders today, on crabs and fish, with a few sheep to graze on the rough, sparse dune grass. The widest part of the island, a mile and a half at low tide, is meadow, which might support a few crops. To supplement their supplies, King Oswald granted Aidan some farmland on the mainland as well. Aidan himself chose the island for his monastery: he preferred, like all the Irish clergy, to live in lonely severity out of the mainstream. However, it was not sufficiently remote for him, and it was his practice to retire during Lent to Inner Farne, one of twenty-eight small rocky outcroppings a mile or more offshore, inhabited only by seabirds and seals, to pray and meditate alone. This little island became renowned a generation later as the retreat of St. Cuthbert, the prior of Whitby and Lindisfarne, who lived here for nine years and later retired to die here.

Lindisfarne — renamed Holy Island by the Normans in the eleventh century, and celebrated in Sir Walter Scott's *Marmion* as a remote bourn for pilgrims — has today all the unfortunate characteristics of a seaside resort. Its gentle green fields are parking lots for hundreds of automobiles from nearby Berwick-upon-Tweed; its flat beach with piles of crab pots and little fishing boats lying aslant on the muddy sand of low tide is the haunt of shrieking barefoot adolescents; its beautiful Norman priory — red sandstone walls open to the sky, early Gothic windows delicately carved with geometric designs, a single slender vaulting rib soaring in a diagonal arch over the grassy nave — is the playground for hordes of children and their picnicking parents. The quiet, enclosed sanctity that invests Iona is absent entirely.

But in the seventh century Lindisfarne was the center of spirituality of northern England. Its founder was a man of kindly prudence who knew how to propitiate royalty, yet who lived with a simple purity that appealed to the lowliest of his congregation. By choice, Aidan administered his enormous diocese from the little island at its edge, but his constant travels brought him the devotion of the people through the whole land. According to the Venerable Bede, the abbot "never thought, nor cared for any possession. He always travelled on foot. He and his followers lived as they taught." [5] Aidan was the valued confidant of his patron, King Oswald, friendly but never fawning nor even markedly respectful. Under Aidan's strict but sensible rule, modelled on that of Columba at Iona, Lindisfarne was for thirty years the center of northern British Christianity. Besides proselytizing and building monasteries, missionaries from Lindisfarne founded schools for both lay and ecclesiastical students, where all branches of learning were taught. Most of the teachers came either from Iona or directly from Columba's monasteries in Ireland, as the rural citizenry of northern England, but lately converted, had not reached the advanced stage of education of the Irish scholars. Out of this Iona-inspired educational system were to come some of Britain's most notable intellectuals, among them Bede and the poet Caedmon. One of the products of the monastic scriptoria is a glorious illuminated manuscript, the *Lindisfarne Gospels,* which stands with the *Book of Kells* and the *Book of Durrow* among the shining exemplars of Irish-English artistry of the early Middle Ages.

While the influence of Irish Lindisfarne — its personnel and its philosophy stemming from Columba's Iona — spread over the north of Britain and even reached down into the south to Suffolk, Sussex and Somerset, the Roman brand of Christianity introduced by Augustine was working slowly northward, to touch the edges of Northumbria. For the first half of the seventh century both parties were too busy with the work of conversion to come into conflict. The most active menace to their cause was the pagan King Penda of Mercia. This strong ruler had extended his kingdom by political and military strategy to include the central heart of England from the border of Wales on the west to the Wash on the east, and as far north as the Humber on the edge of Northumbria. At the height of his power nearly all the Anglo-Saxon kingdoms of England acknowledged his supremacy. Though Penda did not suppress the preaching of Christianity, short shrift was made of clerics who got in his way, and he himself remained a heathen. In 654 he was killed in a battle with King Oswy of Northumbria, the Christian brother of Oswald, Iona-educated patron of Aidan. With the collapse of his kingdom the last great heathen stronghold fell before the proselytizing onslaughts from both sides. The two opposing currents of Christianity met at last, no pagan buffer between them, and the accumulated irritations of years came to a head.

English Christianity as practiced in St. Augustine's territory was the direct child of Rome. By the seventh century the Roman Church, following the reforming dictates of Pope Gregory I, had become a centralized, strongly hierarchical institution demanding absolute conformity of thought and deed. Its ritual was rigid, its standards of obedience to a central organization exacting. No taint of heresy was tolerated and freedom of thought was discouraged. This tight-knit establishment was a necessity to the proper functioning of the ecclesiastical empire that had in a spiritual sense replaced the military and civil empire of the Romans.

In Ireland, untouched by Rome, Christianity had grown up outside these rigid boundaries, as had the Irish-Celts themselves; the island's creed harked back to an earlier Christianity, at once more austere and more tolerant. There had never been the fear in Ireland, as on the Continent, that heresy might be the back door to heathen practices — because there was no fear of heathen practices. In Ireland there was no attempt at centralization, no dictation of thought, no persecution for slight differences in ritual; entire freedom of action existed for every monastery in relation to every other (although the straitest obedience obtained within the walls). Irish Christianity was pure, spiritual, intensely personal, dedicated only to the absolute word of God. Rome's was materialistic, tightly organized, widely social in intent, intolerantly conformist. Ireland might have continued along her own road, forgotten and harmless like an anchorite immured in a desert cave; but the Irish would not have it so. Their country and their beliefs might have been out of the mainstream, but they themselves were very much in it, bearing their message of pure spirituality to barbarians and

Roman Christians alike, ready to fight for it — indeed eager to fight, like their own heroes of pagan times.

And herein lay the conflict. Ireland owed allegiance to Rome only as the original source of her conversion; otherwise there was respect but no abject obedience. Subservience had never been a Celtic trait. The ancient ways of the Irish clergy — their asceticism, their love of nature, their instinct toward martyrdom, their uncomplicated acceptance of the Scriptures — were outmoded on the Continent and even considered suspect, particularly when coupled with observances of the ritual that were different from those practiced by decree from Rome. No one could accuse the Irish of heresy, as there were no truer Christians in all of Europe in their time. But the slight differences in observance became a focus for the vast basic vexation. It was not the people who objected: on the contrary, the generous and purehearted Irish missionaries were loved everywhere by high and low alike. It was the establishment that was galled by these old-fashioned, conservative, exasperatingly positive Celtic saints. Too outspokenly virtuous, they provoked feelings of guilt.

King Oswy recognized that he would have to force the issue. He loved the Irish but understood that the organized discipline of Rome would have greater efficacy in a country so recently converted and still chaotic. In calling the Synod of Whitby in 664, he was precipitating, probably without realizing it, a choice between two civilizations. The Irish tonsure and the Irish dating of Easter were the ostensible points at issue: these tiny lapses in conformity were but excuses for a fundamental spiritual difference. An entire concept of Christianity was at the bar.

Whitby, where King Oswy's fateful meeting took place, was a double abbey for monks and nuns similar to and perhaps modelled after St. Brigid's at Kildare. It had been founded seven years before by Hilda, a royal-born Northumbrian lady who had lived a secular life for her first thirty-three years. Her religious education was mainly Irish, her patron was St. Aidan of Lindisfarne, and her monastery rule was based partly on that of St. Columbanus at Luxeuil in eastern France (which we will describe in the next chapter) — a way of life far more stringent in its prescripts on asceticism and obedience than that in any other Continental monastery. St. Hilda, a zealous educator, attached a school and library to her monastery, which became institutions of high prestige, attended by people from all walks of life. Among the students was Caedmon, England's first poet, who had been a cowherd on the abbey land and who was encouraged by Hilda to write Christian poetry in the vernacular. The abbess herself was wise as well as learned, and her advice was sought by statesmen and rulers.

She was an outstanding example of the effective authority that could be achieved by a woman in the religious field even though no woman could be ordained.

Considering her high connections and her wide prestige, it was natural that St. Hilda's Whitby should be chosen by King Oswy for his crucial synod. With her Irish and Frankish affinities, the hostess of the gathering was predisposed to the Irish cause, but it came to pass that she changed her mind. She had neither the obstinacy of the Celts nor their deep-rooted, conservative certainty; and she could not, after all, escape back to Ireland like her loved Irish brethren. If her work was to continue in the English Church, she would have to learn to live with the victors.

Whitby, when the high prelates came there in 664, was a conglomeration of little buildings — similar to Irish monastic villages — atop the steep hill that dominates the broad mouth of the river Esk, in what is today North Yorkshire. It is a commanding hilltop, the moors and the ocean spread clear on every side, and it had probably been a signal station of the Romans for protection from land attacks and warning against sea raiders. Except for a few foundation stones, nothing remains of Hilda's great establishment — which was, like its Irish and Frankish models, great in spirit and in influence but not in architectural pretensions. A noble early Gothic ruin inhabits its high hill today, the massive pillars supporting nothing, the arched windows, framed in lacy stonework, looking out on sea and sky, the tall roofless walls reflected, along with clouds and seabirds, in the little lake set in its velvet green lawns. It is hauntingly far away from the combination seaside resort and fishing village below it; and equally distant from St. Hilda's austerely plain establishment.

The charges at the Synod of Whitby chiefly concerned the dating of Easter. In the late fifth century Rome had changed the calculation of Easter Day to accord with a more accurate cycle of years. But the Celtic Church, conservative as in most of its Christian practices, elected to stay with the system that had prevailed at the time of St. Patrick. The second bone of contention was the tonsure. The Roman tonsure was that of Roman slaves; later this humble origin was disclaimed and the token image of the crown of thorns substituted as the pious if grisly model. Irish monks shaved the entire front of their heads, leaving the back hair to flow long behind their ears, an unprepossessing style deriving, claimed their enemies, from the dark and mysterious figure of Simon Magus, the Samaritan magician of the early decades of the first century A.D. who tried to buy the Holy Spirit from the Apostles (hence the derivation of the word *simony*) and who reputedly died while attempting to imitate the resurrection of Jesus by having himself buried alive, believing he would rise again on the third day. Not only did the sinister legends of his life condemn him in the eyes of the faithful, but, even more, did his presumed founding of the sect of the Gnostics, who taught that individual salvation comes through self-knowledge rather than through faith. This belief was condemned as dangerously heretical by the Christian fathers of the second and third centuries, but it cropped up throughout the Middle Ages and later, in more intellectual Christian circles, in such forms as Neoplatonism. The coupling of the Irish custom with a noted and pernicious heretic was a device designed to derogate, among the more credulous, the Irish ways: an assigning of guilt by innuendo.

Though the controversy centered on these two issues, other deviations annoyed the Roman party, particularly the unimportance of bishops in the Irish monastic system, hardly higher than servants under the hegemonic abbots.

The chief spokesman for the Irish cause was Bishop Colman, abbot of Lindisfarne, the second successor to its founder, St. Aidan. Wilfred, abbot of Ripon, made the arguments for the English-Roman position. The judge was King Oswy. Bishop Colman was calm, certain, reasoned; his opponent was a pitiless prober, sharp and shrewdly legalistic. Wilfred, though highly educated and well prepared for his case, tended to indulge his temper, barbing his arguments with sneering insults: "The Easter we keep," he said, "is the same as we have seen universally celebrated. . . . The only exception are these men [the Irish] and their accomplices in obstinacy, I mean the Picts and the Britons, who in these, the two remotest islands of the ocean . . . make this foolish attempt to fight the whole world."[6]

Colman replied with equanimity to this Rome-inspired snobbery: "I wonder that you are willing to call our efforts foolish, seeing that we follow that apostle [St. John the Evangelist] who was reckoned worthy to recline on the breast of the Lord."

Wilfred, more cunning and better prepared than his opponent, who had not planned his case, relying on his natural eloquence and the absolute rightness of his convictions, argued right around Colman. He cited the ambiguous complexity of the Evangelist's stand, and claimed that the whole world outside Ireland stood on the Roman side. Colman thereupon invoked the authority of St. Columba, a name revered throughout England — and opened the way for Wilfred's deathblow: "Even if that Columba of yours . . . was a holy man of mighty works, is he to be preferred to the most blessed chief of the apostles, to whom the Lord said, 'Thou art Peter, and upon this rock I will build my Church, and the gates of hell shall not prevail against it, and to thee I will give the keys of my kingdom of heaven'?"

King Oswy, impressed, turned to Colman. "Is it true, Colman, that the Lord said these words to Peter?"

"It is true, O King," answered Colman.

"Have you anything to show," the king went on, "that an equal authority was given to your Columba?"

"Nothing," said the defeated Irishman.

The king then asked, "Do you both agree . . . that these words were addressed to Peter . . . and that our Lord gave him the keys to the kingdom of heaven?"

"Yes."

"Then, I tell you, since he is the doorkeeper I will not contradict him, but intend to obey his commands in everything to the best of my knowledge and ability; otherwise, when I come to the gates of the kingdom of heaven, there may be no one to open them because the one who on your showing holds the keys has turned his back on me."

King Oswy's decision was not as flippant as it sounds today. This devout Christian was not so much simpleminded as simple-faithed. It was a firm and powerful belief from the fourth century well through the Middle Ages that the presence of St. Peter's body in Rome implied his literal residence in that city, and that when appealed to he could dispense advice and make decisions rather in the manner of the Oracle at Delphi. It was unquestioningly believed that the saint held in his hands the actual keys to heaven; hence Oswy, a pious and accepting Christian, was justified in making his own decision on this universally accepted premise.

But it was a tragic decision, and in the end the winners were the losers. Bishop Colman, accepting defeat, departed for Iona and thence Ireland, taking with him the Irish monks of Lindisfarne as well as thirty English brethren, and founded a monastery on the island of Inishbofin off the coast of County Galway. York supplanted Lindisfarne as northern England's spiritual center, and the conformist discipline of the Roman organization was at last supreme in all of England. The demise of Irish Lindisfarne was completed when, in 793, it achieved the unfortunate distinction of being the object of the first Viking raid, in which freebooters sacked and destroyed the monastery and murdered most of the monks. It revived in the eleventh century under the Normans, but in a subsidiary position as a daughter house of the monastery of Durham, tenanted and ruled by monks from that center (and it is from that time that the only remaining ruins date).

With the defection of the Irish after Whitby, a pure and primitive virtue went out of the English Church. Though undoubtedly deviant, stubborn and unsystematic, the Celtic holy men followed their faith with literal absolutism. Their simplicity, humility and charity were joined to a robust love of life and an honest delight in their own pagan past that appealed greatly to the rough Teutonic heathens (the same spirit insured their warm reception by pagan peasants on the Continent). Though they had been defeated and in effect driven away, their influence lingered in a diluted form for many years. The accord of the seventh century between English and Irish, which entered all spheres of spiritual endeavor from scholarship to illuminated manuscripts, was to be reflected in their political rapport, a cordial informal alliance that lasted for four hundred years — until the Normans came.

This is a big accumulation of history to stem from one man. Columba must have had much more than a mind like a computer and a cold eye for the main chance. We have seen that he had the delicate perceptions of a poet. From the evidence of his chief biographer, even allowing for the usual unquestioning adulation and the fact that Adamnan was born twenty-seven years after Columba died, there is revealed a touch of kindliness: a grace that may have been superfluous in the creation of his superbly efficient organization, but that is an intrinsic constituent of sainthood.

He was thoughtful and humble toward his own people, bathing the feet of the brethren after their daily labor, carrying the bags of flour from the mill to the kitchen. One day he saw an old woman cutting nettles near the monastery. When he asked her what they were for, she answered that her one cow was to calve soon; until then she had to live on nettle pottage. "Alas for me," said Columba, ". . . and I hoping to gain the kingdom of God [while all she hoped for was a calf]. . . . forsooth I shall eat no other food save that henceforward." The brethren were distressed, as their abbot ate at best sparingly. But his health did not suffer; and one day he found the cook clandestinely putting butter into the hollowed-out stick with which he stirred the nettle soup. He rebuked the brother with gentleness, adding that "he would not take heaven from him. . . . And Columba did fulfil his vow; for the while he lived he ate naught save for broth alone."

When the first of his original companions lay dying, Columba, who sat beside him, had to leave the hut, too sorrowful to watch. In a short while his grief changed to gladness: as the old monk died, the saint had seen angels and devils contending for his soul, and he saw the angels at last carry his friend off to the "joys of the heavenly country."

Columba's sensitivity to animals was one of his pleasantest characteristics. A story told by Adamnan illustrating this trait is worth quoting for the beautiful simplicity of its language, and for its expression of Columba's unquenchable longing for his native land. "On the third day from this new dawning," Columba told one of the brethren,

> "thou must keep a lookout in the western part of this island, sitting on the seashore: for from the northern regions of Ireland a certain guest, a crane, driven by the winds through long, circling aerial flights, will arrive very weary and fatigued after the ninth hour of the day; and its strength almost exhausted, . . . it will fall and lie before thee on the shore, and thou wilt take care to lift it up kindly and carry it to a neighboring house, and there wilt thou hospitably harbor it and attend to it for three days and three nights, and carefully feed it; at the end of the three days, refreshed, and unwilling to sojourn longer with us, it will return with fully regained strength to the sweet region of Ireland whence it originally came. And I thus earnestly commend it to thee for that it came from the place of our own fair land." . . . Considering for a little while its course in the air, it returned across the ocean to Ireland in a straight line of flight, on a calm day.

The saint would not have been Irish if he had not loved horses. When he was aged and near death he sat down to rest one day on his way from the barn,

> and while the saint sat there . . . behold, a white horse, a faithful servant, runs up to him, the one which used to carry the milk pails to and fro between the byre and the monastery. He comes up to the saint, wonderful to tell, lays his head against his breast — inspired, as I believe, by God, by whose dispensation every animal has the sense to perceive things according as its Creator Himself has ordained — knowing that its master was soon about to leave him, and that he would see him no more, it began to whinny, and to shed copious tears into the lap of the saint as though [the animal] had been a man, and weeping and foaming at the mouth. And the attendant, seeing this, began to drive away the weeping mourner; but the saint forbade him, saying: "Let him alone . . . for he loves me, let him pour out the tears of his bitter lamentation into my bosom. Lo! thou, man as thou art, and possessing a rational soul, couldst in no wise know anything about my departure, save what I myself have just now told thee. But to this brute beast, devoid

of reason, the Creator Himself has . . . revealed that its master is about to go away from him." So saying, he blessed his servant the horse, as it sadly turned to go away from him.

Columba died in 597 at Iona. After the Norse ravaged the island in a series of raids starting in 795, his bones were removed to Dunkeld in the southern Highlands, thence taken back to Ireland, where they were interred, it is said, at Downpatrick, in one tomb with those of Patrick and Brigid.

And Iona — its holy places violated and sacked repeatedly, from Viking to Puritan times, until nothing is left that speaks of Columba — Iona, the little green and rocky island that was the place of his sorrowful exile and his triumphant renascence, still breathes his presence with a serene inviolability that nothing has yet touched.

CHAPTER X
THE TRAVELLERS·
ST. COLUMBANUS
OF LUXEUIL

THE THIRD OF THE GREAT SIXTH-CENTURY TRAVELLERS WAS COLUMBANUS. His mission started, as had the other two, with the desire for penitential exile, which took him to live among the barbarian peasants of the rugged mountain country of eastern Gaul. His final achievement far outshone his primary purpose; for he was the first to expose the Continent to the peculiarly Irish brand of the Christian faith, with its inseparable, contradictory qualities: passion and pure spirituality, self-forgetful humility and stubbornness, kindness and irascibility. Columbanus embodied all these traits; they blended into an exceptional missionary genius that enabled him to convert hostile heathen farmers into enthusiastic Christians, and to infuse with his own glowing spirit the decadent, amoral Christianity of so-called civilized Europe, the draggled remnants of the Roman organization. In addition he was an accomplished classical scholar; the first in a long succession of Irish monk-savants who would bring back to the Continent its lost traditions of learning.

Columbanus was born in Leinster in 543. His mother had had a dream before he was born, in which she saw the sun rising from her bosom, to light up all the world. She took exceptional care of her child of light, refusing to send him out to fosterage, even to close relatives. He was educated at home and, having no other children to distract him, learned well the disciplines of grammar, rhetoric, geometry and the Latin Scriptures. The solitude of his childhood, however, turned him inward and gave him a pensive melancholy; all his life the saint was to seek out the lonely places, where he could dream and pray and commune with wild animals.

His aloneness made him particularly shy of girls, whose company he shunned with repressed horror. Unfortunately, as he was endowed with masculine beauty, girls would not leave him alone. According to his first biographer, the seventh-century monk Jonas, Columbanus was pursued to the point of consternation by "the lusts of lascivious maidens, specially of those whose fine figure and superficial beauty are wont to enkindle mad desires in the minds of wretched men."[1] The tortures of adolescence combined with his natural shyness to produce the obsessive sexual neurosis too familiar among young Irish would-be clerics of this period. Beset with conflicting desire and despair, he finally went to seek the counsel of a woman hermit noted for her flinty chastity. Her advice was unsparing: "For fifteen years," she told him,

"I have been homeless in the place of my pilgrimage, and never by the aid of Christ have I looked back. Yes, and if my weak sex had not prevented, I would have gone on truer pilgrimage across the sea. But you, glowing with the fire of youth, stay quietly on your native soil; out of weakness you lend your ear even against your own will, to the voices of the flesh, and think you can associate with the female sex without sin. But do you recall the wiles of Eve, Adam's fall, how Samson was deceived by Delilah, how David was led to injustice by the beauty of Bathsheba, how wise Solomon was enslaved by the love of a woman? Away, O youth! Away! Flee from corruption. . . . Forsake the path which leads to the gates of Hell."

She spoke directly to the boy's heart. Columbanus ran home and, with a tactless precipitousness that was characteristic, collected a small bundle of belongings and informed his mother that he was leaving forever. Weeping and pleading, she threw herself across the doorsill to prevent his going. Her son advised her not to give way to her grief and, stepping over her supine body, made the chilly announcement that "she would never see him again in this life, but wherever the way of salvation led him, there he would go."

Columbanus's road was not quite so direct as was his callous farewell to his mother. Some preparation was necessary even for a career of purgation. He turned first to the contemplative life of study, for in his adolescent agonies he had found that the cool abstraction of mental exercise was the best antidote to the fevered temptations of the body. He went to Lough

Erne, County Fermanagh, to the monastery of an erudite hermit named Sinell, a disciple of Finian of Clonard. His studies with this scholarly recluse consisted mainly of a thorough grounding in the Scriptures, and included the compiling of a commentary on the Psalter, a formidably learned work that has been lost. In his spare time he wrote sacred poetry, a practice he was to continue all his life.

By the time Columbanus was twenty, Sinell judged him ready for St. Comgall's great school at Bangor. There he mingled with the finest minds of the time, and became himself one of the outstanding products of the extremely progressive Irish education. His continuing study of the Scriptures was augmented by a thorough grounding in the works of Cassian, Jerome, Gildas, Basil, Augustine, Athanasius, Caesarius and Eusebius. Study of the secular classics was included in the broad-minded curriculum, and the young scholar acquired a knowledge, which was to be a continuing pleasure to him, of the great Latin poets, historians and rhetoricians, both pagan and Christian, including Virgil, Ovid, Horace, Juvenal, Martial, Sallust, Prudentius, Fortunatus, Sedulius, Ausonius and Claudian. Though Greek was not a familiar study in Irish schools of the period (nor on the Continent either at this time), Columbanus was one of the few who acquired some knowledge of it.

He must have been happy at Bangor, for he lingered on year after year. Though he had been a lonely, brooding child, he discovered in himself a talent for teaching, and in time he rose to the position of principal teacher, much loved by everyone and specially valued by his abbot. He was forty-eight before the spirit, which had seemed so peremptory in his youth, overtook him once more to escape from human ties and abandon the world he knew for the penitence of exile. During those nearly thirty years he had not only been perfecting his scholarship but had been an attentive observer of the operation of the monastery, developing the techniques of command and a keen eye for the art of diplomacy. For by middle age his motive for renunciation had mellowed into an impulse to be of some good use even amid the sorrows of exile; he had come to believe that his destiny lay in teaching the Gospel to those who knew it not.

But when he spoke to his abbot about his desire to forsake the safe, austere serenity of the cloister in search of a hostile and hazardous world over the sea, "he did not receive the answer he wished, for it was hard for Comgall to bear the loss of so great a comfort." However, the abbot well understood the compulsion for exile and at last consented to let his most brilliant monk depart. He provided Columbanus with a boat and allowed twelve monks to accompany him.

In 591 Columbanus made his landfall on the Breton coast, but this province was not his goal: it was civilized and Christian, having been settled by Celtic refugees from Britain, his own kind, fleeing the Anglo-Saxon invasions. He made his way east and south to Burgundy, a Frankish region in the eastern division of the Merovingian lands, which comprised parts of today's France, Germany, Austria and Switzerland. The Frankish kingdom had been founded by Clovis I at the end of the fifth century and divided into three separate realms in the course of conflict among his sons and even more ruthless feuding between his grandsons. At the time of Columbanus's arrival the combined kingdoms of Burgundy and Austrasia were ruled by Childebert II, great-grandson of Clovis; but the real power was his mother, Queen Brunhilda. This lady, a Spanish princess of beauty, charm and wit in her youth, had matured into a high-handed political dragon who paid lip service to Christianity and who relied on assassination, more convenient and less expensive than war, to keep order in her kingdom.

Columbanus preached, at Childebert's request, a sermon in Latin so affecting that the king asked him to stay. The courts of kings, however, did not attract Columbanus. His objective was bleaker and purer. He attended on the king just long enough to get his permission to settle somewhere in his territory. The grant was seconded by Brunhilda in a gesture of goodwill that, she thought, cost her nothing. She saw no future awkwardness arising from this tiny band of weaponless, apparently shiftless wandering Irish monks who spoke no living language but their own and were very far from home.

Columbanus found his destination in the foothills of the Vosges Mountains in present-day Franche-Comté, near the Swiss and German borders of France, a region of rocky hillsides, great beech forests and steep-sided valleys with fast little rivers curling through them. The monks chose to settle in a green hollow between sharp hills, where there had been a Roman fort, Anegrates, now Annegray. They rebuilt the ruined walls as the cashel of their monastery, and a temple to Diana was consecrated to St. Martin, France's patron saint and a favorite of Columbanus. The square stone foundations of their monastery are still there, along with some simple stone sarcophagi of the same period, on a grassy mound guarded by tall cedars; to the east rises the wall of the Vosges, darkly wooded; on the west opens the broad and fertile valley of the Breuchin River. The countryside is hauntingly like Ireland, and the exiles must have loved it on sight. But in the sixth century it was wilder than Ireland, lacking the tilled fields and the herds of cattle. The forests were inhabited by wolves and bears and, more dangerous, a human population of savage Suevians, Teutonic barbarians from central Germany, a region that had never felt the touch of Rome. Columbanus was not daunted either by the animals, whom he regarded, in the Irish saintly manner, as speaking friends, nor by the people, for he saw rough and uneducated peasants as more teachable than kings, kinder and simpler than courtiers. And the uncompromising solitude of the hills, the rocks and the forests struck a deep answering chord in him.

But the living there was very rough. The monks' Suevian neighbors were almost troglodytic. Living in small, autonomous family groups, they subsisted in the summer on primitive and inadequate farming, piecing out their living by robbing travellers. The cruel Vosges winters discouraged travel and deprived the peasants of their main livelihood. Then came the Irish with their unfortified monastic village and their freehanded piety — an absurdly vulnerable quarry for the starving savages. But the monks had little worth the taking, and they themselves had almost no food. Sometimes they existed for days on herbs and the bark of trees. They tried to make a virtue of this. Once, during a specially lean period, one of the brothers fell ill. The others, having nothing to eat anyway, decided to call their privation a purposeful fast, and to spend their hungry days and nights praying for him. After three days they were all near death; then "suddenly they saw a man standing before their gates with horses loaded with a supply of bread and condiments. He said he had been led by a sudden impulse of his heart to bear aid from his own substance to those who were, for Christ's sake, suffering from so great poverty in the wilderness." He asked them to pray for his wife, who was sick. So eloquently did the grateful monks intercede for this lady that she recovered, her husband found out later, at the very hour that their fervent litany arose.

This was the beginning. The Suevian peasant who had aided them, a tentative believer, told his neighbors and, pagan or not, they began to bring their illnesses and their troubles to Annegray. At first they came only for healing. Columbanus had one of those serviceable saintly talents: he could cure wounds with his spit, even to the extent of suturing a finger almost amputated by a sickle. His patients were happy with this. The doctrines of Christ did not yet attract them: mysticism and pacifism were alien concepts to the Teutonic mentality. But in the course of being repaired, they could not help observing the monks' way of life, and they began to find it appealing.

Mild and forgiving as the Irish exiles had first appeared, they were at least as tough as their new compatriots and far better organized. The pagans saw a group of men bound by a discipline extreme in its rigor, living in cheerful peace and communal sharing. They saw steep, stony land painstakingly cleared by monks working alongside their abbot; they saw healthy corn come up in the carefully cultivated little new fields; they saw the harvest and the threshing and the storing in the barns against winter. They saw unfailing strength and kindness in men whose situation was as critically disadvantaged as their own. They saw, above all, a leader tough-minded and extraordinarily pure, directing all this with an unshakable authority that had nothing to do with aggression. The spirit that motivated these admirable friars began to mean something, particularly to the young men — tired of shiftless husbandry, part-time banditry and a religion no longer meaningful — whose minds were ready to be changed.

Christ had appealed to the lowly country people, but that had been in another age. The Christianity of sixth-century Europe was urban and political, far removed from its source. The barbarian farmers of northern Europe had never had a chance to know the strength of its early simplicity. But the Irish had been nurtured on it. The Irish monastic system, closer in spirit to the Egyptian desert hermitages than to the formalized institution that evolved in Rome-dominated Europe, had produced a breed at once pragmatic and visionary: undilutedly devoted to the original Christian ideal, yet healthy-minded, hardworking and competent. Another trait attracted the barbarians: the Irish were still in touch with their pre-Christian past. It is not known that Columbanus was, like Columba of Iona, deeply versed in the heathen literature of his country. But there must have been, among his disciples, some who knew and loved the old stories and who were happy to exchange their fairy tales with those, equally heroic, of their Teutonic friends. This was almost as good for conversion as the sterner example of Christian merit.

People flocked to the monastery to be healed, conforted, advised or converted. As Columbanus never turned anyone away, the little green bowl of Annegray soon could not accommodate the numbers, and the monks had to seek new quarters. Leaving their high valley they descended the broad vale of the Breuchin, to settle at Luxovium, now Luxeuil-les-Bains, eight miles west, where another abandoned Roman fort stood near a hot spring in a forest glade. The hot spring had been worshipped, apparently, by the various pagans who had occupied the site, because Jonas reports a "great number of stone idols, which in the old heathen times had been worshipped with horrible rites." When Columbanus and his companions came there, however, its only inhabitants were "a multitude of bears and owls and wolves." The monks, using the Roman ruins, built a church dedicated to St. Peter, a school, a refectory and a guesthouse.

None of this remains today, and it is hard to imagine in the comfortable,

S.ᵗ COLOMBAN

Opposite: *St. Columbanus — bronze statue cast by Claude Granges in 1945, at Luxeuil-les-Bains, France*

bourgeois health resort — with its big dim thirteenth-century church, its flamboyantly decorated Renaissance residences, its enormous eighteenth-century bathing establishment and its turn-of-the-century hotels — Columbanus's frugal settlement. But the memory of him lingers, and a vigorous bronze statue cast by the sculptor Claude Granges in 1945 stands outside the church. The saint seems to be declaiming in the wind, his monk's habit flying, long hair streaming back of the tonsured forehead, chiselled face stern, right arm raised in a gesture of vehemently righteous indignation. It was no doubt a familiar pose to his intimates and enemies alike; and it has such ardent life that it could be speaking aloud to the flourishing burghers and cosseted visitors of today's Luxeuil. On its pedestal are the words: *"Tous voyaient éclater en lui la puissance de Dieu"* ("All saw the power of God burst into flame within him"), a translation of Jonas's lines at the climax of a particularly wrath-provoking episode of the saint's career.

To the Luxeuil of nearly 1,400 years ago came streams of people as today, but for the health of their souls rather than their bodies. The penitents and converts included not only the local peasants but the children of nobles "despising the . . . trappings of the world and the pomp of . . . wealth." Besides the hundreds of suppliants who came and went, there were about 220 monks. Though there were many recruits, still more were turned down. The discipline was too rigorous for any except the strongest souls. Columbanus did not want misfits and fugitives who were only on the hunt for cloistered sanctuary. So many applicants came and were accepted, however, that the order had to found a third establishment at nearby Fontanas (Fontaines), where the brothers reclaimed the surrounding marshes to make rich arable land.

With such a multitude of souls to watch over, and his time perforce divided between three monasteries, Columbanus saw that he must devise a written rule so that others could handle the administration in his absence. His *Regula Monachorum* is the first known Irish rule to be written. (The famous eight rules of Ireland have not survived except for short fragments of that of Columba of Iona, and it is possible that, consisting more of a general ascetic code than of specific legislation, they never were inscribed in detail.)

Columbanus's rule is ruthless, almost sadistic, to a modern eye. Mortification is the most important aspect; the soul must humble itself to be worthy of God. Therefore obedience must be immediate and unqualified. Blamelessness of mind was as obligatory as purity of body, and bad thoughts were punished. The daily life, for the lowliest novitiate up to the abbot, was one of unremitting hard work, fasting and prayer. The one meal a day, eaten in silence in the evening after the day's long toil, was a soup of vegetables and meal, with a bit of hard biscuit. Sleep was a necessary evil. To those who came new to him, Columbanus promised no easy salvation. The junior brother was

> not to disagree in mind, not to speak as one pleases . . . not to go anywhere with complete freedom. His part is to say to a senior, however adverse his instructions, Not as I will but as thou wilt. . . . Let him not do as he wishes, let him eat what he is bidden, keep as much as he has received, complete the tale of his work, be subject to whom he does not like. Let him come weary to his bed and sleep walking, and let him be forced to rise while his sleep is not yet finished. Let him keep silence when he has suffered wrong, let him fear the superior of his community as a lord, love him as a father, believe that what he commands is healthy for himself.

Discipline was carried to lengths that seem to us exasperatingly trivial. It covered such picayune lapses from virtue as not waiting for grace at the table, speaking during the meal, giggling during the holy office, sneaking a late bite in the kitchen after the last evening service, cutting the table with a knife. It was downright unkind in its strictures against the involuntary cough at the start of the singing of a psalm, the slip of the tongue when the neophyte automatically referred to a thing as "mine," the accidental fall while carrying the sacrament. "He who neglects little sins gradually lapses from good" was one of Columbanus's aphorisms, accompanied by the exhortation to frequent (two or three times daily) confession.

These fussy prescriptions sound more like the nagging of a perfectionist Victorian parent than rules for presumably responsible adults, and possibly the motive was similar. The converts were entering a new life, and they must be brought up to it, like children. Columbanus designed his code to deal with every aspect of human weakness. If at times his rules seem to get tangled up in their own feet, it is neither from cruelty or bureaucratic silliness, but from the saint's irrepressible zeal for the spiritual purification of the souls entrusted to him.

The relentless regulation of daily life was enforced by corporal punishment: six strokes for minor infractions, up to fifty for the iniquity of lying, disobedience or harmful gossip. Physical chastisement was a specialty of the Irish, and though it was stringent, it was immediate. The contemporary Benedictine practice of imprisonment for wrongdoing was inconceivable to the Irish. Later orders would temper both the strictness of the Irish rule and the harshness of the punishments, but in Columbanus's time they were welcome rather than otherwise.

Frankish Christianity, at the time Columbanus and his monks brought in a breath of fresh air, was in a demoralized condition, a reflection of the general deterioration of manners that followed the breakup of the Roman Empire. The Franks had learned from a Roman establishment already on the decline and itself debauched, the uses of power and the advantages of wealth, and they used them without any mitigating qualities of dignity or self-restraint. Greed was the ruling force and corruption was the life-style. The Frankish kings were not wealthy. Lacking money, they dispensed land, and by the late sixth century the great-grandsons of the strong unifier Clovis I were token monarchs only. The real rulers were the lords and chieftains who had been their beneficiaries, most of them men of little responsibility whose only aim was aggrandizement and whose main pursuit was pleasure. If a king wanted to extend his boundaries, he had to hire an army and go to war. Territories were fought over and changed hands again and again; the farmers became frightened transients ready to flee before the next savage wave of armed ruffians. Consequently, the land suffered, was poorly farmed and became exhausted. City dwellers were in even worse condition. Sieges brought plague as the water supplies became contaminated and people were forced to eat rats and diseased domestic animals. Occupying troops, who surged in when the gates were opened by bribed betrayers, tortured, raped, looted, burned. Among the lower classes, morals were degenerate, security was nonexistent, and hope was dead.

The prevailing rot was bound to corrode religion. Churchmen were as worldly as secular chiefs and their ethics were no different. Bishoprics were bought by wealthy parvenus for social betterment. Clerics, pocketing fat fees, took sides in the power struggles of the local princes; and they also turned a blind eye, when profitable, on the violation of the sanctuary of their own churches. The urban bishops took more interest in show and pomp than in tending the souls of their parishioners, and the country priests were ignorant, superstitious and of flabby moral fiber. Even their Christianity was questionable: they resorted to such druidic practices as reading the future in the entrails of birds. Though Roman Catholicism was the predominant religion, its practice was so adulterated that the Trinity meant little more to the country people than did the deposed heathen deities. Christ and the pagan spirits were worshipped together; for a confused and insecure populace there was reassurance in diversification: if one god didn't work, another might.

Here and there the spirit of the early French saints — Martin, Hilary, Honoré, Cassian — still lived. Tours, Lérins and Auxerre were still great monasteries, and there were others: about forty at the time Columbanus arrived. But on account of the rampant degeneracy of morals out in the world, they had grown inward in an unhealthy way. Asceticism had become a matter of often disgusting self-torture rather than an honest aspiration toward a state of grace. Renunciation of the world reached the zenith of pointlessness when a prospective recluse had herself sealed for life inside a wall, only a small opening left for food.

With religion in the monasteries unproductive and often mentally unhinged, and religion outside materialistic and depraved, the Irish monks must have appeared — after some initial hostility — as saviors. They lived in chastity, silence, poverty and humility under a sternly enforced discipline; yet their way of life was one of healthy tranquillity. They made the land produce, and what they did not keep for their frugal needs they gave away. They healed the sick and helped the poor. But they had no prejudice against the rich: all souls were equal to them. There was no ulterior motive in anything they did, and all their actions were suffused with the transcendent serenity that came from their leader.

Columbanus's boyhood pensiveness and his preference for solitude had stayed with him and mellowed as he grew old. His work in the monasteries would have become frantic but for his penchant for going off by himself for long walks, sometimes spending several days in hidden places in the forest "so he might . . . wholly be free from disquieting cares, devote himself to prayer, and might be ready for religious thought. He was so attenuated by fasting that he scarcely seemed alive. Nor did he eat anything except a small measure of the herbs of the fields, or of the little apples. . . . His drink was water."

A grass-grown lane leads steeply upward through the woods to one of these secret places, a cave on a hillside above the village of Sainte Marie in the valley of the Breuchin. It is hardly a cave: a triangular indentation in the rocky hill, just wide enough for a man to lie down in, narrowing to a point at the back where water drips constantly, its roof a jutting rock. The saint's bed was of stone and grass, his water came from a sweet cold spring just below the cave. Birds sing in the tall ancient beeches that surround the retreat, the smell of summer flowers floats from the meadow below, a church bell sounds through the valley. Beside the cave is a latter-day concession to pilgrims: a little roofed shrine where the faithful have left flowers and pencilled messages asking small favors of the saint. The scene has an air not so much wild as prettily Arcadian, and no doubt Columbanus was attracted as much by the rustic charm of his retreat as by its complete isolation.

For his sojourns in the forest were not devoted solely to penitence and inward meditation. One of his monks reported to Jonas that "he has often seen Columbanus wandering about in the wilderness . . . calling the wild beasts and the birds. These came immediately at his command and he stroked them with his hand. The beasts and birds joyfully played, frisking about him. . . . He often called [a squirrel] from the tops of the high trees and took it in his hand and put it on his neck and let it go into and come out of his bosom." In the way of Irish saints, he chatted with the animals and sometimes admonished them reasonably, as if they were children. Encountering a bear about to devour the carcass of a stag killed by a wolf, he entreated the animal not to injure the hide because the monks needed it for shoes. "Then the beast, forgetting its ferocity, became gentle and fawning and . . . left the body without a murmur." When his work gloves disappeared from the field one day, the saint knew that the only animal that would have stolen them was the raven, "the bird which was sent out by Noah and did not return to the Ark." While the monks looked for the bird, Columbanus waited quietly; soon a raven flew down and laid the gloves at his feet and "humbly, in sight of all, awaited its punishment." There was none. Columbanus merely told it to go.

Ever the teacher, he sometimes found it necessary to educate an animal. At one time he and his monks had no food except the little apples that grew wild in the fields. A bear was found to be devouring these. So Columbanus "set aside a part of the fruit trees for food for the bear, and ordered it to leave the others for himself." The instruction worked; the hungry monks and the equally hungry bear peaceably shared the orchard. On one of his lonely walks, Columbanus debated with himself which he would rather have attack him, savage robbers or savage wolves. He decided on the latter because their ferocity contained no sin. A pack of wolves attacked him, but so calm and natural was his attitude and so assured his equanimity that they desisted and trotted away. Though the account is of course exaggerated, this was not miracle-working in the unearthly sense, nor were Columbanus's other encounters with the beasts of the forest. An instinctive aptitude for communion with wild animals is a well-known phenomenon in people who live much by themselves in the wilds. Friendliness, fearlessness and, above all, gentleness are quickly sensed by creatures whose perception has to be much more highly developed than ours.

Columbanus would come back from his woodland tours refreshed and calmed, his tenderness toward man enhanced by his cordial contact with other animals. The foibles of people aroused his sympathy instead of his impatience. Men of all degree, from the spoiled duke's son to the uncouth rustic, found his equable temper and sensitive response attractive.

From Columbanus's genius flowed the ordered harmony of his monasteries. It was no wonder that his rule did not appear too severe nor his penances too violent. In addition to the appeal of the leader and the obvious physical and mental health of his monks, the life itself offered no extraordinary hardships. The country people were used to gruelling work and privation, and to the sons of noblemen the stern simplicity was a welcome contrast. In the context of the general brutality of life, the ungentle rule of Luxeuil was not in the least grim. Its strictures were never unjust or vengeful, and all was for the good of the soul. In fact it was a return to the earliest practices of Christianity: to the purity of Christ himself. In the sick and corrupt atmosphere of late-sixth-century France, Luxeuil was a vital spark.

But to the establishment, Luxeuil was a nuisance. There was no provision of French monastic law that Columbanus did not ignore or break. Though he was a saint to his people, he was an obstinate and fractious provincial upstart to the entrenched bishops. Both evaluations were right. The tactless directness of Columbanus's youth was still with him, added to a stubborn independence of mind, a literal adherence to the Creed and an intolerance for compromise.

Far from his native inclination to contemplate the heavens and talk to squirrels, Columbanus found himself engaged in constant and energetic controversy, defending his philosophic stand or correcting others. He was an inveterate letter-writer; the pope himself, Gregory the Great, was the recipient of one of Columbanus's lively and unhumble (yet respectful) communications. As for the church dignitaries: to them Columbanus was an outsider from the scorned British Isles, who had the nerve to display his superiority both in religious observance and in intellectual attainment. They didn't care that he was beloved by the poor and the meek. They cared very much that he was the pet of King Childebert and his son and successor, King Theuderich II of Burgundy. That made them helpless against him.

Monasteries in France were under the direct control of the bishops, unlike those of Ireland. Since Ireland had no cities, the bishop's diocese generally coincided with, and was under, the jurisdiction of the monastery. The bishop was less important than the abbot, and the monasteries were the autonomous centers of religious life. This was the system in which Columbanus had grown up, whose workings he had studied at Bangor, and which he carried over to Luxeuil. He ran straight, and willingly, into trouble. To begin with, the bishop's consent was needed to found a monastery. Then the abbot could have limited governance over only that one community, and he must give yearly reports to his bishop. He must ask his superior's permission to receive gifts or to leave his post. The details of the monks' daily curriculum of fasting and prayer must be overseen by the bishop, who also was the only one who could make important decisions. Not one of these directives did Columbanus follow, and everything he did was unauthorized.

But the hierarchy couldn't get rid of him. Since the royal favor was behind him, the bishops resorted to technical ruses and tried to have him denounced on the score of his reckoning of the Easter date, which was, as noted, different from Rome's official computation. They underestimated their quarry, who was far from their assumption of a timid and innocent rustic. As chief teacher at Bangor and adviser to the abbot, Columbanus was no stranger to political maneuver. He went over the bishops' heads and wrote directly to the pope: "What do you say about an Easter on the 21st or 22nd day of the moon. . . . At that point of time it has arisen after the middle of the night. . . . Why then . . . when . . . the streams of your holy wisdom are . . . shed abroad over the earth with great brightness, do you favor a dark Easter? . . . The festival of the Lord's resurrection is light." * He then pointed out that the Irish system of calculating Easter was the older, being based on the earliest apostolic decisions. His plea was followed by a request for advice: what steps should he take, as father confessor, when a bishop confessed to him that he had bought his bishopric or had sinned against chastity? The letter went on to flatter Gregory's

---

*Columbanus was misled by a forged pamphlet; the Roman celebration of Easter had been set in the late fifth century for the first Sunday after the full moon following the vernal equinox.

framing of the pastoral rule ("the work is sweeter than honey to the needy"), and ended with a request that the pope send him some tracts he had written on Ezekiel, as well as his comments on the Song of Songs.

It was a discursive, eloquent and persuasive letter, and it put Gregory in a dilemma. The pope deplored the corruption in the Frankish religious institution and had repeatedly censured the bishops for their simony. But he could not afford to alienate the Franks, who were emerging as the dominant power in Europe, and to whom he looked to support his efforts to strengthen the Church. On the other hand, he had a personal bias in favor of Columbanus, having been abbot of his own monastery, St. Andrew's, in Rome, and advocate of a regime as austere as that of his Irish compeers. The monastic life was dearer to Gregory than the momentous prestige of the papal palace — but he was pope. He had been elected at a time of extreme crisis, when Europe was devastated by floods, famine and plague, and the miseries of nature were compounded by war as the Lombards invaded Italy. The European Church itself was in a shaky condition, with Europe dominated by barbarians and the center of religious authority in Byzantium, where the patriarch of Constantinople claimed the title of universal bishop. As well as having to face problems immediately urgent, Gregory had the long-range objective of strengthening Western Christianity by converting the barbarians and reestablishing the dominance of Rome. To achieve his goals he needed an undivided Church whose members right down through the ranks would recognize the central authority of Rome. Brilliant, dedicated and practical, Gregory was to realize all his aims, emerging as the first of the medieval popes, keystone of the absolute rule of Rome that was to endure for centuries. As a monk, he was also instrumental in strengthening the monastic movement, freeing the monasteries from the rule of the bishops and fostering a great missionary campaign among the barbarians.

With the latter aims in mind, he had no wish to put down the Irish monks, whose monasteries had the independence he envisaged for all, and whose work among the barbarians of northeastern France was outstandingly successful. The date of the celebration of Easter was, at this crucial time, a minor matter to the pope. But the quarrel in France was not. He had the delicate task of placating the irritated French bishops, whose backing he needed for a unified Church, and at the same time tactfully protecting a stubbornly zealous abbot whose convictions were near to his heart but whose manner was intractable and whose methods were impolitely forthright. Instead of entering the controversy by replying to Columbanus's missive, thus giving the quarrel undue importance, he slid around it by putting the Irish abbot under the protection of the powerful abbot of Lérins.

Though Columbanus was safe for the time, the French bishops did not give up. A few years later the matter of Easter was brought up again at a council of bishops at Chalon-sur-Saône. Columbanus did not attend but wrote another of his passionate letters:

> If there be some variety of traditional practise, as there is over Easter . . . let us then seek together, and let us see which be the more true tradition. . . . I have entered these lands a pilgrim. . . . I beseech you . . . that I may be allowed . . . to enjoy the silence of these woods . . . even as up till now we have been allowed to live twelve years among you. . . . Let Gaul . . . contain us side by side, whom the kingdom of heaven shall contain. . . . But do you, holy fathers, look what you do to your poor veterans and aged pilgrims . . . . it will be better to comfort them than to confound. . . . Far be it that I should maintain the need to quarrel with you, so that conflict among us Christians should rejoice our enemies. . . . Each should remain before God in the condition in which he is called. . . . If the patterns of clergy and of monks are different, . . . Let each maintain what he has grasped, but let all maintain the Gospel, and both parties, like single harmonious members of one body, follow Christ. . . . Refuse to consider us estranged from you; for we are all members of one body, whether Franks or Britons or Irish.

The moving appeal did not touch the bishops, for they no longer needed the pretext of the date of Easter. They had found an easier way to dislodge the objectionable Irishman. Columbanus, outspoken and uncompromising as usual, had alienated his royal friends.

Theuderich II, king of Burgundy, liked Columbanus and often visited him at Luxeuil. Though the abbot warmly returned the friendship, he deplored the young king's moral habits — he had four children by four different ladies — and advised him to take a wife. Theuderich amiably agreed and found himself a rich and very proper princess, Ermenburga, daughter of Witteric, the Visigothic king of Spain, which was a thoroughly Christian country and the most civilized place in western Europe. At this juncture Theuderich's grandmother, Brunhilda, came back into the picture. She had been living with her other grandson, Theudebert II, king of Austrasia, but her combination of high-handedness and craftiness finally exasperated him and he evicted her. She took refuge in Theuderich's court in Burgundy and, unregenerate, immediately began scheming again.

She saw Ermenburga as a threat to her dominance; behind the Spanish princess she saw the influence of Columbanus, in whom she recognized a potential enemy, and she concocted a plan to get rid of both of them. It is probable that she had the bishops behind her: they were certainly on her side, they were not above back-door conspiracy, and their morals were no better than anyone else's. Setting to work on Theuderich, she poisoned his mind so effectively that a year after his marriage he sent his bride back to her father — without her dowry — and took up again with his concubines. Then Brunhilda brought two of the bastard children to Columbanus and asked him to baptize them. He refused angrily, calling them "children of a brothel." He followed this outburst with a letter to Theuderich threatening him with excommunication if he did not mend his ways. Theuderich retaliated by threatening to cut off the monastery's alms, on which its continued existence depended. Columbanus replied that he did not want alms from sinners.

The quarrel grew sillier: Columbanus went to remonstrate personally with the king but stopped in the courtyard, refusing to enter the palace. Theuderich, hearing he was there, had a meal prepared and sent out to him. Columbanus cursed it and "all of the dishes broke into pieces so that the wine and liquor ran out on the ground and the food was scattered here and there. . . . And all saw the power of God burst into flame within him." (This scene, with its flavor of a medieval miracle play, was the occasion memorialized in Granges's dramatic bronze portrait in Luxeuil, shown on page 180.)

Theuderich, furious, had Columbanus thrown into jail at Besançon. The irrepressible abbot promised liberty to all the felons awaiting death if they promised to repent. They agreed enthusiastically, the gates of the jail fell open, and they all streamed out into the town — but not to commit more crimes. A very surprised jailer found the whole company in church atoning to God for their sins. Not trusting to their continued mildness and fearing a revolt, he herded them back into prison and quietly allowed Columbanus to go home.

But Theuderich, goaded by Brunhilda, kept his anger fresh. He went to call on Columbanus, complaining that the abbot had secret rooms forbidden to outsiders, and demanding entry to them. Columbanus refused, saying he would not expose the privacy of his monastery to enemies of religion. The king boldly walked past him and the abbot, stung into fury, threw out the curse that if he stepped into one of those private rooms the kingdom and the whole royal family would be destroyed. Theuderich, already inside, backed out, startled, but added angrily as he left: "You want me to honor you with the crown of martyrdom; do not believe that I am foolish enough to commit such a crime. But I will follow a wiser and more useful plan." He sent soldiers to oust Columbanus and all his monks. Refusing to leave "unless he was dragged out by force," Columbanus caused the soldiers to go blind and stray in dazed circles. One of them appealed to him, saying that they would all be executed if they did not carry out their orders. So "he finally decided to yield, in order not to imperil others, and departed amid universal sorrow and grief."

Luxeuil was not to be closed; only the Irish monks were to go. In fact, the monastery grew and prospered. Though the Irish were no longer there, their spirit survived in the Gallic brothers they had trained; and Luxeuil monks went out from there to found other houses for both men and women in France, Germany and Flanders. Though there never was a formal Columbanian order in Europe, less than a hundred years after the founding of Luxeuil there were ninety-four monasteries patterned after Luxeuil and based on Columbanus's rule. Luxeuil, with its cloisters, its school and its great classical library, was the center of this spiritual empire, and remained so until the middle of the eighth century, when the Benedictine rule became the official monastic standard and Luxeuil lost its status as the fount and inspiration of French monasticism.

At about this time, too, the Arabs, who had invaded and conquered Spain in 711–715, spilled over into France, where they occupied Aquitaine and moved east to destroy the three original Columbanian monasteries of Luxeuil, Annegray and Fontaines. They were followed by the Viking raids of the ninth and tenth centuries, and the houses were hit again and again, finally losing their power of recovery.

The Irish monks were expelled in 610. They had been at Luxeuil for nineteen years, and Columbanus, nearly seventy, was condemned to wander over Europe once again. He was not a vindictive man, and his anger never lasted beyond its immediate object; so no doubt he did not rejoice at the working out of his curse: the destruction of Theuderich's family and the ugly demise of Brunhilda. War broke out between the two brothers, Theuderich and Theudebert. Theudebert was defeated and his kingdom of Austrasia was united with Burgundy, while he himself was murdered by his formidable grandmother. Then Theuderich was killed in a fire and the old lady legally assumed the throne she had controlled backstage through three generations. She did not keep it long: Lothair II, king of Neustria, the western division of the Merovingian lands, invaded Burgundy, defeated Brunhilda's forces, and captured the queen. "Brunhilda he . . . placed first on a camel in mockery and so exhibited to all her enemies around about; then she was bound to the tails of wild horses and thus perished wretchedly."

Even if it had been in his nature, Columbanus did not have leisure to gloat. He and his elderly little troop were beset by difficulties and adventures on the long roundabout journeys and temporary resting places of the next four years. When they left Luxeuil, soldiers stayed with them to see them definitely over the border of Burgundy. Reaching the Loire, they were put on a boat to go down to the Atlantic and so, it was intended, back to Ireland. Columbanus wanted to stop at Tours to pray at the tomb of St. Martin, but the officer in charge of their exodus refused permission. The boat then reversed itself without the assistance of the crew, who were forced to bring it inshore. Columbanus spent the night praying at St. Martin's shrine, breakfasted with the bishop of Tours, and went back to the boat, to find that all the little wealth that the monks had left to them had been stolen. Columbanus was not one to take misfortune passively. He went back to the church and remonstrated with the holy relics, saying (much as he would have reproved a refractory bear) that he had not prayed by the shrine all night in order that the saint should allow him to suffer loss. The name of the thief was made manifest and the money returned.

At Nantes he was to take ship for Ireland, and he wrote a moving and beautiful last letter to those he had left behind at Luxeuil:

> To his most sweet sons and dearest disciples . . . Columbanus the sinner sends greetings in Christ. Peace be to you. . . . Look to it that you be of one heart and one mind . . . for we have been more harmed by those who were not of one mind amongst us. . . . If you see some progress of souls with you, stay there; if you see dangers, come thence; by the dangers I mean the dangers of disagreement . . . on account of Easter. . . . Perhaps they wish to divide you, if you do not keep peace with them, for now without me you seem to stand less firmly there. . . . I confess that I am broken on this account, that I wish to help all. . . . Thus do you [Attala, his successor] be wiser; I do not wish you to undertake so great a burden, under which I have sweated. . . . You have learned that all advice is not suitable for all, since natures are diverse. . . . Be many-sided and adaptable for the direction of those who obey you with faith and love; but you must fear even their very love, because it will be dangerous to you.

But there are troubles on every side, my dearest friend; there is danger if they hate, and danger if they love. . . . I wanted to write you a tearful letter, but for the reason that I know your heart, I have simply mentioned necessary duties, hard of themselves . . . and have used another style, preferring to check rather than to encourage tears. . . . So my grief is shut up within. See, the tears flow, but it is better to check the fountain; for it is no part of a brave soldier to lament in battle. . . . Do you examine your consciences, whether you are more pure and holy in my absence; do not seek me through love, but through necessity alone.

It happened that this affecting farewell was previous. Divine intervention in the shape of a huge wave prevented the ship from leaving the harbor. The captain hastened to land his dangerous passengers, whose contact with the powers above was too tangible for comfort. The storm abated at once and he sailed quickly for Ireland without the saintly travellers.

The little band made its way slowly back across France on foot, stopping here and there at the request of local rulers, founding embryo monasteries as they went. They came to Metz, the capital of Austrasia, the eastern sector of the Merovingian lands, where at that time Theudebert II still reigned (the family catastrophe would occur later that year). The brother of Columbanus's enemy welcomed the saint kindly and asked him to make a home there. Old as he was, Columbanus still considered an urban life among Christians too comfortable, and he asked Theudebert's permission to settle somewhere in his territory among barbarians. With the king's consent he set out on a journey by boat down the Moselle to Coblenz, where the river meets the Rhine, thence southeast up the Rhine. In his usual spirit of blithe courage he composed a rowing song, *Carmen Navale*, to hearten his aging companions. It is written in rolling hexameters reminiscent of Virgil, even containing some direct quotes from the *Aeneid* and the *Georgics*:

> *Lo, cut in forests, the driven keel passes on the stream*
> *Of twin-horned Rhine, and glides as if annointed on the flood.*
> *Ho, my men! Let ringing echo sound our Ho!*
> *The winds raise their blasts, the dread rain works its woe,*
> *But men's ready strength conquers and routs the storm.*
> *Ho, my men! Let ringing echo sound our Ho!*
> *For the clouds yield to endurance, and the storm yields,*
> *Effort tames them all, unwearied toil conquers all things.*
> *Ho, my men! Let ringing echo sound our Ho!*

Bear, and preserve yourselves for favoring fortune,
Ye that have suffered worse, to these also God shall give an end.
Ho, my men! Let ringing echo sound our Ho!
Thus the hated foe deals as he wearies our hearts,
And by ill temptation shakes the inward hearts with rage.
Let your mind, my men, recalling Christ, sound Ho!

The cheerful party sang its way up the river to Lake Constance, arriving in the winter of 612. There they resolved to stay, and built a monastery on land given to them by Theudebert near the ruins of the Roman fort of Brigantium, now Bregenz, Austria. It was mild and pleasant farming country surrounded by high forested mountains, and it was inhabited by Allemanni, Teutonic heathens who lived by hunting and made a practice of drinking great quantities of beer as part of their rites in the worship of Wotan. Columbanus set out at once to evangelize them, which he did with literal directness by burning their idols and breaking up their beer casks. The pagan worshippers objected, at times with force. Once the plainspoken proselytizer was nearly killed when a furious group of barbarians set upon the monks, who ran away. Columbanus, older and slower than his companions, was caught, thrown to the ground, and pelted with rocks. The saint chided his attackers angrily, and they let him go. He must have had an almost hypnotic intrepidity.

Somehow they lasted a year; then the locals, complaining that the monks were interfering with the chase, demanded that they leave. But they had made some headway, and at least one of them, Gall, was saddened at the eviction order. Gall was the companion dearest to Columbanus, his closest friend at Bangor and one of the original group of exiles. He had two valuable assets: he spoke the Teutonic language and he was an expert fisherman. His task at the monastery on Lake Constance was making and mending nets, as well as using them, and the brothers always had plenty of fish to eat. Gall's knowledge of the local tongue did not help much in the beginning, for he too, like his master, was prone to breaking pagan idols and throwing them in the lake. But when the time came for them to leave, Gall asked to be left behind. He was ill with fever and he felt too old and tired to undertake yet another strenuous journey. Columbanus, always quick to anger, chose to regard the fever as an excuse, accusing his old friend of liking his comfort too much. Gall persisted in his resolve, and Columbanus, in an inexcusable burst of rage, gave his consent with the appalling condition that Gall must not say mass until his, Columbanus's, death.

Though only seven years younger than his friend, Gall had always regarded Columbanus, his first teacher, more in the light of a father than an equal. Being of a modest and obedient temperament, he took the cruel sentence as no more than his due. He stayed behind to fish the waters of the Steinach River at his lonely retreat in the Appenzell Mountains west of Lake Constance; to gain, gradually, the trust and affection of his pagan neighbors; and to found there the monastery that bears his name. He continued to honor his abbot's bitter restriction until one day, two years after his friend's departure, he told his deacon to prepare the altar, as he had seen in a vision Columbanus surrounded by angels. The word arrived soon that Columbanus had indeed died on that day, and Gall was free to celebrate mass. But his humble nature did not change: he refused successively the bishopric of Constance, which he felt should rather go to a native of the country, and the abbacy of Luxeuil, as being too privileged and exalted a position. He came to be greatly beloved, and his monastery was to become one of the most illustrious centers of learning of the Middle Ages, with a library of classic Greek and Roman manuscripts that is renowned to this day. In that library is a German phrase book penned by St. Gall himself; and his memory lives in the name of the city that rose on the banks of the Steinach — the little river of rocks and whirlpools, where an otter helped a solitary monk catch fish under the shadow of the wild mountains.

In the autumn of 613 Columbanus and his remaining monks set out to cross the Alps. It was a brutal journey in an inimical season for these old men. They traversed the melodramatic and forbidding Glarus Alps, threading a narrow river valley where the great mountains rose on each side shutting out the daylight, their snow-covered peaks lost in the low-hanging winter clouds, cascades of ice on their wrinkled sides, their lower slopes blackly forested and hardly less steep than the harsh rock towers above. Reaching the high Lukmanier Pass, the travellers descended out of winter into the mellow air of Lago Maggiore, thence south to the flat Plain of Lombardy, where the Lombard duke Agilulf held court in Milan.

The Lombards were Arians, believers in a Christian heresy attractive to the barbarians, which in effect set up Christ as a demigod.* Duke Agilulf's wife and son were Catholics and the duke himself, although of the Arian heresy, liked the lively Irish monk and invited him to stay. He even offered to turn Catholic, but such was the confusion of dogma in northern Italy

*Arianism is discussed on pages 71–72.

at that time that the duke confessed to Columbanus that he didn't know what Catholicism was. This was meat and drink to Columbanus. Ever the teacher, he set out to educate not only Agilulf but the entire Plain of Lombardy — the area stretching across northern Italy from Turin to Trieste — which the Lombards had successfully invaded. As usual he took the tactless course of flouting his benefactor. But, though Agilulf was unconvinced by Columbanus's hotly argued logic and resounding sermons on the unambiguity of the figure of Christ, he evidently liked the vehement old man enough so that he allowed him to go on preaching. When Columbanus declined to stay on in the city, his tolerant patron offered to give him any land in his territory he chose on which to found a monastery.

As always, Columbanus sought the mountains. Going south over the long plains, he came to the Trebbia, a wide silted river that wound through fields, then forests increasingly hilly, until it reached the northern foothills of the Apennines. There it made a deep bend in a pass between wooded hills, where a little mountain stream, the Bobbio, tumbled out of the heights to join it. The meeting of the two rivers formed a gracious curved valley, a place to pause before crossing the high mountains; and here Columbanus chose to stop. Hannibal had passed a winter in this place after defeating a force of Roman troops in the battle of the Trebbia in 218 B.C., and St. Peter was reputed to have built a church here.

In this unpeopled mountain pass Columbanus founded his last monastery, restoring the old church and building his huts around it. After the violent deaths of Brunhilda and all her family, Lothair II, now king of the reunited Frankish realms, invited the Irish monks back to Luxeuil. But Columbanus declined: he had become deeply involved in the challenging task of convincing Italy's heretic conquerors of the manifest truth of the Catholic doctrine. The Lombards, disdaining Rome and all she stood for, had the wealth to reduce taxes, and many of the faithful were thus won over to the cause of the onetime enemy. Columbanus's work was all uphill, a situation he still relished despite his advanced age and growing weakness. Bobbio itself became, even in the short time that remained to its founder, a place renowned all over Italy and beyond. Situated on a pass through the Apennines, it was a haven for travellers, who spread word of its sanctity and sometimes stayed on. The foundation was laid for its growth as a medieval sanctuary of holiness and learning whose library, reflecting Columbanus's learning and love for the classics, would be famous all over the Western world.

But Bobbio grew too populous for Columbanus. He retired to a cave high on the slope of nearby Monte Penice, where he could end his life in the lonely and uncomfortable surroundings he had always preferred, with his chosen companions the wild animals of the forest. He died a year after he founded Bobbio, on 21 November 615, and was buried there. His body lies in a fifteenth-century marble tomb in the crypt of the beautiful Romanesque church of brick and yellow-gray native stone that replaced the original building. In the adjacent museum are fragments of a stone sarcophagus made for his remains in the eighth century — heavy slabs decorated with his symbols, the dove and the sun, worked into an intricate and stylized design of interlacing.

Though he was in Bobbio such a short time, it is easier to summon up the memory of Columbanus here than in busy, successful Luxeuil. The little unassuming town does not intrude. It has a medieval air: its old buildings, of the same yellow-gray stone as the church, with red-tiled roofs, climb the steep hill above the bend in the river; its winding streets are too narrow for automobiles. It seems imbued with the quietness of its surrounding fog-shrouded mountains, and the spirit of its founding saint is very near.

Columbanus was Ireland's first notable emissary of the centuries-long flow of faith, ideas and learning from the island at the far edge back to the mainland whence they had arisen. So it is only fitting that he should have been so typically Irish, almost a symbol of late-sixth-century Irish Christianity, with all its irritating foibles and shining graces. He had the certainty of the rightness of his principles, together with an absolute refusal to compromise and a readiness to jump with both feet into any conflict that threatened the immaculacy of his ideals. He was quarrelsome, not out of a fractious disposition but because of his committed devotion. His somewhat self-righteous moral superiority was gall to the back-sliding French bishops; it was also a threat to their entrenched establishment. For the people, from kings to farmers, flocked to Columbanus, seeing in his brand of Christianity a toughness and purity that had long been absent in their demoralized land. He went back to essentials.

But more than the upright sternness of his moral temper, people were attracted by his underlying tenderness, his compassion and the aura of mysticism that emanated from his intensely perceptive quality of mind. His nature was a contradictory combination of delicacy and obduracy: outspoken, tenacious integrity was joined to a brooding abstraction. Columbanus could seem to perform miracles of healing and prophesy; many of these, as is true of other Irish saints, can be attributed to sentient insight. Actually, the miracles are fewer and the narrative more factual than had been the case with any of the saints' lives heretofore. This is due to his thorough, careful (though biased) biographer Jonas, who had the advantage of having entered Bobbio as a monk three years after its founder's death, thus having access to firsthand material.

Besides the quality of Columbanus's personality, the other important aspect of his influence was his scholarly attainment. He was far in advance of his contemporaries in his familiarity with and appreciation of the non-religious Latin classics. But his years of disciplined study and teaching had given him more than a deep and wide knowledge; they had influenced his mental processes, inclining him to the moderation and logic of the great pre-Christian thinkers, giving structure to his ideas and esthetic form to his style. He was spontaneously expressive in words, and the classical discipline directed and shaped that expression. He became a graceful if overwordy writer (the latter was a quality he admitted and deplored). His forte was not in original thinking — he laid no claim to being an innovative philosopher — but in the felicity and imagination of his writing. His prose has an impulsive energy, seemingly extemporaneous. Actually it was very carefully thought out; the style in every work was artfully fashioned for the purpose it was to serve. His sermons have a natural, fervent verbosity, as if the man's very heart were pouring into his words. One can almost hear the strong voice speaking:

> Oh human life, feeble and mortal, how many have you deceived, beguiled and blinded! While you fly, you are nothing, while you are seen, you are a shadow, while you arise, you are but smoke; daily you fly and daily you return, you fly in returning and return in flying, unequal in outcome, identical in origin, unequal in pleasure, identical in passage, sweet to the stupid, bitter to the wise. . . . You are the roadway of mortals, in their life, beginning from sin, enduring up till death.

St. Columbanus had a tendency toward the neat turn of phrase, and loved to express moral truths in adages. His work is full of highly quotable aphorisms, a delight to his simpler parishioners: "The man to whom little is not enough will not benefit from more." "He tramples the world who tramples on himself." "Be hard among pleasant things, be gentle amid harsh things." "Do not be afraid to disagree if need be, but agree about the truth."

He wrote some poetry when he had leisure, generally hortatory little lectures in meter. He was a competent versifier, writing in smooth Latin hexameters and making use of internal rhymes and other poetic devices. His poetry is animated and lucid, but it is not particularly original. Though addicted to the written word and skilled in its use, he never pretended to a creative intellect. He owed much to the classical Latin poets, particularly Virgil. It is a revealing sidelight on a complex character: that a monk steeped as he was in the rigorous discipline of self-denial, a supremely stubborn Christian of the purest stamp, should choose to exercise his mind in his idle hours by perusal and imitation of pagan works from a conspicuously earthy age. And this was at a time when such works were considered sinfully frivolous in Continental cloisters, the souls of their fleshly pagan authors relegated to perpetual damnation. Columbanus did not care about such strictures. He was in all sensible matters a nonconformist, and he was totally unafraid.

Altogether, although he was a man who knew his own shortcomings, who lost his temper too easily (and gained it back as quickly), and who was ready to admit his mistakes, in all the vital circumstances of life he was honest, direct and outstandingly courageous.

Columbanus and his monks infused a refreshing spirit of religious dedication into Europe. It was welcome and much needed, but because of its very purity, the Irish influence could not last. The near-monolithic certainty of Irish Christianity that the soul must prepare itself for the hereafter, despising all earthly considerations, was too transcendental. At this time in history, immediate regard for material exigencies was a compelling necessity for the religious establishment in Europe. After the Lombard conquest and the consequent severance of ties with Byzantium, the pope needed to build up a unified Church in order to bring back coherence and confidence to a divided and demoralized Europe, and to bulwark the faithful against the crude indifference of the barbarian regimes. For this he needed uniformity in the ranks and unquestioning obedience to his dictates. He also needed temporal power, as he was dealing with politicians. Gregory deeply sympathized with the outlook of the Irish monks and surely felt a spiritual identity with Columbanus; but a corrupt, conniving politician like Brunhilda, who had money and influence and who acknowledged the authority of Rome, was more important to his aims. The Irish were of no help to him in these areas. They despised temporal power and ignored politics; their obedience (outside the monastery) was sketchy at best; though they respected and even revered the pope, they regarded him as no more than an equal. Their only consideration was the conversion of souls and their guidance up the divinely mystical road to heaven.

Herein lay a further cause of the Irish monks' ultimate failure. Their very intensity defeated them. The great virtue of Irish monasticism was also a drawback; its passionate commitment and its extreme rigor. The Irish had the penitential fever. They threw themselves into religion as if they had just awakened to it, and compared with the rest of Europe, they had. They wanted to experience the ecstatic suffering of the early Christians and to cleanse their souls with the unconditional fervor of the saved sinner — and they wanted everybody else to do this too. Their unmitigated enthusiasm for martyrdom must have seemed obsolete and even somewhat embarrassing to a blasé Europe that had been through it all a long time before and now wanted only peace. The Irish saints' burning ardor appealed to many, and they achieved outstanding successes. But it was too extreme and it could not last.

There was an alternative for aspiring anchorites who found the Irish rule too demanding: the discipline of Benedict. The gentle saint of Nursia, who lived a generation earlier than Columbanus, had in the early sixth century devised a rule for his monasteries that was temperate, workable and very calm. His monks did not fast unduly; they slept normal hours, with a pillow rather than a stone under their heads. Obedience and penance were there, but were not immoderate. The emphasis was on peace, but without its concomitant, idleness. Though travelling was discouraged — St. Benedict himself never left Italy — and learning was not considered important, the monks must be continuously active at hard manual labor. The days were a succession of pious and silent monotony and thought-dulling toil, with the only hope the ending of all days and the final and utter peace.

Benedict's rule seems unambitious, as if it were tailored to a tired and defeated people. But it apparently answered a deep need in its time, and Pope Gregory and succeeding popes found it extremely useful. It was a flexible discipline (in Gregory's own words, "conspicuous for its discretion") that could be contained and directed by Rome. Under the aegis of the irrepressible Irish, the monastic movement — loftily self-determining, anti-episcopate, too intense for the general run of novitiates — was a threat to the increasing centralization of authority. So successful was the Benedictine order, with its moderation and its emphasis on good sense — and its backing by Rome — that by the middle of the eighth century, two hundred years after its founding, it had absorbed all other European houses and become the fundamental monastic code of western Europe.

Its rise spelled the effective end of Irish dominance of the European monastic system. But there was never any friction between the two orders. Benedictine and Irish houses existed side by side for two centuries, and when Luxeuil and the others were at last taken over by the Benedictine order, no bitterness accompanied the change.

Though Irish supremacy was superseded, Irish influence did not die. Columbanus had introduced new ideas that gradually took hold and supplanted Continental usages. The most important was the practice, which we noted earlier as peculiar to the Irish, of private confession. The old Continental method of public penance had given the priests the unprecedented power of openly stigmatizing people whom they wished out of action. The Irish method was at once more humane and more effective: the sinner need not hide his delinquency for fear of public shame but could expurgate his transgressions whenever he needed. Another change energetically opposed during Columbanus's lifetime but later adopted by the authority of Pope Gregory was the independence of monastic houses from the direct control of the diocese. This further cut down the power of venal bishops and left the monasteries to follow their devotional courses undisturbed, their direction under the control of their abbots, men whose worldly outlook was presumably disinterested and whose aims were extraterrestrial.

The Irish spirit lived on in less tangible ways. For many of the barbarian peoples of eastern France, Austria, Germany and Switzerland, Columbanus had been the first contact with practicing Christianity. It was a beautiful introduction, and though the ascendancy of his order did not last, he himself was beloved, and his memory is still revered. In the field of scholarship his impact was more profound and enduring. The European Dark Ages were lethal to learning: the mass of the people could not read, the aristocracy was too busy with war and intrigue to bother, and the cloistered monks — the only ones with a pretense of education — shrank from defiling contact with the devilish products of pagan minds. Columbanus's Irish education had taught him to be unafraid of the snares of alien philosophies and appreciative of the elegance and wisdom of these same pagan minds. Europe is deeply in debt to this scholarly and undauntable man for helping to keep alive the classical learning that was sinking in a swamp of ignorance and intolerance. His mission, though primarily evangelical, was the beginning of the great procession of Irish erudition that was to amaze and inspirit Europe for the next four centuries.

At a distance of more than thirteen hundred years, this first envoy of the Irish genius is exceptionally clear: a figure no larger than life, standing at the edge of sunrise — a saint endearingly, humanly fallible.

PART THREE

THE
BREAKDOWN

CHAPTER XI
THE VIKING INVASIONS

THE FIRST ORDER OF IRISH SAINTS, ACCORDING TO THE EIGHTH-CENTURY historian mentioned earlier (page 101), was composed of St. Patrick's nonmonastic clergy, bishops on the Roman pattern — though far more actively evangelistic and peripatetic than the contemporary Continental clergy. The second order consisted of the founders of the great monasteries, whose lives and accomplishments have been the subjects of the foregoing pages. The third order consisted of holy men "who made their dwelling in desert places, and who lived on herbs and water and alms." The ways of these anchorites and hermit communities were a narrowing and deepening of the monastic life. Evidently finding even stern Irish monasticism too comfortable — or perhaps judging that the energetic monks were too much with the world for the true, private knowing of God — they left the fold for the hard, silent life of island or mountaintop. Sometimes a man went out alone, as did Cormac from Columba's Iona, to seek a state of grace in the unmapped lands over the ocean. Sometimes several gathered to found their own unsociable communities, where each man spent most of his time alone in his cell, joining with his brethren only for services in the little church, for essential labor in the common garden and for wordless meals. Such was probably the nature of the foundation on Skellig Michael.

The three orders overlapped in time, as in function, and the period of the third order ended, it is written, with the yellow plague of 664. But there was an extension, a new and vital company of ascetic contemplatives, that emerged in the middle of the eighth century and continued through the ninth. These dedicated ascetics were known as the *celi De* (sometimes anglicized to "Culdees"), companions of God, and their sect arose in answer to the increasing worldliness and laxity of the great monasteries.

Columba and Columbanus and the other founders, besides being men of shining faith and spirituality, were brilliant organizers, zealous in the management of their communities, dexterous in their dealings with the local lay rulers, often themselves members of the ruling family. The monastic foundations, under this deft and inspired management, became Ireland's most important centers of wealth and culture, her only towns. Their agricultural methods were the most efficient; their craftsmen were the most highly skilled; their schools and libraries were the outstanding repositories of knowledge and the recourse of teachers and students from all over the Christian world. Their incomes derived from tithes, which were collected by abbots in countryside progressions like those of kings; further, the monasteries were free from military imposts and from the demands of secular wars or any other form of lay interference. So the larger ones were independent, autonomous and enormously wealthy. It was a predetermined result that these prestigious institutions, however idealistic the aims of their saintly founders, should become secular and politically powerful.

Subject to no central authority, each monastery was a self-sufficient entity with its own absolute ruler. This ruler, the abbot, was usually chosen from within the family of the patron saint or, failing descendants, that of the chief landowner. So important was the family in the Irish social scheme that it was considered less crucial that an abbot should be in orders than that he should be descended from a common uncle or cousin. Lay abbots were more usual than not, and by the eighth century, sons were succeeding fathers. Sometimes a busy landowning abbot would have more than one institution under his care, to the detriment of all.

The lay connections of monasteries extended to all conditions of life: they were trading centers, schools, penitentiaries, repositories of food in times of famine. Their multiple role as Ireland's only towns made them peculiarly vulnerable in distressful times. Long before the Viking raids started, needy Irish rulers saw the monasteries as fat and helpless prey. Not entirely helpless at that: occasionally the monastic population joined in secular battles, and some shockingly bloody contests took place between monasteries themselves. In 764, for instance, Durrow lost two hundred monks in a battle with Clonmacnoise (which postulates a monastic population of well over a thousand).

Despite the abuses that grew out of too close a connection with lay affairs and despite the spiritual decay consequent on the frictionless life of property and privilege, the undercurrents of piety still moved within the monastery walls. Wealth was used to foster libraries and scriptoria; lay abbots essayed to promote peace in their territories; monasteries were still places of hospitality and sanctuary; austerity and discipline, while not commonly enforced, were venerated in theory. When a reforming movement started within the Church, it was not only tolerated but generally welcomed.

In their religious revival the *celi De* looked back to Ireland's early saints. The philosophy and the ascetic practices of the reformers were those of St. Brigid and St. Brendan and other exponents of the primitive Church in Ireland, and their rule followed the stern precepts of St. Columba, St. Columbanus and St. Finian of Clonard. The movement was spontaneous and unorganized, arising in several places at once and thriving within the walls of the most consequential monasteries. A form was given it by several strong and strict leaders, who founded separate institutions to practice and teach their brand of pious asceticism. The chief among them, and the first, was Maelruain, an interesting and attractive figure whose innate kindness tempered the severity of his rule.

Nothing is known of Maelruain's background and youth. It is clear from his writings that he must have been well educated in the spheres of religion and literature, and he was well enough considered (and probably high enough in the social scale) so that in 774 King Cellach of Leinster gave him land for a monastery at Tallaght, five miles southwest of present-day Dublin. Tallaght, on the west slope of the Dublin Mountains, near the Dodder River, is notorious in legend as the place of Ireland's first pestilence, when nine thousand of Partholon's people died in one week. A mass plague-burial took place, it is written, and one can see on the hills around the village the ancient tumuli that supported the myth. Even less remains of the eighth-century anchoritic community than of the prehistoric disaster. Tallaght was too close to the convenient harbor around which the Vikings built their first Irish settlement of Dublin, and the monastery was early reduced.

Along with his own predilection for the asceticism of the early saints, Maelruain had a precedent for his establishment in the Order of Canons founded on the Continent some twenty-five years earlier. This was a rule for an intermediate class of clergy between cloistered monks and secular priests: people who, though not fettered by monastic vows, wished to live in common within the salutary bounds of a severe discipline. Maelruain's early disciples, men disaffected by the decadence of life in the rich monasteries, would likely have been in this class.

Maelruain's rule, composed in 780, probably originally in meter, was one of the famous Irish disciplines. Though it lacked the picayune, almost testy prescriptions of St. Columbanus's rule, it was exacting to an extreme: almost no area of a man's thoughts or deeds, even his unconscious actions, was left unsupervised. Great emphasis was placed on prayer, both in private and in community. Private prayer was often performed in cross-vigil and punctuated by repeated genuflections. Besides the quantities of regular prayers for the canonical hours, the reciting of the Psalms was prominent on the daily agenda. "There are three adversaries busy attacking me," wrote the leader, "my eye, my tongue and my thoughts: the Psalter restrains them all." [1] No one was absolved from this daily observance: "He that works with the sickle or the flail, he that uses the mallet or makes the ditch, each has to recite the hundred and fifty Psalms as his additional daily work; and none of them goes to his evening meal until he has finished those hundred and fifty Psalms."

Nighttime prayer was also enjoined; and two monks must always stay in the church all night, spacing the vigil so that no one should do without his necessary sleep (for "he does not forbid anyone to sleep his fill, provided that he diligently observes the Hours, both day and night"). Although his instructions on private prayer were exacting, Maelruain advised moderation in performance: a man should "chant every other fifty [of the Psalms] sitting and standing alternately. If anyone were to remain seated longer than this he would fall asleep; and if he remained standing longer he would be tired out." And he frowned, with a touch of humor, on excess:

> There was a certain anchorite . . . great was his labor: two hundred genuflections he used to perform at matins and one hundred every canonical hour, one hundred at nocturns — seven hundred in all. . . . "By my word," said Maelruain, "a time will come to him before his death when he shall not perform a single genuflection." This came to pass: his feet were seized so that he could not perform a vigil for a long time before his death on account of the excessive amount he had performed in other days.

Along with the daily communal worship, the Gospels were read aloud at mealtimes "so that [the monks'] attention should not be occupied with their supper."

Frequent confession was advised, and it was suggested that the penitent take a hard master: ". . . seek out the fire that you think will burn you the fiercest." If a man fall into such small errors as "murmuring, idle words, backbiting, anger," he need not wait until Sunday but should confess without delay. Penances were castigation and fasting, but in these, too, moderation was practiced. For the very poor who had committed sins, it was "not easy to lay a fast upon them, since they would have scarce any food . . . after the fast." And for the sick there should be "alternate revival and mortification, lest the perpetual confinement should cause their death." Even the most stringent of penances for the healthy did not include "black fasting" (eating nothing). An extreme ascetic who once wished to enter his order was turned away by Maelruain, who said, "Those who are here, while they do their proper share of work, are able to eat their rations. Thou . . . wilt not fit among them. Thou wilt neither do active work nor be able to eat thy rations."

Even when not doing penance the brethren at Tallaght ate sparingly, their food consisting of milk, honey, kale, curds, fish, cheese, eggs, apples and leeks. Occasionally, in the case of scarcity of other food, the flesh of wild deer and wild hogs was permitted. Restraint was counselled in the act of eating as well as in the diet: ". . . drink by sips; for this quenches thirst, and a man finds less sensual pleasure and satisfaction in sips than in a draught, when he is thirsty." There was a penance for vomiting if it was caused by eating or drinking to excess. And drinking of beer and liquor was entirely prohibited: "As long as I shall give rules . . . the liquor that causes forgetfulness of God shall not be drunk here." In general, the regulation of each man's eating habits was left to his own good sense: "Everyone should regulate his pittance for himself, knowing the proper amount, that it cause not sickness if it be too little, neither encourage vice if it be too much."

Sensuality in all forms was condemned. The stricture applied even to music. Though the hymns were chanted, music in its purely pleasurable aspect was censured. In denying a piper permission to play for the monks, Maelruain said: "These ears are not lent to earthly music, that they may be lent to the music of heaven." Such words might have been spoken by St. Brendan. And in matters of sex, Maelruain could even have given that primitive ascetic lessons. In reaction against the lax monastic morals of his day, Maelruain decreed absolute chastity for all who had taken vows, from the novice to the bishop. If a priest sinned against chastity he must not say mass, and his penance was long and heavy.

The company of women must be drastically shunned: a very holy woman, who had fasted and mortified her body until only a little drop of yellowish water came out when she pierced her flesh with a needle, said, "So long as there is this much juice in his [the cenobite's] body, let him bestow no friendship or confidence upon womankind." If a man must speak even with a devout nun, if she was young, he should not look upon her face, and he should have an older man with him. Even desire in thought was to be mortified: "If it happened to a man to pollute his body . . . either through looking at a woman who might please him, or through filthy thoughts in his heart, . . . Maelruain ordered a week's penance to be imposed on him."

The sanctity of Sunday was absolute, like the Jewish Sabbath, and it started the evening before: "Once it happened to me," wrote the chronicler of Tallaght, "that I chanced to stay in the bath a while after evensong on Saturday. [Maelruain] told me to go without condiment of butter or bacon on the Saturday evening and the Sunday following." No task might be undertaken on Sunday: no cooking or splitting wood, no penitential castigation, no "lifting a single apple from the ground." But on other days there must never be a moment of idleness. There were "three profitable things in the day: prayer, labor and study; or it may be, teaching or writing or sewing clothes, or any other profitable work . . . ; so that none be idle, as the Lord has said: 'Thou shalt not appear in my sight empty.' " Next to the godliness of labor was the virtue of teaching, and education was a prime element of the movement: "The kingdom of heaven is granted to him who directs study, him who studies and him who supports the student."

In their daily lives, Maelruain's monks must above all practice quiet and continuous restraint in all areas: "Do not eat till thou be hungry; do not sleep till thou be ready for it; speak to none till there be cause." They must eschew worldly disputes and avoid law courts and assemblies. Nor must they ask for news of the world, "since it might harass and disturb the mind of him to whom it was told." They must stay in the cloister and work and pray and teach. Travelling was to be avoided: "Abide always in the place where thou were wont to be. . . . Anyone who deserts his country . . . is a denier of Patrick in heaven and of the faith he brought to Erin." Of all Maelruain's rules, this last must have been the hardest to observe.

As this resumé suggests, the rule of Tallaght was a harshly restrictive regime. Nothing of a man's weakness was left unspecified; his very thoughts were subject to regulation and the motions of his daily life were minutely governed. But rigorous as was the multifaceted discipline he imposed on his followers, Maelruain's movement was a healthy one. In general, the outlook, aside from a perhaps excessive emphasis on religious observance, was toward physical and mental health, hard work and self-restraint. Like the rule of Columbanus at Luxeuil, it was vital in its time, and many welcomed its unsparing rigor. Much of its success was due to the character of its leader. Maelruain was a man of sense, moderation and charity, and he must have had a lambent spirituality that drew out the best in men. For the *celi De* movement, though it mortified the bodies of its followers, did not quench their spirit. Some of the loveliest nature poetry to come out of Ireland was produced by its votaries; much of the appealing sculpture of the high crosses was the direct result of the *celi De* emphasis on teaching; *celi De* anchorites, skilled and patient craftsmen, were often appointed master scribes and illuminators in the great monastic scriptoria where Ireland's magnificent codices were created. (We will look at this artistic renaissance in some detail in later chapters.)

Tallaght and the other new houses — Finglas, Terryglass and Loch Cre, all founded by disciples of Maelruain — were established along the lines of the old monasteries, collecting agricultural tithes from the surrounding farmers and each following its own rule (not necessarily similar to those of its sister houses) under the absolute direction of its abbot. Aside from these, the *celi De* reform took place as a voluntary movement within the walls of the established houses, countenanced, even encouraged by them. But, although the movement brought a new spirit into the Church — an inspiration that lasted beyond its actual survival — the *celi De* sect never developed a machinery for renewing itself. It had no power of enforcement; its influence was spiritual and depended on the inclination of the abbot who ruled the house. A responsive abbot could maintain the high level of ascetic piety; an unsympathetic successor could reverse the trend in a day, bringing back the old easygoing patterns. The constitutional structure of the Irish Church remained unchanged: responsible to no central authority, each house autonomous and subject to the convictions and temperament of its leader.

We have noted how monasteries were enmeshed with the world even to the extent of joining battle with one another. The *celi De* themselves were guilty in this direction. Feidlimid, king of Cashel in the mid-ninth century, besides being one of Ireland's most powerful kings, was a bishop and a devoutly pious ascetic of the *celi De* sect. He tried first with political scheming, later with the sword, to enforce his opinions on the venerable, rich, reactionary monasteries such as those at Durrow, Fore, Kildare and Armagh. Enraged when Clonmacnoise refused to accept his candidate for abbot, he attacked the monastery, plundering, burning and killing. His deplorable savagery demonstrates the fragile nature of the reform movement: the fatal absence of any sort of restraint over unconscionable violence even in the pursuit of an idea, or of any sane and central method of settling disputes between sovereign monasteries. Feidlimid's un-Christian conduct brought him legendary retribution: according to the annals of Clonmacnoise, St. Ciaran himself, founder of the beleaguered monastery, appeared to the miscreant one night and pierced him in the belly with his crosier, causing a fatal internal wound.

The excesses of Feidlimid were a symptom not only of the malaise of the Church but of the dishevelment of Ireland's political structure. Far ahead of the rest of Europe as she was in intellectual attainment, her political organization remained that of a primitive society, its structure based on the family. Being an island untouched for over a thousand years by foreign invasion either peaceful or bellicose, she had developed a remarkable sense of racial and cultural unity; but there was no idea of nationality or the state — nor had that modern concept yet developed anywhere in Europe. Ireland's kings, including the so-called *ard-ri*, over-king, functioned as such only within the boundaries of their own *tuaths,* or tribal territories, and even locally there were no police nor any sort of central authority to enforce the law. The position of *ard-ri* was an honorary one; it meant chiefly that the assignee collected tribute from lesser kings, who also had to entertain him when he made his annual progress and supply a quota of fighting men for several weeks each year. The *ard-ri*, a title bestowed on weak kings as well as strong ones, was by virtue of his family connections over-king of the groups of *tuaths* that added up to the provinces of Connacht, Leinster, Munster, Ulster and Meath.

Until the tenth century, there was no high-king of all Ireland. The title was an invention of medieval historians, whose lists extend back into pagan times, for the purpose of establishing a precedent for the claims of Brian Boru and his successors. The heirs of the Ui Neill family in the northern provinces and of the Eoganacht in the southwest contended throughout the early medieval period for the position of the most powerful king in Ireland, and occasionally one of them laid claim to the sovereignty of the entire country. But their hegemony, imposed by political and military maneuver, generally lasted only for the life, usually brief, of the stronger scions of those families.

Besides the lack of central authority, a universal characteristic of early medieval times, Ireland fostered a more dangerous source of dissension in her method of selecting kings. There was no predetermined order of succession to the kingship. The only qualification was that the king-designate must be of the ruling dynasty, but in theory he could be chosen from anywhere within the *fine* (that is, the five generations of brothers, uncles, sons and cousins that constituted the legal family). Within two generations the dynasties became so unwieldy with crowds of potential heirs that whole segments of them were discarded by the then-ruling sector. The spurned segments dedicated their lives to working their way back into the succession, using any means that came to hand including blinding or otherwise maiming the legitimate heir to bar him from the kingship, calling in the neighbors to help, or seceding from the province to found a rival kingdom unpleasantly close to the border. The result was an almost constant state of war. Despite the fact that the wars rarely amounted to more than a skirmish, over by sunset, the Irish polity was in a condition of continuous unease and the lives of rulers and their eligible successors were alarmingly short. Therefore there could be no stability: no matter how well-intentioned, strong and clever a king might be, he could die the next day, and the inevitable debilitating struggle would be on again.

The most ominous aspect of the weakness of the political system was that dynastic cousins who had been eliminated tended to call in outside help to unseat their favored relatives. This was an irresistible temptation to neighboring rulers, who saw a chance to enlarge their territories; and it would later prove a windfall to hostile invading forces from outside the island.

Somehow, though the seeds of disaster were within her, Ireland kept herself in balance. Her laws were unenforceable; yet they were obeyed. War and violence were endemic; yet the people prospered, the herds grew fat, and the barley was sown and reaped. The clergy engaged in pitched battles and the unordained sons of abbots succeeded to the primacy; yet the monastic schools continued to turn out artists, poets and philosophers to delight and astonish the world. But the balance was precarious and an unanticipated shock could upset it.

The first signal came in 795. A Viking ship landed on Recheainn Island off the northeast coast (probably Rathlin Island, County Antrim), and sacked and burned the monastery there, which was said to have been founded by St. Columba. Irish monks were not strangers to this brand of calamity. Two years before, the first Vikings had ventured out of the fjords of western Norway in their shallow-drafted, highly maneuverable longboats, and raided the northeast coast of England, destroying the monastery at Lindisfarne. From there they had sailed north to the islands of Shetland and Orkney, thence around the tip of Scotland to the Atlantic coast, to hit Iona, which they plundered for the first time in 795.

During the twenty-five years following the raid on Recheainn, Irish monasteries all around the coast were targets. Bangor and Downpatrick on the east coast were attacked, and the island of Inishmurray off Sligo on the west, even barren Skellig Michael (which surely had little worth the plundering and could but meagerly sustain its few anchorites). The undefended monastic villages proved a source of continuous bonanza to the pirates, who could slip into the shallowest bays and narrowest estuaries, to loot, burn, murder and skim out again before anyone could raise enough outcry to summon help. At first the terrorized Irish regarded the visitations not so much as a national disaster than as an unavoidable local curse, like a plague. "From the fury of the Northmen deliver us," was a ninth-century prayer. A scribe of the period took time out from his copying to write a verse in Irish in the margin of his text:

> Bitter is the wind tonight: it tosses the ocean's white hair:
> I fear not the crossing of a clear sea by the fierce heroes from Lothlend.[2]

Though they were terrifying to the helpless monasteries along the edges, the Norse raids, in the first quarter-century, did not cause any major national disruption. The buccaneers, savage and efficient though they were, had only one objective: the monasteries' wealth of gold and silver altar pieces, reliquaries, book covers and caskets. Along the way, having no love for Christians, they threw the holy books into the sea, set fire to the churches and killed a few monks. Their raids were hardly worse — and not too different from — the familiar cattle raids. The Irish themselves, during that same period, had a far more conspicuously flagrant record of attack, plunder and murder. The recorded figures show twenty-six Norse acts of violence compared with eighty-seven by Irishmen.

After 830, however, the Viking nuisance turned into a full-fledged horror. Increasing numbers of attackers thrust their way inland, plundering monasteries far from the sea and taking numerous prisoners, of whom they held the important ones — bishops, priests and men of learning who had high honor prices — for ransom, and sold the rest as slaves. The Norse invaders were still focussing on the monasteries — vulnerable concentrations of population, stock and portable valuables.

In 837 a new phase began as sixty ships sailed into the mouth of the Boyne at today's Drogheda and sixty into Liffey Harbor (Dublin Bay). The first Norse settlements, built in 841 — one at Linn Duachaill, now Annagassan, on the Louth coast; one at Black Pool (Dubhlinn, later anglicized to Dublin), below a bridged ford (Ath Cliath, Dublin's present-day Irish name) — were stockades around their fleets. The effect of the increased attacks and the subsequent settlements of the barbarians was devastating. The Irish kings did not seem to be able to gather themselves to retaliate, and the country was paralyzed by confusion and despair. Even the Irish attacks on one another, disagreeable as they were, could not be compared with the new, thoroughgoing savagery. The native kings had not been strong enough to inflict serious damage, and the objects of their attacks, the rich monasteries, were well able to mount a defense, even to counterattack. Also, the kings were held back by a certain Christian fastidiousness: they would not touch the bones of a saint, for instance, and the possibility of religious penalties deterred them from the worst atrocities. The Norse invaders had no such delicacy; in fact they seemed to go out of their way to destroy or deface everything with a Christian connotation.

A consequence of the pervasive demoralization was that internal inhibitions broke down. The country collapsed into a state of near-anarchy: a man like King Feidlimid of Cashel, whose reign coincided with the new Viking fury, probably took the cue for his excesses from those masters of atrocity. The distraught populace blamed everything on the invasions, and accounts of Viking enormities soared into poetic flights of exaggeration:

> The whole of Munster . . . was plundered by them. . . . they made spoil-land, and sword-land of her . . . and they ravaged her sanctuaries, and they rent her shrines, and her reliquaries, and her books. They demolished her beautiful ornamented temples. . . . neither veneration, nor honor, nor mercy . . . for sanctuary, for God, or for man, was felt by this furious, ferocious, pagan, ruthless, wrathful people. In short, until the sand of the sea, or the grass of the field, or the stars of heaven are counted, it will not be easy to recount . . . what the Gaedhil . . . suffered from them. . . . They killed the kings and the chieftains, the heirs to the crown. . . . They killed the brave and the valiant . . . and the greater part of the heroes and warriors of the entire Gaedhil; . . . and they reduced them to bondage and slavery. Many were the blooming, lively women . . . and the gentle, well brought up youths, and the intelligent, valiant champions, whom they carried off into oppres-

sion and bondage over the broad green sea. Alas! many . . . were the bright eyes that were suffused with tears, and dimmed with grief and despair, at the separation of son from father, and daughter from mother. . . . Though there were an hundred hard steeled iron heads on one neck, and an hundred sharp, cool, never-rusting brazen tongues in each head, and an hundred garrulous, loud, unceasing voices from each tongue, they could not recount . . . all the Gaedhil suffered.[3]

The foregoing account, strongly reminiscent in style of the bravura of the pagan sagas, was written more than a century after the height of the Viking terror, and its aim was to make everything appear as awful as possible. The probable chief author was Mac Liag, leading poet of Ireland and Brian Boru's secretary and trusted aide; his main object was to glorify his hero, and the more appalling the situation was made to appear, the more radiant became the valiancy of Ireland's deliverer. But although *The War of the Gaedhil with the Gaill* is a romantic tale in the tradition of the hero-sagas rather than a factual historical record, it exaggerates conditions that did exist: the Norse were exceptionally ferocious, and Brian in a very real sense — though not quite by Mac Liag's definition — would come near to being the savior of his country.

By 845 the Irish kings had begun to take the field against the enemy. The first signal success was achieved by Malachy I, over-king of the Ui Neill, who fought a battle with the Norse, captured a pagan leader named Turgesius, or Thorgils, and drowned him in Lough Owel. A lurid series of events was later concocted around the figure of Turgesius by the authors of the propaganda piece quoted above, in which he was depicted as a conspicuously fierce Viking gorilla who had "assumed the sovereignty of all the foreigners in Ireland," and had the aim of subjugating or exterminating the native chieftains, to replace them with his own people, and of destroying the Christian religion in favor of the worship of Odin and Thor. With the latter aim in mind, he is said to have established his wife, Ota, at Clonmacnoise, where she delivered her blasphemous heathen oracles from the high altar. The aim of this Gothic invention, of which there is much more, was to denigrate the Ui Neill, who were demonstrated to have been dilatory in the defense of the Church, in contrast with Brian's intrepid Christian gallantry.

By 853, when Olaf the White, son of a Norwegian king, came to rule over the Norsemen in Ireland from the new Norse capital of Dublin, the worst of the raids was over. In the years following, the Norse established more settlements, mostly in the south, and primarily trading centers and seaports, the nuclei of towns: among them were Waterford, Wexford, Limerick and Cork. Though the Norse population was small and restricted in area, the newcomers were solidly established, and their towns became little Irish-type states embroiled like their neighbors in the disputatious gambits of local politics. So amicable had the relations become that when a fleet of Danish invaders, probably from England, attacked the Norse settlements on the east coast, the Dublin Norse were aided in their defense by the Irish king of Ulster.

Besides business and trade dealings and alliances in the inevitably continuing dynastic feuds, there was a lively cultural exchange and a good deal of intermarriage, resulting in a new generation of mixed Irish-Norse children. The conversion of alien pagans to accepted Christians can be attributed to this social integration.*

The tenth century again saw increased raids on Ireland, as marauding Vikings found themselves firmly persona non grata by their now-settled relatives in France and England, and all of Iceland's choice coastal lands, mecca for landless younger sons and political outcasts, were preempted. Ireland was still open territory, pregnable because of the fatal weakness of her political system, her kings and their families divided among themselves, her resident Norse population sparse and scattered. Late in this century a large fleet of "Black Gentiles" — Danes (the name refers not to their personalities but to the prevailing color of their hair; the Norwegian invaders were known as "White Gentiles") — entered the mouth of the Shannon, entrenched themselves on King's Island, now part of Limerick, and invaded and plundered all of Munster. They set up an infamous despotism over the inhabitants, the most outrageous feature of which was the "nose-tax": an ounce of silver was exacted for every nose, and he who refused to pay either went into slavery or lost his nose. Great and severe were the cruelties and depredations of the Munster conquerors (wrote Brian's annalist, previously quoted) and invincible were "their valor, their strength, their venom and their ferocity." But the liberator was at hand.

In the eighth century a small clan, the Dal Cais (originally the Deisi), had established itself in the eastern part of County Clare, the hilly region of the Shannon at the point where the river begins to widen into Lough Derg. Two brothers, Mathgamain, the elder, and Brian, descendants of

---

*A sidelight on Norse history of the time is the sizable migration of Irish-Norse to the new country of Iceland, founded in the ninth century, which is attested to by the many Irish names found in that country, particularly in the southern part. Perhaps this is a touch of poetic justice, since the original Viking settlers of Iceland had frightened off the colonies of Irish anchorites they found there.

the founder, emerged in the mid-tenth century as able guerrilla leaders against the intolerable regime of the Norse invaders of Munster. The brothers made their sorties over the flat, fertile countryside of Tipperary and melted back into their rugged home territory, ideal for their purposes, where the aliens, unfamiliar with the twisting hidden valleys and forested hills, could never root them out. Inevitably the brothers gained popularity not only with their own clansmen but all over beleaguered Munster. The Eoganacht family, which for centuries had ruled Munster from its head-quarters at Cashel, was badly weakened by more than usually disabling dynastic feuds, and its loss of strength and power had left the province an easy prey to the invaders. The failure of effective central leadership also left a nearly open field for a strong and ambitious leader. Though the Dal Cais was but one of several contiguous minor kingdoms acknowledging the suzerainty of the Eoganacht, its position was strategic: it controlled the great waterway of the Shannon and its lakes. The brothers, brilliant military tacticians as well as agile political activists, had enough influence and popularity to step into the empty space.

In 963 Mathgamain succeeded to the throne of Munster at Cashel. He and Brian continued to harass the Norse, finally inflicting a decisive defeat on their leader Ivar, king of Limerick, in a battle at Sulchoid in Tipperary in 967. In 976 Mathgamain was murdered and Brian succeeded him. He ruled Munster from Kincora, the family seat at Killaloe, today an attractive small town on a hillside at the southern end of Lough Derg. From his fortress on the hilltop (now the site of the parish church) Brian had a view over the long tree-girt lake — on one side of it the mild and bountiful fields of Tipperary, on the other the wooded mountains of his native Clare. Brian Boru, or Boromha (the sobriquet, also applied to the countryside around Kincora and meaning "tribute of cows," was bestowed by Mac Liag on an occasion when the king gave his poet the whole of his tribute), reigned competently over Munster for thirty years, during which time he consolidated his strength, subdued his enemies, and made strong inroads on the territory of the Ui Neill, whose king, Malachy II, claimed the high-kingship of all Ireland.

In 997 Brian and Malachy met near Clonfert and made an agreement that Brian would be king of the southern half of Ireland and Malachy of the northern. But Malachy's position was weakened by the same variety of fatal dynastic division that had undermined the Eoganacht. He lacked the support of his relations, the northern Ui Neill, and five years later Brian found it politic to break their agreement. In 1002 he persuaded the Ui Neill king to resign his throne, and had himself declared king of all Ireland.

"*Brian Imperator Scottorum*," he directed his scribe, Mac Liag, to enter in the *Book of Armagh,* in imitation of Charlemagne, a sovereign greatly admired by Brian. Like his hero, Brian saw himself as a feudal king claiming the real fealty of his subordinate princes. He had the foresight to realize that from this position he could far more efficaciously deal with the unscrupulous and capable foreigner than if he attempted to preserve the traditional limited Irish kingship, with its nominal overlordship of minor but independent kings, each supreme in his own state, and its shaky, unpredictable armies, "ropes of sand" that the tide of family squabbles could erode in a day.

Though he was an adroit manipulator, on occasion conscienceless, Brian never broke the law. He usurped no thrones: Munster came to him on the death of his elder brother, who had a legal claim on it; northern Ireland and with it the high-kingship of Ireland were his prize when Malachy gave in, willingly enough, to the pressure of circumstance. Brian's later assumption of the position of king in fact as well as in name flouted tradition and affronted many, but he never overstepped the bounds of Ireland's ancient laws. Within the framework of custom he forged a new and vital force: for the first time Ireland had a king who transcended the constricting boundaries of the *tuath* and the clan. This was an awesome accomplishment for an outsider from a minor kingdom with not much background and no powerful partisans. His astonishing success was due to military skill — an undefeatable combination of ingenuity, courage and caution — allied with political dexterity and a competent mastery of administrative techniques.

Though the eulogies do not particularize, being more concerned with the heroic aspects of Brian's military exploits and the luster of his peacetime reign, he must also have been blessed with a singularly attractive personality, a generous heart and an equable temper. The Norse sagas are warm in their praise of the enemy king: "The noblest of all kings, . . . King Brian would always forgive men he had sentenced to outlawry, even when they committed the same offence thrice; but if they transgressed yet again, he let the law take its course. From this it can be judged what kind of a king he was."[4]

Along with his native genius, Brian had in his favor another factor, which he exploited with virtuosity: the mortal divisions of his rivals, so deeply embroiled in family dissensions that they had no energy left for ruling Ireland or even for protecting themselves. Brian was the first king who gave Ireland something like a national consciousness. If he had gone further in his break with hidebound custom and provided the country with a sensible rule for the succession, the sorry history of the next 150 years — with its end result of Ireland's last, most tragic and ruinous invasion — might have been quite different.

Brian is credited with being a patron of the arts and learning as well as a reformer in ecclesiastical affairs. As a statesman he realized the inspiriting effect of a lively culture; as a politician he understood the value of a peaceful and unified Church. But he was not, like Charlemagne, a monarch who consciously and zealously sponsored a renaissance. Poets flourished, libraries were restocked, artists went back to work, not because Brian subsidized them or even specifically encouraged them, but because Ireland had peace. The Norse were no longer an enemy bringing distress and confusion but a settled people with trade and towns and a culture of their own. Brian appreciated the economic value of the new towns, most of which were in his own Munster territory, with their population his subjects. Though Dublin remained autonomous, Brian tried to keep on friendly terms with the little kingdom and exerted what control he could over its government.

Brian's operative attitude toward the Church was political. He used the power of the important monasteries in his struggles with the leading dynasties; he even took hostages from them "as a guarantee of the banishment of robbers and lawless people therefrom" — a euphemism for enjoining them not to shelter Brian's enemies. He helped to establish Armagh as the administrative center of the Irish Church, and in 1005 he recognized St. Patrick's original see as the "apostolic city" of Ireland, a first step on the way to Church reform. For Brian a greater concern than reform was that ecclesiastical unification would be advantageous to his centralized secular authority. Actual reform would not come until a century after Brian's death. In his time the two most important Norse cities, Dublin and Limerick, refused to acknowledge the primacy of Armagh; their prelates, mainly Irish clergy trained in England, were oriented to Canterbury. And the great monasteries clung to their traditional autonomy. But however tentative the reforms and however practical Brian's attitude, the Church revived under his rule for the same reason that the arts flourished — law and order had taken the place of chaos and despair.

At the end of three decades of effective supremacy, Brian's troubles were not over. The Leinstermen, whose lands lay between Ulster and Munster on the east and were bounded on the west by Connacht, had always resisted the rule of the Ui Neill. The ascendancy of Munster was even less acceptable, particularly in the person of Brian Boru. After thirty years they still despised the regal patriarch as a presumptuous parvenu from an insignificant state, who had no real ancestors.

The king of Leinster at this time was Maelmorda. He had a sister, Gormlaith, an immoral, awesomely ill-intentioned princess: ". . . the fairest of all women, and best gifted in everything that was not in her own power. . . . She did all things ill over which she had any power."[5] Gormlaith had been married three times, the last time to Brian, who divorced her in 995 — an act, undoubtedly warranted, that earned him her unsleeping hatred. By her first marriage, to King Olaf of Dublin, she had had a son, Sitric, who had succeeded to the throne of Dublin on his father's death. Through this relationship the Dublin Norse and the Leinstermen were allies.

With the combination of the independent pride of the Leinstermen, the intransigence of the Dublin Norse and Gormlaith's active malice, the faintest breath of an insult to someone's honor could precipitate a war. With spiteful ingenuity Gormlaith worked one up, inflaming her brother King Maelmorda against his overlord Brian, to the extent that he summoned all the disaffected Irish clans to help him throw off the yoke of the upstart. Maelmorda's nephew King Sitric of Dublin, willingly recruited, called in Norse allies from Orkney and the Western Isles, promising several of them separately and secretly the hand of his mother in marriage — with her easy acquiescence, and probably a nod toward the shade of her similarly redoubtable predecessor, Queen Maeve — plus the kingship of Ireland (or more plausibly, that of rich Dublin).

Brian collected a great army from Munster and Connacht, which included the deposed but still friendly Malachy and his Ui Neill forces. The Leinstermen and their Irish allies constituted two-thirds of the opposing army; the remaining third consisted of their Norse friends from over the sea. After a false start during which Brian besieged Dublin unsuccessfully for three months and his army, with Christmas coming, began to melt away, preparations were made for a decisive encounter.

The battle of Clontarf (today a seaside town two miles north of Dublin) took place on 23 April 1014, Good Friday: the date was chosen by the Norse allies, who believed that as a pious Christian Brian would not be able to give battle on a holy day. Brian was indeed able to give battle, though at age seventy-three he was not able to take an active part in it. He stayed in a tent in Tomar's Wood at the edge of the battleground, receiving news of the course of the conflict from his bodyguard. It was the longest and bloodiest battle of Ireland's history, lasting from dawn until dark; and multitudes of the leaders were slain, including Brian's son and his nephew. Altogether, according to the accounts, which are impossible to verify, nineteen thousand fell on the field or were drowned in the retreat. Brian's forces were victorious, and toward the end they enclosed the remaining

Norse in a semicircle, preventing their escape. The Norse had nowhere to fall back but into the sea, where thousands of them drowned. The disastrous flight was visible from Dublin, and King Sitric's wife, who was Brian's sister, remarked to her husband, "It seems to me that the foreigners have gained their patrimony."

"What meanest thou, woman?"

"Are they not rushing into the sea, which is their natural inheritance? I wonder are they in heat, like cattle; if so they tarry not to be milked."[6] Sitric slapped her so hard that he knocked out one of her teeth — but to this the course of history was impervious.

The battle was won but the leader was lost. A Viking, Brodar (one of those who had been promised the prize of Gormlaith), escaped from the encircling net of the enemy into Tomar's Wood, and there he found King Brian nearly unattended, most of his men off chasing fugitives. Brodar slew the king and fled deeper into the wood, but was caught by Munster soldiers, who executed him at once. (The Norse account in *Njal's Saga* claims that Brodar's stomach was slit and his entrails fastened to a tree; he was then led round and round the tree until his body was empty. This atrocious barbarity was so untypical of the Irish, to whom the idea of torture was totally alien — and so familiar to the Norse — that it was undoubtedly an invention.)

Brian's body, in accordance with his will, was conveyed to Armagh for burial, and his elaborate funeral was attended by thousands, who truly mourned their slain king. Sorrow was intensified by Brian's hero's-death in battle at the moment of victory; but all of Ireland knew that an incomparable peacetime leader had been lost. Brian was much loved, and the love has grown with time until he has become a towering, near-legendary figure. Exaggeration aside, the hero worship is deserved, for he gave Ireland a new, proud consciousness of herself as a nation.

As for the battle of Clontarf, it too has been hyperbolized and oversimplified into the decisive Irish-Norse confrontation, resulting in the final and total collapse of the invader. In truth it was hardly an Irish-Norse conflict at all, but an internal affair, a milestone in the never-ending struggle of the great dynasties for the sovereignty of Ireland. Long before Clontarf the Norse had ceased to be a power in Ireland. They had been exaggeratedly feared on account of their uncontrolled savagery and their superefficient weapons. But they had never come anywhere near conquering the country — nor had they wanted to. With the years they metamorphosed from warriors to traders, but they remained in all guises people of the sea. Unlike King Canute, the Danish conqueror of England, they had no designs on the subjugation of the country: their city-states were of interest to them only as ports and trading centers, never as headquarters for a serious penetration of the island.

The Norsemen's most effective invasion of Ireland was the peaceful and lasting infiltration of economic and cultural progress. Besides the weaponry skills they brought, which the Irish learned to use effectively against the Norse themselves, and besides the new techniques learned from the magnificent Scandinavian shipbuilders, which modernized the fishing industry and stimulated trade, the Norse introduced the invaluable convenience of coinage. When they had first arrived, the invaders had had no coins either. The knowledge came from the Continent, and about 995 the Norse of Dublin began minting their own silver coins.

Most important of all the Norse contributions, economically, was the development of secular towns, bringing to Ireland at last the incalculable benefit of centers for trading, business and government administration. Dublin, the chief Norse city in Ireland, became one of the most vital of the Scandinavian trade centers. Before Russia was opened up to Western commerce, the Continent's furs came from Iceland and Greenland, and the premier Irish port, with its fine harbor strategically placed on the Irish Sea, convenient to Scandinavia, England and the Continent, became the focal point of this lucrative trade. It was, of course, a Norse monopoly: Dublin was a Norse, not an Irish, city. But the Irish could not help benefiting from the flow of money, new ideas and new commercial contacts.

Though in the early years the horror of the Norse attacks had paralyzed creative endeavor, as comparative peace evolved confidence welled again, and with it came new springs of imaginative creativity. During the years of the Norse influence the Irish learned the advantages of stone in art and architecture: these were the years of the little stone churches (with their earliest use of the true arch), of the lovely soaring round towers and the appealing pictorial high crosses. Also in these years — once the Norse got over their penchant for appropriating movable wealth — there came a renaissance in metalwork. Celtic artists with centuries of traditional skill behind them incorporated Scandinavian animal designs into their intricate curvilinear abstractions, with breathtaking results.

In spite of the overall strengthening effect of the Norse infusion, bringing artistic and economic regeneration, Ireland's political course did not become smoother. There still remained a fatal flaw, and it would be the direct cause of the final breakdown.

CHAPTER XII
THE ANGLO-NORMAN INVASION

As a result of the Norse occupation, Ireland emerged from her primitive chrysalis, shedding her simple rural and pastoral economy and her hidebound political conservatism to become — almost — a full-fledged medieval European nation. Not quite: the ancestral dynasticism still held priority. Local loyalties were more important than the nascent national unity, and the sovereignty of a strong king was bitterly contested by the scions of the old houses, who set their presumptive family rights above communal safety. Slowly the concept of an operative central monarchy was making inroads into age-old tradition. Brian was Ireland's first strong king, but he was not her last nor by any odds her strongest. In the 150 years between his death and the Anglo-Norman invasion, several effectively commanding sovereigns emerged. Unfortunately, such rulers were rare, and there were also decades of no over-king at all or of weak ones whose pretensions to power were fatally corroded by the crippling effect of family bickering.

One of these forceful kings was Murtagh O'Brien (great-grandson of Brian Boru), who ruled from 1086 to 1119. His domination, based on personal ability and goodwill, was dissipated on his death, because he had made no serious effort to repair Ireland's dilapidated political organization, and his failure to ensure the succession led to a relapse into the old divisive dynastic struggles. But he was an authoritative and beneficent king. Among the good acts that had a lasting effect was his presentation of Cashel to the

St. Patrick's Rock at Cashel, County Tipperary — seat of the kings of Munster — presented to the Church by King Murtagh O'Brien in 1101

Church in 1101, to be the metropolis of the bishop's see. His interest in Church reform, like that of his predecessor Brian, was more practical than pious. His gift of Cashel, at the same time that it benefited the Church, deprived the still-threatening Eoganacht of their family seat and ancient capital. Giving away the venerable Munster capital was in any case no sacrifice for O'Brien, who ruled from his own family seat of Kincora.

In the political chaos that followed his death in 1119, the supremacy of Munster that Brian Boru had established was irreversibly reduced. But another strong king arose over its ashes, Turlough O'Connor. He had been helped to his throne of Connacht by Murtagh O'Brien himself, only to initiate, on O'Brien's death, a fierce dispute over the succession with the O'Brien heirs, which O'Connor finally won. He combined military strength with political acumen: playing on the fortuitous divisions of his rivals and setting up puppet kings over adjacent kingdoms, he succeeded in 1136 to the throne of all Ireland.

Turlough O'Connor and, to an even greater extent, his son Rory, who was Ireland's last high-king before the Anglo-Norman invasion, gave Ireland the closest thing to a feudal administration that she had ever known, extending the royal jurisdiction in a centralized and expanded government over most areas of daily life, and cutting far into the claims and prerogatives of the great landed families. But the concept of real kingship was too young in Ireland. Local loyalties were still more compelling than an incipient monarchy, and when external attack came, as in the time of the first Viking invasions, the country found no resources within herself to enable her to deal with catastrophe.

The reign of Turlough O'Connor brought a more lasting benefit than the all-too-fleeting concept of national cohesion: that was the reform of the Church. One result of the Norse occupation was that through increased trade Ireland had a closer contact with the rest of Europe. Travel was easier in the new fast ships, and not only Irish clerics and scholars — always known for their inclination to roam — but laymen and even princes travelled abroad. The most immediate source of fresh ideas was England. When the Norse in Ireland became converted to Christianity they established sees in Dublin, Limerick, Waterford and Wexford. Because of their close connections across the Irish Sea, these new religious establishments were more attuned to English than to Irish practices, and since the Synod of Whitby (discussed previously), the English Church had been effectively Romanized. The Norse wisely chose Irish clerics as bishops for their newly established dioceses, but they chose Irish who had been trained in Winchester and Canterbury. So not only did clerics travelling on the Continent begin to understand that the Irish Church had idiosyncrasies that were inconsistent with the current rulings of the "coarb of Peter" (the Irish designation of the pope), but the English-trained priests came home with concrete ideas of how the Irish Church must be reformed to come into line with medieval Catholicism.

But more was required than a new set of formalities to replace the old. The Irish Church needed to reform not only its structure but its soul. The monastic system had become a top-heavy power structure bristling with abuses. The authority of abbots, as we have seen, was irresponsible, the morals of the clergy were lax, continued embroilment in secular affairs had brought the Church into disgracefully unchurchlike attitudes and activities. The unofficial sect of the *celi De* had brought a cleansing breath of air into religious life, but its influence, never translated into administrative action, proved evanescent when the Viking terror arrived. The raiders were intent not only on pillage but apparently also on the extinction of Christianity. The beleaguered Church lost her energy for reform: the restorative spirit evaporated and the establishment, in self-defense, fell back into the old safer, stronger hierarchical system. The worldliness that resulted had already been deplorably in evidence before the Vikings, and by the time the invaders had become a settled part of the population the Church structure had hardened into reactionary rigidity.

But in spite of the moral deterioration of those centuries there still burned a small bright flame, the spirit that had set the Celtic Church apart and above the Continental brand of Christianity: the legacy of transcendent dedication and purity bequeathed by the saints. This luminous heritage would enable the Church to reform itself from within.

The origin of the reform movement came at first from the Norse dioceses. Gilbert, first bishop of Limerick, and Malthus, first bishop of Waterford, were both Irish monks trained in England under the aegis of St. Anselm, the intellectual and sensitive Italian monk who had become the great reforming archbishop of Canterbury. Malthus was even consecrated bishop of Waterford there. Though they had been imbued with the English tradition of Romanization and convinced it would be good for Ireland, these loyal Irishmen, despite their affection for their mentor, owned to no allegiance to Canterbury. The strong efforts of the English archdiocese to bring the Irish Church into its primacy were initially successful in Dublin. But the bishops of Waterford and Limerick were determined that their native Church, while following England's lead, should maintain her historic independence.

In 1101 a synod was called at Cashel to consider measures for the reform of the Church. At that time King Murtagh O'Brien, as noted, surrendered Cashel "to God and St. Patrick." Cellach, archbishop of Armagh, an Irish-trained cleric who was a zealous reformer, appointed Malthus bishop of Cashel, and a few years later created an archbishopric there. The synod, attended by the leaders of the reform movement — Cellach of Armagh, Gilbert of Limerick, O'Dunan of Meath, Malthus of Waterford and, of course, the reforming King Murtagh O'Brien — did not envision any revolutionary changes, but recommended reform within the framework of the monastic system. Measures were passed to protect the right of sanctuary from abuse — the Church was not to harbor anyone who had committed treason or had murdered within his family — to abolish simony, to insure that abbots be celibate, to tighten the marriage laws (but concubinage and divorce remained untouched, though these practices were opposed to the law of Rome).

It was a first step. The next, taken at the Synod of Rathbreasil in 1110, recommended radical changes. It was convened by Gilbert of Limerick, who by now was papal legate and as such regarded himself as the leading churchman in Ireland, and it proposed what amounted to a new constitution for the Irish Church. There were to be twenty-four dioceses, each under the entire jurisdiction of a bishop, who would have in his charge not only the parish priests but the monasteries with their abbots, who must also be in holy orders. This was revolutionary indeed; it was also, in its time, unfeasible. In the first place, it postulated the immediate and total overthrow of the monastic practices of six centuries. The Church would have to replace lay abbots whose families had virtually owned the monasteries from the beginning, with suitable men in holy orders; and would also somehow have to get rid of the superfluity of old-style subordinate bishops who had always performed their holy offices at the bidding of the abbots. In the second place, Gilbert's paper plan for the dioceses was impracticable because it ignored the tribal boundaries of the *tuaths*. In his division, furthermore, he disregarded Dublin, the wealthy and increasingly important Norse city whose diocese was the oldest in Ireland. Dublin's bishops (calling themselves, without papal sanction, archbishops) considered themselves superior to the old-fashioned Irish Church, and looked for their counsels across the sea to Canterbury. The Irish reformers retaliated by ignoring them, arbitrarily including Dublin in the diocese of Glendalough. Gilbert's diocese of Limerick, on the other hand, was given undue prominence, its Church of Mary designated at the principal church of Ireland.

However unworkable its provisions, Rathbreasil laid the groundwork. It brought Ireland, though as yet only on paper, into the fold of the Catholic Church; it also prescribed corrections for the abuses that had caused the deterioration of the preceding centuries. If Gilbert was overweening in his assumption of preeminence, and too sanguine in his expectations, he and his fellow reformers saw what was needed.

But reform could not be imposed from above — that was never the way of the Irish. To bring the Church at all its levels to the mood of reform would take a man with the rare, selfless and essentially modest commitment of the early saints. Such a one there was; he was still a boy at the time of Rathbreasil.

After the death of Murtagh O'Brien, when Turlough O'Connor was striving to displace the O'Brien hegemony in Munster, one of his tactics was to give a helping hand to the languishing Eoganacht. He placed Cormac Mac Carthy, a scion of that family, on the throne of Desmond, the southern half of Munster, from which he also had jurisdiction over Cashel. In his exile Cormac had taken refuge with Malthus, who had retired from the see of Cashel to the monastery of Lismore, which had been one of the centers of the *celi De* movement. There, in 1121, the exile became friends with a young priest, Malachy, who had come down from Armagh to receive instructions from Malthus in the Roman forms of church administration.

Malachy was born in 1094, the son of a teacher at Armagh. He was taught at Armagh and became a monk there under the direction of a stern and reclusive holy man, Imar, who was in accord with the ideals of the reformers, and so instructed his young charge. Malachy's combination of intellect, piety and personal charm brought him to the notice of Archbishop Cellach, who ordained him priest when he was only twenty-four. Soon after that Cellach made him his vicar, and the fledgling priest proceeded to administer the diocese of Armagh radically and effectively, in accordance with the decrees of Rathbreasil. But, conscious of his youth and his insufficient knowledge, he resigned his post to study with Malthus, where he became friends with Cormac Mac Carthy, the refugee king.

After a few years there, Cellach conferred upon Malachy the ancient abbey of Bangor, where St. Comgall's illustrious school, "the nursery of saints," had flourished in the sixth and seventh centuries, but which the Vikings had attacked repeatedly until it was finally abandoned and fell into decay. Malachy, indifferent to material wealth, refused the land and the tithes, and set about personally rebuilding the abbey in wood, with the help of ten monks from Armagh. In 1124, ordained by Cellach as bishop of two tribal territories, a diocese newly formed for him, Malachy made the abbey the seat of his see. It was an administrative center at the farthest edge of his territory, on the shore of the ocean, but he loved it: there he was in the company of the shades of St. Comgall and St. Columbanus. Also, he had a lingering affinity for the old Irish ways, and did not regard himself so much as bishop as abbot, coarb of Comgall. However, he administered his diocese after the Roman convention with the same zeal that he had shown in Armagh. He travelled constantly, always on foot, with a group of disciples, talking and preaching to the people of the towns and the countryside, much loved for his kindness, his humility and his eloquence. Though a reformer who saw the need of bringing Ireland into line with Roman usage, he was far more a throwback to his spiritual ancestors than the standard type of a medieval bishop. In temperament he was closest to Aidan of Lindisfarne, who likewise ruled a large territory from its remotest corner, journeying on foot among the people to gain by personal contact their devoted obedience.

Malachy was driven out of Bangor in 1127 by King Conor O'Loughlin, a savage scion of the northern Ui Neill, and went with his monks back to his mentor Malthus at Lismore. There he renewed his friendship with Cormac Mac Carthy, once more in exile. When Cormac again regained his throne, he gave his friend land for a monastery on the Iveragh Peninsula in County Kerry. Malachy founded there the Order of Austin Canons, whose brethren, while observing an old-fashioned strict mode of monastic living, practiced among the people a blend of pastoral and educational work — a way of life so beneficial and constructive that the order spread to many cathedral towns.

In 1129 Archbishop Cellach died, having, in a revolutionary move, left the succession of the see of Armagh not to the customary relative, but to Malachy. Though Cellach himself had been of the family that had long supplied the abbots of Armagh, he believed fervently that the custom of appointing hereditary lay abbots should end. In an effort to secure this result in the person of Malachy, he left the enforcement of his will to two kings, Conor O'Brien, king of Thomond, and Malachy's friend Cormac Mac Carthy of Desmond. The combination of the machinations of the two kings with Malachy's personal magnetism and known abilities realized Cellach's will only after eight years of struggle. In 1137 Malachy became coarb of Patrick at Armagh — only to resign the position at once in favor of a designated successor, Gelasius. Five years before, Malachy had made the condition that when he had accomplished what was needed — that the scandal of hereditary succession in this most important see of Ireland should be abrogated once for all — he would go back to Bangor.

But he did not retire to grow old peacefully in the place he loved best. Two years later he went to Rome in order to request of the pope the pallia (insignia of office, without which an archbishop cannot legally perform his functions) for the archbishops of Armagh and Cashel. On the way he stopped at Clairvaux, in Burgundy, the monastery of St. Bernard, a learned, witty and attractive young nobleman who had become the most rigorously ascetic of monks and had revitalized the Cistercian order (founded in 1098), an offshoot of the Benedictine. The two men had much in common; both were intellectual and sophisticated, yet passionately dedicated to the return of monastic life to an idea of self-denying discipline that had gone out of style. This meeting was to result in the founding of the Cistercian order in Ireland, with its headquarters at Mellifont Abbey, of which we will speak in a later chapter.

Malachy's audience with Pope Innocent II did not gain him the pallia, which, according to canon law, must be demanded by a council of bishops. But the pope, much impressed by the Irish bishop, appointed him papal legate in Ireland. Malachy, now in effect the chief prelate of Ireland, worked hard to reform his country's Church until, in 1148, he convened the Synod of Inispatrick, at which the assembled bishops formally demanded the pallia. Malachy was sent again to get them, but he never arrived at Rome. When he reached Clairvaux he caught a fever and died two weeks later. It was at Clairvaux rather than in Ireland that Malachy's cult originated, and in 1190 Pope Clement II canonized him, recognizing him as one of the few official Irish saints.

The reformation of the Irish Church — in which Malachy played so large a part (though he was himself a personification of the best of the old independent Celtic ways) — was not fully accomplished at the time of his death. But his efforts bore fruit four years later when Ireland received her pallia by special legate. The pope overgenerously granted four instead of the two requested, to the annoyance of the bishops. Besides Armagh and Cashel, there were to be two more archbishoprics, Tuam and Dublin. This meant that the Irish bishops had to accept the hated Norse Dublin; it also meant that Dublin must give up her Canterbury connection. Ireland at last had one unified Church, divided into proper town-based dioceses, each ruled uniformly and absolutely by a bishop responsible only to his arch-bishop, like all the other Catholic Churches in Europe. A few loose ends were left, which were tied up a few years later when the Anglo-Normans arrived with their strong-arm efficiency.

The Celtic Church as an independent entity was no more. For better or for worse, Ireland was in the European fold. In the narrowing and con-forming something was lost — the freedom, tolerance and imagination that had set Irish clerics apart for six centuries. But this had been lost even before the Vikings, and in general it can be said that Ireland was better for the reformation. Abuses were remedied, lax morality was corrected, uni-form monastic standards were set, a new-old spirit of piety informed the Church at all levels.

There was a notable cultural regeneration as well. Irish scholars of the eleventh and twelfth centuries began gathering their country's pagan lore into omnibus volumes, and to this period of compilation we owe our knowledge of the pre-Christian Irish-Celts. Although literary inventiveness was at a low ebb after the soaring creative flights of less troubled times, there were provocative developments in art and architecture. Along with the new connections in England and on the Continent came a fresh look at ecclesiastical architecture; and Ireland's conservative, almost primitive style of church building evolved into a happy blend of Continental and traditional that became known as Irish Romanesque. Its first and chief treasure is the little church on St. Patrick's Rock at Cashel known as

Cormac's Chapel (shown on page 303); and this gem of stonework is directly attributable to the friendship between St. Malachy and Cormac Mac Carthy, king of Desmond. St. Malachy was the spiritual father of an even more advanced architectural style when in 1142 he founded Ireland's first Cistercian monastery, Mellifont, modelled on St. Bernard's Clairvaux. This ambitious structure, much larger and more complex than anything seen in Ireland before, introduced the basilica style of church building that had already existed on the Continent for over a century.

In the following chapters we will take a more detailed look at the literary and artistic renaissance that accompanied Ireland's church reform. Now we have to review one last sad step in her political history.

Ever since Brian Boru had voided the never-strong convention of the hereditary succession of the Ui Neill to the high-kingship, the local kings of Connacht and Leinster had considered they had as good a right to the succession as the descendants of the Dal Cais upstart. Consequently, for nearly a century and a half after Brian's death Ireland was lacerated by the destructive bickering of the rival septs, and most of her kings ruled "with opposition" — that is, their supremacy was not universally accepted. The efficacy of the few strong kings who emerged above the disharmony was a function of their particular talents and the pro tem loyalty of their supporters, rather than of any change in Ireland's fatal localism. The great families, having no tradition of national unity in their background, still deemed it more important to seize the kingship for their local dynasties than to pay allegiance, for the sake of a still-dim concept of nationality, to one central authority.

Rory (Roderick) O'Connor, son of Turlough O'Connor, was the last king of independent Ireland. He was also her strongest king to that date. There was no one in Ireland who could challenge him, and he made effectual progress toward the concentration of authority. But his supremacy was undermined by the continuing disaffection of the great clans, among whom the Leinstermen were the most vindictively active. In 1014 this determinedly independent group had called on the foreigners — the Dublin Norse and their overseas friends — to help them put down the parvenu. They had been badly beaten at Clontarf — but not decisively enough. The weakness of succeeding kings gave them a chance to recoup, and when their time appeared to come again they did not hesitate once more to summon foreign aid.

The precedent for their action was so ingrained in the Irish mores that no one regarded it as a serious national threat. The old Irish tradition of sloughing off dynastic segments in order to narrow the possible choices for the kingship had throughout her history been a source of potential disaster. The discarded princes had customarily sought aid from their neighbors; that this perilous expedient might bring dangerously acquisitive confederates did not occur to the disgruntled aspirants, single-mindedly intent on overthrowing a rival.

Diarmait Mac Murrough, who was king of Leinster when Rory O'Connor became high-king of Ireland, was a man of selfish ambition, small morals and a large capacity for resentment. He was also contentious, cruel and savage to a degree extraordinary even in the far-from-gentle times in which he lived. Already execrated for his iniquities (among other misdeeds he had gained his throne by killing two princes and blinding a third; he had forced the abbess of Kildare to leave her convent and marry one of his people; he had carried off, with her temporary consent, a woman of the Ui Neill who was someone else's wife), he had incurred the enmity of Rory O'Connor by supporting his Connacht rival to the high-kingship. When O'Connor gained the throne, his Leinster adherents expelled Mac Murrough from his kingship. In the eyes of succeeding Irishmen, Diarmait's subsequent action has no redeeming features. But at that time it was the least of his crimes, and he had respectable precedents. Doing what many disappointed Irish chieftains had done before him, he called on another king for assistance.

In 1166 he went to England to appeal to King Henry II to help him regain his kingdom and even, he fatuously imagined, seat him on the high throne of all Ireland. The English king, first of the Plantagenets, great-grandson of William the Conqueror and heir to a large part of France, had an entirely different idea of what was entailed in medieval kingship than had this ousted local chieftain. Diarmait's supplication was vindictive and provincial; Henry's positive response was sharp-sighted and coldly practical. An energetic and realistic king, he had for some years had his eye on the vulnerable, divided land so close over the sea. Besides the bountiful productivity of Ireland's countryside and the undefended wealth of her monasteries, the preeminence of Norse Dublin in the world's commerce aroused Henry's envy and cupidity. England was losing too much trade to the active and well-placed Scandinavians. If Henry occupied Ireland, or at least her eastern coast with its thriving harbor cities, he could break the Norse control of the fur trade and divert a large part of this lucrative business to the English port of Bristol.

Ireland's need for ecclesiastical reform had been Henry's excuse to take the first step. Backed by the English bishops, who at that time had the myopic cooperation of some of the Irish reformers themselves, Henry had sought the pope's sanction for an invasion of Ireland, presumably for the good of the immortal souls of her people. Pope Adrian IV, no doubt politically motivated, acceded, and in 1154 the only English pope "gave" Ireland to the Plantagenet king in order that he should inaugurate reforms — most of which in the meantime were being carried out by the Irish themselves without outside assistance. At that moment, however, Henry was not prepared to launch an army across the Irish Sea. Diarmait's misguided appeal twelve years later provided a convenient opportunity for the English king to carry out the project with the least possible disarrangement to his enormous, carefully balanced kingdom. He sent the Irish chieftain to Wales to raise a group of volunteers from among the drifts of bankrupt Norman knights who were idling there hoping for a smile of fortune and ready for any gamble.

In Bristol Diarmait approached an indigent aristocrat named Richard de Clare, earl of Pembroke — known as Strongbow — and promised him, in the venerable tradition, the hand of his beautiful daughter Eva and the throne of Leinster, which he had no legal or moral right to pledge. Several other Norman cavaliers of high family and low fortune were promised smaller prizes, such as the city of Wexford. All the recruits were both impoverished and adventurous and, aside from the promises, they knew that the plundering would be good.

Diarmait then returned to Ireland and conventionally offered hostages to Rory O'Connor for his good faith and that of his foreign allies. The high-king credulously accepted them and even gave the treacherous exile leave to take possession of Hy Kinsella, his ancestral kingdom in South Leinster, which Diarmait proceeded to reinforce with an advance detachment of his Welsh recruits. The gullibility of the high-king is almost incomprehensible; somewhere within him there apparently existed a premedieval Irish chieftain who still believed in the observation of honorable formalities even in the most realistically purposeful of conflicts. The Anglo-Normans, however, did not go by the old rules — nor had the Norse, as history should have warned him.

In 1170, when Strongbow landed near Waterford with an army of about three thousand men, the Irish king belatedly realized that Diarmait and his friends were breaking the rules. In the beginning the Irish were quite unprepared. They were gallant and skilled fighters, but their military discipline was loose and their weapons were old-fashioned. The steel-armored battalions of the enemy were impervious to the sword, and the English detachments of highly trained longbow archers raised havoc in the crowds of leather-clad warriors. In addition the Franks, as the Irish called the invaders because they were French-speaking, had the ramrod discipline that had made the Roman legions invincible to the barbarians, and they cut through the poorly armed, unordered, desperately courageous Irish hordes with the same inexorable efficiency. Irish soldiers fell before the unswerving phalanxes like grain before a reaper; Irish towns, unwalled and defenseless, surrendered with barely a scuffle. But the Norman soldiers gave no quarter, butchering and plundering the terrorized populace with an organized fury that outdid the comparatively simple ferocity of the Vikings.

In a touching and fruitless effort to placate destiny, the Irish clergy called a council at Armagh, at which "it was unanimously resolved that . . . the divine vengeance had brought upon them this severe judgement for the sins of the people [who] had long been wont to purchase natives of England . . . and reduce them to slavery; and that now they also, by reciprocal justice, were reduced to servitude by that very nation. . . . It was therefore decreed . . . that all Englishmen throughout the island who were in a state of bondage should be restored to freedom." [1] The abolition of slavery was an astonishingly progressive act for its time, but it did not soften any English hearts.

The struggle was not absolutely unequal, however. The Irish, falling back everywhere, would not be conquered. Like wild animals they knew their countryside, its bogs, its forests, its hidden valleys and overhanging hills. They waged a constant and effective guerrilla warfare, attacking the enemy from behind, decimating his flanks, destroying his outposts, retaking villages, negating his conquests. The swift Norman successes netted, in this initial invasion, secure ascendancy only over the thirty-mile area surrounding Dublin. It would take four agonizing centuries, baneful to both nations, before Ireland would become a colony of England; and the hate would never die.

At the time with which we are concerned, Henry II was at fault. More interested in his French domains — he was from beginning to end primarily a French king, never even caring to speak English — than his English responsibilities, he was criminally shortsighted in his treatment of his new conquest. He never sent enough troops to penetrate the country and subdue the intransigents. He did not exert his personal authority, except briefly, nor did he leave an adequate royal representative to impose English law, secure the fealty of his colonials, and give the Irish a stable government — or any tolerable government at all. He never attempted, as had his ancestor, William of Normandy, to make his conquest a colony whose people would enjoy the rights of citizens. Irish nationals, outside the law, remained the enemy and were vengefully treated as such for centuries.

In 1171 Henry made an initial gesture toward pacification. Concerned over the arrogant rapacity of his earls, who were appropriating Irish kingdoms wholesale and apparently forgetting that they owed allegiance to the king back home, he made a personal invasion with a large army. Part of his purpose was to secure their fealty, but he also succeeded in placating the Irish by a politic, and false, display of magnanimity. Weak, anarchic Ireland, at first overawed by the king's strength, then won over by his evident kindness, probably would at this point have welcomed a strong and reasonable government, even by a foreigner. But Henry only stayed for six months, and when he departed, his promises melted as the ruthless Norman earls took charge again.

Ireland was brought down — her isolation irretrievably breached, her spiritual freshness succumbed to despair, her creative energy dried at the source. The primitive political system, hardly changed since pagan times because it had never been seriously threatened, had outlived itself. With the hostile encroachment of organized feudal forces, the ancient order toppled like an old tree decayed at the roots.

The denouement was inevitable, but its vicious circumstances were tragic: with the end of an outworn and rotten political structure, there also came an end to the most extraordinary intellectual, artistic and spiritual development the Christian community had seen. For six centuries Ireland had been a beacon; it is time to look at her gifts to the Western world.

PART FOUR

THE FLOWERING

CHAPTER XIII
EDUCATION

IN 591 COLUMBANUS LANDED ON THE SHORE OF FRANCE, BRINGING TO THE Continent the first intimations of the happy congruence of cultures that would constitute Ireland's golden age. Although it was for its time an extraordinary flowering, in the country of its origin it cannot be called a renaissance. There was no rebirth because there had never been a death. The radiant growth of art and literature and scholarship that flourished in Ireland from about the seventh to the twelfth centuries was already there in essence; its seeds were dropped in pagan times and they germinated during the early years of Christianity. No large-scale invaders had trampled the fertile soil for many centuries. When Christianity gently encroached, no fearful clerical purists inhibited the thriving native plant. While Britain and the Continent were set back centuries under the domination of successive waves of barbarians, the dark flood of ignorance and superstition never inundated this green island.

Behind the Christian wealth of art, letters and philosophy in the Middle Ages was the pagan-Celtic veneration for men of learning. We have seen that the Celtic god of literature, Ogma, drew men to him with golden cords fastened to his tongue, that the benign or malignant power of the poet was respected above weaponry, that the *aes dana* was the only class outside of royalty whose members could cross the boundaries of the *tuath*, that the education of a prince in the skills of the mind was as important as his training in the art of warfare. The reverence for the written (originally

239

spoken) word did not wane with the advent of Christianity. St. Patrick communed with the spirits of heathen poets and assuaged his guilty pleasure with the reasoning that the old warrior tales, written down, would bring innocent joy to unborn generations. St. Columba initiated a full-scale battle after a dispute over a rare and precious Psalter.

In a distinctly pagan tone, not only the contents of books but the books themselves were thought to have intrinsic mystical energy. The wisdom of words transferred itself to their corporeal vessels: thus, according to the Venerable Bede, "in the case of people suffering from snake-bite, the leaves of manuscripts from Ireland were scraped, and the scrapings put in water and given the sufferer to drink. These scrapings at once absorbed the whole violence of the spreading poison and assuaged the swelling." [1] During an onslaught of the yellow plague in 664, the Christian poet Colman set off with some of his pupils for an island beyond nine waves from the land, believed to be the limit of contagion; to insure their safe departure he wrote, the night before they sailed, a hymn as a "shield of protection" against the plague. An interesting sidelight on this hymn is that it was written mainly in Irish, not in Latin, the tongue of Christianity. Presumably the ancestral language exuded a potency lacked by the imported. Pagan persuasions died slowly.

Into the receptive atmosphere of a country already imbued with love of literature and learning came the fresh impulse of Christianity — a simple, mystical and potent creed to take the place of outworn pagan practices, and a vital source of inspiration to the Celtic imagination. The new religion brought with it two inestimable boons: a written language and the legacy of Greco-Roman classical culture.

Even before Ireland was officially Christian, scholars from the Continent were emigrating to the island to escape the barbarians. "The Huns," wrote Jordanes, the sixth-century historian of the Gothic nation, "who were infamously begotten, i.e. by demons, after they had found their way by the guidance of a hind through the Maeotic marshes, invaded the Goths, whom they terrified exceedingly by their unexpectedly awful appearance. And thanks to them the depopulation of the entire Empire commenced. . . . owing to [the Huns'] devastations, . . . all the learned men on this side of the sea fled away, and in transmarine ports, i.e. Hibernia, and wherever they betook themselves, brought about a great advance of learning to the inhabitants of those regions." [2] The Hunnish invasions took place in the latter part of the fourth century, so a generation before St. Patrick, Ireland was already being exposed to the erudition of Continental scholars.

The preference of the fleeing savants for Ireland presupposes a cordial intellectual climate. We have seen that the doctrines of Christianity were known in some parts of Ireland when St. Patrick came; European learning had also penetrated, possibly in a more sophisticated form than the country was ready for. There is a hint of this in St. Patrick's *Confession*: while deploring his own ignorant rusticity and his deficiency in Latin, he decries the "rhetoricians, who do not know the Lord, . . . who appear to be wise, and skilled in the laws, and powerful in speech and in every matter."[3]

The rhetoricians to whom he refers were refugee Gaulish scholars, who had settled in some numbers in Munster and Leinster, the provinces most easily accessible from the Continent. For several centuries there had been a natural reciprocity between Gaul and Ireland. Both were inhabited by Celtic people with a similar language and mental perspective. There was a flourishing trade across the Channel: the Irish exchanged their woolens and hides and their awesome wolf-dogs for the wines of Gaul and silks from the Gallic overland trade with the East. The fugitives sailed in these same trading vessels from the great commercial ports of Bordeaux and Nantes, and they named some of their Irish communities after their own lost cities, as Bordgal in Westmeath, after Burdigalia (Bordeaux). The amiable reception of the Gaulish refugees brought others; and Ireland came to enjoy a Continental reputation as a haven of tolerance as well as a hospitable sanctuary where the beleaguered scholars would find all the customary comforts of civilization.

In exchange for Ireland's openhanded welcome, the immigrants brought to their new home a great wealth: their books. The Greek and Latin manuscripts brought over by homeless exiles became the foundations of Irish monastic libraries. Irish schools had the advantage of the prime teaching of the Continent, and Irish students got the benefit of the entire body of fourth-century learning, a lore that went back to classical Greece. In Europe at that time there had not yet developed the churchly fear and negation of the classics that would be such a detriment to medieval learning. (It was not until 436 that the Council of Carthage decreed that no bishop should read the books of the gentiles.) So from their Continental teachers Irish ecclesiastical students learned to appreciate the heathen poets and philosophers with no moral distinction from the Scriptures and the teachings of the Church Fathers. The thorough grounding in the classics polished their style and deepened their philosophy, producing a new breed of scholar.

On the Continent, meanwhile, with the finest minds in exile and the land overrun by ignorant and heedless barbarians, scholarship languished and the centuries-long debasement of learning set in. Ireland was not only a haven; it became the only place outside of Byzantium where the scholastic habit of mind and the accumulation of classical knowledge were preserved and treasured and used. But for the careful and loving transcriptions of ecclesiastical writings and pre-Christian classics by monks in Irish scriptoria and the study of these works by generations of young students, much of the world's literature would have disappeared. The Irish missionaries who brought their glowing faith back to Europe in the Dark Ages turned out to be much more than evangelists — they were Europe's only remaining humanists.

In fourth- and fifth-century Ireland, however, it is likely that the scholarly exiles looked down on the educational defects of their hosts; probably St. Patrick spoke in his *Confession* not only for himself but for his compatriots. But the immigrants must soon have recognized the inbred eagerness to learn, the enthusiastic welcoming of fresh ideas.

The language of the new learning was Latin, and its great advantage to Ireland — besides the books the scholars brought with them containing the collected lore of Europe — was its alphabet. *Ogam* was a singularly clumsy method of writing; consequently, it was rarely used except for carved funerary or ceremonial inscriptions. Latin never took precedence over Irish in the schools, but on account of its convenient script it enriched the native learning. Now educated people could apply the new, easy writing to their own lore. The result was that secular learning throve alongside religious, and an extraordinary body of written vernacular literature evolved — a picture of an ancient pagan civilization unmatched anywhere in the Western world.

The recording of the oral tradition was historically important, and the conscientious copying of Christian and classical works preserved much of what would otherwise have been lost. A further, fascinating result of the fusion of Christian and pagan learning in Ireland was the rise of a new kind of literature. Inevitably, the creative spirit upwelled and the scribes, not content with mere copying, began to invent their own tales. The traditional voyages to seek *Tir na n'Og,* for instance, were enhanced by borrowings from Homer and other classical sources and filled out with the current geographical knowledge, to produce that most captivating of Christian epics, *The Voyage of St. Brendan.*

More intimate and more touching is the poetry that developed. Though under the deft touch of sensitive monk-poets it became an art of high sophistication, it was often no more than a side issue, even a form of self-indulgence by monks bored with tedious transcription. But the seemingly offhand verses, sometimes simply a few lines scribbled in the margins of painstakingly inscribed manuscripts, give us an engaging vision of the interior lives of those cloistered anchorites, their love of nature and of animals, the personal intimacy of their religious experience, their self-deprecating wit, and, on occasion, their irritated ennui. Not the sternest asceticism could quell the effervescence of the Celtic imagination.

With the stimulus of the new learning, monastic schools arose and flourished. Those of Enda of Aran, Finian of Clonard and Comgall of Bangor were among the first; from these illustrious institutions scholars went forth to teach others both in Ireland and abroad. The Irish schools attracted foreign students as well, particularly from Britain. Ireland's neighbor was in a state of uneasy disorder during the years of the Anglo-Saxon invasions, and would-be scholars found in Irish monasteries the tranquil havens they needed for calm, uninterrupted study. Until the seventh century there were only a few; then, in 664, came an outbreak of plague, and streams of Britons fled to Ireland.

Though those who sought sanctuary were mostly laymen, there was a good rapport between them and their hosts, and the Irish monks were outstandingly generous. "Some of [the English]," wrote Bede, "presently devoted themselves to a monastical life, others chose rather to apply themselves to study, going about from one master's cell to another. The Scots [Irish] willingly received them all, and took care to supply them with food, as also, to furnish them with books to read, and their teaching, gratis."[4] In the university at Armagh, one-third of the students were foreign, most of them British. Many of the British nobility enjoyed an Irish education, the most notable among them being the learned Aldfrith, who became king of Northumbria in 685.

In this period there was manifested a connection with Spain, too. Since the Bronze Age, when Ireland had been part of the "Atlantic Ends of Europe," the seafaring connection of the western islands and peninsulas, the two countries had had intercourse over the ocean trade lanes. When monasticism arose in Ireland, the form it took was a direct throwback to the early Christian North African monastic practices, knowledge of which had been part of the cultural interchange that travelled over the trade routes from Spain. We will see later how Irish art exhibited a kinship with Coptic, an affinity probably traceable to the same source.

In the field of learning, Irish rapport with Spain was associated most closely with the teachings of Isidore of Seville. The seventh-century Spanish archbishop, educator and savant was almost as effective in the development of medieval Christianity as Gregory the Great, mostly in the field of education. In Ireland his influence was subtle and far-reaching. Irish scholars discovered a strong congeniality in the outlook of the Spanish churchman, and some of his writings were known and transcribed there sooner than on the Continent. Isidore had a passion for classification, for etymology, for the mystical qualities of numbers: enthusiasms that were echoed in the Irish-Celtic mind. He further endeared himself to the Irish by his conscientious attention to their North African spiritual ancestors, gathering and preserving the lore of the desert fathers.

The monastic schools of Ireland, though they owed much to the stimulus of the Continental body of knowledge contributed by refugee scholars, had a long pagan tradition behind them. Learning had a mythological origin. In Tipperary there was a fountain called Connla's Well; over it grew nine hazel trees that bore flowers and crimson nuts at the same time. The nuts were filled with knowledge of poetry, art and all the sciences. When they dropped into the water, salmon ate them and crimson spots appeared on the fishes' bellies. The salmon then swam down the seven rivers that flowed out of Connla's Well, called the streams of knowledge, among which were the Boyne, the Suir, the Nore, the Barrow and the Slaney. Those who caught and ate the red-spotted salmon were at once possessed of all the world's learning. Regrettably, women were not tolerated at the holy fountain. Sinann, the granddaughter of Lir, King of the Sea, was a maiden of rare accomplishment. Wishing to add a more masculine substance to her attainments, she went secretly to the forbidden fountain. At her approach the water flooded over its banks in an uncontrollable torrent, engulfing her and sweeping her dead body toward the west. She entered the great river that now bears her name, the Shannon, where it widens into Lough Derg, a narrow twisting lake whose calm waters are dotted with yew-covered islands. The salmon in Lough Derg carry no red spots on their bellies; and Connla's Well, after the visit of the overenterprising goddess, dried up forever.

Despite this uncharitable genesis, women in pagan Ireland did on occasion penetrate the masculine world of the intellect and achieve a more than respectable success. In the list of great lawyers are the names of several women; this presupposes their admittance to schools of higher education, as practice of the complex Brehon Law required many years of specialized and intensive study. Mostly, however, although women enjoyed an unusual degree of equality with men, their formal education was restricted to the domestic arts.

The pagan schools, run by poets and historians of the *filid* class and by the druids, required up to fifteen years of study. The poets were ambulatory and travelled, as we have seen, in company with their pupils. The druids were usually stationary, but the method of teaching was the same: the lore was delivered in verse form to facilitate memorizing. The aspirants studied grammar, law, genealogy, history, astonomy, geography and metrical composition; and graduates emerged with a formidable body of knowledge within their herculean minds. Depending on their specialization, they learned about 275 stories, a prescribed set of complicated metric forms, the entire body of Brehon Law, the genealogies of the kings and chief families, a large number of magic spells and incantations, and the forbiddingly long list of prerogatives, rights, duties, restrictions and tributes of kings. This education — part practical, part mystical — entitled its practitioners to privileges and rewards equal to those enjoyed by the highest of the warrior aristocracy.

The students were undoubtedly assisted in their strenuous course by the humanity of their teachers. Brehon Law defines the relationship: "Instruction without reservation, and correction without harshness, are due from the master to the pupil, and to feed and clothe him during the time he is at his learning." In return, the pupil had a lifelong obligation to his teacher: "To help him against poverty, and to support him in old age, these are due from the pupil to the tutor." [5] The humaneness of teaching and the close and warm relationship between master and pupil carried over into the monastic schools, where austerity was tempered by the genuine platonic love that infused the pursuance of education.

Another practice that passed into Christian usage was fosterage (discussed previously). Most children of the higher ranks and many of the lower were sent to live with another family and received their early education from foster fathers or mothers. As in the teacher-pupil relationship the foster child had continuing obligations to his adoptive parent, and, as previously noted, the loving ties between them were often greater than those within the natural family. The system was closely regulated by law, even to designating the clothing that should be worn and the food provided. The son of a lord could wear silks in two colors, embroidered with gold and silver, and he might have silver on his scabbard and brass rings on his hurling sticks (which were used in the game hurley, a kind of field hockey). The humbler child wore plain black-and-white or saffron woolens. The food specified for all was stirabout, usually concocted of oatmeal — and served with salt butter for the poor child, with new milk and wheat bread for the lord's son, and with fresh butter and honey for the son of a king.

The purpose of fosterage in pre-Christian Ireland was not the training of the intellect, though when the system passed over into Christian usage that became its main function. In the ancient days it was intended primarily to give children a practical education to prepare them for the life they were destined to lead. So the curriculum differed with rank. The son of the chieftain received instruction in horsemanship (his father was required to provide the horse), as well as in the use of sword and spear, and in archery and swimming; he also learned games such as chess and hurley. The farmer's son was taught the husbandry of domestic animals, especially the care of lambs, calves, kids and shoats, kiln-drying, combing wool and other farm-related chores. He was not to have a horse, for in his life he would have no need of the kind of riding that required teaching.

Girls were sent out to fosterage as well as boys, but their fathers had to pay a higher fosterage fee because they would not be of so much future use to their foster parents. The farmers' daughters learned to grind corn with a quern, to knead, dye and weave. The children of the elite learned to sew and embroider; Irish needlework was famous all over the world. Girls, naturally, were taught by the women of the foster home.

On occasion a boy also received education from a female. Cuchulain — who at the age of seven defeated single-handed all the other seven-year-olds of the king's court banded against him — later considered that his art needed refinement. He went to live with Scathach, the Shadowy One, a woman skilled beyond all men in the warrior's art, who lived on an island off the east coast of Scotland. From her he learned

> the feats of the sword-edge and the sloped shield; the feats of the javelin and the rope; . . . the feat of Cat and the heroic salmon-leap; the pole-throw and the leap over a poisoned stroke; the noble chariot-fighter's crouch; . . . the feat of the chariot-wheel thrown on high and the feat of the shield-rim; the breath-feat, with gold apples blown up into the air; the snapping mouth and the hero's scream; the stroke of precision . . . stepping on a lance in flight and straightening erect on its point; . . . and the trussing of a warrior on the points of spears.[6]

The education of Cuchulain and of other young warriors in fosterage has little, at first sight, to do with the intellectual flowering of Christian Ireland — unless one stops to consider the wide-ranging interests of the cloistered monk who penned the swashbuckling paragraph above, who might the next day be transcribing St. Jerome's Vulgate edition of the Bible or composing a hymn in Latin hexameters. The pagan educational legacy was more an attitude than a body of knowledge. It was a respect for learning in all fields, from military skill to the intricacy of poetic meter to the science of herd-raising — along with a benignity in imparting that knowledge, which created a deep and lasting bond between the teacher and the taught, whether foster parent and child or schoolmaster and pupil.

Still another gift from heathen to Christian was the comparative democracy of education. By no stretch of the imagination could ancient Ireland be labelled a democratic country. But a man could rise, through his thrift, his profession or the talent given him by the gods, above the station of his father. If education raised him to the status of a master poet, his honor price was equal to that of a chieftain. The boy whose father could not afford the expenses of a school could pay his way by waiting on the children of the wealthy, who supplied him with food and clothing.

This system was carried over intact to the ecclesiastical schools. Adamnan, abbot of Iona, biographer of Columba and author of a learned geographic treatise, started out as a poor boy working for his social superiors. One day, when he was sent to fetch milk, he met on the road the high-king Finnachta the Festive with his retinue. Trying to get out of the way of the horses, the young student fell and broke the milk cask. Finnachta, a considerate prince, dismounted to survey the damage he had caused. "O good man," said Adamnan, "I have cause for grief, for there are three goodly students in one house, and three more of us are attendants upon them. . . . One attendant from among us goes out in turn to collect sustenance for the other five, and it was my turn today; but what I had gathered for them has been spilled upon the ground, and what grieves me more, the borrowed jar is broken, and I have not wherewith to pay for it." [7]

King Finnachta, touched by Adamnan's plight, said, "Thou shalt receive protection, O student, from me," and he assured him of his friendship. Adamnan became thereafter a favorite of the king, and subsequently was appointed his chief counsellor and director. Whether or not this story is apocryphal (Adamnan was of the Ui Neill and a near cousin to Columba, so he should have been comfortably off), its narration by a contemporary illustrates the startlingly modern seventh-century Irish attitude that the elevation of the lowly-born was an attainable condition; and this was a point of view that came straight from the pagan-Celtic educational system.

Filid schools flourished under Christianity as they never had before, on account of the Latin alphabet and the new emphasis on learning for its own sake. But as the monastic schools took over more and more of the lay curriculum, the *filid* schools narrowed their field of study to a concentration on the native heroic literature and an extreme technical development of Irish writing. The ecclesiastical schools, not so specialized, provided the best general education. Many of the students were of the laity: sons of wealthy farmers and of chieftains, destined for civil or military careers, received instruction in literature, history, law and science. Girls were sometimes admitted and were taught equally along with their masculine peers. Most of the lay students did not proceed to the advanced degrees, as their talents lay elsewhere.

The aspiring ecclesiastical student not only learned the basics of Christian theology but received the benefit of the whole classical lore of the Continent, so fortuitously brought by refugee scholars before the encroaching tide of darkness submerged the ancient knowledge. A young student monk, if he finished his twelve-year course of schooling, had passed the "Seven Orders of Wisdom," which included — besides a fundamental and detailed knowledge of the Bible — arithmetic, astronomy, history and the technicalities of written composition (that is, grammar, criticism and orthography). Much of this knowledge he had committed to memory, including all of the Psalms. He could write Latin prose and poetry, often with skill. As Greek and Hebrew had not been much used in Continental schools, he received only a smattering of these; this slight knowledge was tempting to the ambitious scholar, and he tended to sprinkle his texts with foreign words he had got out of glossaries (sometimes with barbarous and bizarre effect, as in the convoluted nonsense of the *Hisperica Famina,* to be discussed later). He had read the works of the classical poets and satirists, historians and rhetoricians, as well as those of the Church Fathers.

He had also studied the body of ancient law, the *Senchus Mor,* and other classics of native lore, including the mythological sagas. His studies and writings in these fields would prove, for a later age, more valuable and exciting than all his expertise in theology and the classics; for they preserved for posterity a graphic, full-scale picture of the Celtic way of life — a lifestyle that overspread Europe before Rome came to dominate but that was recorded only in biased secondhand accounts. Were it not for the Irish scholars and scribes, who recorded the parallel mores of the Celts in Ireland, the authentic knowledge of a vibrant people would have vanished from the world's memory. It was not only a vital slice of history the scribes immortalized, but a beautiful and eloquent body of literature. In the intellectually tolerant atmosphere of Irish monasticism the proscriptions of Christian morality made only superficial changes in this splendidly barbaric heritage.

But in his own time the Irish scholar's mastery of theology and the classics was more important than his eventual boon to literature. He went out of the monastic school to teach and preach, and to carry the humanity of his own education abroad. For it was not only the actual knowledge that was kept alive when Europe was in the intellectual doldrums of the Dark Ages; it was also the Irish attitude toward learning. "It is the custom of good teachers," wrote an eighth-century commentator, "to praise the understanding of the hearers [pupils] that they may love what they hear."[8] The great teachers were rightly beloved and therefore profoundly influential, in their own and their adopted countries.

The schools were set up informally. So many students were attracted that there was not accommodation for them, and they had to erect their huts outside the monastery wall. There was a great deal of memorizing, as books were few and precious; and students were expected not only to learn by rote but to understand what they recited. They gathered out of doors, holding their books if they owned them, while the teacher — who usually sat or stood on a knoll — read, translated and expounded. In the privacy of their cells or in the scriptorium, they worked long hours, copying the works they would study.

The beginner practiced with a metal-pointed stylus on long narrow tablets of yew wood coated with wax, which could be smoothed clear and used over and over. When he had done his copying he bound the tablets together with a pivot pin at one end so they could be opened and closed like a fan. He then wound leather thongs around them, leaving the ends of the cords hanging loose for use as a handle. Such waxed tablets were also used by schoolmasters to teach elementary reading, by travelling poets, even on occasion for self-defense. A poet could ward off an aggressive dog with his stavelike tablet bundle. St. Patrick and his companion were once attacked by Connachtmen who thought their upraised tablets were swords.

The skilled scribes in the scriptoria worked on parchment (the skin of the cow, sheep or goat) and on vellum (the younger, finer skins of these animals). They wrote sitting down, with the book resting on the knees or, if engaged in elaborate illumination, on a table. For straight calligraphy the pen was a quill from the wing of a goose, a swan or a crow. The inkstand was part of a cow's horn and the ink was of pure carbon, thick and time-defying: the writing on the old codices is still sharply black today. The finished books were encased in leather, labelled on the outside, and hung on pegs along the walls of the monastery library. A student's own books he hung in his hut or carried slung by straps over his shoulder. The more precious manuscripts were enclosed in elegantly tooled leather covers, and sometimes in decorated, jewel-encrusted containers.

The monasteries must have had extensive and widely varied libraries: transcriptions of Irish history, law and romance, copies of the Gospel, lives of the Irish saints, works of the Christian Fathers and the Latin classics. Very little is left. When the Norse invaders of the ninth and tenth centuries raided the monasteries, they seemed to be specially aggravated by books, which, along with crosses and other religious objects, symbolized the Christian religion they were bent on destroying. With intentional malice, as if they were attacking a dangerous enemy, they burned or threw in the water every manuscript they found. The Anglo-Normans who followed them in the twelfth century were equally destructive (though for other reasons). The result of the continuing rapine was that many Irish scholars fled their country carrying the tattered remnants of their libraries. There are today far more manuscripts in Gaelic writing in libraries on the Continent than in Ireland.

Remaining are several huge volumes — miscellanea of tales, poems, biographies, genealogies, histories — copied from older manuscripts long since lost, and mixed together in no particular order. The oldest are the *Lebor na h'Uidhre (Book of the Dun Cow)* and the *Book of Leinster,* both compiled in the cultural reawakening that accompanied the reform of the Church in the twelfth century. The *Book of the Dun Cow,* supposedly inscribed on the skin of St. Ciaran's favorite cow, was written in 1106 by Maelmuiri, at St. Ciaran's great school at Clonmacnoise. It contains the most ancient existent collection of early Irish tales, including the *Tain Bo Cuailnge,* the story of Cuchulain and the war between Ulster and Connacht. Besides the heroic epic the volume includes Dallan Forgaill's *Amra Columcille (Hymn to Columcille)* and many other sacred and secular works. The *Book of Leinster* — written in the middle of the twelfth century at Terryglass, County Galway, by Finn Mac Gorman, bishop of Kildare, and Aed Mac Criffan — has the length of six novels by Sir Walter Scott. At the conclusion of Aed's version of the *Tain Bo* in this compilation is his summary: "Some of the tales are the figments of demons, some of them poetic imaginings, some true, some not, some for the delight of fools."[9] Whatever he personally thought of them, he put them all in the book: these inclusive ana, miscellaneous and disorganized as they are, attest to the dedicated thoroughness of the medieval scribes, an inestimable boon to succeeding generations.

Later volumes left by the Irish scholars are the fourteenth-century *Speckled Book of Mac Egan*; the *Book of Ballymote,* written about the same time; the *Yellow Book of Lecan,* compiled about 1415; and the fifteenth-century *Book of Lismore*. These books contain, like the earlier ones, material copied from manuscripts of a much earlier date. Included are annals, usually of local history, such as the *Annals of Tighernach,* the most ancient, compiled by an abbot of that name in the eleventh century; among other items this treasure trove contains the earliest known reference to the Ossianic lore (more of the poetry of the *Fianna* appeared the following century in the *Book of the Dun Cow* and the *Book of Leinster*). To illustrate the size of these ancient volumes; the Ossianic poems alone number eighty thousand lines. Also comprised is the quasihistorical *Dindshenchas (Lore of High Places),* a kind of historical geography; it is a series of definitions of place names, often farfetched and fanciful, connecting them with events out of the past, real or imaginary.

In a separate category, because it is of a much later date, is the work *Annals of the Four Masters,* a compendium of Irish history largely derived from medieval historical manuscripts no longer in existence, beginning in the year 2242 B.C. and coming up to the seventeenth century, when the book was compiled. This monumental task, accomplished by a group of scholars in the Convent of Donegal, was directed by the Franciscan brother Michael O'Clery, of a renowned family of historical scholars going back to the twelfth century. The distinguished historian was also responsible for the *Trias Thaumaturgus* — the lives of St. Patrick, St. Brigid and St. Columba. Other notable accomplishments of his group are *The Succession of Kings,* a listing from the earliest monarch on record to the death of Malachy in 1022; the genealogies of the saints up to the eighth century; and the *Lebor Gabala (Book of Invasions),* transcribed from a twelfth-century manuscript, which we have noted elsewhere.

These great volumes, few as there are remaining, give evidence of a vast literary activity starting about the eighth century and going on, despite the sufferings of the succeeding centuries, right through the twelfth. Though they contain what to us is the whole substance of early Irish literature, there must have been much more than what is within them. Ideas proliferated and words flowed, in an extraordinary burgeoning. The spirit of the age expressed itself not only on the written page but in stone and paint and metal, and in the realms of science and philosophy.

Behind this inspired outpouring was the Irish tradition of education, with roots in the pagan past, changed and revitalized by the earliest Christians, fostered and perfected in the monastic schools. In the next chapters we will look further at some of the wealth that emanated from this tradition.

CHAPTER XIV
THE POETS

ROMANCE, LEGEND AND POETRY ARE THE ELEMENTS OF IRISH LITERATURE.
The tales tend to have an episodic and unfinished quality, partly because
many of them were originally oral and partly because the Irish were not
able to develop a stable literary form. With the exception of the *Tain Bo
Cuailnge,* there are no long-sustained epics; there is also no drama as such,
though there is much that might have evolved into the organized coherence
of drama, given the right literary conditions. A formalized literature that
is still creative needs an abiding external serenity, and this is a luxury
Ireland never had. Though there was comparative quiet within the monastery walls, the climate outside was precarious even in times of peace. The
Norse invasions destroyed the tranquillity of the monasteries: the creative
spirit suffered under the repeated blows of the raiders and the desperate
uncertainty of daily existence. The intrusion of the Anglo-Normans in the
twelfth century and the subsequent cruel domination of England finally
crushed the native genius that never had a chance to flower to its full.

Yet within their limits the Irish, whether inscribing the old tales and
adding their own interpolations or composing fresh stories with a Christian
import, were unendingly creative. Their writings — visionary, fanciful,
dreamy — sparkled with ideas. Their use of words was felicitous and their
imaginative ingenuity captivating. But at the same time, the early clerical
poet-historians were serious and dedicated scholars. At the beginning of
the seventh century, students at the monastic schools, led by Bangor, began

to take an active interest in their country's ancient literature and history, and by the middle of that century the best of them were engaged in transcribing the old lore into the vernacular. In their retelling of the ancestral stories, there was no boundary between history and legend — and this was a medieval trait not confined to the Irish scribes.

The oldest stories, as they have been classified in modern times, belong to the so-called Mythological Cycle, and they form the basis for the medieval account of Irish history known as the *Lebor Gabala,* or *Book of Invasions.* The poet-historians of the eighth and ninth centuries amplified the existing myths with the fruits of their own fertile imaginations, using the current Christian practice of tracing their origins back to Adam and tying in subsequent events with happenings in classical times in Rome, Greece, Palestine, Egypt and Macedonia. The system was in its time a respectable form of history: a summary of the chief events of the known world set side by side in columns. It was known as synchronized history, and its practitioners were highly regarded. It had been an established method on the Continent before Irish history was first chronicled in writing, and Irish scholars saw no reason why they should not add their column, meshing Ireland's traditional history with the recorded annals of the classical world. The result is a spirited romance in which can be discerned faint shapes glimpsed through a mist of fancy: outlines of actuality.

The history begins before the Deluge, when an unnamed race inhabited Ireland. One of its leaders, Ladhra, had sixteen wives and expired "from an excess of women,"[1] becoming the first to die in Ireland. The whole race was destroyed in the Flood. Afterwards came Partholon (a direct descendant of Adam), who had somehow survived the Flood. He created nine lakes, and in his time occurred the first adultery in Ireland, the first judicial ruling and the first battle.

The battle was against the people known as the Fomorians.* This race surfaces time and again through the *Book of Invasions,* always uncouth and vicious, always seeping in from the shore and being driven back again by the more civilized and better equipped newcomers. In Partholon's time these savages lived on coastal islands, ate very poorly, and fought against Partholon's race "with one foot, one hand and one eye."[2] It is hard to avoid the supposition that the Fomorians represent a faint memory, handed down through centuries, of Mesolithic man, who had crept around the edges of the country catching what food he could with his rude stone

---

*See pages 55–56 for a discussion of the Fomorians.

weapons and eking out a static existence for some three thousand years, to present his infelicitous countenance and his paltry resistance to more progressive successors. Some scholars surmise, however, that the Fomorians were remnants of an older pantheon that had been worshipped in Ireland before the importation of the Celtic deities — because the despised Fomorians were not always ineffectual. In a fierce battle on the sea beach, they almost entirely destroyed the next invaders, the sons of Nemed, who came from Scythia with a fleet of thirty-four ships after plague had wiped out all nine thousand Partholonians (on the site, as aforementioned, of Maelruain's Tallaght).

The Nemedians, like their predecessors, improved the land, making new lakes and clearing twelve plains. But they were so harassed by the Fomorians, who demanded two-thirds of their corn, their milk and their children, that they finally abandoned Ireland. These two agricultural peoples, the Partholonians and the Nemedians, one guesses, might correspond to the Neolithic farmers who had come from Spain and Brittany. The next arrivals, the Fir Bolg (an offshoot of a Continental tribe, the Belgae), brought a warlike aristocracy, introducing metal weapons and the system of monarchy — the Bronze Age had come to Ireland. The Fir Bolg are at the edge of history. They did not disappear from the story like those who had gone before, but left descendants. Patrician as they were in their time, however, the remnants of this race were scorned and enslaved by Ireland's last pre-Christian conquerors, the Milesians, the sons of Mil. These people have been identified as the latest wave — small in number, momentous in effect — of Iron Age Celts, the warrior aristocracy whose mastery of Ireland was to last well over a thousand years.

Between the Fir Bolg and the Milesians the historians inserted the invasion of the wholly mythical Tuatha De Danann (previously discussed), investing the old Celtic gods with human form and slotting them neatly into the synchronized history. Besides their conquest of Ireland and the magic-ridden battles this gave rise to, the Tuatha De Danann participated in a series of romantic and heroic adventures in which there was no dividing line between the supernatural and the earthly, and in which unreality approaches the absurd.

With all their fairy-tale fantasy, however, some of these stories have moments both lyrical and poignant. One of the more affecting is *The Children of Lir,* the story of four children changed to swans by their jealous stepmother and forced to wander the waters of the earth for many hundreds of years before the spell can be lifted. As the day of their delivery approaches, they fly to the home of their father, only to find the place deserted and the castle crumbled into ruins. In despair they fly to the island of Inishglora, County Mayo, where they sing music so sad and sweet that all the birds of Ireland come to hear them. And now the Christian scribe takes a hand, bringing in as their savior St. Caemhoch of Inishglora, a disciple of St. Patrick. The sound of the bell of matins fills the enchanted children with fear and then with joy as it tolls the end of their curse. The four white birds change slowly to four aged, wrinkled humans near death — but their souls ready for salvation. As St. Caemhoch baptizes them, they die under his blessing, and their souls rise before his eyes, young, radiant, beautiful as the pagan children they have once been.

Historically, the next set of tales, the Ulster Cycle, belongs to the Heroic Age — the high period of Milesian (Celtic) flowering, which took place about the time of the birth of Christ. The main subjects of these tales are war and chivalry. Although the gods occasionally appear and magic plays a minor part, the emphasis is on human courage and the ideal of a hero who can never become old and never father a race — yet cannot be killed by mortal means. At various times in this account we have mentioned Cuchulain, the hero par excellence. From the age of seven, when he is introduced into the palace of King Conchobar, Cuchulain displays the arrogant, fearless defiance of fate that was the hallmark of the Celtic tribal hero. Refusing the protection of his elders, he wields his wooden toy weapons against the 150 boys of the king's court, come to chastise the bold newcomer. "They flung three times fifty javelins at him, and he stopped them all on his shield of sticks. Then they drove all their hurling-balls at him, three times fifty of them: he dodged so well that none of them touched him, except for a handful that he plucked down as they shot past."[3]

Through all his short life Cuchulain exhibits such insouciant valor in the face of odds — and he never fights except against odds. He must, according to Celtic philosophy, die of violence on the field of battle, yet he is invincible. So the narrator resorts to trickery: the hero is brought low by the artifice of sorcerers, who employ the only means to defeat him, his own fate. He is forced to deny his destiny, to break an oath, and then he is open to the enemy's sword. Even in death he is defiant. Mortally wounded by a spear thrust into his stomach, he asks his enemies if he may go to the lake to drink. Given leave, "he gathered his bowels into his breast, and went forth to the lake. And there he drank his drink, and washed himself, and came forth to die, calling on his foes to come to meet him . . . and he went to a pillar-stone . . . and he put his breast-girdle round it that he might not die seated nor lying down, but that he might die standing up."[4]

The *Tain Bo Cuailnge,* of which Cuchulain is the chief hero, is the longest of the heroic epics. Though its warrior heroes were of a class and a set of beliefs in direct opposition to the Christian ethic, such was the happy tolerance that existed between the monk and his pagan past that the cloistered scribes presented this saga, diluted only peripherally by Christian qualms, in its true savage magnificence. Legend has it that a prestigious group of saints was responsible for the re-creation of the old tale: St. Ciaran, St. Columba, St. Caillin and St. Brendan went together to the tomb of Fergus Mac Roigh, one of the Red Branch Knights, and fasted and prayed until the hero rose from his grave and dictated the entire epic, which was then inscribed by St. Ciaran on parchment made from his dun cow. Charming as is the vision of the gentle saints and the ghost in full war panoply, it is accurate only in so far as it illustrates the enthusiastic commitment with which the Christians preserved the lore of their forebears. As with St. Patrick and the aged poets, the myth demonstrates the amicable terms on which even the holiest and most self-denying Christians coexisted with their barbaric legacy. The *Tain Bo* was not actually committed to writing until the seventh century, and the *Book of the Dun Cow,* as aforementioned, was a product of the early twelfth century.

The tale of the Irish Achilles and associated stories of the Red Branch Knights are Ireland's signal contributions to pagan literature. Their form is prose and verse; the main burden of the narrative being in prose, with verse interpolated at dramatic moments to heighten the mood. Though their form and style may derive from the oral storytellers, the wording — the spontaneous passion of its feeling, the sensitive grace and imagination of its metaphors — must have come largely from the pens of the medieval transcribers. Their nearest kin are the Icelandic sagas, which were composed later. Probably the Icelandic scribes used the Irish form as a model, since, as we have seen, there was much association between the two peoples after the tenth-century founding of the nation of Iceland. The Irish sagas are more primitive than the Icelandic, lacking their terse sophistication. The Irish — romantic, visionary and disorganized — never learned to be terse in their literature. But they were livelier and more poetic than their rather stolid imitators.

Though most of the Ulster Cycle is concerned with men and battle, at least one tale is still renowned as a classic of ill-starred love: a version of the Tristan and Isolde legend, the story of a young maid betrothed without her choice to an old king and overcome by an inescapable passion, on the eve of her wedding, for the king's young knight, who in turn is torn between love and duty. This is *The Exile of the Sons of Usnech,* the story of Deirdre and Naisi.

Before Deirdre was born she cried out in her mother's womb, and Cathbad, King Conchobar's druid, foretold that she would be a maid of great beauty who would bring division and banishment, death and sorrow to the men of Ulster. The Red Branch Knights said that she should be killed at birth, but the king refused, decreeing that she be brought up in total seclusion, to become his wife when she should be old enough. She was reared in a house apart, and knew no man but the king until she was a maid ready to be married. One day she saw her nurse out in the snow, skinning a calf for her dinner; a black raven came down to drink the blood. Deirdre said to her, "That man only will I love, who hath the three colors that I see yonder, — his hair as black as the raven, his cheeks red like the blood, and his body as white as the snow."[5]

". . . That man is not far away," answered the nurse. "He is yonder in the stronghold . . . and the name of him is Naisi, the son of Usnech."

A little later Naisi sat singing on the rampart near Deirdre's dwelling. Though forbidden to leave her home, she went out to him. They fell in love at once, but he drew back when he found out who she was. Then Deirdre "sprang upon him, and she seized him by his two ears. 'Two ears of shame and mockery shalt thou have,' she cried, 'if thou take me not with thee.'" Her importunity won him; he called his two brothers to him, and the four of them fled away. Then Cathbad's prophesy was fulfilled as the men of Ulster were divided between their loyalty to the king and their friendship with the gallant sons of Usnech. The fugitives were hunted all over Ireland and finally found sanctuary with the king of Alba (Scotland), where Naisi became the king's right-hand warrior. But the brothers, always longing for Ireland, were lured home with false promises of pardon. They were slain by treachery, and Deirdre, brought back to be the king's unwilling bride, mourned for a year.

> During all that time she smiled not a smile of laughter, she took not her sufficiency of food or sleep, and she raised not her head from her knee. And if any one brought before her entertainers, she used to speak thus:

> . . . Though ye think the mead sweet
> That warlike Conchobar drinks,
> I oft have known a sweeter drink,
> Often on the edge of a spring.
>
> Our board was spread beneath the tree,
> And Naisi kindled the cooking fire;
> Meat, prepared from Naisi's game
> Was more sweet to me than honey.
>
> Though well your horns may blow music,
> Though sweetly your pipes may sound,
> I say without fear, that I know well
> I have often heard a sweeter strain.
>
> . . . .
>
> For this cause, no more I sleep;
> No more I stain my nails with pink:
> No joy can break the watch I keep;
> For Usnech's sons come not again.

The king, bitter at her unforgiving sorrow, doomed her to live with Eogan, the murderer of her lover. They bore her between them in a chariot toward Eogan's castle. As she turned to look at her tormentors, Conchobar taunted her, saying, "Ha, Deirdre, it is the same glance that a ewe gives when between two rams, that thou sharest now between me and Eogan!" At that she leaped from the chariot, shattering her head on a rock, and so she died.

It says much for the unnamed freethinking eighth-century scribe that he could pen Deirdre's lament, that inconsolable cry of love and sorrow, in the chaste peace of his womanless cloister. He even forbore to save her soul at the end, as those of the children of Lir were saved, but suffered her to meet her pagan fate unedited.

While the doings of the gallant, gaudy and bellicose Ulster heroes seem to be at sharp variance with the stern purity of those who recorded them, the third cycle in time — the Ossianic, or Fenian — portrays a way of life that was, as previously noted, not so alien to those early ascetics. Finn's army of the forests lasted about a century, from the reign of Conn of the

Hundred Battles (177–212 A.D.) to that of Carbery of the Liffey (279–297 A.D.), and reached its highest point in the time of Cormac Mac Art, (254–277 A.D.). Finn himself was killed beside the Boyne in 283, and his son Ossian, after a sojourn in *Tir na n'Og,* returned to mortal life about 150 years later, along with his cousin Cailte, to regale St. Patrick with stories of that dedicated company (as is recounted in *The Colloquy of the Old Men*). We have seen St. Patrick entertained against his better judgment, and how nearly the life-style of the *Fianna* approached that of the early Christian monks.

The antecedents of Finn's band may have further endeared them to their later chroniclers. The forest soldiers, it is thought, may have derived from an older race subjugated by invaders: the Picts mastered by the La Tène Celts or, following the synchronized history, the Fir Bolg defeated by the Milesians. The subordinate people retreated to the wild places of the south and east, the provinces of Munster and Leinster, to pursue a style of life simpler and rougher than that of the new aristocracy, and eventually to progress from the status of outcasts to a warrior company esteemed and loved by the common people whose substance they shared and whose safety they defended. For the tales of the *Fianna* were from the beginning, and continued to be, the property of the peasantry, while the heroic sagas of King Conchobar and his cohorts of Ulster appealed to the Celtic gentry whose capital, Emain Macha, was in the north.

The learned poet-historians, disdainful of the peasant literature, paid little attention to the Fenian lore until the eleventh century, when they began to note its universal appeal, and translated the old stories into a new art form: the narrative poem or ballad with dramatic overtones. The cycle contains one exquisite prose narrative, *The Pursuit of Diarmait and Grainne,* another version of the Tristan and Isolde legend. The idyll of their love takes place in Ireland's fields and forests, and it has a back-to-nature charm that must have represented an appealing escape to the Irish of those years, suffering under the repeated spoliations of the Vikings and sorely divided among themselves. The language of the saga is both more modern and more romantic than the somewhat stiff and antique cadences of the Ulster love story. Grainne's sacrifice of wealth and honor, for instance, has a poignant lyrical simplicity as she says to Finn, her unwanted fiancé: "There is one on whom I should gladly gaze, to whom I would give the bright world, all of it, all of it, though it be an unequal bargain."[6]

As opposed to the entirely pagan character of the Ulster Cycle, the poems of the Ossianic Cycle have Christian overtones. We have quoted from *The Colloquy of the Old Men,* in which St. Patrick, diverted by the adventures of Finn, tends to forget his Christian duty ("Cailte, my soul, tell us another tale."). Purity, courage, selflessness and love of nature are the characteristic burdens of Cailte's lays: these were qualities to appeal to Ireland's heroic first saint, as well as succeeding ones. This gently humorous piece, an engaging example of the friendly meeting of pagan and Christian life patterns, has a decided dramatic impact: it could easily have been acted out, as the old man, last of the pagans, didactically lectured the fascinated, mildly disapproving first of the Christians.

Finn himself was said to have been a poet, an example to all his young men, who, before they could join the woodland army, must pass the test of a master poet. Though he was a warrior and a demigod, the subject of his verse was not derring-do but the face of nature, as in his invocation "May-Day":

> May-day, fair aspect, perfect season; blackbirds sing a full lay when the sun casts a meager beam.
> . . . .
> Summer cuts the stream small; swift horses seek water; tall heather spreads; delicate fair foliage flourishes.
> Sprouting comes to the bud of the hawthorn; the ocean flows a smooth course; (summer) sends the sea to sleep; blossom covers the world.
> Bees of small strength carry bundles of culled blossoms on their feet; the mountain, supplying rich sufficiency, carries off the cattle.
> . . . .
> A flock of birds settles on land where a woman walks; there is noise in every green field through which a swift bright rivulet flows.
> . . . .
> The frail man fears loudness; the constant man sings with a heart; rightly does he sing out "May-day, fair aspect!" [7]

While the medieval chroniclers reproduced the tales of the Heroic Age nearly intact, in all their pagan splendor, and while they did justice to the magic deeds of Finn, interpolating but little of Christian morality, there was one class of adventure inherited from the oral storytellers that was an irresistible target for Christian infiltration: the voyages.

We have seen that *Tir na n'Og,* the Land of Youth, was the paradise of the pagan world, attainable within mortal life, "wherein there is nought save truth, and there is neither age nor decay nor gloom nor sadness nor envy nor jealousy nor hatred nor haughtiness."[8] On occasion a pagan hero journeyed to this magic place, either in the kingdom of the *sid* beneath the earth or across the western sea. But when he returned he did so at his peril. Time passed quickly in *Tir na n'Og,* while centuries elapsed on earth. Ossian, coming back to seek his father and the noble *Fianna,* found his erstwhile home a ruin overgrown with nettles and thorns. Descending from his magic steed to help a distressed group of men move a great stone, he touched the forbidden earth and straightway shrank to a wizened, blind, helpless old man.

One of the loveliest of all Irish saga-poems is the eighth-century *Voyage of Bran,* from which we have quoted. When Bran returned from his happy voyage, one of his men leaped out of the curragh and "as soon as he touched the earth of Ireland, forthwith he was a heap of ashes, as though he had been in the earth for many hundred years."[9]

The attainment of immortal bliss at the cost of earthly contentment was so close to Christian thought that it required only a slight twist of mental outlook to recast the tales in Christian terms, to send the saints on voyages to find across the sea islands of exile where the worship of God was more beautiful even than in the stern peace of the home cloister. Common to both pagan and Christian versions is that universal human chimera, the search for the intangible ideal; the need to slip away, if only for a short while, from mundane reality.

The bridge from the heathen tales of *Tir na n'Og* to the Christian adaptations — culminating in the romantic, poetic, humorous and inspired medieval account of St. Brendan's voyage — is *The Voyage of Maelduin.* This is the story, first written down in the eighth century, of the foster son of an Irish queen who seeks the murderer of his father over the sea, engaging in exploits of daring and visiting strange islands. On one the voyagers are pursued by ants as big as foals; on another they encounter a wild beast with sharp nails on his hooves; on another devils are having a horserace; on another they are greeted by an old man clothed only in his own hair, who tells them he is a pilgrim and is fed by angels. At last they come to the "land of women," where age will never touch them and they will live forever without toil. Though this is basically a pagan adventure, its only concession to Christianity being the questionable one of Maelduin's discovery that he is the son of a nun, it was a model closely followed by the tenth-century *Navigatio Sancti Brendani.*

The author of the much acclaimed saintly romance had, as noted earlier, a long tradition behind him. The preoccupation with voyages and mythical islands both pagan and Christian far predated the Irish-Celts. The medieval literature owes much to Indo-European myth as exemplified in the *Odyssey*, the *Aeneid*, Plato's description of lost Atlantis, the search of Jason and the adventures of Sinbad the Sailor (in which first appears the trembling island that turns out to be a whale). There are also references to real journeys: tales brought back by fishermen and hermits of new lands and strange sights in the unknown ocean, exaggerated by the baroque imaginations of the survivors but containing recognizable elements of reality. The *Navigatio* is full of the echoes of its antecedents. But it is a happy synthesis, and its circulation engendered such excitement in medieval Europe that it was the direct inspiration for real-life voyages of exploration. With little exaggeration one may say that the shores of India and the islands of the New World owe their discovery to St. Brendan's semilegendary travels, and beyond him to the pagan longing for *Tir na n'Og*.

Allied to the voyages are the visions. These were almost entirely a Christian phenomenon in Ireland, though, as with the voyages, there were classical antecedents; also, the dreams and auguries of druids, wherein they saw the fates of kings, had similar illusory qualities. Many of the saints had visions, nearly inevitable consequences of the hermit life. The extreme austerity of the meditative existence — when the anchorite ate nothing but wild berries, nuts and mushrooms, some of them probably hallucinatory; when sleep was short and the waking hours were spent in intense concentration on God — heightened inward awareness to the point where what the mind's eye saw became an outward reality. St. Brendan, on his mountaintop, clearly saw "the beautiful noble island, with three trains of angels rising from it"; entirely confident of the validity of his vision, he set forth to find it.

Among the most famous visions in literary history are those of St. Fursey in the early seventh century. He was a pupil of St. Brendan, therefore early conversant with the visionary way of things. Always of a pious and contemplative turn of mind, when he became deathly ill of fever after days spent in cross-vigil, fasting and prayer, his delirious thoughts naturally turned to heavenly matters, and he had several visions so ecstatic that he could hardly bear to come back to life. In one of them his feet grew cold and his hands stiffened in the attitude of cross-vigil. In all outward signs he was dead, and his soul seemed to leave his body. Three angels appeared, whose white wings extended to heaven, and there was a diabolic howling as a black cloud approached with an army of demons within it.

Their bodies were black and twisted, their necks of "squalid leanness,"[10] their heads enormously bloated. They shot fiery arrows at him, which were deflected by the angels. Angels and devils then fought over Fursey's soul and the forces of darkness were defeated.

Another vision followed, in which Fursey saw the earth, a shadowed valley far below him with four great fires in it — the fires, the angels told him, of man's sins, which destroy the world. They then led him down into hell, where he was burned on the neck by a jet of flame from a damned soul; thence he was conducted into heaven. There two long-dead saints appeared to him and told him to return to the world. With the utmost reluctance his soul descended from heaven and alighted on the roof of a church. At the church door he saw his own body with a crowd of mourners around it. The soul watched, afraid to reenter the senseless body, but an angel told him he must go back to life. At that the breast of his body opened and the soul flew into it.

Though St. Fursey's visions were a function of sickness, they were regarded not only by himself but by his many devoted followers as evidence of God's miraculous favor. His fervent passion alienated some, who were skeptical of his authenticity. Pope Martin I doubted him, but when Fursey went to him and showed him the suppurating wound on his neck, which could only be soothed by spring water the saint himself had blessed, the pope, won over by his impassioned sincerity, fell on his knees before him and begged his pardon.

St. Fursey founded monasteries in Britain and Gaul, the most renowned being at Lagny on the Marne in northeastern Gaul and Péronne to the southeast, a daughter house of Lagny, founded after Fursey's death and known later as "Peronna Scottorum" (Péronne of the Irish). St. Fursey's visions entered medieval literature and are believed to have been models, if not literally followed, at least reflected in Dante's *Divine Comedy*.

Another literary vision that may have been a source of inspiration to Dante was that of St. Adamnan. In "*Fis Adhamhnain*," a sermon in Gaelic attributed to him (but probably not written until about two hundred years later), Adamnan regales his listeners with an account, full of happy imagery, of his chimeric journey to heaven and hell. His soul, guided by its guardian angel, goes first to heaven — a land surrounded by a wall of fire that does not harm those blessed souls who pass through it — where the saints of the east and west and north and south are ranged in separate choirs. Three birds are perched on the throne of the King of Heaven; they sing His praises, accompanied by a choir of archangels. Outside the gate are those who await the Last Judgment. A veil of fire and a veil of ice hang in the gateway and strike against each other, a noise terrible to the ears of sinners. But to those within, the sound is as of faint music.

A soul condemned to hell is swallowed by twelve fiery dragons, one after the other, the last depositing it in the devil's maw. The subsequent inferno, Adamnan's next visit, has grades of torment leading to the inner horror of fire, which is inhabited only by devils. The traveller's soul is brought back in a twinkling from the netherworld to the beautiful Land of the Saints. There, like the soul of Fursey, it wishes to stay; but the voice of an angel commands it to return to its body at home, and to tell everyone there about the joys of heaven and the agonies of hell.

The visions of Adamnan, Fursey and other holy men, though the motif was not original with them — Virgil's Aeneas, among other classical travellers, was familiar with other worlds and conversant with similar shades — served a purpose beyond the enrichment of medieval literature. They dramatized religion in a way that brought it attractively alive to people who were not yet so far away from the interaction of the deeds of gods and mortal men. Probably this was not a conscious motive on the part of the visionaries: they truly believed they had seen angels and demons. After all, they were children of the same era.

While Irish prose literature of the Middle Ages owed much to its pagan antecedents, in the field of poetry creativity knew no precedents. Medieval poets, both lay and clerical, were innovators. They gave their imaginations free play, untrammelled by obeisance to ancestral formulae. This is not to say that they were casual or unconventional. Irish medieval poetry developed along strictly formal lines, and its practitioners were artists of extreme skill. But in subject matter and in use of words, the vernacular poetry of the eighth to the eleventh centuries has a sophisticated harmony that is almost unequalled in any language since. Translation fails it. If one tries to reproduce the alliteration, the internal rhymes and the strict meters, the delicate melodic cadences are lost. If one translates literally, the sensitivity comes through but the polished elegance of the contour escapes. The verse is a felicitous combination of the music of words to delight the ear and subtlety of thought to divert the mind.

The development of Irish poetry of the Christian era was not a primal phenomenon but a slow native flowering. We have detailed the regardful awe in which pagan poets were held. With the coming of Christianity the position of the *filid* became anomalous, as the emphasis on satire and eulogy gave way to the new spirituality. The earliest Christian poetry was in

Latin, and it bore little relation to what had gone before. But the background and the skill were there, and gradually, as pagan poetry became absorbed into the new thought, the two streams converged, culminating in an unsurpassed body of medieval poetic literature.

The earliest Christian poet was St. Patrick. Of the few poems attributed to him, only one may be partly genuine — the *Faedh Fiada (Cry of the Deer)*, noted earlier. It is a moving, fervently pious hymn with a decided heathen cast: a haunting echo of Amergin's chant as he stepped ashore in Ireland's last mythical invasion. The Christian saint invokes the forces of sun, moon, fire, wind, rocks, lightning, ocean — along with the power of God — to defeat, among other evils, "the spells of women and smiths and wizards."[11] If Patrick did write it — it has the style and language of the fifth century — it exhibits not only his glowing imagination but an intuitive appreciation of the pagan background of his adopted country. So close were his Christian converts to their antecedents that they believed, and the tradition survived for centuries, that the recital of this first Christian song heard in Ireland was a potent defense against physical or spiritual peril.

St. Columba was, as we have seen, a master poet. But of the two hundred poems attributed to him, only three hymns in Latin can be ascribed with any degree of certainty. One of them, the *Altus Prosator,* contains the world's earliest known example of rhyme. It has been described as an early *Paradise Lost,* full of profound meanings and recondite learning.[12] He is said to have composed it in penance for his responsibility for causing the battle of Culdreimhne. It too had magical properties ascribed to it by the saintly poet himself: he who recited it devoutly would be attended by angels all his life, and evil spirits would shun him; he would live in peace and suffer neither hunger nor nakedness; he would not be assaulted by enemies, and death would come to him gently.

The most personal of Columba's poems, the affecting songs of exile (exemplified on page 160), were probably not written until the eighth century, as their language and meter were not developed before that period. Monastic poets often attached another's name to their imaginative work. This was not a deceptive device, nor was the unknown poet seeking a borrowed glory. It was merely a fancy: authenticity of authorship had little relevance in medieval times. Perhaps the anonymous author wished to fill out the contours of St. Columba's character, handed down from hearsay. The poignant lines do indeed add a dimension.

Though St. Columbanus is better known for his prose, he also wrote poetry — verse-sermons, most of them authentic, in correct Latin hexameters. His boating song (*Carmen Navale,* pages 193–194) may or may not be of his own composition. It is tempting to consider it genuine, as its lilting joyful strains seem an echo of the very voice of the courageous saint.

In the early Middle Ages the relations between monastic and lay poets were mutually derogatory. The cloistered scholars regarded secular poets as itinerant minstrels who extorted a living from their reluctant hosts with the threat of satire. The laymen in their turn were often failed scholars and as such sneered at the attainments they lacked. Sometimes their scorn was stinging, as in *The Vision of Mac Conglinne*, a tale in prose and poetry. This story details the undertakings of a vagabond student who "conceived a great desire to take to poetry and give his studies the go-by. For he had had too much of the life of learning. [He decided to go to Munster,] for the scholar had heard that there was enough and to spare of every sort of white meat for him to get there. And he had a hungry lust after white meats." [13] The poem is a parody of literary scholarship, more gross than sharp, but with a certain crude wit. Though written in the twelfth century, it harks back to a much earlier period.

An exception to the general disaffinity between lay and clerical poets was the sixth century's Dallan Forgaill, St. Columba's invaluable aide at the Convention of Drumceatt in 575 (see pages 161–163). Together Dallan and Columba fashioned a bridge between secular and clerical learning and laid the basis for Ireland's remarkable educational system. Dallan Forgaill's poetry is the earliest in Gaelic that is still extant. Though he was a secular poet, he became a churchman and appears in the roster of Irish saints. His most famous poem, the *Amra Columcille,* had, like other spiritual poetry of the early years, a benign magic: it was said that the poet's eyesight was restored as he sang the hymn, and that "every day whoever will recite it . . . will reach the good bright kingdom which God granted Dallan." [14]

By the early Middle Ages secular poetry had become a sophisticated art and bards were skilled, highly respected practitioners. Recognized poets had gone through many years of education and most of them were proficient in other fields besides their specialty. Some became the confidants of kings as well as court poets. Such a bard was the late tenth century's Mac Liag (aforementioned), Ireland's chief poet when Brian Boru took the throne of all Ireland in 1002. Though he was engaged by Brian as secretary, historian and adviser, he was primarily a poet. His dedication to his king is expressed in a moving lament upon Brian's death:

> Oh where, Kincora, is Brian the great,
> And where is the beauty that once was thine,
> Oh where are the princes and nobles that sate

To feast in thy halls and drink the red wine,
Where, O Kincora?

They are gone, those heroes of royal birth,
Who plundered no churches, who broke no trust;
'Tis weary for me to be living on earth,
When they, O Kincora, lie low in the dust,
Low, O Kincora. 15

The poetry of the early Christian era, as well as that which preceded it, used alliteration as its only adornment. In the sixth century Irish scholars began composing hymns in Latin, and in these the use of rhyme appeared for the first time anywhere. Soon they began writing in Irish (anticipating by centuries the use of the vernacular on the Continent), and by the seventh century forms were becoming elaborate: groups of alliterative quatrains, prescribed numbers of syllables and internal as well as end rhymes. But up to the eleventh century, poetry nevertheless remained a flexible art. There was a wide variety of form, and poets continued to experiment: a poet could develop his own meter and rhyme scheme to suit his subject. So, despite the complexity of the framework, medieval poetry has a spirited freshness, an absence of cliché and an attractive spontaneity. Indeed poetic composition was often indulged in by the serious-minded scholar as a release from the tediously weighty work of the scriptorium. Scraps of verse appear, like doodling, in the margins of ecclesiastical codices and other solemn manuscripts: the copyist, suffering from spring fever or an access of acedia — the debilitating torpor that was an occupational illness of the monastic life — turned briefly away from his pedestrian labors.

The eighth century was a time of extraordinary creativity in the monasteries. Anchorites following the rule of the *celi De* — their senses sharpened by hours of contemplation and abstention from food and sleep, their minds free of all worldly distraction — could survey the world of nature that was their only physical reality with the ecstatic eye of the visionary. The result of their supersensitive cognizance is a wealth of sophisticated, subtle and imaginative poetry. They looked out at the earth and into their souls, and expressed what they saw with beguiling candor and an entire absence of egotism.

One cloistered recluse looks back, with a trace of irritation at his present portion, to the days when he was free:

There was a time I thought more sweet
than the voice of a little bell beside me

> the singing of the blackbird from the hill,
> the belling of a stag in the storm.
>
> There was a time I thought more sweet
> the howling of the wolves
> than the voice of a cleric within
> a-baaing and a-bleating.[16]

Another sees nature as perhaps too tempting, a threat to his state of grace:

> A wall of forest looms above,
> and sweetly the blackbird sings;
> all the birds make melody
> over me and my books and things.
>
> There sings to me the cuckoo
> from bush-citadel in grey hood.
> God's doom! May the Lord protect me,
> writing well, under the great wood.[17]

The sin of acedia is limned with telling directness by the guilty one himself:

> Shame to my thoughts how they stray from me! I dread great danger from
>   it on the day of lasting doom.
> During the psalms they wander on a path that is not right: they run, they
>   disturb, they misbehave before the eye of great God.
> Through eager assemblies, through companies of foolish women, through
>   woods, through cities — swifter than the wind,
> Now along pleasant paths, again through hideous. . . .[18]

Probably the most famous example of gentle monastic humor is the poem about Pangur Ban, the monk's pet cat. This is not primarily a poem about a cat; the poet rather looks dispassionately at his overacademic self, comparing his industrious quest for the precise word with the strenuous zeal of the cat chasing mice:

> I and white Pangur practise each of us his special art: his mind is set on
>   hunting, my mind is on my special craft.
> I love . . . to be quiet beside my book, diligently pursuing knowledge.
> White Pangur does not envy me: he loves his childish craft.

*When the two of us . . . are alone together in our house, we have
something to which we may apply our skill, an endless sport.*
*It is usual, at times, for a mouse to stick in his net, as a result of warlike
battling. For my part, into my net falls some difficult rule of hard
meaning.*
*He directs his bright perfect eye against an enclosing wall. Though my
clear eye is very weak I direct it against keenness of knowledge.*
*He is joyful with swift movement when a mouse sticks in his sharp paw.
I too am joyful when I understand a dearly loved difficult problem.*[19]

Only the occasional monastic poem was humorous or cynical. Most of
them expressed a moving, simple love of God and nature. But even the
religious poetry was often couched in personal terms, and the relation
between the anchorite and his God was rarely abstract. An engaging example, revealing in its aristocratic overtones, is the ninth-century poem
that has the name of St. Ita (St. Brendan's unsparing foster-mother) attached to it, in which Jesus comes to her in the form of a child:

*It is little Jesus who is nursed by me in my little hermitage. Though a
cleric have great wealth, it is all deceitful save Jesukin.*
*The nursing done by me in my house is no nursing of a base churl: Jesus
with Heaven's inhabitants is against my heart every night.*
. . . . .
*It is noble angelic Jesus and no common cleric who is nursed by me in my
little hermitage.*[20]

Another example of religious love-poetry is a poem of the eighth-century
Blathmac, son of Cu Brettan — a tender lament with Mary after the death
of Christ:

*Come to me, loving Mary,
that I may keen with you your very dear one;
. . . .
That with you I may beat my two hands
for your Son being in captivity;
. . . .
Your womb has conceived Jesus —
it has not marred your virginity . . .*

. . . . .

> *Come to me, loving Mary,*
> *you, head of unsullied faith,*
> *that we may have talk together*
> *with the compassion of unblemished heart.*[21]

This poem — primitive, intimate, deeply religious — is typical of the personal approach that so irritated the purist pedants of the Continent, who saw an unprovable taint of heresy in the naive Irish assumption of a direct line to heaven.

The sternest celibate, seeking solitude, found in his exile a rapport with his surroundings that approached sensuality, as in this dialogue between king and hermit:

GUAIRE: *Hermit Marban, why do you not sleep upon a bed? More often would you sleep out of doors, with your head . . . upon the ground of a fir-grove.*

MARBAN: *I have a hut in a wood; only my Lord knows it; an ash-tree closes it on one side, and a hazel, like a great tree by a rath, on the other.*

. . . .

Little hidden humble abode, with the path-filled (?) forest for estate: will you go with me to see it? My life, even without you, has been very happy.

. . . .

Bees, chafers . . . barnacle geese, brent geese. . . .
The wind's voice against a branchy wood, on a day of grey cloud; cascades in a river; roar of rock: delightful music!
Beautiful are the pines which make music for me, unhired; through Christ I am no worse off at any time than with you.

. . . . . .

GUAIRE: *I will give my great kingdom . . . to live with you, Marban.*[22]

The pagan echo is clear: the poet could almost have been Ossian. Yet looking the other direction in time, the scribe anticipates St. Francis, aware of God in all creation and praising Him with delight in His works. In another poem to nature an anchorite is less openly sensuous; yet still, equating God with nature, he sees his salvation in the wild places (a sentiment almost literally echoed by Yeats nine hundred years later):

I wish, O son of the living God, eternal, ancient King, for a hidden little
*   hut in the wilderness that it might be my dwelling,*
All-grey shallow water beside it, a clear pool to wash away sins through
*   the grace of the Holy Spirit.*[23]

Most of the religious poems that have survived are short mood pieces like the above, or straight hymns. A notable exception is the *Saltair na Rann (Psalter of Verses)*, one of the most captivating products of the *celi De* emphasis on education. It is a series of 150 poems, composed about 987, that retell the story of the Bible from the day of Creation until the Last Judgment. Though deeply religious, the work has an accent peculiarly Irish. Into the holy company, for instance, is injected Gaidel Glas, the first ancestor of the Gaels, who was grazing flocks in Egypt at the time of the crossing of the Red Sea. He was married to the daughter of the pharaoh but he refused to join the Egyptians in pursuit because he understood the power of God that was in the children of Israel. He also, however, feared reprisals from his father-in-law, so he took ship and set sail, arriving eventually in Ireland. The imagery is inventive, after the way of Irish poets. The winds were given colors by the Lord when he created them: "From the east comes the crimson wind; from the south, the white; from the north, the black; from the west, the dun."[24]

The story of Adam and Eve has an ingenuous parochiality in the *Saltair na Rann*. When God was good to his children in Paradise, the tale goes, the devil was jealous. He went to the serpent and flattered it, saying that as Adam was created later, it need not submit to its junior. He then asked permission to enter the serpent's body in order to tempt Eve. When God exiled his children, they had no food, dwelling, fire or clothing; and Adam went to stand in the river Jordan and asked the river and all its creatures to fast with him against God.* The stream stood still and all its creatures gathered around Adam and prayed with him, until God forgave him. Doomsday, at the end of the book, is a portentous revelation of seven signs, one for each day of the week: ". . . the sea rises up and gives a shout. . . . Heaven will be bent, and will be crushed against the earth. . . . Hosts of stars will fall down from their seats. . . . The sun and moon will be quenched."[25]

Secular poets adopted the meters and rhyme schemes developed in the monasteries. Though their themes were sometimes similar — they had the

---

*This is an interesting Christian adaptation of the pagan custom of fasting against wrongdoers, as described on page 32.

same love for nature — the emphasis was different. In place of the meta-
physical tenor of even the most nature-oriented clerical poetry, lay poems
were directed toward purely human emotions: anger, sorrow, love. One
of the most beautiful of love poems is the song of Liadan, which is
contained in a prose saga about a maiden who took the veil, while the
lover she abandoned, Cuirithir, tried to forget her by entering a monastery.
She followed him there, and to escape her he went abroad on pilgrimage.
Bereft by her own fault, she sings this song, in which the intensity of the
passion is enhanced by the spare economy of words and the absence of the
easy cliché:

> *No pleasure*
> *that deed I did, tormenting him,*
> *tormenting what I treasure.*

> *Joyfully,*
> *but that God had come between us then*
> *had I granted what he begged of me.*

> *Not unwise*
> *is the way that he is taking now,*
> *enduring pain and gaining Paradise.*

> *Great folly*
> *where once I showed such gentleness*
> *to set Cuirithir against me!*

> *Liadan I;*
> *they say that I loved Cuirithir,*
> *nor would I, if I could, deny.*

> *The while I bless*
> *that I was in his company*
> *and was treating him with tenderness.*

> *A woodland breeze*
> *was my melody with Cuirithir,*
> *sounding harmony of reddening seas.*

> *It seemed thus:*
> *the last thing I would ever do*
> *was a deed to come between us.*

> *Cry clearly:*
> *if any lovers this heart cherishes,*
> *he its darling, loved most dearly.*
>
> *A cry of pain*
> *and the heart within was rent in two,*
> *without him never beats again.*[26]

Satire was the feared weapon of the pagan poet, and its use persisted through the early Christian era. Though it lacked the magic — it raised no boils on the victim's face — it retained the power to sting. Its knife was humor, as in this four-line lampoon:

> *I know him;*
> *He'll give no horse for a poem;*
> *He'll give you what his kind allows,*
> *Cows.*[27]

In another not-so-gentle satire, the poet attacks the silliness of the woman who mourns the death of her pet goose.

> *O Mor of Moyne in Mag Siuil, loss of a bird is no great occasion for grief. If you consider that you yourself must die, is it not an offense against your reason to lament a goose?*[28]

Sometimes the poet expresses poignancy and acerbity at the same time, as in an old woman's wry plaint for her youth:

> *Ebb-tide has come to me as to the sea; old age makes me yellow; though I may grieve thereat, it approaches its food joyfully.*
> . . . .
> *When my arms are seen, all bony and thin! — the craft they used to practise was pleasant: they used to be about glorious kings.*
> . . . .
> *I speak no honied words; no wethers are killed for my wedding; my hair is scant and grey; to have a mean veil over it causes no regret.*
> . . . .
> *Alack-a-day that I sail not over youth's sea! Many years of my beauty are departed, for my wantonness has been used up.*
> . . . .
> *I am cold indeed; every acorn is doomed to decay. After feasting by bright candles, to be in the darkness of an oratory!*[29]

The medieval poetry from which we have quoted is carefully wrought in its original language; the rhyme schemes are complex, the meters neatly realized. Yet such was the creative imagination of the poets that their words sing despite the intricacy of the framework. This was not universally true. Sometimes the obsession with form obscured the meaning or rendered it absurd. The need to pad the verse to balance the meter correctly led to meaningless parentheses; the desire for the correct rhyme scheme rendered the wording awkward. Another pitfall was the Irish penchant for the arcane: poets and scholars delighted in abstruse riddles and paradoxes, and they attached recondite symbolism to such abstract concepts as numbers and letters. The letter *A,* for instance, they regarded as being placed first because it led the name of the first man, Adam, and the first patriarch, Abraham; further, it was symbolic of the Trinity, three strokes making one letter. Numbers had figurative qualities — the number one signifying the unity of God, two the marriage bond, and so on. At times literary craftsmen became so involved in metaphor, allegory and counterfeit semantics that all sense was lost.

The ultimate example is the seventh-century tract entitled *Hisperica Famina (Western Sayings,* or, as one scholar parodied its gaudy rhetoric, *Occidental Talkitudes).*[30] The work is a fantasy of crabbedness that has no equal in medieval literature; its vocabulary is bizarre in the extreme and its style so grotesque that one cannot even decipher whether it is prose or poetry. It begins with a teacher glorifying his own skill; he goes on to advise a would-be pupil, a countryman, to go back home and tend his sheep. There ensues a collection of essays on mundane subjects such as a teacher would present to his class: on the adventures of one day, on the four elements, on the furniture of a classroom. The work ends with a story to be narrated by the pupil in the same knotty jargon used by the teacher. Though the subject matter and the syntax are almost foolishly simpleminded, the language itself has an awesome unreason. It is a farrago of classical, ecclesiastical and colloquial Latin with wrong endings, punctuated by misused and misunderstood Greek and Hebrew words. It is impossible to unravel the purpose of this piece of inflated turgidity. It was obviously created by a cultist or a group of them with a compulsive attraction to esoteric glossaries and an astonishing ingenuity in mixing them up; but there may have been design behind it. While it illustrates the chaotic extreme to which the Irish passion for involution could lead, it has at least one element of a secret language: a cryptic vocabulary. Perhaps its inventors designed through deliberate obscurantism to deceive the less educated into regarding them as more erudite scholars than they were. As literature, however, it is a cul-de-sac of fustian.

Yet the extravagant imagination that produced the *Hisperica Famina* also gave birth to the *Navigatio Sancti Brendani;* and the intoxication with the sound of words, carried to absurdity in the one case, in others was sublimated to the expressive grace of Liadan's love song, Columba's paean to Derry, Deirdre's lament.

CHAPTER XV
THE SCHOLARS

THE VOICE OF IRELAND SANG THROUGH HER POETS AND STORYTELLERS, DELIGHT-
ing her populace from king to sheepherder. It also spoke in the accents of
the learned, and it was in this aspect that Ireland reached across to Britain
and the Continent. The veneration of learning, a heritage from pagan days,
fostered through the importation of classical culture and the growth of the
monastic schools in the early years of Christianity, gave rise to an extraordinary development of scholarship in medieval times. The Irish were intense and eager learners; they were also dedicated and impassioned teachers.
As they loved to gain knowledge, they loved to share it, sometimes with
an enthusiastic self-approbation, as if they were the chosen, which was a
source of exasperation to the less naive. Generally, however, Irish philosophers, scientists and classicists were sought after by the courts of Europe
and welcomed in the schools. The savants from the outer island, once
regarded as an uncouth hinterland, brought back to the Continent the
disciplines of learning that had been buried during the centuries of
barbarism.

Scholarship in early Christian Ireland was, as we have seen, divided
between the lay schools, which traditionally taught orally in Irish, and the
monastic, where the first language was Latin. The introduction of the Latin
alphabet and the consequent facility of writing did much to stimulate the
development of the lay schools, and a mixture of cultures resulted, of
supreme benefit to both.

The rise of a new class of intellectual elite is typified by the bizarre story of Cenn Faelad, a seventh-century chieftain who received a head injury in battle. The skull fracture was cured by a trepanning operation in which the abbot Briccine, a famous surgeon, removed a part of the warrior's brain, the "brain of forgetting." The patient was taken for convalescence to the abbot's house in Toomregon, County Cavan, where he stayed for a year. The house was at the meeting of three streets, where three professors lived. "And there were three schools in the place; a school of Latin learning, a school of Irish law and a school of Irish poetry. And everything that [the convalescent] would hear of the recitations of the three schools every day, he would have it by heart every night. And he fitted a pattern of poetry to these matters and wrote them on slates and tablets and set them in a vellum book." [1] This strange story illustrates the beginning of the application of Latin learning to oral lore; Cenn Faelad's studies, initiated in such an odd way, brought him to the forefront of Irish scholarship as the first acknowledged student of the vernacular. He went on to compile texts, revising the ancient Irish grammars to lay a foundation of comparative philology, and drafting a law tract that incorporated much of Brehon Law, Ireland's pre-Christian common-law code. He is the first poet to be mentioned in the annals.

Cenn Faelad's change from warrior to academician, besides standing as a symbol of Ireland's intellectual development, says something also for the high state of medical knowledge in early Christian Ireland, another legacy from pagan times.* Trepanning is an operation requiring delicate skill and an anatomical knowledge of the brain. Removal of the "brain of forgetting" was a quaint way of describing the effect of such an operation on the subsequent behavior of the patient. After a fracture, memory is often lost; the operation, relieving the pressure and removing the injured part, allows the memory to return so that the patient becomes as he was before. In this case the warrior chieftain was for a year unable to follow his assigned course and indulge his bellicose proclivities. In enforced idleness his mind, always quick and active, found a new, engrossing outlet. In the course of his absorption he uncovered his true bent — and so his destiny changed dramatically.

While seventh-century Cenn Faelad was breaking ground for scholarship in the vernacular, which was revolutionary in his age, the monastic schools were at the same time continuing and perfecting the classical ideals of

---

*Pagan medical practices are discussed on pages 45–46.

academic education. One of the earliest and brightest exponents of monastic learning was Adamnan of Iona. He has already been mentioned as the poor student whose milk crock was broken by a king, as the literary visionary and as the biographer of St. Columba. In all his guises he was first and foremost an intellectual — a scholar and a teacher. If his vision was delightfully imaginative, it also served to instruct. His *Vita S. Columbae* at first sight appears to have little relation to the modern ideal of disinterested scholarship. Adamnan was writing for his own time, a time when factual data, social comment and chronology had no place in a spiritual biography. The *Vita* is largely a recital of miracles, with the bare facts of the saint's life condensed into a paragraph at the end of the second preface. But this also was a method of instruction in his day, to give the student a picture of the attributes of holiness for inspiration and emulation. While spiritual enlightenment was the motive of his chronicle and pious marvels its material, the basis of the *Vita* is authentic. Writing in his old age, a hundred years after Columba's death, he had access to word-of-mouth information only slightly removed from its original source. His account was in its time considered a high achievement in religious biography. To today's reader, once he understands that he is not to seek factual information, it is lively in its style and touching in its all-accepting reverence.

Adamnan was born in Donegal, Columba's county, in 624. Though like Columba he was highborn, of the Ui Neill family, he did not have the exalted prospects of his princely cousin. In fact, if the story of the milk jug is to be believed, he was inured to poverty from childhood. While still young he gained a reputation as a quiet and thoughtful student, and he rose to a position of renown as a scholar. Among his pupils, probably, was King Aldfrith of Northumbria, who had sought refuge in Ireland during one of the many power struggles within his uneasy kingdom, and had become one of the stellar foreign exponents of Irish education. The Anglian king became a good friend, as did King Finnachta the Festive of Ireland, who had inadvertently broken the milk jug, and through these two royal benefactors Adamnan came to wield great political influence.

In 679 he became abbot of Iona, ruling there until his death in 704. He was on the move continually, convening synods, negotiating affairs, and serving as ambassador between the courts of his two powerful friends. He became much concerned over the differences between the Roman and the Celtic Churches in the matters of the date of Easter and the shape of the tonsure. He was convinced that Ireland should follow the Catholic rule in these matters and tried to persuade the brethren at Iona. They persisted in their time-honored usage and Adamnan, being gentle and peaceable, did not try to enforce his convictions. He did, however, succeed in getting his views adopted at the Synod of Tara, which he convened in 697; and the enactments of that gathering were known as *Lex Adamnani*.

Besides introducing the Roman usage into the Irish Church, this synod produced a law pivotally important to Irish society. The lot of women in Ireland was, as most everywhere else, primitively inequitable. The female slave had no rights whatever, even being forced to build her hut outside the home enclosure. Her mistress was not much better off:

> The work which the best of women had to do, was to go to battle. . . . On one side of her she would carry her bag of provisions, on the other her babe. Her wooden pole upon her back. Thirty feet long it was, and had at one end an iron hook, which she would thrust into the tress of some woman in the opposite battalion. Her husband behind her, carrying a fence-stake in his hand, and flogging her on to battle.[2]

More than a hundred years earlier, Columba had introduced a law against the serving of women in battle, but it had never been enforced and had fallen into abeyance. Adamnan was brought to reinaugurate his predecessor's reform through the agency of his mother. The following vignette of early Irish family life illustrates that while Irish women may have been deplorably exploited, they were far from spineless. One day, while crossing the Plain of Bregia with his mother, Adamnan said:

> "Come upon my back, dear Mother."
> ". . . I must not," she said . . . "because you are not a dutiful son."
> "Who is more dutiful than I am? . . . Carrying you about from place to place, keeping you from dirt and wet [literally urine]. . . . I know of no duty which a son of man could do for his Mother that I do not do for you, except the humming tune which women perform. . . ."
> "That is not the duty I desire, but that you should free women for me from encounter, from camping, from fighting, from hosting, from wounding, from slaying. . . ."
> Then she went upon her son's back until they chanced to come upon a battlefield. Such was the thickness of the slaughter into which they came that the soles of one woman would touch the neck of another. . . . They saw nothing more touching or more pitiful than the head of a woman in one place and the body in

another, and her little babe upon the breast of the corpse, a stream of milk upon one of its cheeks, and a stream of blood upon the other. . . .

Adamnan . . . adjusted the head upon the neck and made the sign of the Cross with his staff across the breast of the woman. And the woman rose up. . . . "Well now, Adamnan," said she. "To thee henceforward it is given to free the women of the western world. Neither food nor drink shall go into thy mouth until women have been freed by thee."[3]

This directive, enforced by his mother, who placed a chain around his neck and a stone in his mouth so he could not eat, caused Adamnan not to rest until he had done their bidding and freed women from their martial servitude. His action caused a revolution in the social customs of the Irish — a nearly final step in the eradication of the more inhumane of pagan practices, which would not be entirely uprooted until the abolition of slavery in the twelfth century (seven hundred years before the rest of Europe and the United States took the same action).

Although Adamnan was an untiring and effective negotiator in affairs that he felt were important to his calling, he was not, like Columba, a political activist. He was primarily a scholar. He knew Latin as well as he knew his native tongue, and he had some command of Greek and Hebrew. Though his universe was bounded by Northumbria on the east and Donegal on the west, his curiosity ranged over the known world. A Gaulish bishop, Arculf, was shipwrecked off the coast of Britain, and Adamnan, hearing that the cleric was returning home from a visit to the East, invited him to Iona for the winter. Arculf told him in detail of his journeys to Jerusalem, Damascus, Constantinople, Alexandria and the islands of the Mediterranean. He told him of the salt of the Dead Sea, of the overflowing of the Nile, of the source of the Jordan River, of Mount Etna, which was "fiery by night and smoky by day" and thundered so violently "that one would think the land of Sicily was being shaken by an earthquake,"[4] of the desert where St. John the Baptist had lived near a clear spring, and where people ate locusts cooked with oil, of the trees whose leaves, when ground between the hands, had the taste of wild honey. Adamnan wrote it all down on waxen tablets; then he checked and added and perfected. Finally he inscribed the finished work on parchment with the title *De Locis Sanctis (Of Holy Places)* and presented it to King Aldfrith.

This work and his *Vita S. Columbae* are the only two works definitely known to be by Adamnan. He is said to have written a life of St. Patrick, no longer extant, and a work called *An Epitome of Irish Laws in Meter,* as well as some hymns and the aforementioned sermon on his vision.

From this small sampling it is evident that Adamnan must have been a scholar who drew continuing pleasure from satisfying his curiosity. And it follows that he must have communicated his pleasure to his students. They could not have helped being fascinated by his wide-ranging interests, his zestful details and his lively style.

Adamnan was a luminous example of the early Irish teacher-missionary. He combined a deep commitment to his calling with a sparkling zeal for teaching; he was withal kindly and direct in his dealings with people, and simple in his way of life. He was among the first of a long line of inspired teachers and scholars who imparted to their generations an extra civilizing dimension, who contributed, some of them profoundly, to the world's knowledge and, not least important, who added to life a generous measure of enjoyment during a few bleak centuries. After the ninth century, most of these academics practiced their arts abroad on account of the afflictions of the Viking invasions. A few stayed home, keeping scholarship alive in troubled Ireland.

Among them was the early tenth century's Cormac Mac Cuilennain, bishop of Cashel and king of Munster, an accomplished poet, historian and scholar knowledgeable in Latin, Greek, Hebrew and Danish. Most of his writings are lost; the remaining work attributed to him is one of the most provocative and diverting works in the Irish language, *Cormac's Glossary,* from which we have quoted on occasion. It is the first vernacular dictionary of any European language; and besides its historic importance, it is a matchless repository of facts and legends of the mores of early Christian and pre-Christian Ireland.

Cormac was one of the few savants who chose to pursue their scholarly researches at home. The Irish love for wandering, which had sent abroad the missionaries of the sixth and seventh centuries — Columba, Columbanus, Fursey, Gall, Adamnan — brought a new spirit to Britain and Europe out of Ireland. These enthusiastic and dedicated holy men were the forerunners of the Irish renaissance on the Continent, which reached its height in the eighth and ninth centuries at the courts of Charlemagne and Charles the Bald. The aim of these first teachers was primarily conversion. But, well educated in the fine monastic schools of home, they brought their books and their high ideals of scholarship with them. Most of the monasteries they founded had schools and libraries connected with them, the most celebrated being those at Luxeuil in France, Saint Gall in Switzerland and Bobbio in Italy. The Irish won renown for their high standards of education and scholarship; the aristocracy flocked to their schools, and it became the fashion to have an Irish scholar or two in residence at kingly courts, to enhance the prestige of rulers rich in temporal power but poor in intellectual attainments.

St. Virgil of Salzburg, who flourished a generation before this vogue for scholars reached its full strength, was another in the distinguished line of missionary-teachers. Like Adamnan, he was primarily an intellectual; unlike the gentle teacher of Iona, he was a dissenter — positive in his opinions, tactless in his methods. He had a remarkable aptitude for science, which led him to convictions considered unbecoming if not downright heretical among the conformist Continental clergy of his time.

His name had been Fergal, which he chose to spell "Fergil" in homage to the classical poet, and which was later Latinized to "Virgilius." Nothing is known of his antecedents in Ireland except that he received a good education and came to the Continent well versed in mathematics and classical lore. His primary desire, like that of his earlier compatriots, was exile — to preach in a land of heathen darkness. His first known stop, about 742, was at Quierzy on the Oise in northern France, where Pepin the Short held court. Pepin's goal was to reunite the huge Frankish kingdom that had become fragmented and decentralized; in 751, sanctioned by the pope and crowned by Boniface, archbishop of Mainz, he became king of the Franks, the first of the Carolingian dynasty. (His son Charles, Charlemagne to be, was about eight years old at the time of Pepin's coronation.) Virgil's erudition, intelligence and spirit appealed to the new king; and Pepin, upon his return from the suppression of an uprising in Bavaria by Duke Odilo, sent the Irish monk there to arrange a peace. Virgil decided forthwith that Germany would be the field of his missionary endeavors.

Though there were still worshippers of Thor and Odin in northern Germany, the exile did not exactly find himself in a land of unruly barbarians. Most of southern Germany had already been converted into thoroughgoing Catholic conformity by Boniface (originally named Wilfrith), known as the Apostle of Germany. Pope Gregory II, with the concurrence of his patron, Pepin, had given the British-born monk the threefold mission of evangelizing Germany, organizing the already existing Christians into submission to the papacy, and counteracting the influence of the schismatic Irish monks there. The archbishop, who had been raised and schooled in Devonshire, stronghold of the Rome-oriented Augustinian missions, must have been appalled to see yet another independent-minded Irish monk turning up in what was almost his private territory — an Irish monk, moreover, who was backed by the enthusiastic favor of Boniface's own patron, Pepin the Short.

The two holy men had diametrically opposed notions of how to run a church, and each was passionately motivated. Boniface, for all his established position, was at a disadvantage. Though he was assuredly gifted with intelligence adequate to the conversion and organization of multitudes of pagans and schismatics, he had neither the guile, the mental grasp nor the education to deal with a stubborn Irish genius.

The differences between the two churchmen were something more than a personality clash, though that undoubtedly exacerbated the hostility. Virgil was the product of an older type of Christianity that had taken root in Ireland and developed independently of the distant Vatican. Irish abbots owed allegiance to none but their God, and cooperation between them was a matter of Christian choice rather than superimposed discipline. When they went abroad they took their individuality with them, stayed outside the mainstream, and won the devoted love of their constituents on personality unrestricted by jurisdiction from above. Virgil was impatient of orthodoxy for its own sake, and he must have been difficult to deal with.in an organization run from the top, like Boniface's. The German archbishop had custom and conformity on his side. He also had the course of history with him, an inevitable motion toward concentrated authority as the savage nomadic tribes one by one became settled farmers and urban dwellers, more interested in the peace of their new security than in the fierce pride of their old independence.

Duke Odilo was attracted, as Pepin had been, by the gifted and lively Irishman, and he made him abbot of St. Peter's monastery in Salzburg. In 745 Bishop John of Salzburg died, and it probably was intended that Virgil should succeed him. Possibly this purpose was quenched by Boniface; but it is more likely that Virgil himself declined. He had the Irish ways and he knew, as Columba had so brilliantly demonstrated, that he could rule better from a modest position than an exalted one. He chose to remain a simple priest, and wielded all the power he pleased in Salzburg as abbot of his monastery, while Boniface fumed in Mainz, looking for ways to pull the thorn out of his flesh.

A charge of heresy seemed to Boniface the most telling form of attack. The Irish had always skirted on the edge of it, and Virgil, with his profound learning and his freethinking outlook, was so far ahead of his period as to appear dangerously different in his faith. The archbishop's first move was to attack the Irish priest for incorrect use of Latin in the baptismal service. Virgil used an ungrammatical and colloquial form of Latin, and Boniface claimed that this debased the service to the point of heresy. He made representations to Pope Vitalian, whose response was negative: Virgil was only using a country form of Latin in order more easily to communicate with his simple congregation. The pope himself used it in daily speech, even in sermons when he was preaching to the common people. This adulterated Latin, spoken by most of the country people in the Carolingian and Lombard lands, was the ancestor of today's Latin languages. It is still spoken in isolated parts of Switzerland, Austria and northern Italy, where it is known locally as Romansh, Ladin, Rhaetic or Friulian, depending on the district.

Losing the first round, Boniface found what seemed an invincible weapon. Virgil, applying his scientific deductive faculties to his classical learning, had become convinced that, since the earth was round, there must be life on the other side in the shape of humans walking around like ordinary mortals anywhere. He was teaching this heterodoxy of the antipodes to innocent young Christian pupils and writing papers on it for wider dissemination. This, it seemed to Boniface — who was but expressing the generally held opinion — was flagrant heresy. Though Boniface was ultraconservative in believing the earth was flat,* his logic in proving the flouting of God's truths was in tune with his times. If creatures existed on the other side of the earth, whatever its shape, they would have to move about head downward. Such unnatural beings could not belong to the human race and could not have been created by God or saved by Christ. Therefore whoever postulated them was offending against God and the true Church. According to his lights, he had irrefutable right on his side.

But Virgil foiled him again. Using the same debased Latin that served him in his clerical intercourse, he wrote his theories in a detailed scientific treatise on cosmography. He signed this work with the nom de plume Ethicus Ister, which has been translated either as "The Philosopher from the Danube" or as "A Man from Ethica Terra" (signifying Tiree near Iona in Scotland). To certify the authenticity of the work, he put forth that it was derived from a Latin version of a Greek text written by St. Jerome some 350 years earlier. As a final touch — possibly to administer a gratuitous bee sting to Boniface, still smarting from his previous defeat in this area — he claimed that the manuscript had been copied by a Merovingian

*Such irreproachable Christian scholars as the Venerable Bede a generation before and Isidore of Seville over a century earlier had accepted the axiom of a spherical earth, based on their studies of Greek theory as far back as Pytheas of Marseilles, who set out on his voyage to prove it in 300 B.C.

scribe who could write only corrupt and ignorant country Latin. To dis-associate himself incontestably from the work, he added a diatribe against Irish schools, books and teachers. The information contained in the tract, such as the existence of antipodes, was thus unimpeachably vouched for by authority of an eminent Father of the Church, one of the most presti-gious scholars in early Christian history. None of Virgil's contemporaries could prove that this authority was straight fabrication, there being no authentic list then extant of the works of St. Jerome.

The doctrine of the antipodes was clearly acceptable after the publication of this brilliant piece of chicanery — which continued its success as a work of geographic reference for some four or five centuries — and fault could no longer be found with the Irish priest who so persuasively taught it. For he must have been an eloquent and stimulating teacher. He left a long-lasting reputation for learning and missionary zeal among the Slavs of Carinthia.

Boniface was murdered in 754 by ax-wielding pagans while on a mission of conversion to the Frisians of northwestern Germany. Perhaps the death of his rival changed Virgil's outlook, or perhaps age had brought him to more conventional views of the administration of the Church, for within the year he accepted the call to be consecrated bishop of Salzburg. Little record remains of his career in this office, except that he labored to bring about closer collaboration between the bishops and the abbots of Bavaria. This was directly in line with the aims of Boniface, and contrary to the Irish tradition of independence from orthodox ties with the Vatican. Though Virgil's scientific theories were beyond the imaginations of many of his contemporaries, his head was never in the clouds. He was a realist, and he must have understood that the fate of the independent Irish missions in Germany had been foreshadowed when the Synod of Whitby in England a century before had ordained the decline of Irish influence in that country. The welfare of the Church was his concern above all, and if cooperation with the establishment was the inexorable historical movement, he was not going to be an anachronism. He was perceptive enough to see the necessity for spiritual centralization as temporal power was being concentrated in the person of Charles, son of Pepin, now king of all the Franks, and rapidly expanding his realm to include most of western Europe in what would soon be called the new Roman Empire.

Virgil died in 784 and was buried in his cathedral. When the Early Italian Baroque cathedral was erected in 1628 on the site, his remains were re-interred under the magnificent high altar.

Time, erasing discord, has bequeathed only halos. Boniface, the supreme organizer, the faithful proconsul of the papacy, the holy martyr, became an unofficial saint immediately after his death, his cult arising at Fulda and his feast recognized by the Catholic Church in the nineteenth century. In 1233 Pope Gregory IX, friend of St. Francis of Assisi, exalted Virgil to sainthood. St. Virgil is one of the rare Irishmen to receive the official benison.

In 795, eleven years after Virgil's death, the Vikings made their first raid on Ireland, signalling the start of two centuries of intermittent but savage plundering. As previously noted, the buccaneers had a particular detestation for books as symbols of the religion they were intent on destroying, and the distressed monks began to gather their ravaged libraries and flee to the Continent. The forced emigration of learned men from their once-peaceful sanctuaries was an eventuality of serious detriment to Ireland and of inestimable benefit to western Europe. The monks and scholars who brought their books to the courts and monasteries of the Continent to preserve them from the specialized virulence of the Norse invaders were the chief agents of a great revival of learning in France, Germany, Switzerland and Italy.

But the Europe of these ninth-century émigrés was different from the Europe of the time of Columbanus. Already in Virgil's lifetime the independence of the Irish-run monasteries was giving way to deference to the central authority of Rome. There were few barbarians or lapsed Christians left to attract the exiled missionary, and the fervor of the heaven-inspired hermit, which used to attract disciples who became the nucleus of a new order, was out of date. The exiles, unable to find a haven for their pious aspirations, wandered the roads and wound up, if they were lucky, in the entourage of a prince who welcomed them not so much for their holiness as for their erudition, regarded as an ornament to his court.

Companies of Irish refugees became a familiar sight in ninth-century France and Germany. As they had left Ireland with nothing but their books, they were destitute and unkempt in appearance, with long hair and rough homespun garments, carrying walking sticks, water bottles and the leather satchels that contained their precious manuscripts. But their poverty and homelessness did not hide their scholarly attainments nor still the unconquerable optimism of their spirits. An apocryphal story that dramatically expresses this truth is that of two Irish scholars who came to the coast of France in an English merchant ship. Seeing the merchants set out their wares and the crowds gathering around to buy, and having nothing to offer for sale but their learning, the two pilgrims began to cry out: "Whoever wants wisdom let him come to us and get it: we have it for sale." When Charlemagne heard of the learned hawkers, he had them brought to his court, and one of them, Clement, stayed until his death.

Of all the royal benefactors who sponsored these displaced savants, Charlemagne was the ne plus ultra. He was the acme of a Teutonic prince of his period: six feet tall, with a strong, lithe figure, large expressive eyes and a happy temperament. His favorite pastimes were swimming in the hot springs near Aix-la-Chapelle and hunting in his great homeland forests. He liked to dress in the old Frankish style, and in his eating habits he also reverted to his nomadic hunting ancestors: disliking ceremonious banquets, he preferred heavy, masculine meals consisting mostly of broiled venison served on a spit. He was educated, having studied Latin grammar, rhetoric, dialectic and astronomy; he could speak Latin and understand some Greek, and he liked to have his clerics read aloud to him from St. Augustine's *City of God,* which was his source of divine revelation. But despite an energetic curiosity and a deep admiration for learning in others, he never could learn to write, having come to this faculty too old. His greatest aspiration was to reconstruct the Roman Empire as the supreme Christian edifice on earth; in pursuing this dream, he assiduously emulated the civilization of Byzantium, attempting to rival the Eastern emperors even in the details of daily existence (he was very proud, for instance, of the splendid furniture of his chapel at Aix-la-Chapelle, which was a direct imitation of the golden eating couches in the imperial palace at Constantinople).

As his empire grew through conquest, Charlemagne determined to match the high prosperity of his political gains with a corresponding enrichment of culture, and he enhanced his court with all the cultivated foreigners he could entice there. The intellectual renaissance he fostered was permeated with religious considerations, as the emperor was motivated by a deeply Christian piety. His task, he had written to Pope Leo III on his coronation as emperor, was to defend the Christian Church by force of arms against pagan and infidel, and to strengthen it within through knowledge.

In politics, Charlemagne was aggressively enterprising. As king of all the Franks, he expanded his rule to include all the Germanic lands except Scandinavia and Britain; he took possession of the south slope of the Pyrenees down to the river Ebro, to create the Spanish March; and he conquered Lombard Italy, to become king of the Lombards. In 800 — with the active collaboration of his tame pontiff, Pope Leo III (earlier driven from Rome by a conspiracy and riot, Leo had sought refuge at the Frankish court and was restored to the Vatican by Charlemagne's troops) — Charlemagne was crowned emperor of the revived Roman Empire in the West. Though the new Rome was largely a Franco-German realm, Charlemagne saw it as the practical realization of his dream of reviving in the West the empire of Constantine and Theodosius. On the other side, it was seen in Byzantium as the deliberate impudence of a powerful upstart; and the clear rebuff marked the first serious break between the two vital centers of Christianity.

The two Irish knowledge-peddlers were an example of the emperor's avid search for the flower of scholarship. At his chief court, Aix-la-Chapelle, he founded an institution known as the Palace School, which for two generations attracted the finest minds of the time, to teach and to write. The level of scholarship at this school was a direct reflection of the simple, naive enthusiasm of its patron and of the callowness of his era. No great originality of thought issued from there: its scientists were imitators, copying and synthesizing what they found among the ancients; its poets and philosophers were unsophisticated. But the general impression is of a sprightly humanity, an innocent Christian goodness. They all — teachers and pupils alike — took a fresh enjoyment in their intellectual exercise and delighted in the imparting and absorbing of knowledge.

As an example: in the year 810 there were rumored to be two eclipses of the sun. A reclusive Irish monk named Dungal wrote to the emperor that he could explain the reports, and Charlemagne invited him to Aix-la-Chapelle. Calling on his knowledge of the writings of classical astronomers, Dungal demonstrated accurately that the double phenomenon could have happened, but he doubted that it actually occurred in that year. He went on to expound the causes of eclipses, explaining the convergence of the orbits of earth and moon in the path of the sun. His knowledge was in all details correct, but it exhibited no original research — and this was the mark of early Carolingian scholarship.

One of the pleasantest exponents of this ingenuously eager period was the Irish geographer and astronomer Dicuil. The little that is known of him has been deduced from his writings. He may have come from islands north of Britain and Ireland, as his section on them in his chief work, *Liber de Mensura Orbis Terrae (Book of the Measurements of the Earth),* has the wealth of descriptive detail that denotes familiarity. He was born not later than 770 and settled as an émigré in the kingdom of the Franks early in the ninth century, when he was between thirty and forty years old. Charlemagne was still emperor when Dicuil taught at the Palace School, but died in 814, the year that the Irish scholar began writing his first known work. This was an astronomical treatise, found in 1879 by a German scholar, Ernst Ludwig Dümmler, in Valenciennes, France. It is a beautiful manuscript, inscribed in a fine hand and elegantly illuminated. The contents of its four books, written in Latin in a mixture of prose and verse, are mainly astronomical observations derived from Pythagoras, the sixth-century-B.C. Greek philosopher, mathematician and astronomer; Donatus, the fourth-century-A.D. Roman grammarian, teacher of St. Jerome; and other classical and contemporary sources not quoted by name.

Dicuil informs the reader of the rules for finding what month it is (counting from April) and what day of the month; he explains how to figure from the phases of the moon the dates of Lent and Easter; he discusses the existence of the nineteen-year lunar cycle and other cycles of sun, planets and stars. In a somewhat fanciful manner, he computes the distance between heaven and earth and between the seven planets. Though his particulars of solar, lunar and planetary matters include all that was then known, he purposely leaves out the effect of the moon on the tides, explaining that since he lives far from the ocean, this is a phenomenon better dealt with by coastal dwellers. He is not always content with quotation and calculation. Occasionally there is the glint of a questioning spirit: the then-current theories of the apparent motion of the sun and the stars seem to him inadequate, and he notes that if a better explanation of these phenomena were to be found, he would espouse it.

Dicuil's best-known work is his geographical treatise, named above, written in 825. The first geographical work produced in the Frankish lands, it is a brisk and entertaining dissertation comprising practically all the known facts and fancies of the inhabited earth. Along with the locations and dimensions of the lands from India to Iceland, including northern Africa and the islands north of Great Britain, there are lively descriptions of the creatures to be found therein. His sources are many and mostly classical: they include the famous map of the Roman Empire ordered by Julius Caesar and completed in the reign of Augustus by his son-in-law Marcus Vipsanius Agrippa; the geographical works of Pliny the Elder; quotations from Artemidorus of Ephesus, Clitarchus, Herodotus, Pytheas and many others. Though the facts are admittedly secondhand, sometimes third- or fourth-hand, its breezy style and its abundance of bizarre and provocative detail render it a work of diverting charm.

Consider the elk of Germany, "whose upper lip hangs down so much that it can feed only by walking backward." Or the hyena of Africa, "whose neck and spine form a rigid continuous unit: he can turn only by moving all his body round. . . . It follows the abodes of shepherds and by listening continually it learns their names so as to be able to express an imitation of the human voice, so that it can savage by night men who have been lured out of doors by its cunning." Or lions, which "have intercourse back to back." Or the cerulean worms of the river Ganges, which have "two arms not less than six cubits long, of such great strength that when elephants come to drink they grip them with a snapping hand and drag them off into the depths." Some humans, he informs us, are as strange as the dumb animals, such as the inhabitants of islands "on which men are born with horses' feet [and so] are called Hippopodes. In others they have very large ears, which cover completely their naked bodies."[5]

His information is not all fantastic. When it comes to Egypt his account is fully practical, comprising the dates, measurements and functions of the inundation of the Nile and including the consequent states of mind of the people: fourteen cubits brings joy, fifteen security and sixteen delight. We have seen, in the discussion of St. Brendan's voyage, that he was among the first to publish an account of the settlement by Irish clerics of little-known Iceland. The Faeroe Islands, also settled by Irish eremites, yielded their secrets to Dicuil through "a man worthy of trust," who had landed on those remote shores after a journey of "two days and a summer night in a little vessel of two banks of oars." Dicuil's informant told him that the Irish holy men had been driven from those islands by Northmen a hundred years before, and "just as they were always deserted from the beginning of the world, so now . . . they are emptied of anchorites and filled with countless sheep, and very many diverse kinds of sea-birds."

Though his information on these northern islands was up-to-date, he was oddly behindhand about Ireland; but perhaps he was pleased by the exaggerated compliment paid his homeland by the third-century Latin grammarian Gaius Julius Solinus, which he quotes: "Hibernia . . . is so rich in pastures as to endanger the cattle unless they are now and then removed from their feeding grounds." And finally, his single withering sentence on Scandinavia reflects the Irishman's natural repugnance toward the land of the Vikings: "Of the Germanic islands, Scandinavia is the greatest, but there is nothing great in it beyond itself."

While Dicuil was not an original thinker, he was a lively, well-informed scholar whose work was deservedly popular, and his acclaim enhanced the Irish reputation for erudition. By the middle of the ninth century, Irish scholars were in fashionable demand all over Europe. One of the principal centers of learning, from which wits and savants radiated to kingly courts, was the city of Liège, an important bishop's seat, later capital of an independent church-state. Here in the mid-ninth century resided the scholar Sedulius Scottus (the Irishman), leader of a group of Irish prodigies whose wit and learning were greatly in demand. Sedulius was a poet and philosopher well versed in the classics: as well as being a Latin scholar, he was one of the first to reintroduce on the Continent the lost knowledge of Greek. He was also au courant with the kind of intellectual flattery that insured that his standard of living was that of a prince: he was a master of polished verse in the intricate meters of Virgil and Horace, composed in honor of prelates and kings. His *De rectoribus christianis,* a treatise on the ideal Christian ruler, was considered the mirror of the enlightened sovereign of the early Middle Ages.

The most rewarding sphere of intellectual activity for Sedulius and his coterie was the court of Charles II, grandson of Charlemagne and king of the West Franks, who was crowned Roman emperor in 875, two years before his death. Charles, nicknamed the Bald, was forced to devote much of his reign to bloody squabbling with his relatives in an unceasing effort to maintain the scope of his inheritance. But like his grandfather and his father, Louis the Pious, he recognized the prestige of culture, and he succeeded in attracting to his court the cream of the intellectual elite.

The brightest luminary of Charles's court, and a philosopher centuries ahead of his time, was Johannes Scottus, later called Eriugena ("born in Ireland"). His family background and place of birth are unknown. He was probably born around 810, and he received a fine education, including Greek, in Ireland. In 847, driven out by the rampages of the Vikings, he crossed over to France. His reputation as a Greek scholar preceded him. Though the monastic schools of Ireland were not very strong on Greek, it was taught there, whereas on the Continent the knowledge was forgotten. And though the Irish were indifferent scholars of the language, they were responsible for its European revival in the Middle Ages. Eriugena had more than a smattering of Greek: he was familiar with the classic philosophic literature. At the invitation of Charles the Bald he joined the gathering of intellectuals at the Palace School at Laon, northeast of Paris (an offshoot of Charlemagne's Palace School at Aix-la-Chapelle). "Little of stature but of merry wit,"[6] brilliant and temperamental, withal modest and pious, the Irish scholar quickly became a favorite of Charles, and was soon the school's most interesting and exciting teacher.

An example of the wit that endeared him to the emperor is his possibly apocryphal remark at the banqueting table. "What separates a Scot from a sot?" asked the emperor.

"This board," promptly retorted the philosopher.

The general attitude toward Eriugena was at first one of amazement. One of his duties as a Greek scholar was to translate into Latin the Greek manuscripts attributed to Dionysius the Areopagite (said to be St. Paul's first convert), which had been brought from the East by refugees. Because Greek was a lost language in the West, the manuscripts had lain unread for a century in the abbey of St. Denys in Paris, until Charles the Bald commissioned Eriugena to translate them. He completed the task, and his translation is still extant, as is a report of the subsequent remark of Anastasius, librarian of the Vatican Library: "It is wonderful that this uncivilized man, dwelling on the confines of the world, should have been able to understand such things and to translate them into another tongue."

Though the works supposedly written by Dionysius the Areopagite were subsequently found to have been composed by an anonymous author, probably a Syrian monk, early in the sixth century, in Eriugena's time their provenance was not questioned. Their ingredients are Christian, Greek, Oriental and Jewish, and these diverse influences merge into a beautifully organic Neoplatonic system. This creation exerted a deep influence on Eriugena. He was already inclined toward Hellenism from his studies of Greek philosophy, and the Dionysius manuscripts had a profound attraction for him. Much of the thought contained in them was later incorporated by Eriugena into his own system.

His first original writing, completed before the Dionysius translation so momentous to him, was a treatise on the Eucharist. It is no longer extant, but from the records of contemporaries it is evident that he proposed that the Eucharist was symbolic, a stand that was apparently not immediately recognized as heretical. For later, in 850, he was asked by Hincmar, archbishop of Rheims, to refute the extreme doctrine of selective predestination put forth by the German monk Gottschalk. Here the Irish freethinker ran into trouble. In defending freedom of will in this work, *De Divina Praedestinatione,* he reflected the heresy of Pelagius.* But Eriugena went far beyond the fifth-century preacher of moral responsibility, asserting boldly that philosophy and religion are basically the same, both being the embodiment of reason, and foreshadowing in his argument the Neoplatonic view of God and creation that was to be the dominant thesis of his chief work.

---

*Pelagius and his heresy are discussed on pages 75–77.

Several high churchmen disputed his orthodoxy, and the dissertation on free will was condemned by two councils, Valence in 855 and Langres in 859. That of Valence dismissed this *pultes Scotorum* ("Irishmen's porridge") as "an invention of the devil."

Eriugena's masterwork, the sum of his philosophical studies and the realization of his all-absorbing spiritual bent, is *De divisione naturae (On the Division of Nature)*. This profound and complex philosophical essay, written between 862 and 866 and published probably in 867, is in the form of a Socratic dialogue — the disciple questioning, the master explaining. The philosophy it expounds is that known as idealism, and Eriugena is in the tradition of thinkers from Heraclitus and Plato through the rational idealists up to Henri Bergson. Its four books develop the nature of God as an unknowable, immaterial essence from which all creation ensues. God takes form only in appearances, which occur within our minds, as all nature is a realization of this first inscrutable principle. It is the metaphysics of monism: there is only one ultimate reality, of which all phenomena of mind and matter are manifestations.

In a simplification of Eriugena's thesis, God has no being, because He is not perceivable. While superior to everything, He permeates everything. Only in His creations does He achieve reality: pervading the whole of existence but adhering to no part of it. Therefore He is incomprehensible to the thing created, and becomes comprehensible only through His creatures. Man, created in God's image, knows through his own intellect (which is the godhead in him) that God exists; but all man knows is the appearance of God — as the air, dominated by light, seems to *be* light. The essence of God is reason, and the qualities of His manifestations are virtue, truth and beauty. His perfect wisdom is seen in the perfect order of the universe, which is His appearance made reality.

The philosophic system built on this premise is a fourfold division of reality, or *nature*: (1) that which creates and is not created; (2) that which is created and creates; (3) that which is created and does not create; (4) that which neither creates nor is created. The first is God, the primal cause and Creator of all. He was not created: in a logical paradox, as He is superior to mere existence, He cannot therefore exist; He is nothing and He is everything. The second is the Logos, the primordial causes or types of things, in which God is made visible; these are also eternal. The primordial causes are goodness, life, wisdom, truth, intelligence, reason, justice, health, peace and so on. From all these flow all of life and the material things on earth. The third is the phenomenal world, which has infinite variety, but of which every part relates back to the primordial causes, and so to God — as in the center of a circle all radii are one. The fourth is again God, as the End to which all things must return. This is best seen in man, who is made in the image of God.

And here the philosopher runs into difficulties. Man is God's ultimate creation, the direct realization of the first unknowable essence; therefore the ideal man is the embodiment of God. This doctrine, of the essential beauty and goodness of the human spirit as the mirror of God, while profoundly attractive to the rational thinker, encounters problems when a philosopher as deeply pious as Eriugena attempts to fit into it the tenets of the Catholic Church. One of the Church's basic premises is the doctrine of original sin, which presupposes the existence of evil; and Eriugena has to resort to some contortions in logic to avoid the charge of heresy. He reasons thus:

All creation comes from God, who is the first principle of goodness, truth and reason. Nothing can exist in heaven or on earth that does not flow from this first principle; therefore there can be no evil. Since man himself is a mirror of God, his spiritual essence being simple, spiritual, celestial and sexless, he also can contain no evil in his original state. As evil is not of natural origin, it must come from man's perverse will, or more properly, his libidinous appetite, moving against divine reason. But since man issues directly from God and is created in His image, of one indivisible nature, God cannot punish what He made. There can be no hell, no eternal agony of worms and fire.

But God — says the philosopher, hedging — can punish what He did *not* make. As man's libidinous will, which is not substantial and not created by God, leads to evil, God can afflict him with fantasies that, while not substantial, are not altogether without existence. Hell, therefore, is the torment of the living: it consists of the devouring flame of man's conscience, the soured putrefaction in his mind of his vices and bad habits, and the anguish of his insatiable desires, which nothing can satisfy. The heaven of the good is just as incorporeal as are the subjective pains of hell. The good will pass into a state of deification, where they will find joy, peace and equality with angels. Their bodies will not be physically changed from an earthly form to a heavenly one, but they will pass over into pure intellect, and from this state return to God, their primal source — the original Oneness become again at last One.

Eriugena's profound and sophisticated logic was so far beyond the comprehension of most of his contemporaries that his difficult magnum opus was largely ignored in his own time: and that is probably one of the reasons why so little is known of his life. His end is as obscure as are his beginnings.

Only legends remain. It is said that he was invited to Oxford by Alfred the Great of England, a patron of learning who welcomed foreign scholars, and that later he taught in a school he founded at Malmesbury Abbey on the Avon in Wiltshire — though it is not even certain that he was a monk or priest. There, about the year 880, it is said, his students killed him with their styles. His body lay unburied until, on advice from heaven, the monks buried him in the abbey church, beside the altar. His tomb, stating that he had attained sainthood through martyrdom, was inscribed *sanctus sophista Joannes* [sic] ("John, sainted teacher of philosophy"), an appellation often applied to him in his lifetime.

While Eriugena's philosophic structure is limited by his medieval perspective and qualified by his devout faith, his overall conception is poignant. He has more than a touch of the poet in the expressive revelation of his mysticism. Seeking to bridge the gap between abstract reason — the form of God and the highest quality of man — and the busy, multifaceted world of materiality, he sees reality as continuous motion within a conformation of eternal quietness: a deeply poetic vision. The quality of his mind was ardent, penetrating and imaginative. He was an original thinker and a brilliant synthesist at the same time, the most outstanding intellect of his century and one of the most remarkable ever to come out of Ireland.

Though Eriugena's erudition and his genius as a teacher were recognized in his time, his contribution to philosophy was not understood until three centuries after his death, when the rigid Catholic thinkers of the Church of the Inquisition saw his appeal to reason as a clear invitation to heresy. In 1225 *De divisione naturae* was condemned by a council at Sens and by Pope Honorius III, and in 1585 Pope Gregory XIII placed it on the Index. To the Church that in the sixteenth century decreed the burning of the collected works of such a profoundly humanistic thinker as Erasmus, the intellectual freedom of Neoplatonism was anathema.

Yet the deification of reason, the classical ideal, lived brightly, and still lives, beyond the confines of Catholic theology. Ideas akin to those of Eriugena are the basis of the work of Spinoza, Berkeley, Hegel and Kant; and the medieval sage, who came into his own so long after his death, still holds a lustrous place in the annals of philosophy.

CHAPTER XVI
ART IN STONE

WHILE IRISH SCHOLARS WERE ASTONISHING AND DELIGHTING THE WORLD abroad, an even more brilliant renaissance was occurring at home in the growth of the visual arts. Its roots were in native Celtic design and its development was determined by contact with Germanic and Scandinavian imagery and the high sophistication of the art of the East. Irish Christian art and architecture, starting piously plain with unadorned little wooden churches, simply carved grave slabs and the dedicated, painstaking work of the scribes, evolved in several unique directions: to the graceful, small-scale Irish Romanesque churches of the twelfth century, with their spend-thrift abundance of stone decoration; to the splendidly etched and filigreed metalwork shrines for books and relics from the eighth century on; to the entrancing imagery of the early medieval high crosses, with their combi-nation of storytelling charm and prayer expressed in stone; and to the incomparable virtuosity of the illuminated codices of the seventh, eighth and ninth centuries, masterpieces of sensuous delicacy.

The earliest monasteries followed the style of the farm settlements: a circular wall of earth or stone with a ditch outside it surrounded a group of wooden buildings. The focus of the community was the church, a small rectangular building, sometimes of oak, sometimes of wattle and daub, roofed with thatch or shingles. Its usual size, according to a commentary on the old Irish Brehon Laws, was ten by fifteen feet. This tiny building

Interior of Gallarus Oratory — dry-stone chapel in the primitive style on the Dingle Peninsula, County Kerry

was surrounded by the even smaller huts of the monks; a guesthouse, refectory and sometimes a school completed the village.

As the monastery grew larger, the monks did not build bigger buildings but added more small ones. One enclosure might have three or four little churches in it, while the students and novices built their huts outside the wall. None of these wooden structures have survived. But in some parts of Ireland, where the stormy climate and the rocky terrain are not kind to the growth of timber trees, the monks built perforce of stone. Such are the Dingle Peninsula of County Kerry and the islands off the south and west coasts, the kinds of wild remote places the early anchorites sought for the apotheosis of their souls. Though it is impossible to assign dates to these early buildings, it is thought that they reproduced in stone the more usual wooden structures. The cells were usually built on a rectangular ground plan of overlapping stones massive at the base and smaller as they narrowed toward the top in a beehive shape, like those on Skellig Michael. Space was left for a low doorway not as high as a man; the only other opening was at the top, where a flat stone finished off the dome. The churches were somewhat larger, with a higher doorway and a little square window at the back. But the ground plan and the stone corbelling were the same.

This principle of building in stone — primitive, functional and almost eternally durable — was native to Ireland, going back, as we have seen at Newgrange, at least to the third millennium. The early Christian churches, though their dates can only be guessed at, clearly echo their ancient heritage. A perfect little church in a later refinement of this style is Gallarus Oratory, possibly not built until the eleventh or twelfth century, on the Dingle Peninsula, County Kerry. It stands by itself in a slightly sunken green field with a dry-stone wall around it: a low stone-corbelled building on a rectangular base, its sides curving upward to meet at the top like the keel of an overturned boat. For added reinforcement its end walls also slant inward toward the roof. It is of fitted stones, small stones inserted to fill in the uneven gaps between the larger ones, and at its apex is a straight line of flat stones. The impression is of the utmost skill and neatness; every stone is in place as if the chapel had been built last week.

The beehive shape, a throwback to Ireland's earliest architecture, is found only in the south and west of Ireland, where the people were the most conservatively tenacious of the old ways (this area has always been the stronghold of the Irish language). In the rest of the country, when stone came to be used in place of wood, religious building followed the conventional form of rectangles with perpendicular walls and pitched roofs. These churches, like their predecessors, were small, plain and unpretentious, direct imitations in stone of the earlier (and still prevalent) wooden churches. In some cases the architect even went so far as to render the steep-pitched shingled roof in stone. This was an Irish specialty and its examples are rare, probably for a good reason: the sharp slope of massive stones had a tendency to sag in the middle. If there were more of them than the surviving examples, their roofs have probably fallen in. To reinforce them the builder sometimes added an arch under the roof and a floor below that, making a small attic room with curved walls.

An attractive example of this style of architecture is St. Kevin's Kitchen in Glendalough (shown on page 121). Probably built in the twelfth century, the church is a little stone oblong with a high-sloping roof; over the doorway is a small tower like a fat chimney, which gave the structure its name. The only decoration, inside or out, is above the altar: a twelfth-century granite high cross with a primitive carving, perhaps of St. Kevin, at its foot — a squat figure with a big head, like a gingerbread man. Set in the narrow lush valley, shadowed by forested hills and surrounded by the old gray buildings of the monastic village, St. Kevin's Kitchen is the quintessence of early Christianity. In the perfection of its minuscule proportions, it is truly spiritual, an idealization in stone. It breathes the same spirit of exalted simplicity that informed the Irish missionaries abroad and endeared them to their converts, from uneducated peasants to worldly princes.

On Saint Macdara's Island, County Galway, is another of these remarkable buildings that imitate wood in stonework. This one even reaches verisimilitude to the extent that the wooden roof supports of the inspiration — the antae projecting from the gable — have been copied in stone, and the stone "shingles" of the roof, where they are larger than the corresponding wood shingles would have been, have horizontal etched lines to resemble overhanging wooden shingles.

St. Feichin's Church at Fore, County Westmeath, though it has lost its roof, has the small-scale proportions of the early churches. It is on a hillside overlooking the twelfth-century Benedictine priory that sits sheltered by tall oaks in a field below. This little building, like the others, is severely plain; its most extraordinary feature is its lintel, a single oblong-cut stone weighing two and a half tons, over the low door. Etched in the center of this massive slab is a cross enclosed in a circle, the only concession its designers made to decoration.

One of the most appealing of the little churches, partly because of the remote tranquility of its setting, is the one at Toureen Peakaun, County

Tipperary, site of a monastery founded in the seventh century and named
for its second abbot, a famed anchorite named St. Beccan. It is far out of
the way, not even on a road; a footpath leads through a farmyard of
manure and barking dogs, then follows a slow curving stream to a hillslope
bright with field flowers. The crooked stones of an old cemetery lean
through the high grass, and between the slabs is a miniature church adorned
only by two round-arched Romanesque windows and crosses built into its
walls. Roofless, simple, austere, it lies dreaming on the sunny hillside, and
the hustling present slides away, replaced by the quiet echo of ancient
piety.

Though the taste of monastic Ireland tended toward chaste simplicity,
not all of its early churches were uncompromisingly plain. Way back in
the fifth century, St. Brigid, as noted earlier, built at Kildare a wooden
house of God that was generous in its size and lavish in its decoration. This
church was probably sui generis — no others, nor descriptions of others,
survive; and it may well have been a monument celebrating the unstinting,
outgoing fervor of that delightful saint's prodigal nature.

With that one known divergence, most early ecclesiastical architecture
remained conservatively stark. Considering the popularity of plainness, a
parallel development of exuberantly decorated churches is at first sight
surprising. At the same time such irreducible little chapels as that at Toureen Peakaun were going up, other churches, hardly larger, displayed an
esthetic reversal, the effect of a new form of artistry. In the eleventh and
twelfth centuries, architects and stonecutters were exploiting their talents
in the direction of ornamental stonework in a style initially borrowed from
the Continent — a style that later developed, under the imaginative ingenuity of native artisans, into a peculiarly insular form known as Irish
Romanesque. Behind the new style in stonework were the Irish ecclesiastical reforms of those centuries, which had brought new contacts with
Europe. Travelling clergymen, admiring the Romanesque basilicas of continental Europe, with their gracious proportions and their profusion of
decorative carving, took a fresh look at their own old-fashioned, unimag-
inative building. In Europe the development of Romanesque architecture
(named for its low round arches, borrowed from classical Roman buildings)
was as much a matter of ground plan as of ornamentation. The Continental
churches of the early eleventh century followed the Roman basilica form:
aisles on either side of the nave, a rounded apse behind the altar and
occasionally transepts, giving the building the form of a cross.

Ireland held on to the basic rectangles for another century, although there was at least one spectacular exception. The old-style ground plan was evidently pleasing to the conservative Irish mentality: it imitated the ancestral wooden structures, and the smallness enhanced the intimacy that traditionally existed between the priest and his congregation — an intrinsic attribute of Irish worship. But though these stone boxes can hardly be dignified by the appellation architecture, their simple forms, like clean canvasses, were invitations to imaginative artists in stone to fill them with extravagantly fanciful ornamentation.

Since the churches had no aisles to provide freestanding columns with capitals for decoration, the stonemasons were limited, usually, to doorways and chancel arches. These they covered with a prodigality of fantastic and beautiful carvings often difficult to relate to Christian motivation: grotesque animals, human and animal masks, geometric figures, intertwined foliage — only rarely an identifiable saint or scriptural scene. Some of the abstract designs recall Irish-Celtic and pre-Celtic motifs; the animal themes are reflections of Scandinavian metalwork; the geometric chevrons were borrowed from Norman England; the interlaced foliage has a haunting resemblance to the stonework on fourth-, fifth- and sixth-century Egyptian Coptic churches. The spirit that infuses these intricate carvings is similar to the craft of the monastic scribes, out of whose meticulous artistry grew the astounding labyrinthine carpet pages of the *Book of Durrow* and other illuminated codices. Hardly an inch is left vacant: it is as if the small areas of stone available to the artist were a challenge, to see how much he could squeeze in without creating a chaos. Actually, these decorated doorways and arches are not confusing at all; they are, in all their imaginative complexity, miracles of harmonious symmetry.

The first known exception to the rule of the box-shaped churches is an exquisite little church in Tipperary: Cormac's Chapel, one of the earliest results of the new look at architecture. This church was at the same time the inspiration and the epitome of Irish Romanesque. It is probably the first church in Ireland that can be called a work of architecture; it was also, for nearly a century, probably the only one that can be characterized as such. Though many of its features were immediately imitated, conservative Irish architects clung persistently to the modest foursquare structures they had grown up with.

Built between 1127 and 1134, a product of the friendship between St. Malachy and King Cormac Mac Carthy of Desmond, Cormac's Chapel is among the buildings on the spectacular bastion of St. Patrick's Rock at Cashel (shown on page 225). The diminutive church is tucked against

Cormac's Chapel on St. Patrick's Rock at Cashel, County Tipperary — the epitome of Irish Romanesque architecture

the south transept of the thirteenth-century cathedral, which partly over-shadows it. Unlike the larger building, which is of the local limestone, the chapel is of sandstone brought from fifteen miles away, a material at once enduring and amenable to carving. Both Malachy and King Cormac had English contacts through their older mentor Malthus, who, as earlier noted, had been a monk in England. Consequently, Cormac's Chapel shows a strong kinship with Anglo-Norman architecture, particularly in the deco-rative stone carving. There are some traits, less evident, of German Romanesque; the intertwining carven animals are borrowed from Scandinavian art; and at least one feature is uniquely Irish: the high-slanting stone roof, which, as mentioned above, was probably a direct imitation of the early wooden churches. Though the provenances of Cormac's Chapel are fragmented, its totality is supremely original. Conceived and executed with creative ingenuity, the chapel ends up, for all its derivations, being abso-lutely itself.

The building is in the form of a cross, the transepts formed by two square towers of unequal size at the junction of nave and chancel. Its steep, sharp-angled stone roof makes it tall in proportion to its length (which is only 46 feet 9 inches in the interior), an effect that enhances the chapel's miniature grace. The roof, 3 feet thick, is supported by an arched stone attic where the monks from the surrounding abbeys came to copy their manuscripts. This chamber in turn rests upon the barrel vaulting of the chancel ceiling, a new concept in Irish architecture. The north door, which was the main entrance, is dead-end now because it abuts on the cathedral; over it is a relief of a dwarfed centaur shooting with a bow and arrow a large, patently evil lion — a vigorous and primitive carving with a strong pagan flavor. The south wall is decorated outside with blind arcades above and beside the doorway, whose rounded arch has three lavishly carved orders. The interior is gloomy now because of the adjoining cathedral, but when the chapel stood alone it was full of light: the ingenious designers canted the narrow windows so that sunlight came through every hour of the day from dawn until sunset. There are no side aisles, but in the nave and chancel are arches, arcades and columns, which provided an inviting field for the inventive stonecutters. Everywhere one looks there are geo-metric figures, interlaced foliage, little human heads peering around the capitals or coming out of the arches. The whole stone tapestry was origi-nally painted in many colors, and with the sun slanting through the slim windows the effect must have been astonishing.

At the west end of the nave is a stone tomb on which a serpentine quadruped coils all over the outside, its body shackled by intertwining thin snakes in an eerie design that appears to have no beginning and no end — perhaps a representation of infinity. This extraordinary carving owes its inspiration to the Scandinavian metalwork of the eleventh century known as the Urnes style, and it is one of the fortuities of the Norse penetration.

Despite the diversity of its decoration and the oddity of its proportions, the overall impression of Cormac's Chapel is of a harmonious entity. To us today it is the prototype of Irish Romanesque, a style that, though it echoes Continental church architecture, has a small-scale perfection unique in Ireland. But in the twelfth century the style was too revolutionary to be swallowed all at once. There is no other church of the period (at least none still standing) with the originality of this chapel on the hilltop. It was a new and exciting departure, however, and Irish architects at once began to imitate it, accepting its novelties piecemeal. Without abandoning the elementary lineaments of their churches, they incorporated the decorative features of Romanesque. Within the limits of their conservatism, they achieved marvels of carven imagery.

Around the doorway of Clonfert Cathedral, County Galway, erected in the twelfth century on the site of St. Brendan's favorite monastery, is one of the most breathtaking of these stone fantasies. Flanking the narrow portal is a row of columns richly and variously incised with chevrons, circles, rosettes, lozenges, interlaced foliage and stylized figures. On their capitals are rows of animal heads and scroll foliage. The seven orders of the arch surmounting the door are carved with foliage-covered bosses and foxlike animals with rounded molding in their jaws. Above the arch is a sharp-pointed gable; in the lower part of its triangle is a blind arcade with carved human heads under its arches, and in the narrowing angle above, decorated triangles alternate with more heads. There is not an unadorned space, from the carven knob atop the gable to the twisting pattern that winds over the squared columns at the outer edge of the portal — yet the skillful balance of the whole delights the eye.

The luxuriant carving of the doorway contrasts with the simplicity of the rest of the building. It is a small single-chamber church of the conventional shape, with an attractive square bell tower that was added in the fifteenth century. The only concession to elegance inside are the tall graceful triple Roman arches surrounding the east windows in the chancel, each triplet surmounted by a larger round arch. A further decoration, added at the same time as the bell tower, is a Gothic chancel arch adorned with smiling angels and, with the appearance of a profane afterthought, a pretty little mermaid, off center, carrying a mirror.

This entrancing church is not a ruin like, sadly, so many of Ireland's

Stone carving on a tomb in Cormac's Chapel, showing the Scandinavian influence on decorative art

Interior of Clonfert Cathedral with sculptured reliefs of angels and a mermaid

Opposite: Doorway of Clonfert Cathedral, County Galway, decorated in the Irish Romanesque style

historic monuments, victims of the vicissitudes of the island's turbulent history. Though partly destroyed in the sixteenth century, it was restored and has since been lovingly cared for; and congregations gather here every Sunday as they have, presumably, since it was built, to uplift their souls in contemplation of its barbarically opulent doorway in the pure setting of the simplest stone harmony.

A different aspect of Romanesque design is revealed at Ardmore Cathedral, County Waterford, built toward the end of the twelfth century on the site of St. Declan's monastery. Though dignified by the name "Cathedral" because it was the center of an episcopal see, the church has the familiar small plain dimensions. Unassuming as it appears, however, it has some surprising characteristics. One new departure for the period is the arch over the west portal: with all its Romanesque breadth and shallow curve, it comes to an unmistakable Gothic point at its apex — one of the very early Irish uses of this style, already prevalent on the Continent.

Its outstanding feature is the panel on the outside of the west wall. A pleasing pattern of Romanesque arcades contains sculptures in high relief of scenes from the Scriptures, many of which are obliterated. Those still decipherable have a captivating medieval literalness: Adam and Eve cling to the Tree of Knowledge with one hand while attempting to hide their nakedness with the other; Solomon on his throne, holding a large sword, threatens the baby held toward him by one mother, while in back of her the other stretches out her arms in appeal, as a bearded musician sits high behind them playing on his little harp; the devil slyly interferes with the scales weighing the souls on Judgment Day; three tall robed magi holding scepters walk across the stone coping toward a modest, childlike Virgin sitting beside an ass.

This appealing panel, the only Romanesque one of its kind known in Ireland, was inspired by a conception different from the elaborate fancies of Cormac's Chapel and its imitators. Most Irish Romanesque carvings were flights of imagination designed chiefly for decoration. The storytelling Ardmore panel seems to have been instructive in intent, and its nearest relations are the high crosses, carved in an earlier century, which we will look at later. By the twelfth century, when more of the Romanesque churches were built, the storytelling element was out of style and rococo embellishment was in.

In 1142 the first Continental monastic order was introduced into Ireland, signalling, as we have seen, the start of a profound change in Irish monasticism, and forecasting the end of the old ways. St. Malachy invited the

Cistercians to build a foundation at Mellifont (from *Fons Mellis,* "fountain of honey"), County Louth. As a result of the twelfth-century reform of the Irish Church, which brought it finally under the wing of Roman Catholicism, Irish culture, reflecting the new contacts, became tinged with the fashions of the Continent. The churches built by the new orders were direct reflections of styles current in the countries of their origins, and they were radically different from the time-honored quadrangular buildings. Their dimensions were much bigger, and they were cruciform, with a vaulted chancel, transepts and side aisles separated from the nave by arcades. Not only was the architecture different; the layout of the monasteries followed a neatly coherent plan sharply divergent from the amorphous, random collections of cells and tiny churches, grown up any way through the years, that had comprised the early Irish monastic villages. Perhaps something was lost — a spirit of spontaneous piety — in the gaining of order and harmony. But perhaps also the tenor of the times demanded a stricter obedience to an imposed structure than had been needed in the surer, more self-reliant days when Ireland was free.

Of the parent abbey, Mellifont, only foundations and a few fragments remain. It was built on the same plan as its elder sister in Burgundy; in fact, St. Bernard of Clairvaux, St. Malachy's mentor and friend, sent a master mason to help in the building. The church, two hundred feet long, is a basilica on the Continental model, with pillared aisles and a transept. It lies on the north side of the cloister — a peaceful, sheltered area, the center of the monks' precisely ordered existence. Around it are the remains of the chapterhouse, refectory, kitchen, dormitories and other buildings. All the buildings face inward to the cloister, so that the whole complex is effectively closed away from the outside. Contemplation and spiritual removal from the earthly bustle were to be prescribed rather than, in the old way, to upwell spontaneously from a tranquil heart. In the twelfth century, Irish hearts were no longer tranquil.

The skeleton of Mellifont lies in a green basin surrounded by low wooded hills, a place of equable, undramatic serenity. Its foundations delineate its form, and some remains still stand, notably a cloister arcade of slender twin pillars and Romanesque arches, and a striking octagonal lavabo, two stories high, which enclosed a fountain where the monks washed their hands before eating.

Mellifont was the progenitor of some thirty-five Cistercian monasteries in Ireland during the next hundred years. The most beautiful still-remaining ruins are those at Jerpoint, County Kilkenny, started in 1158, completed

Interior of Jerpoint Abbey with sculptured stone relief of the Weepers

Opposite: *Jerpoint Abbey, County Kilkenny — Cistercian abbey in the twelfth-century transitional style*

around 1180 and lovingly rebuilt, with additions, in the fifteenth century. Built around a cloister on the same plan as Mellifont, it is in a transitional style: the aisles of its basilica-form church have shallow-pointed early Gothic arches whose columns are carved, Romanesque fashion, with stylized flowers and abstract interlacing; and some of the portals are Gothic, while the round-arched west windows are Romanesque. The spacious cloister is enclosed by an arcade with some remarkable figure sculpture in its pillar niches; though this arcade is in the Romanesque style, it was not built until the fifteenth century.

Inside the church there are several thirteenth- to sixteenth-century carved tombs with wonderful figures on them, particularly one of the Weepers — two richly dressed figures with long wavy hair and big oval eyes who flank a smugly pious praying angel with a halo of faultless curls. The composition, as well as the hieratic, staring faces, recalls Byzantine icons, a resemblance probably not accidental (as we shall see when studying the illustrated codices).

Though Jerpoint is a mélange of styles, each successive builder or restorer, up to the careful and unobvious reconstruction of recent years, managed to make his contribution without marring the happy proportions of the original conception. The result is that the dark stone buildings, rising against the glowing green of the cloister lawn, have a rare harmonic perfection. Though originally completed in a time of frightening unrest, the abbey has a transcendent spirituality, which attests that the vital ardor was not yet defeated.

Another of Mellifont's daughter houses, founded between 1175 and 1195, is Corcomroe Abbey. It is set in the startling landscape of the Burren, limestone hills and plateaus near the Atlantic coast in County Clare: a strange land of flat layers of pale gray rock bare of vegetation and sheared off evenly like paving flags. From level stone valleys rise exactly rounded hills formed of even rock tiers, their tops flattened as if they had been sat on. The uncanny geometric scenery is extraordinarily light, the effect of sunlight on nearly white stone; it has the aspect of simplistic surrealist painting. Once in a while a narrow valley appears, almost shocking in the intensity of its green and the wealth of its flowers, its fertility the result of underground streams and lime-rich soil. In one of these opulent valleys are the ruins of Corcomroe, originally and aptly named Sancta Maria de Petra Fertilis (Saint Mary of the Fertile Rock). The abbey, of the local limestone, is in a state of ruin, which gives it an eerie similarity to its encircling hills. Like Jerpoint, the sizable church is part Romanesque, part Gothic, and it has the cruciform shape, which was by that time standard. There is some lovely carving in the chapels and on the column capitals, of masks and floral designs; and in a wall niche is a severely simple tomb, a mere slab of undecorated rock with a prone figure upon it — a sculpture so primitively hewn that, although it was made around 1300, it appears of a much earlier provenance.

Though for the most part the Irish were not enterprising architects before the coming of the Continental orders or the advent of the Anglo-Normans — superior church-builders, who arrived at the same time — they displayed an innovative skill in one direction: the building of the round towers, unique to Ireland. These slim tapered structures, which demonstrate a capable knowledge of architectural engineering, make it clear that the reason the Irish built small plain churches was not because they didn't know any better. The towers are of mortared stones expertly cut and fitted; they are 14 to 17 feet in diameter at the base, narrowing toward the top, and they rise to a height of from 70 to 125 feet (the height depended on the length of the church they sheltered and was dictated by a prescribed arithmetical proportion). The tower doorway, which traditionally faces that of the church, is above the ground, at about twice the height of a man, and is reached by a ladder. Inside there are usually four stories, which used to have wooden floors, connected by ladders, each landing lit by a narrow window facing in a different direction. Below the conical stone roof is the top landing, which has four windows facing the cardinal points. The towers had two purposes: they served as bell towers — their old Irish name is *cloigtheach* (bell house) — and as refuges in times of danger. In peaceful times the assigned monk climbed the ladders to the top landing and rang his handbell at each of the four windows to summon the brethren in from the fields.

There were probably over a hundred of these fine slender towers, of which only about a dozen still stand more or less to their original height. The earliest known, at Castledermot, County Kildare, was constructed probably in 919; the latest, probably the one at Ardmore, dates from the late twelfth century; so they spanned the entire period of the Norse depredations and the beginning of the Anglo-Norman invasions. During those grievous times the round towers often became sanctuaries. The books and valuables of the monastery were transferred there and the monks climbed to the high-placed door, pulled up the ladder, and barricaded themselves inside. As asylums the towers were nearly impregnable; but they were

Opposite: *Round tower on St. Patrick's Rock at Cashel, County Tipperary*

efficacious only depending on how much time the intruders could afford to sit under them and lay siege or set fires before help arrived and they were cut off from retreat to their ships.

The oldest tower still intact, that at Castledermot, is of uneven granite blocks, topped with a battlemented parapet added in medieval times, an inconsistent military touch. It is only sixty-six feet high (though it may have originally been taller), and the small church to which it was proportioned no longer stands. Its irregularly cut old gray stones give it a primitive look, though considering how long it has stood, the technique of its building must have been sophisticated. Rising next to an ordinary nineteenth-century pebble-dashed church, the ancient tower looks somehow lost — a survivor from another age, protecting nothing.

The tower on St. Patrick's Rock at Cashel is more in tune with its surroundings. It rises, moss-grown and romantic, on the other side of the cathedral from Cormac's Chapel, and may have been built earlier than the Romanesque church, for its Romanesque doorway has only elementary decoration. But this tower is also out of proportion. Though it narrows gracefully to its stone roof cone at a height of ninety-two feet, it has an oddly squat look, because the simple, low-roofed church it once sheltered has been replaced by the complex, impressive thirteenth-century cathedral.

St. Kevin's monastery at Glendalough has one of the finest of the remaining towers. From a distance, its pale stone soaring out of the dark valley 103 feet to a perfect cone (rebuilt in the last century with the original stones) appears both beacon to the wanderer and sentinel for the low clustered buildings of the monastic city. Close to, it loses none of its thin elegance; but it stands alone (its personal church having presumably fallen), a classic monument rather than an integral part of its community.

The tower that is still in its right place, unravaged by time and juxtaposed to its original church, is that at Ardmore. In contrast to the fine Romanesque decoration of the church, the tower has a Greek simplicity. It rises ninety-five feet in four tiers of perfectly cut mortared stones, each tier separated by a string molding, and it is topped by a flawless pointed stone cap. As a tower should, it dominates the scene: visible for miles atop St. Declan's hill, its restrained purity is stark against the flowered grass of the surrounding churchyard and the shallow, pale-waved ocean beyond.

The predilection of the Norse raiders for carrying away everything of value that they could lift and destroying everything else with a religious connotation led the Irish in self-defense to express themselves in the non-portable and indestructible medium of stone. The replacing of wooden churches with stone began about the time of the Viking invasions, as did the construction of the defensive bell towers. The art of metalworking declined, particularly in the production of religious objects such as shrines for saints' relics and holy books. Goldsmiths and metalworkers turned their talents to the carving of stone, intrinsically worthless and impossible to transport, and an unusual and imaginative art form developed: the great stone high crosses, three times the height of a man, decorated with sculptured reliefs. This form of religious art had its genesis before the first Viking raid, but its finest flowering occurred through the ninth century.

The stone crosses typically associated with Ireland — those with an open ring where the shaft and arms cross (as shown on page 321) — were modelled on processional wooden crosses. When these heavy wooden crosses were carried, there would have been a strain at the crosspiece; this had to be reinforced with stays traversing the four angles, and the designers chose a circle as the most attractive shape for the purpose. The cross was covered with bronze sheets etched with figures and designs and fastened to the wood with studs. In the eighth century Irish artisans began to translate this entire operation into stone. Though the style of the early designs is in some cases associated with the revival of art in the Carolingian Empire, the literal translation from wood into stone was an Irish innovation unknown elsewhere in Europe.

The most striking examples of these identical reproductions are the eighth-century crosses at Ahenny, County Tipperary. The shaft and crosspieces of the two remaining crosses are incised with a delicate and elaborate network of interweaving abstract patterns such as would have covered a metal sheet — and are similar also to the geometric motifs in the *Book of Kells* (the art of the illuminator, as we will see later, was closely allied to that of the metalworker). Ornamental stone bosses punctuate the design; these represent the metal coverings of the nails fastening the metal sheet to the wood. The crosses stand on heavy pyramidal bases covered with figure sculpture of an entirely different style: on one frieze a palm tree shades a man in the act of running after a group of bizarre prancing animals; on another an outré funeral procession includes a headless man carried on a horse, chariots with riders and a cleric carrying a ringed cross (presumably wooden) of the same shape as the one on which he is carved — as if the artist had decided to provide the viewer with a clue. These sculptures, far from the spirit of the *Book of Kells* and the art of the Irish metalworkers, show no Celtic derivation, but have the atmosphere of southern Europe: they exhibit a late Roman and Gallic influence.

The inspiration of the *celi De* movement, beginning in the second half of the eighth century, was, as noted earlier, the source of medieval Ireland's most beautiful and sensitive poetry. The reform movement also found graphic expression in art, especially the art of the stone-carver. Education was one of Maelruain's first directives, both teaching and learning being among the most godly of virtues. The first requisite of education was the teaching of the Scriptures, and what better place to proclaim the holy message than on great stone monuments accessible and comprehensible to all?

So the decoration of high crosses received a new direction, toward storytelling rather than abstract design. In this primary method of instruction, well suited to an unlettered audience, scenes from the Old and New Testaments acquainted the viewer with the stories of the Bible and uplifted his spirit with the illustration of God's never-failing benevolent power as well as His practical help. One can picture the priest standing before the cross and expounding the tales pictured above him in language suited to his unsophisticated congregation. If he was talented his recital might have the captivating inventiveness of the aforementioned *Saltair na Rann* — which is the spirit of the high crosses transposed into poetry. It is thought that the scenes were originally painted in colors, which would have made them even more piquant.

In the early ninth century the chief center of the high crosses was the valley of the river Barrow in County Kildare, where there are still several outstanding crosses, mostly intact. The local stone in that area is granite, a rigid medium for the carver, and the stiffness of the scenes imparts a primitive innocence. Castledermot has two crosses, on which scenes from the Old and New Testaments are contained in square-framed panels along the shaft and on the crosspiece, leaving, in the Celtic manner, no blank spaces: Adam and Eve beneath a simplistic tree whose two branches, hung with apples, adjust themselves sinuously around the edges of the frame; Daniel in the Lion's Den, David and Goliath, the Sacrifice of Isaac, the scenes of the Passion and others. All the figures have stiff bodies, big heads and a certain staring ingenuousness due not to the sculptor's lack of skill but to the intransigence of his material. The broad base of one of the crosses has a design of interlocking spirals reminiscent of the Stone Age designs at Newgrange, a pattern that also bears an astonishing resemblance to the work of Mycenaean goldsmiths of the second millennium B.C. —

Ninth-century granite high cross at Moone, County Kildare, with primitive reliefs representing scriptural scenes

which might be fortuitous, as the spiral, an imitation of nature, is a nearly
universal figure. The fat coils lack the fine execution of the abstract carving
on the Ahenny crosses, but they have their own crude grace.

The most attractive of the Barrow crosses is the one at Moone, which,
though the representations are no less naive than those at Castledermot and
other Barrow localities, has an entirely original and ingratiating charm.
The cross is unusual in its shape, its tall slenderness accentuated by a long,
tapered base. On the shaft are panels containing graceful, active and nearly
recognizable quadrupeds. The Bible tales, scenes of spirited imagery, are
on the four sides of the base. They include Adam and Eve — two small fat
people framed by arches of apples; Daniel in the Lion's Den — a figure in
a square garment, like a paper doll, in a frame of seven openmouthed lions,
four down one side from his ear to the hem of his dress, three down the
other; the Twelve Apostles — twelve identical square men with pear-
shaped heads and circle eyes, looking like three rows of cookies; the Miracle
of the Loaves and the Fishes — five loaves, two fishes and two eels all by
themselves in a pure and simple design.

Homage is paid to those early anchorites St. Anthony and St. Paul,
patrons of the monastic life. One panel shows their meeting in the desert:
seated facing each other on straight-backed chairs, they break bread together. Another depicts the Temptation of St. Anthony — the rectangular
saint beset by two rectangular visions, one with the head of an animal, the
other of a bird. The panel below these two religious ones has an unscriptural
scene of animals with the heads of horses and the bodies of serpents locked
in an inextricable coil of combat; unlike the squared representations of
humans, the artist carved his animals in sinuous curves. All the scenes are
executed with a kind of childlike artfulness so that they fit exactly into their
frames: the animals arch into the corners; the humans have round heads
(the males' are elongated by their short oval beards into teardrop shapes)
and rectilinear torsos to fill the squares, and all their feet are turned sideways, like those on Egyptian friezes.

In fact the art is clearly reminiscent of that of ancient Egypt: the artist
was concerned with depicting what he saw intellectually with his mind's
eye rather than in reproducing in a naturalistic style the shapes seen by the
visual eye alone. The stonework lacks the formalized skill of the Egyptians'
art, but it has an individualistic freshness deriving from the sculptor's
unregimented imagination, a luxury never permitted to the intensively
trained Pharaonic artists.

The acme of the scriptural high crosses came in the late ninth century,
possibly into the tenth, at Monasterboice, County Louth, and Clonmac-

noise, County Offaly. Monasterboice, founded in the sixth century by St. Buite, a shadowy figure who was a friend of St. Finian of Clonard, became famous much later as the abode of Flann Mainistreach, Latin master of the monastery, who died in 1056 (he was a noted scholar and presumed author of historical works in poetry on the Tuatha De Danann, the kings of Tara and others). The founding of the Cistercian abbey at nearby Mellifont in the twelfth century caused the decline of the importance of Monasterboice. Today the peaceful, deserted remains of the monastic village lie amid a patchwork of crooked little fields climbing up and down the rounded hills and shallow vales of the Boyne valley. A tall round tower with a jagged top rises out of a grove of wide-spreading horse chestnuts that shade the ruins of two little churches and a graveyard. In the graveyard are three high crosses, of which the most beautiful and the best preserved is the South Cross. It was erected, according to an inscription on its base, by one Muiredach, possibly one of two abbots of that name who lived some eighty years apart. The cross is of sandstone, a more malleable material than the granite of Moone and Ahenny, and which has the added virtue that it withstands the weathering of the centuries. Most of the panels retain much of their pristine clarity of detail, and it is even possible to visualize the extra sparkle that would have been imparted to this spirited work by the original colors.

Muiredach's Cross is massive and tall (17 feet, 8 inches), giving the sculptor room for many figures and a wealth of lively detail. Though there is the customary Celtic antipathy for empty spaces, such is the balanced artistry that there is no sense of crowding. Both the east and west faces have scenes from the Old and New Testaments; around the base, which is time-eroded, are animals and interlaced designs. Though the scriptural scenes are similar to those on the more primitive granite crosses, the figures have not the innocent doll shapes, but express varying identities.

On the bottom panel of the east face are the familiar Adam and Eve under curving lines of apples — but this time they are patently a man and a woman. Beside them Cain flourishes a bludgeon toward the skull of his brother. Above them huge Goliath kneels before David, surrendering his weapons. Then comes Moses smiting the rock to bring forth water for a doubting congregation seated before him, their arms uncompromisingly crossed over their breasts. Over that is the Adoration of the Magi, and the center of the cross is occupied with a sweeping portrayal of the Last Judgment. Christ stands in the center holding crossed over his breast a double crook in his right hand and a cross in his left, an arrangement

Muiredach's Cross at Monasterboice, County Louth — one of the high points in the art of the scriptural high crosses

Detail of the late-ninth-century Cross of the Scriptures at Clonmacnoise, County Offaly. The bottom panel may represent St. Ciaran and Prince Diarmait planting the first stake of the church.

similar to the pose of Egyptian Osiris.* On Christ's left, a little musician plays a pipe; beyond him a devil with a trident drives the sinners away from the Savior, while an assistant kicks them into hell. On Christ's right, David plays his harp, which has a bird sitting on top of it, and leads the faithful, who, hands joined, approach their Lord. Below the figure of Christ, the archangel Michael weighs the souls: a small soul rests in one pan of the scale, while the other is being tipped up by a devil lying on his back and prodding it with a stick. The top of the cross is fashioned into a model of a rectangular church with a steep shingled roof; on one of its walls St. Anthony and St. Paul meet again in the desert, and on the other Moses prays at the battle of Rephidim, his tired arms held up in the air by Aaron and Hur, to insure Israel's victory. The west side of the cross has scenes from the Passion, the depiction of which is as fine and animated as on the other side.

The whole production is a delightful masterpiece of character and drama to bring the Bible to life for the ignorant. It is more than that: its busy detail is transfigured by consummate artistry into a euphonious composition, an authentic work of art.

The other great cross of the Midlands is the Cross of the Scriptures at Clonmacnoise, sometimes called Flann's Cross because of a request for a prayer inscribed on it, possibly for Flann. As in the case of the abbots at Monasterboice, there were two Flanns, of the same periods as the two Muiredachs, and scholarly opinions differ as to which one was commemorated. Whatever its date, the similarity of the two crosses is so striking that they must be nearly contemporaneous.

The cross at Clonmacnoise is slimmer than that at Monasterboice, so the scenes are simpler and the figures fewer. Its much larger circle dominates the cross section, and has, as at Monasterboice, one side dedicated to the Crucifixion, the other to the Last Judgment. The shortened arms of the cross have an odd upward tilt, imparting an attractive discord to the prevailing vertical-horizontal mode. The lowest panel of the west face is a lovely and expressive composition: two soldiers are asleep, their heads touching, bent over the tomb of Christ; behind them, like a counterpoint, Martha and Mary keep watch, while below the tomb is the body of Christ swathed in a shroud whose stylized folds are ornamented with three raised crosses. Over Christ's exposed head hovers a bird, touching the mouth

---

*This pose turns up frequently in the high crosses and in the contemporary illuminated manuscripts; as we will see when we examine the latter, much, both in symbolism and decoration, may have been borrowed from Coptic art — which in turn was an offshoot of Egyptian temple art of an earlier time.

with its beak to breathe into it the life of the Resurrection. The inspired piety of the scriptural scenes is counterpoised by carvings on the base, almost erased, which, amid running Celtic patterns, depict chariots, horses and other earthly themes.

These two beautiful crosses, while the finest surviving examples, are not the only ones. Across Ireland — at Durrow in the Midlands, at Kells north of Dublin, at Drumcliffe on the west coast, at Donaghmore and Arboe in the north central — are magnificent scriptural crosses, their crisp detail dimmed by time but still eloquent. Several of these are at monasteries founded by St. Columba. The spirit of Iona, and back of that the transcendent genius of its founding saint, found renewed life in Columba's Irish monasteries when in 807 the monks fled from Alba back to Ireland to escape the disastrous Viking attacks (taking with them not only their ideals and their skills but such matchless material possessions as, probably, the unfinished *Book of Kells*).

The period of these splendid sculptures, from the middle of the ninth until the early tenth centuries, was the culmination of the scriptural crosses. It was also the end of them. It is not known what occasioned this: perhaps the Viking invasions reached a point of thoroughgoing malevolence, touching every facet of life, which discouraged all forms of creative effort; perhaps there was a reversion to wooden crosses. Whatever the cause, for two centuries no stone crosses are known. When they reappeared in the twelfth century, it was in a different part of Ireland, the southwest, and the style was different. Scenes from the Scriptures were replaced by one or two large figures carved in high relief, a form very close to freestanding sculpture. This art, brought to Ireland by the Anglo-Normans, belongs to a period outside the scope of this work.

But there is at least one surviving wooden sculpture dating from the thirteenth century that is purely Gaelic, bearing no trace of the influence of the Anglo-Norman conquerors: that is the aforementioned oak effigy of St. Molaisse of Inishmurray. The elongated brown figure has a long and saintly face, high cheekbones, hair cut round and tonsured, a cowled habit and eyes cast down as if in prayer. It has an elemental spirituality, the reticent piety of a simpler age than that in which it was carved. In historical perspective, it seems at sharp odds with the shattered morale of those years.

CHAPTER XVII
ART IN METAL AND THE ILLUMINATED GOSPELS

ON A DIFFERENT PLANE FROM THE INSPIRED, OFTEN MAGNIFICENT BUT IN-trinsically cumbrous art of the stoneworker is the delicate, intricate perfection of Irish metalwork and the closely associated art of manuscript illumination.

The metalworker's craft goes back centuries before St. Patrick. From 2000 to 1500 B.C. finely chased lunulae made in Ireland of gold from the Wicklow Hills were being exported to the Continent. Later, starting in the third century B.C., came the art of the Celtic metalsmiths of the La Tène period, incorporating Stone Age and Bronze Age patterns into designs of stylized figures and abstract curving tendrils that covered every space. To the Celtic styles were added forms imported from Roman Britain, notably the penannular brooch, or ring-brooch, a broken ring attached to a pin, used as a garment fastener. By the early Christian centuries metalworking was a highly esteemed art, its practitioners ranking just below poets in the social order. Celtic chieftains decorated themselves and all their belongings with barbaric splendor. Shields and sword scabbards were of etched bronze; horse trappings were enamelled in vivid colors; warriors wore massive gold neck torques enchased with the La Tène coils and spirals; women had incised golden balls at the ends of their long braided hair; both sexes fastened their cloaks with heavy gold, silver and bronze penannular brooches decorated with jewels.

When Ireland was converted to Christianity, many of the secular chieftains became priests; and while they spiritualized their personal lives, they did not change their taste, handed down from pagan forefathers, for the elegance of finely wrought metals. The native love for personal jewelry was transmuted to the adornment of the new religion and the metalworkers' skills were employed to the greater glory of the Church. Chalices, crosses, shrines for books, bells and relics took the place of the accoutrements of warriors and their ladies — all incised with designs, overlaid with filigrees of gold thread, inlaid with enamel, embossed with precious stones. The dark interiors of the small plain churches must have been irradiated by the golden fires at the altars.

One of the most exquisite of the altar treasures that has been found to date is the Ardagh Chalice, made in the eighth century. It is seven inches high and nine and a half in diameter, a simple cup shape attached by a narrow stem to a conical base. Its pure lines and its surface areas of plain silver set off the fine elaboration of its decorated gold bands and panels with red and blue cloisonné enamel bosses. The areas of ornamentation are a band of gold interlacing interspersed with enamel bosses below the rim, the incised gold casing of the stem, gold-filigreed panels beneath the handles; and, as a loving exercise in nonessential perfectionism, the underside — which could only be seen by the priest when he raised the cup in consecration — has three intricately wrought gold friezes of Celtic-style animals, spirals and interlacing around a rock crystal boss.

The main work of the metalsmiths in the religious field was the making of reliquaries for the enshrinement of articles belonging to saints, as well as of parts of their bodies. From the fourth century until well into the twelfth, the cult of relics was the most pervasive and possibly the most vital aspect of Christianity. Representing the saints' continuing contact with the faithful, relics were a potent source of spiritual energy, antidote to suffering and illness and cogent defense against the swarms of demons, the dethroned pagan gods, who invisibly inhabited the earth ready to snatch at the unprotected. The cherished trophies were encased in luxurious caskets of precious metals and jewels, usually fashioned in the shape of the object within. They represented a great part of the wealth of individual churches and monasteries as well as being an attractive lure to converts and pilgrims. Often attached to the altar, they were essential for the saying of mass; they were more binding than the Gospel for the swearing of oaths in judicial courts; warriors wore them into battle to insure victory.

In Ireland the cult of relics inspired the metalworkers to soaring heights of elaborate beauty. The most frequently enshrined items were those most characteristic insignia of the saint, his crosier and his bell. St. Patrick, who always carried a consecrated bell and gave one to a disciple whenever he left on a journey, employed three smiths chiefly for the making of bells. One of these bells remains, Ireland's most ancient Christian relic, found, it is said, in 552. It is a little bell, about eight inches high, of two thin iron plates hammered into a quadrangular shape then coated with bronze to increase the resonance. Its original shrine is gone and the present one, made around 1100, is an openwork silver frame divided into panels of gold and gold-plated bronze wire. On the front, the panels have symmetrical designs of slender animal forms, interlaced in delicate patterns similar to the Irish Romanesque stonework at Cormac's Chapel, deriving from the Scandinavian Urnes style. On the sides, the intertwined animals form the shape of a cross (a telling example of the adaptation of pagan imagery to Christian concept), and the filigreed crest covering the handle bears at its back two stylized peacocks, symbol of resurrection and immortality in early Christian mythology. The little shrine is a pefect gem of Irish Romanesque metalwork — subtle, elegant and graceful.

The crosier of the abbots of Clonmacnoise is enshrined in a case of the same period, and it also exhibits one of the more beneficent effects of the Norse infiltration. On the crook is the head of a fierce animal; around it, bands of silver edged with niello outline thick coiling animal limbs ending in tendrils, an adaptation of a Scandinavian style known as Ringerike.

In the early twelfth century a piece of the True Cross was brought from Rome and enshrined in the Cross of Cong, a superb example of Irish Romanesque metalwork. The finely wrought gold filigree cross, about thirty inches high, depicts Urnes-style animals, fat four-legged ones entwined with thin snakelike ones, and Celtic spirals similar to the decoration on the eighth-century Ardagh Chalice. Also in the earlier style are the red enamel bosses and a bright eye of rock crystal in the center. The foot of the cross is grasped on both sides in the jaws of a scaled golden dragon's head with big black eyes. Complex and finicky as is the workmanship of this shrine, the total effect is one of indivisible grace.

Some of the virtuosity of Irish metal craftsmen who worked from the early Christian period into the medieval was displayed in the delicate artistry of articles having no religious connotation. Personal decoration, particularly penannular brooches to fasten the cloak at the shoulder, still held a high place among the wealthy laity. The earliest ones found, dating to the fifth century A.D., are simple broken-ring pins with little decoration, in a style imported from Roman Britain. By the eighth century they had evolved into highly decorated gems of fine workmanship. The loveliest

The Tara Brooch, an example of exquisite eighth-century metalwork

and most intricate that has been found is the early-eighth-century Tara Brooch (which has nothing to do with the seat of northern Ireland's high-kings but was named by a dealer in the last century). It is of bronze covered with gold filigree and incised silvered panels, and is set with amber and glass bosses. The front is a symphony of gold filigree interlace design with a stylized animal head on the crescent, fashioned of spirals. On the back (which could only be seen by the wearer before he put it on, like the seldom-seen embellishment on the bottom of the Ardagh Chalice), coiling animals and birds of Germanic or Scandinavian inspiration battle restlessly around two silvered bronze panels engraved with abstract Celtic curlicues. The articulation is brilliantly clear: the work is so fine that it seems the artist must have been nearsighted. Though many of the particularities are derivative of British or Continental styles, the synthesis is totally individualistic; it has a felicitous harmony that was not derived but freshly created.

After the ninth century, the art of metalworking declined, with some exceptions. Many of the artists, as previously noted, were forced to change their medium when it came to pass, during the Norse invasions, that their products were too attractively conveyable. But they had made their mark on Irish art, inspiring stone-carvers of the following centuries, who transferred the subtleties of the metalworker's craft with manifest success to the inflexible medium of stone.

The same delicate craft animated the work of the illuminators, and metal jewelry transposed to parchment is one of the more striking components of the illuminated Gospels, Ireland's crowning achievements of the seventh to ninth centuries. Some of the decoration of these codices is almost two-dimensional jewelry, direct translation to parchment of such gems as the Ardagh Chalice and the Tara Brooch.

Manuscript copying had always been an important part of the curriculum of the Irish monasteries and of the foundations of Irish missionaries in Britain and on the Continent. The rarity of books made their production essential, and every monk had to put in his hours in the scriptorium writing out copies of the Gospels and the Psalms. In the beginning these volumes were not illuminated, being only for daily use. But such was the overriding value of books to the Irish that by the late sixth century Ireland had already developed a distinctive script and an original style of ornamentation. In addition to every monk's daily stint in the scriptorium, as routinely prescribed as his labors in the field, the bigger monasteries had special scribes, chosen for their scholarship and skill with the pen, whose chief task was the creation of finely wrought artistry on parchment. There developed a reverence for writing for its own sake as an art form, chiefly, in the beginning, in the decoration of the capital first letters of paragraphs. The peculiarly Irish development of this style may have started at Columbanus's Bobbio, whose Irish monks had continuing contact with the homeland as well as with the East. Some of their inspiration must have come with study of manuscripts from the Coptic scriptoria, such as would have been in Bobbio's renowned library. Illuminated Irish manuscripts from the earliest period exhibit Coptic motifs along with patterns from Celtic and Anglo-Saxon metalwork in a fortunate blend of north and south, Christian and pagan, that was to culminate in the consummate artistry of the *Book of Kells*.

Of these three chief sources of inspiration — Coptic, Celtic, and Anglo-Saxon — two interplay creatively in the earliest surviving illuminated manuscript, the *Cathach* of St. Columba,* a Psalter written probably in the late sixth or early seventh century. The decoration of the capitals combines the free rhythms of La Tène scrolls expanding and opening out of each other like the designs in Celtic filigree metalwork, with writhing open-mouthed animals of Anglo-Saxon derivation. Only faint beginnings of the remaining component of Irish manuscript art, the Coptic influence, are evident in the patterns of dots adorning these figures.

The *Cathach* initials have a further original characteristic. In the usual majuscule script of the Late Antique period, the figured capital stood alone, separated by its size and its elaborate embellishment from the following text. The Irish scribes drew their capital into the body of the paragraph by gradually diminishing the size of its following letters, so that the initial blends into the total scene rather than dominating the page as a single, unrelated ornament. This synthesizing process was to be adapted later, with startling decorative effect, to the illustrated pages of illuminated manuscripts, in which foregound and background merge in abstract integration, a reversal of the classical concept of figure standing out against ground.

The first of the surviving codices containing illustrations is the *Book of Durrow,* a small manuscript of the Gospels, painted probably between 670 and 680 and named for one of St. Columba's earliest and most important monasteries in Ireland, to which it belonged until the seventeenth century. Such was the close artistic association of Ireland and England, however, that the provenance of this beautiful book is in question. It may have been

*See footnote, page 153.

painted in Ireland, Iona or Lindisfarne; its style is an amalgam of Celtic and Anglo-Saxon that came to be known as Hiberno-Saxon. The art of the metalworker is evident in the pulsating Celtic spirals, the Anglo-Saxon intertwined animals biting each other and millefiori inlay decorations — all features borrowed from Irish and Anglo-Saxon goldsmiths.

In addition to these now familiar elements, the third feature is given full play for the first time: Coptic interlacing. The intricate knotwork patterns that play such an important part in Ireland's illuminated manuscripts, both as background and as an integral part of the illustrations, are much older than Egyptian Christianity. The Copts themselves, building their churches within the ruins of Pharaonic temples, inherited a long tradition. In the fourteenth century B.C. artists in stone carved interlacing patterns on the tomb of King Tutankhamen. Whether Ireland's use of this classic decorative device — developed by northern artists to a sophisticated complexity far beyond its antique prototypes — came directly from Egypt is questionable; similar patterns occur in Italian and Byzantine art of the period. Their use in the *Book of Durrow* only illustrates the never-ending, both-ways flow of ideas through Europe and the East, in which Irish and Anglo-Saxon artists were not so much end receivers as contributing partners.

The most striking of the Hiberno-Saxon contributions to religious art on parchment are the elaborate carpet pages that introduce each of the Gospels in the *Book of Durrow* — full pages seemingly devoted to nothing but decoration. This art form possibly derives from closely similar Coptic manuscripts and textiles of the sixth century, though there is no positive proof of this. An interesting speculation is that Arculf, the same Gaulish bishop who in the late seventh century entertained and instructed St. Adamnan at Iona with accounts of his eastern travels, also had with him some of the handiwork of those distant artists, and that these became models — first in the sciptoria of Iona, later at Lindisfarne and other Irish-founded English monasteries. Besides the borrowing from the art of the East, these pages show a clear kinship with the curvilinear abstractions of Celtic pre-Christian art.

The style of the carpet pages is anticlassical, abstract and symbolic, unlike anything found in Continental medieval manuscripts.[1] Recognizable figures play no part in the rhythmic, restless designs that, in their kinetic appeal, have more relation to music than to representational art. Trumpets, spirals, stylized animals, key patterns (of Greek derivation) and ribbon interlace ebb and flow over the page with carefully orchestrated effect, enhanced and deepened by the artful blending and contrasting of their colors, unfaded through the centuries. The designs are deliberately occult, based on interior vision rather than outward, comprehensible perception. An expression of perpetual motion they have the dynamic, mysterious vibrance of life itself.

Amid the cadenced abstraction is the one clear Christian symbol, the cross, reminding us that the cloistered artists, for all their apparent obsession with design for its own sake, had a Christian message to proclaim. But even this unmistakable shape is subject to the dominating feature of the carpet pages: the merging of subject with background. In classical art the figure, set off by the surrounding ornament, emerges primary. In the art of the carpet pages, design and figure interact so that neither is paramount and both form together an abstract geometric entity. The cross is clearly there; yet its fusion with its background gives it an aura of purposeful mystical obscurity — an expression, perhaps, of the ultimate incomprehensibility of God.

The human figure is notably absent from the carpet pages but it occurs in stylized form in some of the other illustrations. Whether seventh-century Irish and Anglo-Saxon artists were not trained to grapple with the subtleties of the human figure or whether they deliberately avoided any taint of realism as detracting from the mystical meaning they sought to convey, the representations of man are frozen symbols not unlike the simplistic doll figures on the Moone high cross carved over a century later.

The most vivid of these primal images is St. Matthew's symbol, the Man, facing the beginning of the apostle's Gospel: a flat frontal figure encased in a bell-shaped garment completely enclosing its body except for the neckless head and the feet, both of which point to the right. The garment is covered with a formal millefiori inlay pattern of colored squares, recalling the art of the metalsmiths. There is the hint of a monk's cowl in the curve of the dress at the shoulders, and a clear suggestion of realism in the straight falls of hair, one on either side of the high forehead, representing the Celtic tonsure — a touch that implies the Irish background of the artist. Neither of these effects is naturalistic; they serve as metaphors, to point up the religious character of the symbol. The figure is enclosed by a wide frame of interlacing ribbons repeating the colors of the garment against a black background. In contrast to the static tranquillity of the figure, the border has the unceasing pulsation of rolling waves, an effect of motion so potent that the eye is irresistibly drawn away from the placidity at the center — and back again — as the artist reproduces here the same deliberately ambiguous effect of figure versus ground that infuses the carpet pages.

While the human image is sublimated, the animals appear to have a different spiritual intent. The carpet page facing the beginning of St. John has a central medallion of interlaced ribbons with a square Coptic cross, small and simple, at its core. The rest of the page consists of broad panels of writhing animals, savage and distorted, biting each other's convoluted bodies and even their own. Except for a vague connotation of snakes, the creatures have no relation to any animals in nature, but seem the very distillation of evil — symbols, perhaps, of pagan cults that became demonic as Christianity sent them underground. Destructive as they are, their violence is contained — locked safely into a complex knotted interlacing, imprisoned by the contortions of their own bodies. The artist clearly has a message: the rampant furies of evil are contained by the divine orderliness of the Word, as the devil is captive in hell. As if to confirm the allegory, the viewer's eye, lured by the colors and rhythms of the struggling beasts, is drawn always back to the center, away from the agitation, to rest on the silent, still purity of the little cross.

Although it is a fascinating exercise to unravel the spiritual meanings enciphered in the art of the *Book of Durrow,* it becomes clear, when one looks at these glowing pages in totality, that the Christian symbols are accessories only. The overwhelming effect is sensuous and definitely pagan, the antithesis of idealized classical art. The Christian message is an imposed overlay on a nonrepresentational, essentially barbarian art — an obvious descendant of the abstract art of the Stone Age carvers at Newgrange and the Iron Age creators of the Turoe Stone. The character of this art has been modified but not fundamentally changed by contact with the craft of northern metalworkers and the mystical patterns and ideas that came out of the East. Under the brushes of skilled and sophisticated illustrators, the artistry became refined, subtle and wondrously intricate, but its basis is a concept of art quite alien to the Continental Christian style inherited from Greek and Roman ideals. Nonliteral and intentionally arcane, it substitutes symbols for figures and merges them with their backgrounds in labyrinthine patterns, producing a total figuration that is geometry in motion — with cryptic meanings. For the pagan art from which these Christian pages are derived was also sacred and symbolic, but the religious intention was hidden within the design, just as the Celtic druids concealed the knowledge of their arcane mysteries by their deliberate refusal to develop a written language.

The monks did not so much surrender to an already existing art style as let their own art be formed by it, substituting new symbols for the old. Just so did the monkish scribes, ascetic and exalted as they were, transfer to parchment the oral tales of Cuchulain's ferocious, insouciant heroism and Deirdre's fatal beauty, touching them with only the thinnest of Christian veneer. It adds a dimension to our picture of Irish Christianity to see thus exemplified the sublimated love of life of these cloistered ascetics — their all-embracing tolerance to ideas out of other times and other faiths; their pure delight in the intellectual tools, the pen and the brush; above all, their very Irishness, their motivation to preserve the best of their insular civilization in all its earthly exuberance.

Awesomely intricate as it is, the *Book of Durrow,* being among the earliest of the Hiberno-Saxon illuminated manuscripts, lacks the skill and scope evident in later works. Its coloring, though brilliant, is limited; its figures, primitive. Through the eighth century the work coming out of the monasteries of the British Isles shows an increasing deftness of technique and ever more agile play of wide-ranging imagination. The scriptoria were very active, and undoubtedly many more books were made than survive today. Mostly these were pocket Gospels carried by the priests on their travels, very personal little books, brightly and simply illustrated with decorated script and portraits or symbols of the Evangelists. There were also the few lavish and elaborate codices, the great jewels of the church, intended chiefly as ornaments to the altar, to be brought out only on special occasions.

The *Lindisfarne Gospels,* made in the early eighth century, is one of these sumptuous volumes. Though painted not long after the *Book of Durrow,* this manuscript already exhibits a new virtuosity, particularly in the figure delineation. Lindisfarne, Irish in origin, was peopled mostly by Irish-trained English clerics by the time of the painting of its famous Gospels. So close were the spiritual and political ties between Ireland and northern England at this time that the *Lindisfarne Gospels* can be considered, along with several of the other great eighth-century manuscripts whose provenance is less certain, as being the product of a combined culture. Unlike the others, its creator, who was probably not only the scribe but the painter as well, is known, along with several of his auxiliaries. "Eadfrith," it is written at the end of the codex, "Bishop of the Church of Lindisfarne, originally wrote this book in honor of God and St. Cuthbert. And Aldred, unworthy and most miserable priest, glossed it in English with the help of God and St. Cuthbert. And Aethelwald, Bishop of the Lindisfarne Islanders, bound it on the outside and covered it . . . and Billfrith the anchorite, wrought the ornaments on the outside and adorned it with gold and gilded silver. . . ." [2] This modest signature indicates that the book was a worthy altar embellishment for the central church of Celtic Christianity in England.

The *Lindisfarne Gospels* has carpet pages similar to those of the *Book of Durrow,* but they are more meticulously drawn — clear and delicate, like finely woven tapestries. The animals incorporated into the interlacing have not lost any of their barbaric savagery, but they are more articulated. As in the *Book of Durrow* they are gracefully captive in the toils of their own twisted bodies. Unlike those of the earlier book they consist of more than bodies: to the sinuous torsos of the animals are attached curled paws and doglike heads with enormous, realistic teeth; the birds are equipped with many-colored wings, immense grasping talons and the fierce decurved beaks of birds of prey.

The *Lindisfarne Gospels* is innovative among insular manuscripts in another direction, having the first known full-page illustrations. In this case they are portraits of the Evangelists, striking in their classical delineations of the human figure. The page preceding the Gospel of St. Matthew presents the Evangelist seated on a bench writing in a book. His togalike mantle falls realistically about his body, a skeleton of bold lines deftly suggesting folds. His body is shaped naturally to the bench, the feet articulated, the hands long and slender and full of motion. His head, in three-quarter profile, is a real human head, an idealized portrait quite Greek in feeling. In fact the whole classical conception of the figure, so different from the stylized man-symbol in the earlier work, is directly attributable to Byzantine models that were finding their way to English monasteries.

There is an even wider variance here with the spirit of the *Book of Durrow* than the classical delineation of the figure. This is a picture, not a pattern. Decoration is at a minimum, confined to the bench and to the border of Matthew's undergarment. The artist's skill is directed instead to the literal and dramatic representation of ideas. Above the Evangelist's head, his symbol emerges from his halo, suggesting that the divine inspiration comes from within; the winged figure blows a trumpet to indicate its resounding voice. A curtain falls in front of Matthew; from behind its drawn-back folds, the head and shoulders of another man project — a figure holding a book, a halo around the graceful curls of his hair. The text identifies him as Christ; the curtain probably represents the "veil of mystery" before the sacred inner temple of the Eastern Church.

Full-page illustrations, first appearing in the *Lindisfarne Gospels,* play an even more important part in the *Book of Kells* — the end product of two centuries of illumination and the sublime achievement of insular art. In this transcendent work features of earlier codices are improved upon with the skill that came from long familiarity, and are blended with an imaginative originality unsurpassed by any other work of parchment art in the Western world.

Argument, often stormy, surrounds the history of the *Book of Kells,* there being strong claimants for its generation in Ireland, Iona, Lindisfarne or some other insular foundation of Irish origin and mixed personnel. The answer will probably never be known, though some experts reason that evidence favors its inception at Iona in the late eighth century and subsequent removal to Kells, where it was completed in the first quarter of the ninth century.

In 795 Iona was pillaged by Norse raiders; in 801–802 they came again and burned the monastery to the ground; returning in 806 they murdered sixty-eight monks. For the first time in the history of Irish Christianity Irish monks suffered red martyrdom. In 807 the abbot, Cellach, with the remaining monks, moved to Ireland taking with them the bones and other relics of St. Columba and whatever valuables they had managed to hide from the ravagers — among them, presumably, the unfinished manuscript. They went to the site of one of Columba's monasteries at Kells, County Meath, and built there a new monastery, to be the headquarters of the league of Columban houses.

Kells, being inland, was considered safe from the marauders, who, in the early years, limited their invasions to hit-and-run assaults on the monasteries immediately accessible by sea. But Kells was struck the year after its founding and its church destroyed. A new church was completed in 814 and the monastic village, probably fortified, succeeded in fending off subsequent attackers. Undoubtedly, also, successive abbots paid tribute for the privilege of being left alone. At any rate, the monastery at Kells had years of peace in the early ninth century — time enough for the production of the great book. For the creation of such a complex, profound and subtle work of art is a luxury that presupposes a number of conditions: security from outward disturbance; wealth to afford the years of dedicated specialization of a corps of scribes and painters; a scholarly intimacy with the Christian thought of the time; and a large library of books from abroad, which, being rare, would take years to accumulate. The scriptorium at Kells, fortunate in its relative tranquillity, could meet these conditions and finish — though it was never absolutely finished — the work that had begun at Iona. But the monastery was not permanently inviolate. The Norse sacked it in 919, 950 and 969, and in the following century it was raided repeatedly by the Irish themselves. In 1170 it was burned to the ground by the Anglo-Normans at the instigation of their Irish ally, Diarmait Mac Murrough.

Despite the brutal history of Kells, the manuscript survived almost intact. In 1006 it was stolen, and turned up two and a half months later buried "under a sod" with the gold of its wood-and-metal cover wrenched off. The inside pages were unscathed, though some missing leaves at the beginning and the end may have been torn off at this time. Though the book miraculously had weathered the violence of successive plunderers, when Cromwell's army came rampaging over Ireland in the seventeenth century, destroying whatever relics of popish idolatry turned up in its path, some of the Protector's cavalry were quartered in the church at Kells, and it was deemed that this was one storm the precious treasure might not ride out. In 1654 the governor of Kells sent the manuscript to Dublin and in 1661 it was presented to Trinity College, where it still is.

The book is larger than the earlier insular manuscripts. At present its pages average 13 by 9½ inches, but clipping by a careless binder probably reduced them by about an inch overall. It has 340 folios (680 pages); probably it originally had 370. The work is divided into two parts: the first consists of the preliminaries — canon tables, *Breves causae* (summaries of the Gospels, plus *Argumenta,* a collection of legends about the Evangelists), and lists of Hebrew names; the second part contains the Four Gospels. The script throughout is lavishly and entertainingly decorated, and there are, besides, a number of full-page illustrations of bewildering but ever harmonious complexity. A close student of the work, Françoise Henry, has discovered the distinct personal style of at least four artists.[3] But she stresses that the book is essentially a work of collaboration, that more than one scribe and painter probably worked on the same page, and that separate pages could be distributed among several artists so that they could work simultaneously on the same Gospel.

However, unmistakable personalities are perceivable throughout, and Dr. Henry has given them designations. The "Goldsmith," so named because of the fine, clear intricacy of his patterns and his use of the metallic colors of gold-yellow and silver-blue, painted the introductory pages of three of the Gospels, a carpet page with a double cross known as the "page of the eight circles" and the full-page Chi-Rho Christogram. He is a meticulous craftsman with a fine sense of balance and subtle use of color. In the ninth century he was old-fashioned: by this time the carpet page was nearly obsolete, and his is the only one in the book. Traditional also is his use of scrolls, spirals and entwined snakes. But although the style is conservative, the techniques of the "Goldsmith" are more delicate and sophisticated and at the same time freer than those of the painters of the *Book of Durrow* more than a century earlier. The later artists were no longer experimenting. They had had time to assimilate elements from different lands and different eras, and were able to combine them with the ease and skill of familiarity.

The carpet page of the eight circles is a masterpiece of eurythmic convolution: a great double cross with richly ornamented circles at its two crosspieces and at its ends, with a background of complex interlacing in muted, varying colors. The cross is separated from the background by bands of sharp yellow and pale red, which also serve to delineate and limit the pulsing mobility of the surrounding designs. The result is a double-vision effect, the mysterious fading in and out of the subject noted in the carpet pages of the *Book of Durrow*.

The pages of ornamental script that begin the Gospels are, like the cross page, classics of design and color. Unlike the latter, they are not pure design; fused into the patterns are symbolic figures alive with hidden Christian meanings. In the page introducing St. Mark, for instance, there is a weird and wonderful composition in the upper right-hand corner: a human figure entwined with the jaws of a lion and two peacocks. The figure is white with red designs all over it, giving the impression of patterned tights. His long thin arms are crossed over his chest in an acute contortion bizarrely reminiscent of the Osiris pose, one hand behind his back grasping the curling tongue of the lion, the other holding a spiral that comes out of an interlace of his own beard, which is also connected with the two birds. This is probably, reasons Dr. Henry, the figure of the Evangelist himself with his symbol, the lion, while the peacocks represent Christ's Resurrection. To us, accustomed to the serenely devotional set poses of later Christian art, this grotesquerie seems almost impious. But to the medieval mind, especially one with the free virtuoso imagination of the "Goldsmith," it was properly reverent to wind the symbols into a pattern. Naturalistic literalness was not an object to the medieval religious artist. His aim was rather to present an intellectual idea in all its complexity, artfully structured into a design that would appeal to the esthetic sense while conveying a pious message.

Chi and Rho, the first two letters of Christ's name in the Greek alphabet (in the Latin they resemble *X* and *P*), are used in monogram as an emblem of Christ. These symbolic initials are the point of departure for the most brilliant achievement of the "Goldsmith," the Chi-Rho page at the beginning of the text in St. Matthew on the birth of Christ. Enlarged and decorated initials are a feature of the *Book of Kells,* as of many illuminated manuscripts. As we saw in the *Cathach,* the decorated capitals developed by Irish scribes became artistically a part of the text rather than standing conspicuously alone. In the *Book of Kells,* also, the capitals are generally worked into the overall design of the text pages. But on the Chi-Rho page the artist evidently became so carried away by his own splendid inventions that the initials sweep over the entire page, leaving the scribe space for only a single two-inch line at the bottom.

The page is designed around the Chi, which loops extravagantly from top to bottom on the left-hand side and on the right thrusts out in a flurry of circles, spirals and curlicues, almost leaving the page. Its curving outlines, banded by mauve and black, are filled in with trellises of interlaced birds and animals so fine and so small that without a magnifier one cannot make out their details (like the metalsmiths, this artist must have been myopic). Worked into the design so intricately that they are hard to disentangle are a wealth of symbols, many of them strange to us. Two pale finedrawn moths outlined in red dots hold a lozenge between their heads. The lozenge is thought to be a Christian symbol, though its meaning is obscure. A sleek dark otter grips a fish in its jaws — the fish being a known early symbol of Christ. Near this is a group of two cats and four smaller animals, which may be kittens from their playful and familiar attitudes toward the cats, though they have a nearer resemblance to mice. Two of the little animals hold between their noses a disc with a cross upon it, while the other two sit on the backs of the cats nibbling at their ears. The disc is probably a symbol for the Eucharist, but the choice of animals, as well as their pose, is unfamiliar.

Though the Chi-Rho page is mainly the subtle and delicate work of the "Goldsmith," these sportive animals do not have his style. They seem rather to be the work of another artist, whose hand appears throughout the text in the hosts of fanciful and athletic birds and animals playing among the words, wandering between the lines or contorted into the shapes of initials. Some of these have ostensible purposes, to indicate a textual addition or correction, or to point the direction of the next line; some of them are simply fill-ins for blank spaces. The artist's observation is keen and his imagination humorous: a hunched cat watches a mousehole, a wolf treads purposefully along the tops of the letters, a bright-hued cock lords it over two cowering hens, a dog bends its neck backward so its head is curled upside down over its back, a long gaunt cat stretched over three lines arranges the letters with its scrawny paws.

There are human figures too: a man rides horseback along the top of a line of text, one large bare foot pointed out in front of the horse, which is apparently licking it; an acrobatic little person twisted into an initial and evidently wrestling with himself holds one leg straight up in the air while the other, folded beneath him, is grasped around the knee by a very long, contorted arm. This artist, familiar with the homely scenes of the farmyard and sharply perceptive of nature, appears to have little but ornament in his mind as he strews his stylized caricatures freely over the pages. But it is probable, considering the obvious symbolism of his creatures on the Chi-Rho page, that many of his animals represent meanings to which we no longer have a clue. Sometimes they also indicate a mood rather than a literal intention. Where Matthew relates, "Then two thieves were crucified with him" ("*Tunc crucifixerant . . .*"), the first initial, *T,* is formed of two animals elongated into tortured shapes, their mouths open in evident roars of anguish — an eloquent orchestration of the text.

Very different from the two foregoing artists is the one called by Dr. Henry the "Illustrator," creator of several of the surviving full-page illustrations: the Virgin and Child, the Temptation of Christ and the Arrest, as well as other illustrated pages. Where the imagery of the animal artist is appealingly personal, the "Illustrator" presents stark, awesome, stylized portraits that stare straight at the viewer with uncompromising solemnity. He eschews the delicate color and subtle, finicky design of the "Goldsmith," instead applying his colors with simple intensity, and impatient of small detail.

We have seen how, a century earlier, the flat, sublimated human images of the *Book of Durrow* gave way to the classic poses in the *Lindisfarne Gospels.* In the *Book of Kells* there is a partial return to the older style, but executed with the skill of more sophisticated and knowledgeable artists. In these illustrations there is a striking revelation of the affinity of the Hiberno-Saxon art with that of the icons and church frescoes of Byzantium. The hieratic, impersonal figures present an intellectual, symbolic expression of holiness rather than that, more familiar to Western eyes, of passion and pathos. They appeal to the mind rather than to the heart. In their inexpressive splendor they turn away the worshipper looking for a recognizable emotion with which to identify, and present him instead with an abstract symbol: it is the Greek *Logos,* which informed the framers of Christianity — an idealized and intellectual representation of the unknowable, that which cannot be pictured by direct communication either in words or in pictures. With all their symbolic abstraction, however, these figures have a spirituality that the direct appeal to the senses could never attain.

One of these iconlike representations is that of the Virgin and Child. The

The Virgin and Child — full-page illustration in the Book of Kells

full-page picture, in the preliminary section of the book, introduces the *Breves causae* of St. Matthew, which starts with the birth of Christ. The Virgin is presented not as a tender mother but as a static, awesome figure to be worshipped, surrounded by angels and enclosed in an elaborate banded frame of interlaced animals (of a careful intricacy that seems to be the execution of a different artist). Her ritually staring face is framed in a figured veil and encircled by a halo decorated with three formée crosses. She is robed in a voluminous mantle of deep purple decorated with dots in groups of three and fastened at her right shoulder with one of those meaningful lozenges; both the garment and the headdress fall in formal Grecian folds around her. She sits sideways on a fantastic chair adorned with twisting animal finials; and although her upper body is flat and frontal, her legs (visible through a diaphanous skirt of clearly Eastern provenance) and her dainty feet are disposed with natural grace.

In contrast to the Virgin's goddesslike immobility, the Child in her lap has an affectionate attitude: his face in side view looking up at hers, one hand raised to her symbolic breasts — concentric circles outlined on her mantle — and the other resting on her own long-fingered white hand. Though this is the first known representation of the Virgin in a Western codex, the placement of the figures has prototypes in icons of both East and West, and exhibits similarities also with scenes of the Adoration of the Magi on Irish high crosses. It has been further pointed out that the pose is exactly like the conventional one of Egyptian Isis holding the child Horus: the seated mother a formal high-crowned goddess facing the viewer with frozen dignity, the child on her knees turning his head toward hers in a position of tender dependence.

Despite its polygenetic derivations, the picture has a bizarrely beautiful harmony all its own. It has a startlingly modern aspect — partly the result of the near-surrealistic drawing, partly of the balance and contrasting clarity of the colors, which emphasize the strangeness of the conventionalized figures. In any age the "Illustrator" would be a master.

The Arrest is another curious ceremonious tableau where inner meaning supersedes objective reality. In a forceful, uncluttered scene, Christ stands between his two captors, each of whom holds one of his arms. The Savior, much bigger than the soldiers, is swathed in a royal purple mantle; his large eyes, of clear deep blue, gaze straight ahead inflexibly; his captive arms are rigidly outstretched in a position approaching that of the Crucifixion. Clearly the imagery, sacerdotal in purpose, points to the voluntary nature of the Passion. This great godlike figure dominating the scene is not submitting to his fate, he is declaring it. The stark little group is positioned under a round decorated arch surmounted by the heads of two open-mouthed beasts with interlaced tongues. The arch is supported by two columns constructed of large and small squares and having elaborate crosses where the capitals should be — an item of architecture drawn by a drafts-man who evidently did not know what a freestanding column looked like. These ornamental, unserviceable columns appear in other illustrated pages; they denote lack of knowledge rather than of observation, as we will see in the next illustration. Ninth-century Irish churches did not have freestand-ing columns.

The third of the masterpieces by the "Illustrator," the Temptation, is a much more complicated and eventful painting than the other two, though it too is conceptual rather than naturalistic. It is a dramatization of the account in St. Luke: "[the devil set Jesus] on the pinnacle of the temple, and said to him, If you are the Son of God, throw yourself down from here; for it is written, He will give his angels charge of you, to guard you, and on their hands they will bear you up, lest you strike your foot against a stone. And Jesus answered him, It is said, You shall not tempt the Lord your God."[4]

A large and noble Christ with the same straight oval-eyed stare and curling gold hair of the figure in the Arrest is presented in bust form filling the entire top of the temple, which is an elegantly detailed copy of one of the little basic Irish churches examined earlier, with a steep roof, antae with animal-head finials, a square door and painted, decorated shingles. Around him hover four angels, two in the corners of the picture, their wings fitting felicitously into the triangles, two floating above his ornate halo (which is very like that of the Virgin, as is his triple-dotted purple mantle). Beside him is the devil, much smaller: a startling, attenuated coal-black figure with cloven hoofs and scraggy black wings — the phantasmic essence of devil. This bold portrayal is one of the earliest in the West. Though the devil turns up, as we have seen, in stone carvings of the Last Judgment, there is no representation of the Temptation on Irish or English crosses, and the devil does not appear in Western codices in any form before the ninth century. His springy pose and his total blackness are clearly Eastern: the athletic little devils in Byzantine frescoes are always black.

Besides the main characters of the drama there are crowds of people looking on whose relevance to the story is unclear. On Jesus's left is a bust-length group all facing him — a striking accent to his centrality — which may anticipate the subsequent verses in Luke, in which Christ preaches in the synagogue. Within the doorway of the church is another holy figure, in the Osiris pose with crossed scepters, attended by two more large groups of onlookers; it could be that this is a representation of the Last Judgment, as Christ is usually presented in that pose on insular stone carvings.

It is a picture full of activity, yet with all its busyness it is not confusing. The sharp contrast of its figures, small balanced with large, crowds pointing up single figures; the subtlety of the interlaced background whose delicacy sets off the striking boldness of the subjects; the intensity of the foreground colors against the subdued gentleness of the frame — all work together to please the eye and satisfy the intellect.

The fourth artist discerned by Dr. Henry is the "Portrait Painter." Though his pictures have not the imaginative mysticism of those by the "Illustrator," he is, in a more straightforward way, a superb artist. He created the portraits of the Evangelists and of Christ, as well as, probably, the "four-symbols page" at the beginning of St. Matthew. This illustration presents the symbols of the Evangelists, formally grotesque, each set in a plain ashen panel framed with bright yellow bands; each panel is surrounded by the wonderfully intricate designs borrowed from insular metalwork. The whole is a masterpiece of balance and color.

His portrait of St. John, an extraordinary composition, is particularly notable for Christian allegory. Though the Evangelist does not have the ritualistic mien of the subjects portrayed by the "Illustrator," his pose is arrestingly ceremonious. He is portrayed full-face, seated in an ornate chair, holding a book in one upraised hand; in the other he bears a very long quill pen, which he is about to dip into a small inkpot. Around his head is an enormous, highly decorated nimbus consisting of concentric circles of elaborate design alternating with bright purple and orange bands. Bordering this magnificently formal figure is an imposing frame of multi-faceted, convoluted beauty, drawing the eye away from the subject. In the center of each of its sides is a square cross decorated with interlacing, and projecting beyond these crosses, seemingly coming out from behind the frame, are parts of a human body: on both the right and the left, a closed hand; at the bottom, a pair of sandalled feet; at the top, a part of a haloed head (the rest of it cut off by a clumsy binder in the eighteenth century). This symbolic fantasy, which appears in other illustrations in the book as well as in other contemporary codices, is undoubtedly the artist's metaphoric imaging of the hidden mystery of the Word, which is beyond imaging — the Godhead that is all-encompassing and unknowable, his presence manifested only in his works.

This is the merest sampling: the *Book of Kells* is so rich in imagery, design and color, and so laden with allusion and symbolism, that it is not possible in a work of this limited scope to do more than hint at its profound intricacy. It represents the culmination of two centuries of insular manuscript illumination. Though its concepts are those familiar to medieval Christianity and most of its features can be found in other works of the period, its totality is unique. The lively profusion and beguiling imagination of its decorated script, and the haunting import and fluent symmetry of its full-page portraits and illustrations give it a place far above illuminated manuscripts of its time or any other.

It seems extraordinary that it could have been produced, even in the quiet oasis of Kells, during years of such pervasive insecurity; and indeed the *Book of Kells* is the last great insular manuscript. The ninth and tenth centuries saw nothing else of this stature: in the first place, its perfection set an inaccessible standard; in the second, many of the great illuminators were killed in the raids or escaped to the Continent. In the eleventh and twelfth centuries there were some interesting productions, but conventions had changed, and these later works do not approach the magnificent complexity of the earlier masterpiece.

EPILOGUE

THE *Book of Kells* IS A PROJECTION OF THE ESSENCE OF IRISH CHRISTIANITY. The streams converge here: the one that came from within Ireland, combining her turbulent, talented Celtic past with the austere and passionate piety of her early monks; the one that rose in the Egyptian desert, bringing with it the exaltation of Eastern mysticism idealized by the fine logic of classical Greece; and the one that came out of prebarbarian Europe, bearing the accumulated knowledge of Western civilization. In her few centuries of light, Ireland produced from these a new and beautiful vision, an entity that had no antecedents, and gave back to the world more than it had lost.

Behind the vision were the men and women who saw it, and it is in their motivation that we must look for its pristine freshness, its radiant imagination, and, above all, its shining spirituality. Because they did not set out to invent something new: to begin with, they were simply and purely seeking a state of grace. If it led them to heights heretofore unscaled, that was not their original quest, but a side result of their self-forgetting piety. It is hard for us, now, to acknowledge, even to understand, the intrinsic confidence with which they put themselves into the hand of God. But in following their lives, we may glimpse the substance of their faith, and that fleeting knowledge carries an essential and profound appeal.

NOTES
BIBLIOGRAPHY
INDEX

NOTES

CHAPTER I • PREHISTORIC IRELAND

1. Much of this chapter's discussion about the establishment of the Celts in Ireland is based on Peter Harbison, "The Coming of the Indo-Europeans to Ireland."
2. C. Hawkes, "Cumulative Celticity in Pre-Roman Britain," *Études Celtiques* 13: 607–628.

CHAPTER II • PAGAN IRELAND • THE PEOPLE

1. *The Story of Mac Datho's Pig*, in Tom Peete Cross and Clark Harris Slover, eds. and trans., *Ancient Irish Tales* (hereafter cited as *Ancient Irish Tales*).
2. *Tain Bo Cuailnge*, ibid.
3. *The Destruction of Da Derga's Hostel*, ibid.
4. Thomas Kinsella, ed. and trans., *The Tain*.
5. Ibid.
6. Brehon Law, as quoted in Patrick Weston Joyce, *A Social History of Ancient Ireland*.
7. Kinsella, *The Tain*.
8. [Cormac Mac Cuilennain], *Cormac's Glossary*.
9. Quoted in Eugene O'Curry, *Manners and Customs of the Ancient Irish*.
10. Brehon Law, as quoted ibid.
11. *The Death of Cuchulain*, in *Ancient Irish Tales*.
12. *The Death of Finn*, ibid.
13. *The Colloquy of the Old Men*, ibid.
14. Quotations concerning Cailte and the nobles throughout this chapter are from Standish H. O'Grady, ed. and trans., *Silva Gadelica*.
15. Quotations concerning *The Colloquy of the Old Men* throughout this chapter are from *Ancient Irish Tales*.
16. *The Wooing of Etain*, ibid.

17. Kinsella, *The Tain.*
18. Ibid.
19. *Senchus Mor,* as quoted in Joyce, *Ancient Ireland.*

CHAPTER III • PAGAN IRELAND • THE RELIGION

1. *The Second Battle of Mag Tured,* in *Ancient Irish Tales.*
2. *The Voyage of Bran Son of Febal,* ibid.
3. [Cormac Mac Cuilennain], *Cormac's Glossary.*
4. *The Second Battle of Mag Tured,* in *Ancient Irish Tales.*
5. Robert Alexander Stewart Macalister, ed. and trans., *Lebor Gabala Erenn.*
6. *The Voyage of Bran Son of Febal,* in *Ancient Irish Tales.*
7. Jocelyn, Monk of Furness, *The Life and Acts of St. Patrick.*

CHAPTER IV • CHRISTIANITY ON THE CONTINENT

1. Luke 14:26–27.

CHAPTER V • ST. PATRICK

1. Quotations concerning the life of St. Ailbe throughout this chapter are from Rev. John O'Hanlon, *Lives of the Irish Saints.*
2. Rev. P. Power, ed. and trans., *Life of St. Declan of Ardmore.*
3. Quotations concerning the life of St. Declan throughout this chapter are from Power, *Life of St. Declan.*
4. *Life of St. Patrick in the 'Book of Armagh,'* quoted in Mary Frances Cusack, *The Trias Thaumaturga.*
5. Ibid.
6. St. Patrick, *Confession.*
7. Quotations concerning the life of St. Patrick throughout this chapter are, unless otherwise specified, from Jocelyn, Monk of Furness, *The Life and Acts of St. Patrick,* and from Whitley Stokes, ed. and trans., *The Tripartite Life of Patrick.*
8. The Venerable Bede, *Bede's Ecclesiastical History of the English People.*
9. Giraldus Cambrensis, *The Topography of Ireland.*
10. St. Patrick, *Confession.*
11. Quotations concerning *The Colloquy of the Old Men* throughout this chapter are from *Ancient Irish Tales.*

CHAPTER VI • THE INNOVATORS • ST. ENDA, ST. FINIAN AND ST. BRIGID

1. John Ryan, trans., in "The Church in Ireland," in Arthur West Haddan and William Stubbs, *Councils and Ecclesiastical Documents Relating to Great Britain and Ireland* (Oxford: Clarendon Press, 1869–1878), vol. 2, pt. 2.
2. Quotations concerning the life of St. Enda throughout this chapter are from Rev. John O'Hanlon, *Lives of the Irish Saints.*
3. Whitley Stokes and John Strachan, *Thesaurus Palaeohibernicus.*
4. Padraic Pearse, *Collected Works: Political Writings and Speeches* (Dublin and London: Maunsel & Roberts, 1922).

5. Whitley Stokes, ed. and trans., *Lives of the Saints from the 'Book of Lismore.'* (Subsequent quotations concerning the life of St. Finian in this chapter are from the same source.)
6. Ibid.
7. Eugene O'Curry, "Manuscript Materials of Ancient Irish History" (lectures), trans. adapted by Hugh De Blacam in his book *The Saints of Ireland.*
8. Charles Plummer, ed. and trans., *Lives of Irish Saints.*
9. St. Broccan's "Hymn to Brigid," as quoted in Stokes and Strachan, *Thesaurus Palaeohibernicus.*

CHAPTER VII • THE FOUNDERS OF THE MONASTERIES

1. Marianus Scotus, eleventh-century Irish scholar.
2. Quotations concerning the life of St. Kevin throughout this chapter are from Charles Plummer, ed. and trans., *Lives of Irish Saints.*
3. Quotations concerning the life of St. Ciaran throughout this chapter are from Whitley Stokes, ed. and trans., *Lives of the Saints from the 'Book of Lismore.'*
4.. Rev. John O'Hanlon, *Lives of the Irish Saints.*
5. "Sancti Venite," trans. Francis John Byrne, quoted in his essay "Latin Poetry in Ireland," in James Carney, ed., *Early Irish Poetry.*
6. O'Hanlon, *Lives of the Irish Saints.*
7. Quotations concerning the life of St. Molaisse throughout this chapter are from "Life of S. Molasius of Devenish," in Standish H. O'Grady, ed. and trans., *Silva Gadelica.*

CHAPTER VIII • THE TRAVELLERS • ST. BRENDAN THE NAVIGATOR

1. Gen. 12:1.
2. Quotations concerning the life of St. Moling throughout this chapter are from Whitley Stokes, ed. and trans., *The Birth and Life of St. Moling.*
3. Quotations concerning the life and voyages of St. Brendan throughout this chapter are, unless otherwise specified, from Rev. Denis O'Donoghue, *Brendaniana*; Charles Plummer, ed. and trans., *Lives of Irish Saints*; and Whitley Stokes, ed. and trans., *Lives of the Saints from the 'Book of Lismore.'*
4. Dicuil, *Liber de Mensura Orbis Terrae.*
5. Ibid.
6. Ari Thorgilsson the Learned, *Islendingabok.*
7. Ari Thorgilsson the Learned, *Landnamabok.*

CHAPTER IX • THE TRAVELLERS • ST. COLUMBA OF IONA

1. Quotations concerning the life of St. Columba throughout this chapter are, unless otherwise specified, from Adamnan, *Vita S. Columbae,* and from Manus O'Donnell, comp., *Life of Columcille.*
2. Dr. Samuel Johnson, *A Journey to the Western Islands of Scotland,* ed. R. W. Chapman (London: H. Milford, 1924).
3. Karl Klingemann, letter of 10 Aug. 1829, in *Familie Mendelssohn, 1729–1847* (Berlin: B. Behr, 1886), vol. 1.
4. Adamnan, *Vita S. Columbae.*
5. The Venerable Bede, *Bede's Ecclesiastical History of the English People.*
6. Ibid. (Subsequent quotations concerning the Synod of Whitby are from the same source.)

CHAPTER X • THE TRAVELLERS • ST. COLUMBANUS OF LUXEUIL

1. Quotations concerning the life of St. Columbanus throughout this chapter are, unless otherwise specified, from [St. Columbanus], *Sancti Columbani Opera,* and from Jonas, Monk of Bobbio, *Life of Columban.*

CHAPTER XI • THE VIKING INVASIONS

1. Quotations concerning Maelruain's rule throughout this chapter are from Edward John Gwynn, ed. and trans., "Teaching of Maelruain" and "Rule of the 'Celi De,'" and from Edward John Gwynn and Walter John Purton, eds. and trans., "The Monastery of Tallaght."
2. Verse in the *St. Gall Priscian,* as quoted in Whitley Stokes and John Strachan, *Thesaurus Palaeohibernicus.*
3. James Henthorn Todd, trans., *The War of the Gaedhil with the Gaill.*
4. Magnus Magnusson and Hermann Palsson, eds. and trans., *Njal's Saga.*
5. Ibid.
6. The exchange between Brian's sister and King Sitric is from Todd, *The War of the Gaedhil.*

CHAPTER XII • THE ANGLO–NORMAN INVASION

1. Giraldus Cambrensis, *The Conquest of Ireland.*

CHAPTER XIII • EDUCATION

1. The Venerable Bede, *Bede's Ecclesiastical History of the English People.*
2. Jordanes, *The Gothic History,* ed. and trans. Charles Christopher Mierow (Cambridge: Speculum Historiale, and New York: Barnes & Noble, 1960).
3. St. Patrick, *Confession.*
4. *Bede's Ecclesiastical History.*
5. Brehon Law, as quoted in Patrick Weston Joyce, *A Social History of Ancient Ireland.*
6. Thomas Kinsella, ed. and trans., *The Tain.*
7. Quotations concerning Finnachta the Festive throughout this chapter are from William Reeves, "Memoir of St. Adamnan," preface to his translation of Adamnan, *Vita S. Columbae* (Edinburgh: Edmunston & Douglas, 1874).
8. Quoted in Joyce, *Social History.*
9. David Greene, "Early Irish Society," in Myles Dillon, ed., *Early Irish Society.*

CHAPTER XIV • THE POETS

1. Robert Alexander Stewart Macalister, ed. and trans., *Lebor Gabala Erenn.*
2. Ibid.
3. Thomas Kinsella, ed. and trans., *The Tain.*
4. *Tain Bo Cuailnge* in *Ancient Irish Tales.*
5. Quotations concerning *The Exile of the Sons of Usnech* throughout this chapter are from *Ancient Irish Tales.*
6. Gerard Murphy, ed. and trans., *Early Irish Lyrics: Eighth to the Twelfth Century.*
7. Ibid.

8. *Cormac's Adventures in the Land of Promise*, in *Ancient Irish Tales*.
9. *The Voyage of Bran Son of Febal*, ibid.
10. The Venerable Bede, *Bede's Ecclesiastical History of the English People*. (The entire account of Fursey's visions is drawn from the same source.)
11. Whitley Stokes and John Strachan, *Thesaurus Palaeohibernicus*.
12. James Carney, ed., *Early Irish Poetry*.
13. Robin Flower, *The Irish Tradition*.
14. Adamnan, *Vita S. Columbae*.
15. Douglas Hyde, trans., in his book *The Story of Early Gaelic Literature*.
16. Eleanor Knott and Gerard Murphy, *Early Irish Literature*.
17. Ibid.
18. Murphy, *Early Irish Lyrics*.
19. Ibid.
20. Ibid.
21. Carney, *Early Irish Poetry*.
22. Murphy, *Early Irish Lyrics*.
23. Ibid.
24. Eugene O'Curry, *Manners and Customs of the Ancient Irish*.
25. Mary E. Byrne, trans., in St. John D. Seymour, "The Signs of Doomsday in the *Saltair na Rann*."
26. Knott and Murphy, *Early Irish Literature*.
27. Vivian Mercier, trans., in her book *The Irish Comic Tradition*.
28. Murphy, *Early Irish Lyrics*.
29. Ibid.
30. Robert Alexander Stewart Macalister, *The Secret Languages of Ireland*.

CHAPTER XV · THE SCHOLARS

1. Quoted in Theodore William Moody and Francis Xavier Martin, eds., *The Course of Irish History*.
2. Kuno Meyer, ed. and trans., *Cain Adamnan*.
3. Ibid.
4. Adamnan, *De Locis Sanctis*.
5. Quotations of Dicuil throughout this chapter are from his *Liber de Mensura Orbis Terrae*.
6. Quotations concerning the life of Eriugena throughout this chapter are from John J. O'Meara, *Eriugena*. (Much of this chapter's discussion of Eriugena's philosophy is drawn from the same source.)

CHAPTER XVII · ART IN METAL AND THE ILLUMINATED GOSPELS

1. Much of this chapter's analysis of the carpet pages in the *Book of Durrow* is based upon Harry Bober, "Celtic Christian Art: Form and Meaning," lectures presented at New York's Metropolitan Museum of Art, fall 1977.
2. Translation on display with the original manuscript at the British Museum, London.
3. Much of this chapter's analysis of the illustrations in the *Book of Kells* is based upon Françoise Henry, "A Study of the Manuscript."
4. Luke 4:9–12.

BIBLIOGRAPHY

PREHISTORIC AND PAGAN IRELAND

Harbison, Peter. *The Archaeology of Ireland*. London: Bodley Head, 1976.
———. "The Coming of the Indo-Europeans to Ireland: An Archaeological Viewpoint." *Journal of Indo-European Studies* 3, no. 2 (summer 1975).
Hencken, Hugh. "Indo-European Languages and Archaeology." *American Anthropologist* 57, no. 6, pt. 3, memoir no. 84 (1955).
Herity, Michael, and Eogan, George. *Ireland in Prehistory*. London: Routledge & Kegan Paul, 1977.
Herm, Gerhard. *The Celts: The People Who Came Out of the Darkness*. New York: St. Martin's Press, 1977.
Kendrick, Thomas Downing. *The Druids*. London: Methuen, 1927.
Macalister, Robert Alexander Stewart. *Ireland in Pre-Celtic Times*. Dublin: Maunsel & Roberts, 1921.
MacNeill, Eoin. *Celtic Ireland*. Dublin: M. Lester, 1921.
O'Curry, Eugene. *Manners and Customs of the Ancient Irish*. 1873. Reprint (3 vols.). New York: Lemma Publishing Corp., 1971.
O'Rahilly, Thomas Francis. *Early Irish History and Mythology*. 3 vols. Dublin: Dublin Institute for Advanced Studies, 1946.
Peake, Harold. *The Bronze Age and the Celtic World*. London: Benn Bros., 1967.
Powell, T.G.E. "The Celtic Settlement in Ireland." In *The Early Cultures of Northwest Europe*. H. M. Chadwick Memorial Studies, edited by Cyril Fox and Bruce Dickins. Cambridge: Cambridge University Press, 1950.
Raftery, Joseph, ed. *The Celts*. Thomas Davis Lectures. Cork: Mercier Press, 1964.
Sjoestedt, Marie-Louise. *Gods and Heroes of the Celts*. Translated by Myles Dillon. London: Methuen, 1949.

354

HISTORY AND GENERAL

Ari Thorgilsson the Learned. *Islendingabok*. Translated by Halldor Hermansson. Ithaca, N.Y.: Cornell University Press, 1930.
———. *Landnamabok*. Translated by Rev. Thomas Ellwood. Kendal, England: T. Wilson, 1908.
Ashe, Geoffrey. *Land to the West*. London: Collins, 1962.
Bede, the Venerable. *Bede's Ecclesiastical History of the English People*. Edited by Bertram Colgrave and R. A. B. Mynors. Oxford: Oxford University Press, Clarendon Press, 1969.
Campion, Edmund. "Historie of Ireland." In *Ancient Irish Histories*, edited by Sir James Ware. Society of Stationers, 1633. Reprint. Dublin: Hibernia Press, 1809.
De Paor, Maire, and De Paor, Liam. *Early Christian Ireland*. London: Thames & Hudson, 1958.
Dillon, Myles, ed. *Early Irish Society*. Dublin: C. O. Lochlainn (for Cultural Relations Committee of Ireland), 1945.
Duckett, Eleanor Shipley. *The Gateway to the Middle Ages*. 3 vols. Ann Arbor: University of Michigan Press, 1938.
Freeman, Thomas Walter. *Ireland: Its Physical, Historical, Social and Economic Geography*. London: Methuen, 1950.
Giraldus Cambrensis. *The Topography of Ireland* and *The Conquest of Ireland*. Revised and edited by Thomas Wright. Translated by Sir Richard Colt Hoare. 1 vol. London: G. Bell & Sons, 1887.
Harbison, Peter. "John Windele's Visit to Skellig Michael in 1851." *Journal of the Kerry Archaeological and Historical Society* 9 (1976).
Hull, Eleanor. *History of Ireland*. London: G. G. Harrap, 1926.
Johnson, Paul. *A History of Christianity*. New York: Atheneum, 1976.
Joyce, Patrick Weston. *A Short History of Gaelic Ireland*. Dublin: Educational Co. of Ireland, 1924.
———. *A Social History of Ancient Ireland*. 2 vols. London: Longmans, Green, 1920.
Kendrick, Thomas Downing. *A History of the Vikings*. New York: Charles Scribner, 1930.
Killanin, Lord, and Duignan, Michael V. *The Shell Guide to Ireland*. London: Ebury & George Rainbird, 1967.
Lavelle, Des. *Skellig: Island Outpost of Europe*. Dublin: O'Brien Press, 1976.
Lawless, Hon. Emily. *Ireland*. New York: G. P. Putnam's Sons, 1898.
Mac Niocaill, Gearoid. *Ireland before the Vikings*. Gill History of Ireland. Dublin: Gill & Macmillan, 1972.
Magnusson, Magnus, and Palsson, Hermann, eds. and trans. *Njal's Saga*. Baltimore: Penguin Books, 1960.
———. "Eirik's Saga." In *The Vinland Sagas*. Baltimore: Penguin Books, 1965.
Moody, Theodore William, and Martin, Francis Xavier, eds. *The Course of Irish History*. Cork: Mercier Press, 1967.
Morison, Samuel Eliot. *The European Discovery of America: The Northern Voyages*. New York: Oxford University Press, 1971.
O'Corrain, Donncha. *Ireland before the Normans*. Gill History of Ireland. Dublin: Gill & Macmillan, 1972.
Orme, A. R. *Ireland*. The World's Landscapes, no. 4, Harlow, England: Longmans, 1970.
Praeger, Robert Lloyd. *Natural History of Ireland*. London: Collins, 1950.
Ryan, Rev. John, S.J. "The Battle of Clontarf." *Journal of the Royal Society of Antiquaries* 68, pt. 1 (Dublin, 1938).

Todd, James Henthorn, trans. *The War of the Gaedhil with the Gaill*. Public Record Office of Great Britain. Chronicles and Memorials, vol. 48C, 1867.

Whittow, J. B. *Geology and Scenery in Ireland*. Baltimore: Penguin Books, 1974.

CHRISTIANITY IN IRELAND

Adamnan. *Vita S. Columbae*. Translated by W. Huyshe. Dublin: Educational Co. of Ireland (for the Irish Texts Society), 1922.

Bernard of Clairvaux, Saint. *Life of St. Malachy of Armagh*. Edited and translated by N. J. Lawlor. London: Society for Promoting Christian Knowledge, 1920.

Betten, Francis Sales, S.J. *St. Boniface and St. Virgil*. Benedictine Historical Monographs, no. 2. Washington, D.C.: St. Anselm's Priory, 1927.

[Columbanus, Saint.] *Sancti Columbani Opera*. Edited and translated by G. S. M. Walker. Dublin: Dublin Institute for Advanced Studies, 1957.

De Blacam, Hugh. *The Saints of Ireland*. Milwaukee: Bruce Publishing Co., 1942.

Cusack, Mary Frances. *The Trias Thaumaturga*. Edinburgh: Ballantyne, Hanson, 1875.

Gwynn, Edward John, ed. and trans. "Teaching of Maelruain" and "Rule of the 'Celi De.'" In *Hermethena*, no. 44, 2d supp. vol. (1927).

———, and Purton, Walter John, eds. and trans. "The Monastery of Tallaght" *Royal Irish Academy Proceedings,* sec. A-B-C 29. Dublin: Hodges, Figgis, 1911.

Hughes, Kathleen. *The Church in Early Irish Society*. Ithaca, N.Y.: Cornell University Press, 1966.

Jocelyn, Monk of Furness. *The Life and Acts of St. Patrick*. Translated by J. C. O'Haloran. Philadelphia: Atkinson & Alexander, 1823.

Jonas, Monk of Bobbio. *Life of Columban*. Pennsylvania University History Dept., Philadelphia. Translations and reprints, vol. 2, no. 7 (1895).

Lehane, Brendan. *The Quest of Three Abbots*. London: Murray, 1968.

O'Donnell, Manus, comp. *Life of Columcille*. Edited and translated by A. O'Kelleher and G. Schoepperle (from a manuscript [Rawlinson B514] in the Bodleian Library, Oxford). Urbana: University of Illinois Press, 1918.

O'Donoghue, Rev. Denis. *Brendaniana*. Dublin: Browne & Nolan, 1893.

O'Grady, Standish H., ed. and trans. *Silva Gadelica: A Collection of Tales in Irish*. London: Williams & Norgate, 1892.

O'Hanlon, Rev. John. *Lives of the Irish Saints*. 10 vols. Dublin: J. Duffy & Sons, 1875.

Patrick, Saint. *Confession* and *Letter to Coroticus*. Edited and translated by Rev. Charles H. H. Wright. 1 vol. London: Religious Tract Society, 1889.

Plummer, Charles, ed. and trans. *Lives of Irish Saints*. 2 vols. Oxford: Oxford University Press, Clarendon Press, 1922.

Power, Rev. P., ed. and trans. *Life of St. Declan of Ardmore*. London: Irish Texts Society, 1914.

Ryan, Rev. John, S.J. *Irish Monks in the Golden Age*. Dublin: Clonmore & Reynolds, 1963.

Stokes, Whitley, ed. and trans. *The Birth and Life of St. Moling*. London: Harrison & Sons, 1907.

———. *Lives of the Saints from the 'Book of Lismore.'* Oxford: Clarendon Press, 1890.

———. *The Tripartite Life of Patrick*. London: Eyre & Spottiswoode, 1887.

THE ARTS, EDUCATION AND LITERATURE

Adamnan. *De Locis Sanctis*. Edited and translated by Denis Meehan. Dublin: Dublin Institute for Advanced Studies, 1958.

Bain, George. *Celtic Art: The Methods of Construction.* New York: Dover Publications, 1973.

Carney, James, ed. *Early Irish Poetry.* Thomas Davis Lectures. Cork: Mercier Press, 1965.

[Cormac Mac Cuilennain, Bishop.] *Cormac's Glossary.* Edited by Whitley Stokes. Translated by John O'Donovan. Calcutta: O. T. Cutter (for the Irish Archaeological and Celtic Society), 1868.

Cross, Tom Peete, and Slover, Clark Harris, eds. and trans. *Ancient Irish Tales.* New York: Barnes & Noble, and Dublin: Figgis, 1936.

De Breffny, Brian, and Mott, George. *The Churches and Abbeys of Ireland.* London: Thames & Hudson, 1976.

Dicuil. *Liber de Mensura Orbis Terrae.* Edited and translated by J. J. Tierney. Dublin: Dublin Institute for Advanced Studies, 1967.

——. *An Unpublished Astronomical Treatise.* Edited and translated by Mario Esposito. Chicago: Modern Philology, 1920.

Dillon, Myles. *Early Irish Literature.* Chicago: University of Chicago Press, 1948.

Flower, Robin. *The Irish Tradition.* London: Oxford University Press, 1947.

Harbison, Peter. "The Bronze Age." In *Treasures of Early Irish Art, 1500 B.C. to 1500 A.D.* New York: Metropolitan Museum of Art, 1977.

——. *Guide to the National Monuments of Ireland.* Dublin: Gill & Macmillan, 1975.

——; Potterton, Homan; and Sheehy, Jeanne. *Irish Art and Architecture from Prehistory to the Present.* London: Thames & Hudson, 1978.

Henry, Françoise. *Irish Art in the Early Christian Period.* London: Methuen, 1947.

——. "A Study of the Manuscript." In *The Book of Kells: Reproductions from the Manuscript in Trinity College, Dublin.* New York: Alfred A. Knopf, 1974.

Hyde, Douglas. *The Story of Early Gaelic Literature.* London: T. F. Unwin, 1895.

Kinsella, Thomas, ed. and trans. *The Tain.* London: Oxford University Press (in association with Dolmen Press, Dublin), 1969.

Knott, Eleanor. *Irish Classical Poetry.* Cork: Mercier Press, 1966.

——, and Murphy, Gerard. *Early Irish Literature.* London: Routledge & Kegan Paul, 1966.

Macalister, Robert Alexander Stewart. *The Secret Languages of Ireland.* Cambridge: Cambridge University Press, 1937.

——, ed. and trans. *Lebor Gabala Erenn.* 4 vols. Dublin: Educational Co. of Ireland (for the Irish Texts Society): 1938–1941.

MacLean, Magnus. *The Literature of the Celts.* London: Blackie & Sons, 1926.

Mercier, Vivian. *The Irish Comic Tradition.* Oxford: Oxford University Press, Clarendon Press, 1962.

Meyer, Kuno. *Learning in Ireland in the Fifth Century.* Dublin: Hodges, Figgis, 1913.

——, ed. and trans. *Cain Adamnan.* Oxford: Clarendon Press, 1905.

Murphy, Gerard. *Ossianic Lore.* Cork: Mercier Press, 1955.

——. *Saga and Myth in Ancient Ireland.* Cork: Mercier Press, 1961.

——, ed. and trans. *Early Irish Lyrics: Eighth to the Twelfth Century.* Oxford: Oxford University Press, Clarendon Press, 1956.

Neeson, Eoin. *The First Book of Irish Myths and Legends.* Cork: Mercier Press, 1965.

——. *The Second Book of Irish Myths and Legends.* Cork: Mercier Press, 1966.

Nordenfalk, Carl. *Celtic and Anglo-Saxon Painting.* New York: George Braziller, 1977.

O'Meara, John J. *Eriugena.* Cork: Mercier Press, 1969.

Rees, Alwyn, and Rees, Brinley. *Celtic Heritage.* London: Thames & Hudson, 1961.

Seymour, St. John D. "The Book of Adam and Eve in Ireland" and "The Signs of Doomsday in the *Saltair na Rann.*" *Proceedings of the Royal Irish Academy* 36 (1921–1924).

Stokes, Whitley, and Strachan, John. *Thesaurus Palaeohibernicus.* Cambridge: Cambridge University Press, 1901.

Thomson, Derek. *An Introduction to Gaelic Poetry.* London: Victor Gollancz, 1974.

INDEX

Page numbers in *italic* type indicate photographs. Monasteries, church conclaves, books and annals are usually listed under their locations (e.g.: *Kells, Book of;* Whitby, Synod of).